WILLS
OF THE
U.S. Presidents

WILLS
OF THE
U.S.
PRESIDENTS

Biographical Text
Herbert R. Collins
Associate Curator
Division of Political History
Smithsonian Institution

Notes on the Wills
David B. Weaver
Professor of Law
The George Washington University

COMMUNICATION CHANNELS INC.
New York, N.Y.

Copyright © 1976
By
Communication Channels Inc.

NOTES ON STYLE AND THE COMPOSITION OF THE TEXT OF THE WILLS

Spelling, punctuation, and capitalization have been maintained as they are in the original Wills. The layout of the text, including occasional blank spaces between words or sentences, approximates the original Wills. Of course only an exact reproduction can produce true facsimiles of the Wills, but it is the text, not facsimiles, that is the interest of this book. In the case of the Will of William Henry Harrison the several blank spaces within the text are due to words in the original being illegible and the editors elected to leave blank spaces rather than attempt to guess what the words are. A question mark within a parenthesis following a word in the text of a Will signifies that the editors retain some doubts as to whether the word, because of legibility difficulties, is correctly transcribed.

ISBN 0-916164-01-2
Library of Congress Catalog Card Number 75-32100

WILLS OF THE U.S. PRESIDENTS is a **publication of** Trusts & Estates Magazine, **a division of Communication Channels, Inc.**

Produced by Stravon Educational Press

Printed in the United States of America

CONTENTS

Illustrations 7
Preface 9
Introduction 11
GEORGE WASHINGTON 15
   Text of the Will 19
   Notes on the Will 29
JOHN ADAMS 32
   Text of the Will 34
   Notes on the Will 36
THOMAS JEFFERSON 37
   Text of the Will 39
   Notes on the Will 41
JAMES MADISON 42
   Text of the Will 44
   Notes on the Will 47
JAMES MONROE 49
   Text of the Will 51
   Notes on the Will 53
JOHN QUINCY ADAMS 54
   Text of the Will 56
   Notes on the Will 64
ANDREW JACKSON 66
   Text of the Will 68
   Notes on the Will 71
MARTIN VAN BUREN 72
   Text of the Will 74
   Notes on the Will 77
WILLIAM HENRY HARRISON 78
   Text of the Will 80
   Notes on the Will 84
JOHN TYLER 85
   Text of the Will 87
   Notes on the Will 90
JAMES K. POLK 91
   Text of the Will 93
   Notes on the Will 96

ZACHARY TAYLOR 97
   Text of the Will 99
   Notes on the Will 101
MILLARD FILLMORE 102
   Text of the Will 104
   Notes on the Will 107
FRANKLIN PIERCE 108
   Text of the Will 110
   Notes on the Will 113
JAMES BUCHANAN 114
   Text of the Will 116
   Notes on the Will 120
ABRAHAM LINCOLN 122
ANDREW JOHNSON 125
ULYSSES S. GRANT 127
RUTHERFORD B. HAYES 130
   Text of the Will 132
   Notes on the Will 133
JAMES A. GARFIELD 134
CHESTER A. ARTHUR 136
   Text of the Will 138
   Notes on the Will 140
GROVER CLEVELAND 141
   Text of the Will 143
   Notes on the Will 145
BENJAMIN HARRISON 146
   Text of the Will 148
   Notes on the Will 156
WILLIAM McKINLEY 158
   Text of the Will 160
   Notes on the Will 161
THEODORE ROOSEVELT 162
   Text of the Will 164
   Notes on the Will 167
WILLIAM H. TAFT 168
   Text of the Will 170

Notes on the Will 173
WOODROW WILSON 174
   Text of the Will 176
   Notes on the Will 177
WARREN G. HARDING 178
   Text of the Will 180
   Notes on the Will 183
CALVIN COOLIDGE 184
   Text of the Will 186
   Notes on the Will 187
HERBERT C. HOOVER 188
   Text of the Will 190
   Notes on the Will 195
FRANKLIN D. ROOSEVELT 197
   Text of the Will 200

Notes on the Will 211
HARRY S. TRUMAN 213
   Text of the Will 215
   Notes on the Will 232
DWIGHT D. EISENHOWER 234
   Text of the Will 237
   Notes on the Will 245
JOHN F. KENNEDY 247
   Text of the Will 249
   Notes on the Will 259
LYNDON B. JOHNSON 261
   Text of the Will 264
   Notes on the Will 278
Notes on Dying Without a Will 281
INDEX 283

Illustrations

George Washington 15
    Footstool 17
    Cane 17
    Sword 17
Facsimile of
    sections of the Will 18
    Tambour secretary 28
    Circular chair 28
    Facsimile of
    a section of the Will 31
John Adams 32
    The Adams house 33
    Vest 36
Thomas Jefferson 37
    Writing desk 38
    Jefferson with bust of
    Benjamin Franklin 41
James Madison 42
    Montpellier 43
    Tomb of President
    James Madison 47
    Head of cane 48
James Monroe 49
    Elizabeth Kortright Monroe 50
    Oak Hill, home of
    James Monroe 53
John Quincy Adams 54
    Louisa Catherine Adams 55
    Cane 63
John Quincy Adams suffering
    a stroke in the House of
    Representatives 64
    Portrait of
    John Quincy Adams 65
    Sally, the
    White House doll 65
Andrew Jackson 66
    The Hermitage 67

Tomb of
    President Andrew Jackson 71
Martin Van Buren 72
    Angelica Singleton Van Buren 73
    Marble bust 76
    Pitcher 77
William Henry Harrison 78
    Political campaign banner 79
John Tyler 85
    Julia Gardner Tyler 89
James Knox Polk 91
    Polk's house 92
    Tomb of President and
    Mrs. James K. Polk 95
    Polk wallet 96
Zachary Taylor 97
    Sketch of Zachary Taylor 98
    Taylor's home 101
Millard Fillmore 102
    Silver coffee urn 103
    Open book 103
    Silver snuff box 107
Franklin Pierce 108
    Mrs. Franklin Pierce and
    her son Benny 109
    Facsimile of
    a section of the Will 113
James Buchanan 114
    Gavel 115
    Bible 120
    Wheatland 121
Abraham Lincoln 122
    Top hat 124
Andrew Johnson 125
    Three books 126
Ulysses S. Grant 127
Rutherford B. Hayes 130
    Lucy Webb Hayes 131

Desk 133
James A. Garfield 134
    At the bedside of
        the dying President 135
Chester A. Arthur 136
    Fishing reel 137
    President Arthur fishing 139
Grover Cleveland 141
    Wedding cake box 142
    Fishing flies 144
    Spectacles and case 145
Benjamin Harrison 146
    Caroline Scott Harrison 147
    Plate.......................155
William McKinley 158
    Cup and saucer 159
    Headlines announce the
        shooting of McKinley 161
Theodore Roosevelt............162
    Campaign book 163
    Leather chaps worn by
        Theodore Roosevelt 166
    Theodore Roosevelt campaigning ...166
William Howard Taft............168
    Taft in White Steamer 169
Woodrow Wilson 174
    Woodrow Wilson's house 177
    Mrs. Edith Bolling Galt Wilson 177
Warren G. Harding............178
    Woodrow Wilson and
        Warren G. Harding...........179
    Harding's Tomb................182
    Golfing cap, shoes,
        clubs, and ball 183
Calvin Coolidge 184
    Mrs. Calvin Coolidge 185

Calvin Coolidge Homestead 186
    Lamp and Bible 187
Herbert C. Hoover 188
    President Hoover fishing 189
    Hoover birthplace 196
Franklin D. Roosevelt..............197
    Franklin D. Roosevelt in car 198
    Facsimile of a copy
        of a segment of the Will 199
    F.D.R. blanket................212
Harry S. Truman 213
    Facsimile of last page
        of Codicil.................231
    Chicago Daily Tribune
        front page 233
Dwight D. Eisenhower................234
    "I like Ike" button 235
    Mamie Doud Eisenhower 235
    Elephant 236
    Five-star pajamas 236
    Eisenhower home 244
    Bust of
        Dwight D. Eisenhower..........245
    President Eisenhower with a
        sugar-beet farmer 246
John F. Kennedy................247
    Life preserver................248
    Drum 259
    Facsimilie of a section of the Will ..260
Lyndon B. Johnson 261
    Birthplace of
        Lyndon Baines Johnson 262
    Lyndon B. Johnson
        taking the oath of office 263
    Facsimile of a section of
        Page 18 of the Will 280

Pictures were researched by coauthor Herbert R. Collins.

PREFACE

THIS WORK IS NECESSARILY A COL-
LABORATIVE EFFORT. In addition to the
nominal authors—one a political historian, the
other a professor of law—the contributors include 31 Presidents of the United States and,
in many instances, the lawyers whom they consulted in the preparation of their Wills. The
Wills themselves are, of course, the core of interest in this book. They reveal a little known
aspect of these Presidential lives and characters. The material which precedes each Will is
intended to recall to the reader some of the
highlights of the life of the particular President
and to furnish information about the family and
assets of the President, which should make the
provisions of the Will itself more meaningful.
The Notes following each Will deal with one or
more aspects of the document which are interesting from a legal standpoint. The possibilities for such comment on any particular
Will are not exhausted; often they are barely
touched, but spread across the Notes on 31
Wills is a broad range of comment on various
aspects of will-making. The Introduction to the
Wills is an overview sketching briefly the considerations which bear on will-making, the
changing factors affecting that process over
nearly 200 years, and the one aspect of the
Wills which is peculiarly Presidential.

The contributors to this book are not limited to those whose words appear in it. The
starting point in its production was the as-
sembling of the Wills, a task with its own difficulties. Following a testator's death a will is
ordinarily offered for probate, i.e., presented
to an appropriate court for a determination that
it is the last formally expressed wish of the deceased on the way in which his property should
be distributed. Once admitted to probate, a

will becomes part of the public records of that
court and available for inspection by anyone.
Thus, the starting point for collection of each
will was the court records in the place where
the particular President lived at the time of his
death. Though court records proved sufficient
for most of the Presidents, this source was not
always productive, particularly for some of the
early Presidents. Some wills are not offered for
probate; more important, some very old court
records are unavailable. The sources from
which these Wills were obtained are listed at
the conclusion of this preface.

One final caution may be appropriate. No
reader should be tempted to use this work as a
form book, uncritically adopting all or parts of
these Wills for inclusion in a will for himself,
members of his family, or friends. Many of
these Wills have been prepared by able lawyers.
They may well suggest subjects to be covered
in a will and ways in which they might be
handled, but wills are prepared for a particular
testator in the light of the law of the time and
place in which it is to be executed. Differences
in the law or in the individual's situation or
wishes can make an instrument custom-tailored
for one testator an ill-fitting document for
another. Reading these Wills may conceivably
stimulate one to think about his own; it can not
serve as an adequate substitute for the services
of a professional adviser familiar with local law
and with the details of the individual's family,
property, and most important, wishes.

Thanks are due and are herewith gratefully
given to the many people and institutions
whose help and cooperation made this book a
reality. Specifically the publisher wishes to
acknowledge the following: Mr. and Mrs.
Theodor Schuchat who initially conceived this

project and obtained authentic copies of the Wills reproduced in the book; Circuit Court, Fairfax County, Fairfax, Virginia for the Will of George Washington; Norfolk County Registry of Probate, Dedham, Massachusetts for the Will of John Adams; Alderman Library, University of Virginia, Charlottesville, Virginia for the Will of Thomas Jefferson; Archives Division, Virginia State Library, Richmond, Virginia for the Will of James Madison; Circuit Court, Loudoun County, Leesburg, Virginia for the Will of James Monroe; Office of Register of Wills, Clerk of the Probate Court, Washington, D.C. for the Will of John Quincy Adams; County Court, Davidson County, Nashville, Tennessee for the Will of Andrew Jackson; Office of Surrogate, Columbia County, Hudson, New York for the Will of Martin Van Buren; Library of Congress, Manuscript Division, Washington, D.C. for the Will of William Henry Harrison; Charles City County Court House, Charles City, Virginia for the Will of John Tyler; Office of County Court Clerk, Davidson County, Nashville, Tennessee for the Will of James K. Polk; State Archives and Records Commission, Baton Rouge, Louisiana for the Will of Zachary Taylor; Surrogate's Court, County of Erie, Buffalo, New York for the Will of Millard Fillmore; Office of Register of Probate Court, Merrimack County, Concord, New Hampshire for the Will of Franklin Pierce; Register of Wills, Lancaster County Court House, Lancaster, Pennsylvania for the Will of James Buchanan; Office of Probate Judge, Sandusky County, Freemont, Ohio for the Will of Rutherford B. Hayes; Old Records Division, Hall of Records, New York, New York for the Will of Chester A. Arthur; Superior Court, Trenton, New Jersey for the Will of Grover Cleveland; Register of Wills, Marion County Court House, Indianapolis, Indiana for the Will of Benjamin Harrison; Probate Court, Stark County, Canton, Ohio for the Will of William McKinley; Surrogate's Court of the County of Nassau, Mineola, New York for the Will of Theodore Roosevelt; Register of Wills, Washington, D.C. for the Will of William H. Taft; Office of Register of Wills, Probate Court,

U.S. District Court, D.C. for the Will of Woodrow Wilson; Register of Wills, Marion County Court House, Marion County Probate Court, Marion, Ohio for the Will of Warren Gamaliel Harding; Register of Wills, Hampshire County Courthouse, Northampton, Massachusetts for the Will of Calvin Coolidge; William S. Mullen, Chief Clerk and Clerk of the Surrogate's Court of the County of New York, New York, N.Y. for the Will of Herbert C. Hoover; Surrogate Court of the County of Dutchess, Poughkeepsie, New York for the Will of Franklin Delano Roosevelt; Circuit Court, Independence, Missouri for the Will of Harry Truman; Register of Wills, County of Adams, Pennsylvania for the Will of Dwight D. Eisenhower; Louis F. Musco, Register of Wills, Suffolk County Court House, Boston, Massachusetts for the Will of John F. Kennedy; County Clerk, Travis County, Texas for the Will of Lyndon Baines Johnson; U.S. Bureau of Engraving and Printing for the Presidential portraits on pages 15, 32, 37, 42, 49, 54, 66, 72, 78, 85, 91, 97, 102, 108, 114, 122, 125, 127, 130, 134, 136, 141, 146, 158, 162, 168, 174, 178, 184, 188, 197, 213, 234, 247, 261; the Smithsonian Institution for illustrations on pages 17, 33, 36, 38, 41, 47, 48, 53, 55, 63, 64, 65, 67, 71, 79, 92, 95, 96, 98, 101, 103, 107, 113, 115, 120, 121, 133, 135, 137, 142, 144, 145, 155, 159, 161, 163, 166, 169, 179, 183, 187, 189, 196, 198, 212, 233, 235, 236, 244, 245, 248, 259; The Mount Vernon Association for the illustration on page 28; National Geographic Society for the illustration on page 43; Mrs. Gouveneur Hoes for the illustration on page 50; The White House for the illustrations on pages 73, 76, 77, 79, 89, 103, 131, 147, 177, 185, 235; the New Hampshire Historical Society and the Pierce Brigade, Concord, New Hampshire for the illustration on page 109; Probate Court, Merrimack County, Concord, New Hampshire for the illustration on page 113, the National Trust for Historic Preservation for the illustration on page 177; the Lyndon Baines Johnson Library for the illustrations on pages 262, 263; County Clerk, Travis County, Texas for the illustration on page 280;

INTRODUCTION
TO THE WILLS

THE BUREAU OF THE CENSUS estimates that approximately 400,000,000 people have been American citizens since 1790 when they started counting. Of these, exactly 37 have been President of the United States. The interest naturally focused on this small group of men has led to the publication of hundreds, perhaps thousands, of books about them individually and collectively. Many of these have dealt with some special aspect of these men or their careers, but this is the first volume to assemble in one place information about the way in which the property that each of them owned at the time of his death was distributed.

Of the 37, two are ineligible for inclusion in this book, because they are still living. Four, Presidents Lincoln, Andrew Johnson, Grant, and Garfield, died intestate; that is, without a will. Their property passed to members of their immediate families under the intestate statutes of their states. The other 31 each left a will, expressing his wishes on this subject. Those wills, and any codicils amending them, are all included here.

There is great variety in these documents. They range from the single sentence Will of Calvin Coolidge to several which ran roughly 20 typewritten pages in the original. Most reveal a carefully thought out and constructed plan; one, at least, suggests a hastily written, temporary document.

The wills differ in the degree of formality of their execution. One was so loosely done it should not have been admitted to probate.

Five other wills or codicils bore the President's signature, but not those of witnesses, an omission which would invalidate them in, more than half the states. The most recent of these though was signed more than 125 years ago.

The pattern of disposition displayed by these wills varies widely. Of course, the kinds of provisions which can be made depend to some extent upon the wealth of the testator. Three of the Presidents were in serious financial difficulty when they died. The others were all comfortably well off though. Rich is the only accurate description for a few.

The pattern of disposition also reflects the testator's family situation at the time of writing his will. All but one of the Presidents married. Ten outlived their wives. Twenty were survived by widows, some of whom lived for many years. In this respect, the second Mrs. Benjamin Harrison, who married her husband three years after he had left the Presidency, holds the record. She outlived him almost 47 years, dying in 1948 at the age of 89. A number of others lived more than 25 years beyond their husbands.

Six Presidents had no children of their own. A seventh outlived all of his. The surviving children of the others ranged from infancy to middle-age when their fathers died. Five Presidents were survived by a widow and his children of a prior marriage, a situation which can have its own special tensions.

Each will then is the product of the particular family situation, the property available, and that President's ideas of what would be most suitable or desirable for members of his own family. Collectively, they make up a series presenting a great variety of modes of property distribution. At one end of the spectrum there are wills which make only a simple outright gift of everything to a wife. At the other end are those using trusts and powers of appointment in various combinations to provide for a widow, children, and grandchildren for as long as the law permits the wishes of a former owner to control property. Between falls a range of other dispositive schemes.

This variety is not peculiarly Presidential. It reflects the factual differences in family and property, the diverse reactions of testators, and the freedom of choice given to one writing his will under our law. Probably a collection of the wills of 31 other testators from similar backgrounds and with comparable property and family circumstances would show a like variety. The wills in this book then are unique, but they are also representative.

These instruments differ too in the degree of sophistication with which they are drawn. In this respect, the last six wills in the book, those of Presidents Hoover, Franklin Roosevelt, Truman, Eisenhower, Kennedy, and Lyndon Johnson, are different in kind from the 25 which precede them. They are much longer, are obviously drawn by experts, and, in various ways, reflect modern developments which have altered the task of will-drafting, at least will-drafting for the wealthy.

Among these developments are changes in the forms of property and in the methods of transferring it. In the early years of the Republic land was the principal form of wealth. While it is still important, there are now many other kinds of property in which funds can be invested. Many of these are intangible forms barely known to George Washington. The corporation and other forms of business organization have flowered during this period and with them the kinds of property interests which an individual may own. Life insurance, annuities, and other important contractual forms of wealth are also comparatively new. Government-

issued securities are available to investors in all sizes and shapes. Presidents and other citizens have put their money into all of these.

In the same way, the methods of transferring property have grown in number. A will remains an essential element of a well-planned estate, but it may have less significance than before. Other techniques of property transfer can also be used to carry much of the load. Thus, co-ownership of all manner of property by a husband and wife is a widespread practice. (Whether it is wise or not is another matter.) Insurance policy proceeds are typically paid to a beneficiary named in the policy itself rather than under the terms of a will. Other wealth is transferred at death as a survivor benefit provided by contract or law. Gifts may be made during life as well as at death, and, for the wealthy or those with need for special protection, a trust created during life can be a very useful vehicle of transfer. When used in combination with one or more of these other methods, the will's importance is reduced, both in controlling the disposition of property and as a source of information.

Another very significant change which has affected the "modern" wills in this series is the role of the tax collector. Both state and federal governments impose taxes on property transferred by death. Though many state governments have been at it longer, the federal bite is much sharper for estates of any size. The first $60,000 of value owned is free from federal tax, but inflation has progressively diluted the significance of that exemption. The federal rates on "taxable estates" (a term of art) begin at a modest 3% but rise rapidly until they level off at 77% of everything above $10,000,000.

The rate tables are only a part of the tax structure though, and many believe them less formidable than illusory when other characteristics of the law are studied. These make it possible to reduce drastically the tax which the table would seem to require to be paid. To take advantage of them though one must plan ahead and be willing to use the forms of giving favored by the statute. The most important of these special opportunities is the estate tax marital deduction for gifts, in specified forms, to a surviving spouse. A second is the creation of trusts for the use of two or more successive generations. Gifts made during life rather than at death can be advantageous. Gifts to charity in certain forms can be used to promote both public and family welfare.

One need not understand all of the details to feel the tremendous pull which these opportunities for tax reduction exert upon the choices which people of wealth—those who are exposed to the high rates—make. Few people pay taxes joyously during life. They seem no more ready to number governments among their heirs if they can help it. The obvious way to avoid or minimize the share which governments may claim is to use the paths favored by the statute.

Precisely this course is widely followed. For people of wealth, estate planning has become as much a matter of the distinctions in statutes enacted by a bygone Congress as a matter of selecting the most logical and efficient methods of sharing their wealth with the members of their families and others. The evidence here is that Presidents are not immune from this disease. Some families are more guarded about the details than others, but it is no secret that in the case of all six Presidents who have died since 1940, a fair reading of their wills requires the conclusion that tax considerations strongly influenced the property dispositions which they made.

George Washington, one of the wealthiest men of his time, felt perfectly comfortable drawing his own Will—and did a very good job of it. If the last six wills in this volume are to be believed, a man of comparable wealth and status should be most reluctant to attempt this task today. The legal profession, and even specialists within it, dominate the drafting of wills for the wealthy.

The instruments drawn by these specialists display characteristics not found in the earlier wills—though they are foreshadowed to some extent by those of Benjamin Harrison and Theodore Roosevelt. One is that of thoroughness in visualizing all the contingencies which might occur within the family in the future, stating them, and providing clear answers for each possible question. A second is drafting with an eye on the Internal Revenue Code and Treasury Regulations. If one's objective is to take advantage of the smoother paths through the tax thicket, it is, of course, imperative to pay attention to their many twists and turns.

A third characteristic of these documents, contributing enormously to their length, is the development of extensive provisions dealing with aspects of administration of the estate or trust. Usually these are spelled out in great detail and authorize the executor or trustee to do many things which would not otherwise be permitted under the usual legal rules—including many which have no apparent relationship to the needs of the particular estate or trust. The use of standardized forms is the explanation for the latter phenomenon. In fact, in particularly well-organized law offices, these portions of modern wills are prepared in an area of the office where automatic typewriters are encouraged to work on their own.

The effect of these drafting practices is to depersonalize the modern will. It is not phrased in the testator's own language. That would be too dangerous. The specialist chooses language of precise and well-established meaning to express the testator's purposes. Beyond that, where tax considerations or those of administrative feasibility are significant, the advisor's ideas of what the plan of disposition ought to be may override the testator's own ideas of what he would like.

This is not to suggest that the legal profession imposes on its clients in this regard. Lawyers should know better than their clients what is needed in a will to do the best possible job of carrying out their clients' objectives, and they are engaged precisely for that reason. It would be absurd not to guide the client or to fail to select the words which best express the client's ideas. Modern wills are not exercises in creative writing for testators. One consequence though is that little trace of the individual testator's personality survives in the language of the modern will.

The earlier wills are much more interesting in this regard. Many of them were drawn by the Presidents themselves. Without exception they are shorter and more to the point. They deal with gifts of property to members of the immediate family, relatives, and friends, and with appointment of an executor or guardian for minor children. The contingencies are not fully covered. The spinning out of administrative provisions is not evident. Nor does one find those cautious qualifications which are intelligible only in the light of the tax law.

The wills remain essentially functional instruments used to achieve particular purposes rather than as an opportunity for some final message to the family—or to the nation. Subject only to the libel laws, a testator is free to choose the content of his will, but rare is the instrument which contains a hymn of praise, a poem, or an expression of love—in a non-cash form. For better or worse, wills have always been businesslike and are becoming more so if this record is representative. The occasional expressions of patriotic sentiment, or gratitude to survivors, or affection for them found in the earlier wills have largely disappeared.

In most aspects of their wills, Presidential testators appear to be representative rather than special citizens, They have shared their property with others in typical ways. They are no more anxious to support government with their taxes than the rest of us appear to be. They too have delegated to the legal specialists selection of the words in which to express their ideas. In one respect though, they are unique as testators.

Our Presidents have been the only citizens with a claim of ownership to Presidential papers. Until very recently, it would not have occurred to anyone to describe that as a *claim* of ownership. George Washington and all his successors have acted on the assumption that they did own the papers of their Presidencies. For a century and a half they physically removed them; probably most of them believed the papers would not be preserved otherwise. Few did a good job of protecting the papers, though nine Presidents before the modern era did refer to them specifically in their wills.

President Franklin Roosevelt changed the practice. Now libraries and museums, one per President, have sprung up in suitable locations across the nation to house these collections, and just in time, too, for the volume of paper involved has become far too great for a former President to house, manage, and sort without the assistance of his government.

So far, the forms by which the new practice is carried out still reflect the traditional theory. The President gives his papers to the nation through the Administrator of General Services, or simply deposits them with him without transferring title to the government, or, as we see illustrated here, transfers papers to him by will. Whatever method, or combination of methods, is used to transfer the papers, one consequence of the theory of Presidential ownership is that the President may impose on the terms of the transfer conditions or limitations which he believes to be important. The underlying theory may or may not survive. In the meantime, the trail which it has left across these wills is one of the things which makes them interesting and special.

David B. Weaver

GEORGE WASHINGTON

G EORGE WASHINGTON WAS BORN OF EN-
GLISH STOCK ON FEBRUARY 22, 1732, on
his family's estate at Pope's Creek in
Westmoreland County, Virginia. George's
father, Augustine, was a moderately well-to-do
planter and a widower when he married
George's mother-to-be, Mary Ball.

Augustine Washington died when George
was 11, leaving 5,000 acres of land, 22 slaves,
but little cash, and George was brought up by
his half-brother, Lawrence, whom he idolized
and who took over the estate. Lawrence died
in 1752 and left George a share of his estates;
George paid rent on Mount Vernon to Lawrence's widow until 1761 as she had retained a
life interest in the estate.

At the age of 20 Washington was thus already an established Virginia landowner with a
total estate of 2,700 acres. Soon he was to buy
another 2,300 acres—the extent of the original
Washington-Spencer grant from Lord Culpeper
in 1674—increasing his holdings to 5,000 acres.
In the 45 years Washington owned Mount
Vernon it was to grow to over 8,000 acres,
comprising five different farms.

George's formal schooling was sketchy at
best; what learning he acquired he got from his
mother, his parish sexton and a teacher in an
"old-field" schoolhouse. He early showed an
aptitude for mathematics, however, and could
keep accounts, draw up legal documents and
was adept at surveying. Though he never attended college, Washington became a licensed
surveyor at the age of 17.

At 21, Washington was sent west by Governor Robert Dinwiddie to fight in the French and Indian Wars, from which he emerged commander-in-chief of the Virginia militia. Upon his return from the wars at 27 he married Martha Dandridge Custis, also 27, a very rich Virginia widow with two children from her previous marriage. She added substantially to Washington's own not inconsiderable holdings (5,000 acres, 49 slaves), bringing him an additional 17,000 acres of land and 300 slaves. Martha Custis was a small, plump and cheerful woman who nicely complemented her somewhat austere husband. She was descended from a proud old Welsh family, the oldest daughter of Colonel John and Frances Jones Dandridge. Her first husband, Colonel Daniel Parke Custis, had been a prosperous planter.

Upon Washington's return to civilian life he devoted himself to improving the house and grounds of Mount Vernon. Service in the Revolutionary War interrupted Washington's placid civilian life there; he was 51 by the time he returned to his home. In the meantime, he had made what was perhaps his first will. In a letter to Martha, dated Philadelphia, June 18, 1775, he writes: "As life is always uncertain, and common prudence dictates to every man the necessity of settling his power, I have, since I came to this place—for I had no time to do it before I left home—got Colonel Pendleton to draft a will for me by the directions I gave him, which I will now enclose. The provisions made for you, in case of my death, will, I hope, be agreeable."

In 1789, Washington's election to the Presidency again forced him to leave Mount Vernon for eight years, leaving the plantation in the hands of caretakers, except for occasional visits. His salary as President was to be $25,000 annually.

Washington's meticulous record-keeping, as well as his purchase orders, letters, wills, and the appraiser's account of 1800 give a good idea of how he lived. In 1790 when Tobias Lear informed Washington that his restored coach was rich and elegant, he replied that he "had rather have heard that my repaired coach was plain and elegant than rich and elegant."

The house and furnishings of Mount Vernon were simple and unostentatious. The architect Benjamin Latrobe described it thus: "There is a handsome statuary marble chimney piece in the dining room with inverted columns on each side. This is the only piece of expensive decoration I have seen about the house, and is indeed remarkable in that respect. Everything else is extremely good and neat, but by no means above what would be expected in a plain English country gentleman's house of 500 or 600 pounds a year."

Hospitality was the order of the day at Mount Vernon. Both Martha and George Washington were of backgrounds in which entertaining of casual visitors and relatives was deemed a duty and a virtue. Not only did they provide food and quarters but they also showered food and other tokens of friendship upon departing visitors.

Washington spent his final two years at Mount Vernon, enjoying the company of visitors and Martha's grandchildren, whom he adopted as his own and who became known as the "children of Mount Vernon." As he was dying in December, 1799, he directed Martha to bring him two papers from his desk. He then informed her: "These are my wills—preserve this one and burn the other." At the time of his death Washington owned more than 33,000 acres of land: 23,341 in Virginia, 5,000 in Kentucky, 3,051 in the Northwest Territory, 1,119 in Maryland, 1,000 in New York, 234 in Pennsylvania. He listed his stocks as worth $25,212. His livestock consisted of 640 sheep, 329 cows, 42 mules, 20 work horses, some pigs—a total value of $15,653. He also owned and bequeathed slaves. An extremely astute businessman, Washington added to his estates all his life. But he was "land poor," with never much cash available, so that he actually had to borrow 600 pounds to travel to his first inauguration in New York City. His estate was valued at $530,000.

Washington was a remarkably able businessman who increased his land holdings constantly through astute speculation. Although his Mount Vernon lands—like most farm land in Virginia—were depleted through successive tobacco plantings, lands he had begun to acquire as a teenager grew to be worth one hundred times their original value. By 1799 his land holdings alone were worth an estimated $488,137—millions by today's standards—though he had had to sell $50,000 worth of land a few years before to keep out of debt. He estimated that his service in the war cost him 10,000 pounds sterling, for he had to pay many military expenses out of his own pocket; in addition to this, his estates deteriorated in his absence. Besides farming, Washington also owned a distillery, a commercial mill, and several fisheries.

Of the objects treasured by Washington and bequeathed in his will many have survived. The cane which Franklin willed Washington and Washington bequeathed to his brother Charles is now in the Smithsonian Institution, as is the sword he bequeathed his nephew Samuel Washington. The swords bequeathed George Steptoe Washington, George Lewis, and Bushrod Washington are now at Mount Vernon. The sword bequeathed William Augustine Washington is owned by the New York State Library. Mount Vernon also owns the tambour secretary and circular chair Washington left Dr. James Craik as well as the telescope and shaving and dressing table left Dr. David Stuart. The Bible he left Bryan Fairfax is in the Library of Congress and the cane willed Robert Washington is still privately owned. Washington's request in his will to have a new vault built was not honored until 1830.

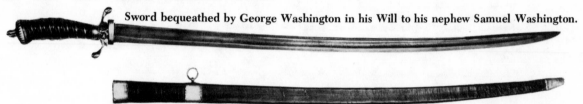

Sword bequeathed by George Washington in his Will to his nephew Samuel Washington.

Footstool used by Washington at Mount Vernon. The cane was bequeathed to George Washington in 1790 in the Will of Benjamin Franklin and subsequently bequeathed by Washington in his Will to his brother Charles.

Facsimile of sections of the Will.

22

the youngest shall have arrived at the age of twenty one years, by three judicious and disinterested men, – one to be chosen by each of the brothers, and the third by these two. – In the mean time, if the termination of my wife's interest therein should have ceased, the profits arising therefrom are to be applied for their joint uses and benefit. –

Third.   And whereas it has always been my intention, since my expectation of having Issue has ceased, to consider the Grand children of my wife in the same light as I do my own relations, and to act a friendly part by them; more especially by the two whom we have reared from their earliest infancy – namely – Eleanor Parke Custis, & George Washington Parke Custis. – And whereas the former of these hath lately intermarried with Lawrence Lewis, a son of my deceased Sister Betty Lewis, by which union the inducement to provide for them both has been increased. – Wherefore, I give & bequeath to the said Lawrence Lewis & Eleanor Parke Lewis his wife and their heirs, the residue of my Mount Vernon Estate, not already devised to my Nephew Bushrod Washington, – comprehended within the fol-

G. Washington

Text of the Will of George Washington

In the name of God amen

I George Washington of Mount Vernon—a citizen of the United States,—and lately President of the same, do make, ordain and declare this Instrument; which is written with my own hand and every page thereof subscribed with my name, to be my last Will & Testament, revoking all others.

Imprimus. All my debts, of which there are but few, and none of magnitude, are to be punctually and speedily paid—and the Legacies hereinafter bequeathed, are to be discharged as soon as circumstances will permit, and in the manner directed—

Item. To my dearly beloved wife Martha Washington I give and bequeath the use, profit and benefit of my whole Estate, real and personal, for the term of her natural life—except such parts thereof as are specifically disposed of hereafter:—My improved lot in the Town of Alexandria, situated on Pitt & Cameron Streets, I give to her and her heirs forever, as I also do my household & Kitchen furniture of every sort & kind, with the liquors and groceries which may be on hand at the time of my decease; to be used & disposed of as she may think proper.

Item Upon the decease of my wife, it is my Will & desire that all the Slaves which I hold in *my own right*, shall receive their freedom.—To emancipate them during her life, would, tho' earnestly wished by me, be attended with such insuperable difficulties on account of their intermixture by Marriages with the Dower Negroes, as to excite the most painful sensations, if not disagreeable consequences from the latter, while both descriptions are in the occupancy of the same Proprietor; it not being in my power, under the tenure by which the Dower Negros are held, to manumit them.—And whereas among those who will recieve freedom according to this devise, there may be some, who from old age or bodily infirmities, and others who on account of their infancy, that will be unable to support themselves; it is my Will and desire that all who come under the first & second description shall be comfortably cloathed & fed by my heirs while they live;—and that such of the latter description as have no parents living, or if living are unable, or unwilling to provide for them, shall be bound by the Court until they shall arrive at the age of twenty five years;—and in cases where no record can be produced, whereby their ages can be ascertained, the judgment of the Court upon its own view of the subject, shall be adequate and final.—The Negros thus bound, are (by their Masters or Mistresses) to be taught to read & write; and to be brought up to some useful occupation, agreeably to the Laws of the Commonwealth of Virginia, providing for the support of Orphan and other poor Children.—And I do hereby expressly forbid the Sale, or transportation out of the said Commonwealth, of any Slave I may die possessed of, under any pretence whatsoever.—And I do moreover most pointedly, and most solemnly enjoin it upon my Executors hereafter named, or the Survivors of them, to see that *this* clause respecting Slaves, and every part thereof be religiously fulfilled at the Epoch at which it is directed to take place; without evasion, neglect or delay, after the Crops which may then be on the ground are harvested, particularly as it respects the aged and infirm;—Seeing that a regular and permanent fund be established for their Support so long as there are subjects requiring it; not trusting to the uncertain provision to be made by individuals.—And to my Mulatto man William (calling himself William Lee) I give immediate freedom; or if he should prefer it (on account of the accidents which have befallen him, and which have rendered him incapable of walking or of any active employment) to remain in the situation he now is, it shall be optional in him to do so: In either case however, I allow him an annuity of thirty dollars during his natural life, which shall be independent of the victuals and cloaths he has been accustomed to receive, if he chuses the last alternative; but in full, with his freedom, if he prefers the first;—& this I give him as a testimony of my sense of his attachment to me, and for his faithful services during the Revolutionary War.—

Item To the Trustees (Governors, or by whatsoever other name they may be designated) of the Academy in the Town of Alexandria, I give and bequeath, in Trust, four thousand dollars, or in other words twenty of the shares which I hold in the Bank of Alexandria, towards the support of a Free school established at, and annexed to, the said Academy; for the purpose of Educating such Orphan children, or the children of such other poor and indigent persons as are unable to accomplish it with their own means; and who, in the judgment of the Trustees of the said Seminary, are best entitled to the benefit of this donation.—The aforesaid twenty shares I give & bequeath in perpetuity;—the dividends only of which are to be drawn for, and applied by the said Trustees for the time being, for the uses above mentioned;—the stock to remain entire and untouched; unless indications of a failure of the said Bank should be so apparent, or a discontinuance thereof should render a removal of this fund necessary;—in either of these cases, the amount of the Stock here devised, is to be vested in some other Bank or public Institution, whereby the interest may with regularity & certainby be drawn, and applied as above.—And to prevent misconception, my meaning is, and is hereby declared to be that these twenty shares are in lieu of, and not in addition to, the thousand pounds given by a missive letter some years ago; in consequence whereof an annuity of fifty pounds has since been paid towards the support of this Institution

Item Whereas by a Law of the Commonwealth of Virginia, enacted in the year 1785, the Legislature thereof was pleased (as a an evidence of Its approbation of the services I had rendered the Public during the Revolution—and partly, I believe, in consideration of my having suggested the vast advantages which the Community would derive from the extension of its Inland Navigation, under Legislative patronage) to present me with one hundred shares of one hundred dollars each, in the incorporated company established for the purpose of extending the navigation of James River from tide water to the Mountains: and also with fifty shares of one hundred pounds Sterling each, in the Corporation of another company, likewise established for the similar purpose of opening the Navigation of the River Potomac from tide water to Fort Cumberland; the acceptance of which, although the offer was highly honourable, and grateful to my feelings, was refused, as inconsistent with a principle which I had adopted, and had never departed from—namely—not to receive pecuniary compensation for any services I could render my country in its arduous struggle with great Britain, for its Rights; and because I had evaded similar propositions from other States in the Union;—adding to this refusal, however, an intimation that, if it should be the pleasure of the Legislature to permit me to appropriate the said shares to *public uses*, I would receive them on those terms with due sensibility;—and this it having consented to, in flattering terms, as will appear by a subsequent Law, and sundry resolutions, in the most ample and honourable manner, I proceed after this recital, for the more correct understanding of the case, to declare—

That as it has always been a source of serious regret with me, to see the youth of these United States sent to foreign Countries for the purpose of Education, often before their minds were formed, or they had imbibed any adequate ideas of the happiness of their own;—contracting, too frequently, not only habits of dissipation & extravagence, but principles unfriendly to Republican Governmt. and to the true & genuine liberties of mankind; which, thereafter are rarely overcome.—For these reasons, it has been my ardent wish to see a plan devised on a liberal scale which would have a tendency to sprd. systemactic ideas through all parts of this rising Empire, thereby to do away local attachments and State prejudices, as far as the nature of things would, or indeed ought to admit, from our National Councils.— Looking anxiously forward to the accomplishment of so desirable an object as this is (in my estimation) my mind has not been able to contemplate any plan more likely to effect the measure than the establishment of a UNIVERSITY in a central part of the United States, to which the youth of fortune and talents from all parts thereof might be sent for the completion of their Education in all the branches of polite literature;—in arts and Sciences,—in acquiring knowledge in the principles of Politics and good Government;—and (as a matter of infinite Importance in my judgment) by associating with each other, and forming friendships in Juvenile years, be enabled to free themselves in a proper degree from those local prejudices and habitual jealousies which have just been mentioned; and which, when carried to excess, are never failing sources of disquietude to the Public mind, and pregnant of mischievous consequences to this Country:—Under these impressions, so fully dilated,

Item I give and bequeath in perpetuity the fifty shares which I hold in the Potomac Company (under the aforesaid Acts of the Legislature of Virginia) towards the endowment of a UNIVERSITY to be established within the limits of the District of Columbia, under the auspices of the General Government, if that government should incline to extend a fostering hand towards it;—and until such Seminary is established, and the funds arising on these shares shall be required for its support, my further Will & desire is that the profit accruing therefrom shall, whenever the dividends are made, be laid out in purchasing Stock in the Bank of Columbia, or some other Bank, at the discretion of my Executors; or by the Treasurer of the United States for the time being under the direction of Congress; provided that Honourable body should Patronize the measure, and the Dividends proceeding from the purchase of such Stock is to be vested in more stock, and so on, until a sum adequate to the accomplishment of the object is obtained, of which I have not the smallest doubt, before many years passes away; even if no aid or encouraged is given by Legislative authority, or from any other source

Item The hundred shares which I held in the James River Company, I have given, and now confirm in perpetuity to, and for the use & benefit of Liberty-Hall Academy, in the County of Rockbridge, in the Commonwealth of Virga.

Item I release exonerate and discharge, the Estate of my deceased brother Samuel Washington, from the payment of the money which is due to me for the Land I sold to Philip Pendleton (lying in the County of Berkeley) who assigned the same to him the said Samuel; who, by agreement was to pay me therefor.—And whereas by some contract (the purport of which was never communicated to me) between the said Samuel and his son Thornton Washington, the latter became possessed of the aforesaid Land, without any conveyance having passed from me, either to the said Pendleton, the said Samuel, or the said Thornton, and without any consideration having been made, by which neglect neither the legal nor equitable title has been alienated;—it rests therefore with me to declare my intentions concerning the Premises—and these are, to give & bequeath the said land to whomsoever the said Thornton Washington (who is also dead) devised the same; or to his heirs forever if he died Intestate:—Exonorating the estate of the said Thornton, equally with that of the said Samuel from payment of the purchase money; which, with Interest; agreeably to the original contract with the said Pendleton, would amount to more than a thousand pounds.—And whereas two other Sons of my said deceased brother Samuel—namely, George Steptoe Washington and Lawrence Augustine Washington, were, by the decease of those to whose care they were committed, brought under my protection, and in conseqe. have occasioned advances on my part for their Education at College, and other Schools, for their board—cloathing—and other incidental expences, to the amount of near five thousand dollars over and above the Sums furnished by their Estate wch—Sum may be inconvenient for them, or their fathers Estate to refund. I do for these reasons acquit them, and the said estate, from the payment thereof.—My intention being, that all accounts between them and me, and their fathers estate and me shall stand balanced.—

Item The balance due to me from the Estate of Bartholomew Dandridge deceased (my wife's brother) and which amounted on the first day of October 1795 to four hundred and twenty five pounds (as will appear by an account rendered by his deceased son John Dandridge, who was the acting Exr. of his fathers Will) I release & acquit from the payment thereof.—And the Negros, then thirty three in number) formerly belonging to the said estate, who were taken in execution—sold—and purchased in on my account in the year   and ever since have remained in the possession, and to the use of Mary, Widow of the said Bartholomew Dandridge, with their increase, it is my Will & desire shall continue, & be in her possession, without paying hire, or making compensation for the same for the time past or to come, during her natural life; at the expiration of which, I direct that all of them who are forty years old & upwards, shall receive their freedom; all under that age and above sixteen, shall serve seven years and no longer; and all under sixteen years, shall serve until they are twenty five years of age, and then be free.—And to avoid disputes respecting the ages of any of these Negros, they are to be taken to the Court of the County in which they reside, and the judgment thereof, in this relation shall be final; and a record thereof made; which may be adduced as evidence at any time thereafter, if disputes should arise concerning the same.—And I further direct, that the heirs of the said Bartholomew Dandridge shall, equally, share the benefits arising from the Services of the said negros according to the tenor of this devise, upon the decease of their Mother.

Item If Charles Carter who intermarried with my niece Betty Lewis is not sufficiently secured in the title to the lots he had of me in the Town of Fredericksburgh, it is my Will & desire that my Executors shall make such conveyances of them as the Law requires, to render it perfect.—

Item To my Nephew William Augustine Washington and his heirs (if he should conceive them to be objects worth prosecuting) and to his heirs,—a lot in the Town of Manchester (opposite to Richmond) No 265 drawn on my sole account, and also the tenth of one or two, hundred acre lots, and two or three half acre lots in the City, and vicinity of Richmond, drawn in partnership with nine others, all in the lottery of the deceased William Byrd are given—as is also a lot which I purchased of John Hood, conveyed by William Willie and Samuel Gordon Trustees of the said John Hood, numbered 139 in the Town of Edinburgh, in the County of Prince George, State of Virginia

Item To my Nephew Bushrod Washington, I give and bequeath all the Papers in my possession, which relate to my Civel and Military Administration of the affairs of this Country;—I leave to him also, such of my private Papers as are worth preserving;—and at the decease of wife, and before—if she is not inclined to retain them, I give and bequeath my library of Books, and Pamphlets of every kind.—

Item Having sold Lands which I possessed in the State of Pennsylvania, and part of a tract held in equal right with George Clinton, late Governor of New York, in the State of New York;—my share of land, & interest, in the Great Dismal Swamp, and a tract of land which I owned in the County of Gloucester;—withholding the legal titles thereto, until the consideration money should be paid.—And having moreover leased, & conditionally sold (as will appear by the tenor of the said leases) all my lands upon the Great Kanhawa, and a tract upon Difficult Run, in the county of Loudoun, it is my Will and direction, that whensoever the Contracts are fully, & respectively complied with, according to the spirit, true intent & meaning thereof, on the part of the purchasers, their heirs or Assigns, that then, and in that case, Conveyances are to be made, agreeably to the terms of the said Contracts; and the money arising therefrom, when paid, to be vested in Bank stock; the dividends whereof, as of that also wch—is already vested therein, is to inure to my said Wife during her life—but the Stock itself is to remain, & be subject to the general distribution hereafter directed.

Item To the Earl of Buchan I recommit "the Box made of the Oak that sheltered the Great Sir William Wallace after the battle of Falkirk" presented to me by his Lordship, in terms too flattering for me to repeat,—with a request "to pass it, on the event of my decease, to the man in my country, who should appear to merit it best, upon the same conditions that have induced him to send it to me." Whether easy, or not, to select *the man* who might comport with his Lordships opinion in this respect, is not for me to say; but conceiving that no disposition of this valuable curiosity can be more eligable than the re-commitment of it to his own Cabinet, agreeably to the original design of the Goldsmiths Company of Edenburgh, who presented it to him, and at his request, consented that it should be transfered to me; I do give & bequeath the same to his Lordship, and in case of his decease, to his heir with my grateful thanks for the distinguished honour of presenting it to me; and more especially for the favourable sentiments with which he accompanied it.

Item To my brother Charles Washington I give & bequeath the gold headed Cane left me by Doctr. Franklin in his Will.—I add nothing to it, because of the ample provision I have made for his Issue.—To the acquaintances and friends of my Juvenile years, Lawrence Washington & Robert Washington of Chotanck, I give my other two gold headed Canes, having my Arms engraved on them; and to each (as they will be useful where they live) I leave one of the Spy-glasses which constituted part of my equipage during the late War.—To my compatriot in arms, and old & intimate friend Doctr. Craik, I give my Bureau (or as the Cabinet makers call it, Tambour Secretary) and the circular chair—an appendage of my Study.—To Doctor David Stuart I give my large shaving & dressing Table, and my Telescope.—To the Reverend, now Bryan, Lord Fairfax, I give a Bible in three large folio volumes, with notes, presented to me by the Right reverend Thomas Wilson, Bishop of Sodor & Man.—To General de la Fayette I give a pair of finely wrought steel Pistols, taken from the enemy in the Revolutionary War.—To my Sisters in law Hannah Washington & Mildred Washington,—to my friends Eleanor Stuart, Hannah Washington of Fairfield, and Elizabeth Washington of Hayfield, I give, each, a mourning Ring of the value of one hundred dollars.—These bequests are not made for the intrinsic value of them, but as mementos of my esteem & regard.—To Tobias Lear, I give the use of the Farm which he now holds, in virtue of a Lease from me to him and his deceased wife (for and during their natural lives) free from Rent, during his life;—at the expiration of which, it is to be disposed as is hereinafter directed.—To Sally B. Haynie (a distant relation of mine) I give and bequeath three hundred dollars—To Sarah Green daughter of the deceased Thomas Bishop, and to Ann Walker daughter of Jno. Alton, also deceased, I give, each one hundred dollars, in consideration of the attachment of their fathers to me, each of whom having lived nearly forty years in my family.—To each of my Nephews, William Augustine Washington, George Lewis, George Steptoe Washington, Bushrod Washington and Samuel Washington, I give one of the Swords or Cutteaux of which I may die possessed; and they are to chuse in the order they are named.—These Swords are accompanied with an injunction not to unsheath them for the purpose of shedding blood, except it be for self defence, or in defence of their Country and its rights; and in the latter case, to keep them unsheathed, and prefer falling with them in their hands, to the relinquishment thereof

And now

Having gone through these specific devises, with explanations for the more correct understanding of the meaning and design of them; I proceed to the distribution of the more important parts of my Estate, in manner following—

First To my Nephew Bushrod Washington and his heirs (partly in consideration of an intimation to his deceased father while we were Bachelors, & he had kindly undertaken to superintend my Estate during my Military Services in the former War between Great Britain & France, that if I should fall therein, Mount Vernon (then less extensive in domain than at present) should become his property) I give and bequeath all that part thereof which is comprehended within the following limits——viz—Beginning at the ford of Dogue run, near my Mill, and extending along the road, and bounded thereby as it now goes, & ever had gone since my recollection of it, to the ford of little hunting Creek at the Gum spring until it comes to a knowl, opposite to an old road which formerly passed through the lower field of Muddy hole Farm; at which, on the north side of the said road are three red, or Spanish Oaks marked as a corner, and a stone placed.—thence by a line of trees to be marked, rectangular to the back line, or outer boundary of the tract between Thomson Mason & myself.—thence with that line Easterly (now double ditching with a Post & Rail fence thereon) to the run of little hunting Creek.—thence with that run which is the boundary between the Lands of the late Humphrey Peake and me, to the tide water of the said Creek; thence by that water to Potomac River.—thence with the River to the mouth of Dogue Creek.—and thence with the said Dogue Creek to the place of beginning at the aforesaid ford; containing upwards of four thousand Acres, be the same more or less—together with the Mansion house and all other buildings and improvemts. thereon.

Second In consideration of the consanguinity between them and my wife, being as nearly related to her as to myself, as on account of the affection I had for, and the obligation I was under to, their father when living, who from his youth had attached himself to my person, and followed my fortunes through the viscissitudes of the late Revolution—afterwards devoting his time to the Superintendence of my private concerns for many years, whilst my public employments rendered it impracticable for me to do it myself, thereby affording me essential Services, and always performing them in a manner the most felial and respectful—for these reasons I say, I give and bequeath to George Fayette Washington, and Lawrence Augustine Washington and their heirs, my Estate East of little hunting Creek,—lying on the River Potomac;—including the Farm of 360 Acres, Leased to Tobias Lear as noticed before, and containing in the whole, by Deeds, Two thousand and Seventy seven acres—be it more or less.—Which said Estate it is my Will and desire should be equitably, & advantageously divided between them, according to quantity, quality & other circumstances when the youngest shall have arrived at the age of twenty one years, by three judicious and disinterested men;—one to be chosen by each of the brothers, and the third by these two.—In the meantime, if the termination of my wife's interest therein should have ceased, the profits arising therefrom are to be applied for thir joint uses and benefit.

Third And whereas it has always been my intention, since my expectation of having Issue has ceased, to consider the Grand children of my wife in the same light as I do my own relations, and to act a friendly part by them; more especially by the two whom we have reared from their earliest infancy—namely—Eleanor Parke Custis, & George Washington Parke Custis. And whereas the former of these hath lately intermarried with Lawrence Lewis, a son of my deceased Sister Betty Lewis, by which union the inducement to provide for them both has been increased;—Wherefore, I give & bequeath to the said Lawrence Lewis & Eleanor Parke Lewis, his wife, and their heirs, the residue of my Mount Vernon Estate, not already devised to my Nephew Bushrod Washington,—comprehended within the following description.—viz—All the land North of the Road leading from the ford of Dogue run to the Gum spring as described in the devise of the other part of the tract, to Bushrod Washington, until it comes to the Stone & three red or Spanish Oaks on the knowl.—thence with the rectangular line to the back line (between Mr. Mason & me)—thence with that line westerly, along the new double ditch to Dogue run, by the tumbling Dam of my Mill;—thence with the said run to the ford aforementioned;—to which I add all the Land I possess West of the said Dogue run, & Dogue Crk—bounded Easterly & Southerly thereby;—together with the Mill, Distillery, and all other houses & improvements on the premises, making together about two thousand Acres—be it more or less

Fourth Actuated by the principal already mentioned, I give and bequeath to George Washington Parke Custis, the Grandson of my wife, and my Ward, and to his heirs, the tract I hold on four mile run in the vicinity of Alexandria, containing one thousd—two hundred acres, more or less,—& my entire Square, number twenty one, in the City of Washington.

Fifth All the rest and residue of my Estate, real & personal—not disposed of in manner aforesaid—In whatsoever consisting—wheresoever lying—and whensoever found—a schedule of which, as far as is recollected, with a reasonable estimate of its value, is hereunto annexed—I desire may be sold by my Executors at such times—in such manner—and on such credits (if an equal, valid, and satisfactory distribution of the specific property cannot be made without)—as, in their judgment shall be most conducive to the interest of the parties concerned; and the monies arising therefrom to be divided into twenty three equal parts, and applied as follow—viz—

To William Augustine Washington, Elizabeth Spotswood, Jane Thornton, and the heirs of Ann Ashton; son, and daughters of my deceased brother Augustine Washington, I give and bequeath four parts;—that is—one part to each of them.

To Fielding Lewis, George Lewis, Robert Lewis, Howell Lewis & Betty Carter, sons and daughter of my deceased Sister Betty Lewis, I give & bequeath five other parts—one to each of them

To George Steptoe Washington, Lawrence Augustine Washington, Harriot Parks, and the heirs of Thornton Washington, sons and daughter of my deceased brother Samuel Washington, I give and bequeath other four parts, one part to each of them.

To Corbin Washington, and the heirs of Jane Washington, Son & daughter of my deceased Brother John Augustine Washington, I give & bequeath two parts;—one part to each of them.

To Samuel Washington, Francis Ball & Mildred Hammond, son and daughters of my Brother Charles Washington, I give & bequeath three parts;—one part to each of them.—And to George Fayette Washington Charles Augustine Washington & Maria Washington, sons and daughter of my deceased Nephew Geo: Augustine Washington, I give one other part;—that is—to each a third of that part.

To Elizabeth Parke Law, Martha Parke Peter, and Eleanor Parke Lewis, I give and bequeath three other parts,—that is a part to each of them.

And to my Nephews Bushrod Washington & Lawrence Lewis,—and to my ward, the grandson of My wife, I give and bequeath one other part;—that is, a third thereof to each of them.—And if it should so happen, that any of the persons whose names are here ennumerated (unknown to me) should now be deceased—or should die before me, that in either of these cases, the heirs of such deceased person shall, notwithstanding, derive all the benefits of the bequest; in the same manner as if he, or she, was actually living at the time.

And by way of advice, I recommend it to my Executors not to be precipitate in disposing of the landed property (herein directed to be sold) if from temporary causes the Sale thereof should be dull; experience having fully evinced, that the price of land (especially above the Falls of the Rivers, & on the Western Waters) have been progressively rising, and cannot be long checked in its increasing value.—And I particularly recommend it to such of the Legatees (under this clause of my Will) as can make it convenient, to take each a share of my Stock in the Potomac Company in preference to the amount of what it might sell for; being thoroughly convinced myself, that no uses to which the money can be applied will be so productive as the Tolls arising from this navigation when in full operation (and this from the nature of things it must be 'ere long) and more especially if that of the Shanondoah is added thereto.

The family Vault at Mount Vernon requiring repairs, and being improperly situated besides, I desire that a new one of Brick, and upon a larger Scale, may be built at the foot of what is commonly called the Vineyard Inclosure,—on the ground which is marked out.—In which my remains with those of my deceased relatives (now in the old Vault) and such others of my family as may chuse to be entombed there, may be deposited.—And it is my express desire that my Corpse may be Interred in a private manner, without—parade, or funeral Oration.

Lastly I constitute and appoint my dearly beloved wife Martha Washington, My Nephews William Augustine Washington, Bushrod Washington, George Steptoe Washington, Samuel Washington, & Lawrence Lewis, — my ward George Washington Parke Custis (when he shall have arrived at the age of twenty years) Executrix & Executors of this Will & testament,—In the construction of which it will readily be perceived that no professional character has been consulted, or has had any Agency in the draught—and that, although it has occupied many of my leisure hours to digest, & to through it into its present form, it may, notwithstanding, appear crude and incorrect.—But having endeavoured to be plain, and explicit in all the Devises—even at the expence of prolixity, perhaps of tautology, I hope, and trust, that no disputes will arise concerning them; but if, contrary to expectation, the case should be otherwise from the want of legal expression, or the usual technical terms, or because too much or too little has been said on any of the Devises to be consonant with law, My Will and direction expressly is, that all disputes (if unhappily any should arise) shall be decided by three impartial and intelligent men, known for their probity and good understanding; two to be chosen by the disputants—each having the choice of one—and the third by those two. Which three men thus chosen, shall, unfettered by Law, or legal constructions, declare their Sense of the Testators intention;—and such decision is, to all intents and purposes to be as binding on the Parties as if it had been given in the Supreme Court of the United States.

In witness of all, and of each of the things herein contained, I have set my hand and Seal, this ninth day of July, in the year One thousand seven hundred and ninety and of the Independence of the United States the twenty fourth.

G. Washington   (Seal)

Tambour secretary bequeathed in the Will of George Washington to Dr. James Craik.

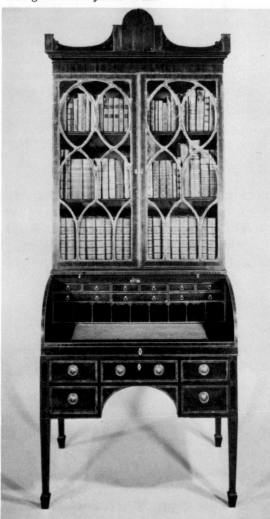

Circular chair bequeathed by George Washington in his Will to Dr. James Craik.

Notes on the Will of George Washington

IN ITS SPECIAL WAY, the Will of George Washington is yet another monument to his greatness and to his high rank among his contemporaries and among all those who have been President. The reader is unlikely to find another here which will impress him more.

Washington wrote this Will in the summer before his death using 15 sheets of specially prepared paper bearing his personal watermark. Each sheet was used on both sides; the pages were numbered and signed by him, probably after the whole was completed. Washington took pains to prepare an aesthetically pleasing document with evenly spaced lines of uniform length. He achieved this by using dashes or waved strokes to complete lines which words would not quite fill out and, where necessary, by cutting short the last word on a line whether division at that point coincided with the end of a syllable or not. Apparently he sought no legal assistance in drawing the Will, but he used appropriate legal terms skillfully, though he expressed some diffidence on that score near the end. There were no witnesses, but none were needed for a Will entirely in the testator's hand, dated and signed by him.

Two or three errors in spelling or in unnecessary repetition of a phrase in a long sentence do appear. The date is incorrectly written at the end as a result of the omission of the word "nine" in writing out the year of execution. Students of his life regard all of these errors as uncharacteristic of the man; they may reflect weariness or illness in the summer before his death.

When he died Washington was reputedly one of the nation's wealthiest men; certainly he was one of its largest landholders. With these holdings and his other assets Washington could afford to make a complicated disposition of his property among many persons—and did.

His wife was wealthy in her own right as the result of her prior marriage to Daniel Parke Custis, but he made generous provisions for her anyway. She was given outright a lot with improvements in the nearby town of Alexandria and the equipment and furnishings of their home at Mt. Vernon. She also received an interest for life in the great bulk of his other property. Following her death, which occurred on May 2, 1802, the Will provided for the division of his extensive holdings in northern Virginia into four large tracts ranging in size from 4,000 to 1,200 acres. These tracts were divided among descendants of his brothers and of his wife, Washington having had no natural children of his own.

He left his home, Mt. Vernon, to his nephew, Bushrod, who had been named to the Supreme Court in the previous year and who was later to be Washington's biographer with John Marshall. By the middle of the 19th century the estate at Mt. Vernon had fallen into serious disrepair, but it was saved by a private philanthropic organization created specifically for that purpose. It was restored to prime condition and is maintained by the organization as an historic shrine for the citizens of the nation and its visitors.

Two of the other specific properties left by Washington have also acquired permanent significance. A handsome plantation home, Woodlawn, was constructed by Lawrence and Eleanor (Nelly Custis) Lewis in 1805 on the land devised to them. It is now a museum house owned by The National Trust for Historic Preservation. Wellington (or River Farm as it is sometimes known) was the home of Tobias Lear, who had been secretary to Washington and tutor to his adopted children (his wife's grandchildren). It had been leased to Lear for life before the Will was written. After his death the property passed to members of Washington's family under the terms of the Will, where it remained for about 100 years. It is a large house on 27 acres near the Potomac and was built around 1750. It was recently acquired by The American Horticultural Society for its national headquarters.

Washington directed that the balance of his substantial wealth, consisting largely of pieces of land scattered throughout Virginia, Maryland, Pennsylvania, and what is now West Virginia and Ohio, be sold and the proceeds divided into 23 shares distributed in specified combinations. All in all, the Will creates a carefully thought out but complex scheme for dividing his principal wealth among those nearest to him.

Washington's benefactions were not, however, confined to family and friends. He owned slaves which he left to his wife for her life, stating though his personal preference for their immediate emancipation but citing essentially humanitarian reasons for waiting. At her death they were to be freed but still treated as a continuing responsibility of the Executors, who were charged by Washington with their care in various ways appropriate to their respective ages and needs. He also made gifts for the support of existing schools and to begin an endowment for the establishment of a proposed national university. The coming of the railroads had a disastrous effect on the value of the Potomac Company shares which he had provided for that purpose. This diminished the practical effect of his gift but not the significance of his vision of the Republic's needs.

Another interesting aspect of the Will is the way in which Washington anticipated some of the problems which might arise in administering assets so widely dispersed. He named his wife, whose health was poor, and five younger male members of his family as Executors. To facilitate their work in liquidating assets which he had directed to be sold, Washington prepared and attached to his Will a separate schedule of these properties. The schedule runs several pages in length and lists each asset to be sold with an estimate of its value and, in some instances, a few descriptive notes.

He recognized that disputes about the meaning and legal effect of Wills do sometimes occur and could indeed affect his own Will. If that should occur, he did not want the matter submitted to a court, the usual forum for such purpose. Instead, he requested that any such question be submitted to arbitration by three "impartial and intelligent men, known for their probity and good understanding." Such a provision would not be legally binding on any one with an interest in the estate—though its moral suasion would be formidable. The provision is primarily of interest for its revelation of Washington's view of litigation. No dispute over the meaning of the Will's provisions ever developed, though one minor controversy of another sort was taken into court.

Washington the patriot is visible in this Will as well as Washington the testator disposing of his property. At various points, from the opening identification of himself as "a citizen of the United States—and lately President of the same . . ." to the closing description of the year of execution as the 24th of the Independence of those United States, one feels his sense of pride as a participant in recent great events. Similarly, his statement of his reasons for wishing to have a national university created at the seat of government shows his continuing concern for the country's future needs and welfare.

As a document, Washington's Will has had an interesting history. It was first printed for public distribution in 1800, the year following his death, and has been published many times since, usually without scrupulous attention to accuracy. Since 1939 The Mount Vernon Ladies Association of the Union has published it in a booklet which also contains Martha Washington's Will and the supplemental Schedule of Property prepared by Washington and attached to his Will. The booklet version is based on the Jackson edition of 1868, which is deemed the most accurate. Extensive annotations describe in detail the persons and properties named in all three documents.

The booklet also includes a Foreword describing the physical characteristics of the Will, the circumstances of its execution, and its history since Washington's death. The last paragraph of the Foreword states:

The Will has been more or less damaged by time and ignorant handling; but the greatest injury developed from its having been folded vertically down the middle when it was placed in an envelope in 1861, by the then Clerk of Fairfax County, and taken to Richmond to preserve it from the Union troops. The wisdom of this precaution was amply attested by what happened to the Will of Martha Washington, which was left in Fairfax Court House. The folding was responsible for a weakening of the paper along the fold and the damage gradually spread until nearly every leaf broke into two pieces. The first and second leaves of the Will became badly mutilated and the last leaf of Washington's "Notes" to the "Schedule

of property" also lost many words of the written text. After the war, when the Will was returned to the Court House from Richmond, some pious, but misguided attempts were made to arrest the disintegration, the most startling of which was the sewing together of the broken leaves with needle and thread. In 1919, under the auspices of the Court, the Will was scientifically repaired and inlaid in the most approved manner by the chief manuscript repairer of the Library of Congress, mounted and handsomely bound as a solid volume. It is now preserved in a specially constructed steel exhibition case, bolted to the wall of the vault in Fairfax County Court House.

Facsimile of a section of the Will.

JOHN ADAMS

OHN ADAMS, THE OLDEST SON OF JOHN AND
SUSANNA BOYLSTON ADAMS, was born on
October 10, 1735, in Braintree (now Quincy),
Massachusetts, where his great-great-
grandfather had received a grant for about 40
acres in 1636. His father was a church deacon,
farmer, and selectman who at the time of his
death in 1761 left an estate appraised at 1,330
pounds, a moderate sum. His uncle, Joseph
Adams, was a schoolmaster and a clergyman
who had gone to Harvard and who became as
a model for John. For 125 years the Adams family had played no significant part in the affairs
of their community, though they were hard-
working, pious, reliable, and public-spirited village folk. Until John Adams of the fifth generation, none had shown any larger ambition.

The Adams family, like Washington's, had
come to America early in the 17th century.
Bringing with them only some household effects,
they had settled into a three-room house
among their Puritan brethren. After the burial
of Henry Adams—the great-great-grandfather
of the President—in 1646, the inventory of the
estate lists a house, barn, cow, calf, some pigs,
furniture and utensils, three beds, a silver
spoon, and some old books—valued at 75
pounds in all.

The first Adams house in Braintree was
built about 1675 and was bought by the senior
John Adams. The future President was born in
this house, known as the cottage, and at his
father's death inherited it. He and Abigail lived
in it until 1785, when he went abroad as U.S.

Minister to Great Britain. While in England in 1787 he purchased a second house, Peacefield, nearby.

The family fortune consisted of $6,000 by the time John Adams came of age and was sent to Harvard. He graduated at 19, third in a class of 24. He proceeded to study law while teaching school, was admitted to the bar, and began his practice by 1758 in Suffolk County, residing in Braintree.

Six years later, at 28, he met a lady of higher social position than himself and soon married the witty and attractive Abigail Smith of Weymouth, Massachusetts. She was the 19-year-old daughter of William Smith, Congregational minister of the church at Weymouth and the granddaughter of Colonel John Quincy, who had been Speaker of the Massachusetts House. This union brought Adams into the company of people of influence in the colony, which helped his law practice.

Thirteen years after his father's death, John bought from his brother the old homestead with the buildings and 35 acres of land for 440 pounds. Previous to this he had already owned some arable acreage and meadowland and had combined his law practice with farming.

His successful defense in 1770 of Captain Preston, who was charged with the murder of the victims of the "Boston Massacre," so impressed the voters of Boston that they elected him to the colonial legislature that same year.

John Adams was sent in 1774 to represent the people of Massachusetts at the First Continental Congress. He helped draft the Declaration of Independence, was Commissioner to France and Minister to Holland and, in 1783, helped negotiate the Treaty of Paris.

In recognition of his services to the American Revolution, he was made Minister to the Court of St. James's. Returning in 1788, he was elected the first Vice President of the United States at a salary of $5,000 a year. The two terms under Washington were frustrating, however, for a man of Adams' intellect and intense ambition.

In 1796, he was elected second President of the United States with a salary of $25,000 annually. During his years in Philadelphia (then the capital), Mrs. Adams spent much of her time in Quincy, leaving the President alone. When they moved into the still uncompleted White House in Washington in 1800, they brought only the bare essentials, leaving the Quincy estate furnished. Adams considered his salary insufficient for Presidential expenses. He served only one term, and passed his last 25 years in peaceful and happy seclusion at Quincy, where he died on July 4, 1826, at the age of 90.

John Adams had sprung from obscurity to prominence but had not accumulated great riches; his estate came to $30,000. On a marble slab in the church where John and Abigail Adams are interred their son placed a marble slab which reads in part: He pledged his life, Fortune and Sacred Honour to the Independence of His Country.

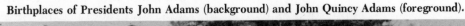

Birthplaces of Presidents John Adams (background) and John Quincy Adams (foreground).

Text of the Will of John Adams

Know all Men by these presents that I John Adams of Quincy in the county of Norfolk Esquire, being of sound mind and disposing memory though in the eighty fourth year of my age, do hereby make my last will and testament.

My debts, which I hope will not be large and my funeral charges, which I hope will be very small, must be paid by my Executors.

I give and devise to my son John Quincy Adams and to his heirs, all that part of my real estate, which lies on both sides of the Ancient County road from Boston to Plymouth, containing by estimation one hundred and three acres be the same more, or less, together with my mansion house, gardens and buildings thereon situated; I also give to him Babel pasture so called, which I purchased of the Executor of Norton Quincy; also the two rocky pastures which we have called the Lanes pasture and the Red cedar pasture, upon the following Condition vis.—that he pay, or secure to be paid with interest, within three years after my decease, to my Executors herein afternamed, for the said real Estate first above, named Ten Thousand dollars; for the said Babel pasture One Thousand dollars; and for both the said Lanes pasture and the said Red Cedar pasture One Thousand dollars. But in case my said son John Quincy shall refuse to accept the said Estate and pastures upon the said conditions then I order my said Executors to make sale of the same, and to apply the proceeds in portions, as herein after directed.

I give and devise to my said son John Quincy Adams, the whole of my library, upon condition that he pays to my son Thomas Boylston Adams, the value of one half the said library, to be estimated, in case my said sons cannote agree concerning the value, by appraisers, to be chosen by my Executors and to be approved by the Judge of Probate of the Court of Norfolk, for the time being. And my will is that a discharge or offset, made by my said son John Quincy, for the amount of such valuation of any debt, due from my said son Thomas, to my said son John Quincy shall be deemed a full compliance with this condition.

All the rest and residue of my estate, real, personal and mixed, I order to be sold by my Executors. After the payment of my debts and funeral expenses, I order that the proceeds of the said sale together with the sums to be paid or secured to be paid by the said John Quincy to my Executors as above provided, be applied and appropriated in the following manner, vis.—in equal portions to my said son John Quincy Adams,—to my said son Thomas Boylston Adams,—to my grandchildren William Smith, John Adams Smith,—Caroline Amelia de Windt, children of my deceased daughter Abigail Smith,—to my grandchildren Susanna Boylston Clark, Abigail Louisa Smith Johnson children of my deceased son Charles Adams;—to my grandchildren Abigail Adams, Elizabeth Coombs Adams, Thomas Boylston Adams, Isaac Hull Adams, John Quincy Adams, and Joseph Harod Adams, children of my said son Thomas Boylston Adams;—and to Katharine Louisa Smith neice of my late consort, who had been brought up in my family.

And my will is that my Executors herein after named shall retain in their hand, all the portions of my estate, herein above devised to my son Thomas Boylston Adams and to his six children abovenamed, that they put the same out to interest and hold the same in trust;—paying the said interest to my said son Thomas Boylston Adams, or to the support of his family, or forming an accumulating fund for the benefit of his children, at their discretion, until his said children attain the age of Twenty one years & as each attain the said age, my will is that my Executors should pay over such child's portion to him or her successively; and after the decease of my said son Thomas my will is that his portion be equally divided among such of his children as shall then survive.

All my family pictures;—all my books, papers, manuscripts and letters of every kind, I devise to my son John Quincy Adams.

I hereby constitute and appoint my son John Quincy Adams and my friend Jonah Quincy of Boston, Executors of this my last will and Testament.

I hereby revoke all my former wills and declare this to be my last will.

In witnesss whereof I have hereunto set my hand and seal this Twenty seventh day of September, in the year of our lord One Thousand eight hundred and nineteen.

John Adams

Signed sealed published and declared
by the said John Adams the testator
to be his last will and testament, in
presence of us, who in his presence and in the
presence of each other subscribe our names as
witnessed. *"fifth"* erased & *"seventh"* inserted
in 3rd line from the bottom before signing.

    M. Davis
    Thomas Greenleaf
    Geo. W. Beale

Notes on the Will of John Adams

JOHN ADAMS WAS ALREADY 84 when he executed this Will. His wife, his two daughters, and one son had already died, but two sons, John Quincy Adams and Thomas Boylston Adams, and a host of grandchildren were living. He wished to divide his property among all of the living members of his family, including a niece of his wife who had been brought up in their home though never formally adopted.

It seems evident from the Will that the older son, John Quincy, enjoyed greater confidence and favor in his father's eyes than did his brother. Thus, the family pictures, books, papers, etc. were given to him alone. Though he was active in public life and frequently absent from Quincy, John Quincy was the son named co-Executor with the responsibilities which that entails. (At the time of the execution of the Will, he was Secretary of State in President Monroe's Cabinet; at the time of his father's death he was President.) Moreover, though the Will directs conversion of his principal assets into cash to facilitate division among 14 legatees, John Quincy was given an option to buy particularly desirable assets either at a price fixed in the Will, or one to be reached by agreement or appraisal.

This Will is the first of many in this book to create a trust. A trust is a protective arrangement in which ownership of property is divided between persons who are to enjoy its benefits (called beneficiaries) and those who accept its responsibilities (called trustees). Here the shares of Thomas Boylston Adams and his minor children were to be retained in the hands of the Executors, who were charged with the duty of investing them, and who were given a broad discretion over when and how to pay out the return produced. The trust device is an extremely flexible one which can be given a very wide variety of characteristics desired for it by its creator, a fact abundantly illustrated by the numerous trusts found in this book.

The Will illustrates how easily an apparently straightforward statement can be seen to be ambiguous on closer scrutiny. Thus, it directs that the funds realized by the sale of various assets "be applied and appropriated . . . in *equal portions* to" (14 named persons each of whose relationship to the testator is described). Did Adams intend 14 equal shares, or does the punctuation which he used require a division into six shares, one for each son, one for the wife's niece, one for the children collectively of each of two deceased children, and one for the children of Thomas Boylston Adams? This is the stuff of which disputes are made. Of course, if all of those who have an interest are adults and can agree upon a single interpretation, any dispute is avoided—though hard feelings may not be.

Division of property among descendants of a common ancestor can raise difficult questions where they are or could be members of different generations. Those contemplating such division must first decide on a method of division which seems to them most suitable; then the draftsman of the will must clearly describe the pattern chosen. The problem is encountered in a number of these wills, and it may be instructive to compare the language here which speaks simply of "equal portions" with that used in other wills in this series for a similar purpose.

Vest worn by President John Adams.

THOMAS JEFFERSON

THOMAS JEFFERSON WAS BORN ON APRIL 13, 1743, at Shadwell, Albemarle County, Virginia. He was the son of Peter Jefferson, a surveyor and planter with 30 slaves, and of wealthy and socially prominent Jane Randolph Jefferson. Peter Jefferson had been a justice of the peace, a vestryman in his parish, and a colonial legislator. The ancestral Jefferson came from Wales to Virginia in the early 1600's.

Thomas inherited some 5,000 acres of land at the age of 14, when his father died. As had been arranged, he entered William and Mary College at the age of 17. There, one of his teachers, George Wythe, a leading jurist, persuaded Thomas to study law under him following his graduation. He soon took over the management of the family estate and was appointed a justice of the peace and vestryman, like his father before him.

Thomas Jefferson was learned in many areas. An avid and innovative farmer and inventor, he was also a talented musician, architect, philosopher, writer, lawyer, and politician. He spent 25 years in building the 33-room Monticello on a mountain overlooking Charlottesville. When he married the 23-year-old widow Martha Wayles Skelton in 1772, his house was still unfinished. From his father-in-law, John Wayles, a successful Williamsburg lawyer, Jefferson inherited 40,000 acres of land and 135 slaves in 1773. The former though was subject to heavy indebtedness which caused him endless money troubles.

At 33 Jefferson drafted the Declaration of

Independence and three years later, in 1779, he became Governor of Virginia. In 1782 his wife died, leaving him with three daughters; he did not remarry. Jefferson succeeded Benjamin Franklin as Minister to France in 1785; while he was there his youngest daughter Lucy died. Upon his return in early 1790 he witnessed the marriage of his eldest daughter Martha to Thomas Mann Randolph. In the spring of that year he left Monticello for New York to become Secretary of State at an annual salary of $3,500. Jefferson found himself at odds with the Secretary of the Treasury, Alexander Hamilton, and finally resigned his office late in 1793.

His political ability and the confidence of his party would not allow him to live a private life at his Virginia estate. In 1796 he was elected Vice President under Adams at a salary of $5,000 a year. In 1801 he won the disputed election in the House of Representatives and became the third President of the United States with a salary of $25,000. His most notable act as President was perhaps the Louisiana Purchase in 1803, which doubled the nation's territory. After his second term, Jefferson returned at the age of 66 without regret to Monticello and private life. But his public activities had been largely financed by himself, he was openhanded to a fault, and he had no funds left to carry out his dreams.

A man of expensive tastes, Jefferson was bedeviled by financial worries most of his adult life. First, he had to pay twice over the debt on the property which he inherited from his father-in-law because his British creditors refused the first payment as depreciated currency. Then too, he was temperamentally incapable of turning away numerous people who dropped in at Monticello for free meals and lodgings. Though his estate was worth around $200,000, the land was poor and brought him only a modest return: the farm $4,000 a year, his mill, naillery, cooper's shop and the hiring out of slaves another $2,000. By the time of his retirement in 1809 he still owed about $25,000, partly because he had signed a $20,000 note for a friend who proceeded to go bankrupt. In 1814 he had to sell his library to Congress for $23,950. In 1826 he petitioned the Virginia legislature to hold a lottery to dispose of all his property, including Monticello. When this became known, friends all over the country contributed to a fund to help the former President and the lottery was abandoned.

Jefferson lived at Monticello in retirement for 17 years before he died on July 4, 1826. The furnishings at Monticello were sold to help satisfy his debts of $40,000. His surviving daughter and her children lost their home and means of support. In gratitude for her father's service, the states of Virginia and South Carolina each voted Martha Jefferson Randolph the sum of $10,000. For many years Monticello was unoccupied, and it fell into ruin before an effort was made in the 1920's to acquire the estate and restore it as a national shrine.

The gold-mounted walking staff of animal bone and the silver watch alluded to in his will are still owned by Jefferson's descendants. His papers are in the Library of Congress and the University of Virginia.

Portable writing desk upon which Thomas Jefferson wrote the first draft of the Declaration of Independence in Philadelphia in 1776.

Text of the Will of Thomas Jefferson

I Thomas Jefferson of Monticello in Albemarle, being of sound mind and in my ordinary state of health, make my last will and testament in manner and form as follows.

I give to my grandson Francis Eppes, son of my dear deceased daughter Mary Eppes, in fee simple, all that part of my lands at Poplar Forest lying West of the following lines, to wit, Beginning at Radford, upper corner near the double branches of Bear creek and the public road, & running thence in a straight line to the fork of my private road, near the barn, thence along that private road (as it was changed in 1817) to it's corssing of the main branch of North Tomahawk creek, and from that crossing, in a direct line over the main ridge which divides the North and South Tomahawk, to the South Tomahawk, at the confluence of two branches where the old road to the Waterlick crossed it, and from that confluence up the Northernmost branch (which separates McDaniel's and Perry's fields) to it's source; & thence by the shortest line to my Western boundary. And having, in a former correspondence with my deceased son in law John W. Eppes contemplated laying off for him with remainder to my grandson Frances, a certain portion in the Southern part of my lands in Bedford and Campbell, which I afterwards found to be generally more indifferent than I has supposed, & therefore determined to change it's location for the better; now to remove all dout, if any could arise on a purpose merely voluntary & unexecuted, I hereby declare that what I have herein given to my 2d grandson Francis is instead of, and not additional to what I had formerly contemplated.

I subject all my other property to the payment of my debts in the first place.

Considering the insolvent state of the affairs of my friend & son in law Thomas Mann Randolph, and that what will remain of my property will be the only resource against the want in which his family would otherwise be left, it must be his wish, as it is my duty, to guard that resource against all liability for his debts, engagements or purposes whatsoever, and to preclude the rights, powers and authorities over it which might result to him by operation of law, and which might, independantly of his will, bring it within the power of his creditors, I do hereby devise and bequeath all the residue of my property real and personal, in possession or in action, whether held in my own right, or in that of my dear deceased wife, according to the powers vested in me by deed of settlement for that purpose, to my grandson Thomas J. Randolph, & my friends Nicholas P. Trist, and Alexander Garrett & their heirs during the life of my sd. son in law Thomas M. Randolph, to be held & administered by them, in trust, for the sole and separate use and behoof of my dear daughter Martha Randolph and her heirs, and, aware of the nice and difficult distinctions of the law in these cases, I will further explain by saying that I understand and intend the effect of these limitations to be, that the legal estate and actual occupation shall be vested in my said trustees, and held by them in base fee, determinable on the death of my sd son in law, and the remainder during the same time be vested in my sd. daughter and her heirs, and of course disposable by her last will, and that at the death of my sd. son in law, the particular estate of the sd. trustees shall be determined, and the remainder, in legal estate, possession and use become vested in my sd. daughter and her heirs, in absolute property, for ever.

In consequence of the variety and undescribableness of the articles of property within the house at Monticello, and the difficulty of inventorying and appraising them separately and specifically, and its inutility, I dispense with having them inventoried and appraised; and it is my will that my executors be not held to give any security for the administration of my estate. I appoint my grandson Thomas Jefferson Randolph my sole executor during his life, and after his death, I constitute executors my friends Nicholas P. Trist and Alexander Garrett joining to them my daughter Martha Randolph after the death of my sd. son in law Thomas M. Randolph.

Lastly I revoke all former wills by me heretofore made; and in witness that this is my will, I have written the whole with my own hand on two pages, and have subscribed my name to each of them this 16th day of March one thousand eight hundred and twenty six.

Thomas Jefferson

I Thomas Jefferson of Monticello in Albemarle make and add the following Codicil to my will, controlling the same so far as it's provisions go.

I recommend to my daughter Martha Randolph the maintenance and care of my well-beloved sister Anne Scott Marks, and trust confidently that from affection to her, as well as for my sake, she will never let her want a comfort.

I have made no specific provision for the comfortable maintenance of my son in law Thomas M. Randolph, because of the difficulty and uncertainty of devising terms which shall vest any beneficial interest in him which the law will not transfer to the benefit of his creditors, to the destitution of my daughter and her family and disablement of her to supply him: whereas properly placed under the exclusive right of my daughter and her independent will, as if she were a femme sole, considering the relations in which she stands both to him and his children, will be a certain resource against want for all.

I give to my friend James Madison of Montpellier my gold-mounted walking staff of animal horn, as a token of the cordial and affectionate friendship which for nearly now an half century has united us in the same principles and pursuits of what we have deemed for the greatest good of our country.

I give to the University of Virginia my library, except such particular books only, and of the same edition, as it may already possess, when this legacy shall take effect. The rest of my said library remaining after those given to the University shall have been taken out, I give to my two grandsons in law Nicholas P. Trist and Joseph Coolidge.

To my grandson Thomas Jefferson Randolph I give my silver watch in preference to the golden one, because of it's superior excellence. my papers of business going of course to him, as my executor, all others of a literary or other character I give to him as of his own property.

Thomas Jefferson

Notes on the Will of Thomas Jefferson

JEFFERSON WAS NEARLY 83 when he prepared this Will. He had been widowed for more than 40 years. Four of his six children had died as infants. Two daughters lived to marry and have children of their own, but one of them was already dead. When he came to write this Will, his family consisted of one middle-aged daughter, her husband, and the children of both daughters. He also felt some responsibility for a sister.

Jefferson was trained as a lawyer and was an experienced draftsman. The provisions of his Will reveal a grasp of the distinctions then made by the law in the legal status of married and single women—specifically, with respect to property which they might own or acquire. At common law a married woman was much worse off than one who was unmarried. In legal theory her personality was merged with that of her husband, and he acquired ownership of her personal property and the right to enjoy and control her real estate. As a corollary, his creditors acquired the ability to reach and to satisfy his debts from assets which had originally been transferred to his wife.

In the 17th and 18th centuries legal doctrine had evolved a technique to escape from these consequences. By transferring property *in trust* for a married woman, a donor or testator would avoid the automatic creation of the husband's interest in such property recognized by the common law and avoid the potential claims of his creditors as well. Thus, Jefferson, making provision for his daughter, felt obliged to transfer assets to a trustee for her benefit rather than to her directly. Unlike the trust in the Will of John Adams, this one does not reflect any lack of confidence in his daughter, for it was to last only as long as the son-in-law should live. His death would terminate his daughter's status as a married woman. Thereafter his creditors could make no claim to property which she would receive free of the trust following her husband's death.

This form of protection for a married daughter is no longer necessary today. Under statutes called Married Women's Property Acts, enacted in all states in the 19th century, married women now may own their property separately from their husbands. One consequence is that their property is not available to satisfy claims against their husbands unless they have previously consented to share that risk. Jefferson's concern for protection against his son-in-law's creditors, in fact, proved pointless since Jefferson's estate itself was insolvent at the time of his death, and its assets were held to satisfy the claims of his own creditors.

The provisions of the Will dispensing with an inventory and appraisal of the contents of his home at Monticello, and also relieving the Executors from any need to provide security, are often included in wills. These procedures afford protection to those with an interest in the estate, but they entail some expense and delay. Thus a testator may seek to simplify the process of estate administration and cut its cost by directing their omission. The direction is not effective, however, if creditors of the estate establish that one or more of these procedures are needed for their protection.

The provisions of the codicil disposing of his cane to Madison, his old colleague and successor as President, and enlarging the library of the University of Virginia introduce some oblique reference to some of his concerns and activities in his public life, but the Will is disappointing in this respect. His interests of this nature continued throughout his life. He may simply have thought his Will a specialized document inappropriate for such considerations.

Jefferson with bust of Benjamin Franklin (detail).

JAMES MADISON

JOHN MADISON, THE GREAT-GREAT-GRANDFATHER of James Madison, settled on the Chesapeake Bay coast of Virginia, between the North and York rivers, in 1653. James Madison was born on March 16, 1751, the oldest of 12 children of James and Nelly Conway Madison who, while not exactly wealthy, were comfortably fixed.

James got his early education from a Scottish schoolmaster named Donald Robertson and from Reverend Thomas Martin, clergyman of his parish then residing in the Madison home. He entered the College of New Jersey (now Princeton) at 18 and graduated three years later, in 1772, though he stayed another year to study Hebrew. His formal education completed, he returned to Orange County, Virginia, where his family owned Montpellier, a plantation of between 3,000 and 4,000 acres. Here he continued to study history, law, and theology, while tutoring his brothers and sisters. He also became absorbed by public life, and in 1776 he was chosen a delegate to the state constitutional convention in Williamsburg.

When the national Constitutional Convention met in Philadelphia in 1787, Madison, then 36, and already a member of the Continental Congress, attended as a member of the Virginia delegation. With the establishment of the House of Representatives in 1789, Madison became a member of that body, a position he held until 1797.

It was during this time that he met and married Dolley Payne Todd, widow of a

Philadelphia lawyer and the daughter of a boardinghouse keeper. She became an accomplished hostess. Mrs. Madison had one surviving son by her first marriage, but she inherited all of her first husband's property. And as both she and her son were quite extravagant, they soon appreciably diminished the family fortune.

Meanwhile James Madison continued his political career, serving as Secretary of State from 1801 to 1809 and then becoming President of the United States with an annual salary of $25,000. The burning of the Executive Mansion during the War of 1812 occurred during the Madisons' residence there. While it was being rebuilt, the Madisons resided at the nearby Octagon House, where Mrs. Madison continued to entertain lavishly.

In 1817 the Madisons returned to Montpellier, where they lived for the next 20 years. In 1819 the former President bought a house at 16th and H Streets in Washington, D.C. During the 16 years Madison had lived in Washington, he continued to supervise the administration of the estate in Montpellier and after his return he devoted his full time to the estate while continuing to entertain lavishly. Only a year after her husband's death on June 28, 1836, however, Mrs. Madison was forced to part with the plantation, and move into the house in Washington. The step was made necessary largely because of her son's prodigality. Madison had spent 20 years of hard economic times and $40,000 in a vain effort to pay off debts incurred by this spendthrift stepson.

To assist Mrs. Madison in her financial difficulties, Congress purchased her husband's papers in two lots, one in 1837 for $30,000 and the second (according to a reference in Dolley Madison's will) for $20,000 in 1848. The walking stick made from the timber of the frigate *Constitution* mentioned in Madison's will is now in the Smithsonian Institution at Washington.

Montpellier, Madison's home.

Text of the Will of James Madison

I, James Madison, of Orange County, do make this my last will and testament, hereby revoking all wills by me heretofore made—

I devise to my dear wife, during her life, the tract of land whereon I live, as now held by me, except as herein otherwise devised, and if she shall pay the sum of nine thousand dollars ———— within three years, ———— after my death, to be distributed, as hereinafter directed, then I devise the same land to her in fee simple. If my wife shall not pay the said sum of money within the period before mentioned, then and in that case, it is my will, and I hereby direct, that at her death, the said land shall be sold for cash, or on credit as may be deemed most for the interest of those entitled to the proceeds thereof. If my wife shall pay the said sum of money within the time before specified, as aforesaid, so as to become entitled to the fee simple in the said land, then I bequeath the said sum of money to be equally divided between all my nephews and nieces which shall, at that time, be living, and in case of any of them being dead leaving issue, at that time, living, then such issue shall take the place of its or their deceased parent—

It is my further will, that in case my wife shall not pay the said sum of money within the time before named, and it shall therefore be necessary to sell the said land at her death, as before directed, then after deducting the twentieth part of the purchase money of the said land—which deducted part I hereby empower my wife to dispose of by her will I bequeath the residue of the purchase money, and in case of her dying without having disposed of such deducted part by her will, I bequeath the whole of the purchase money of the said land to my nephews and nieces, or the issues of such of them as may be dead in the manner before directed in regard to the money to be paid by her in case she shall pay the same.

I devise my grist mill with the land attached thereto to my wife, during her life, and I hereby direct the same to be sold at her death, and the purchase money to be divided as before directed in regard to the proceeds of the tract whereon I live.

I devise to my niece, Nelly C. Willis, and her heirs, the lot of land lying in Orange County, purchased of Boswell Thornton, on which is a limestone quarry, and also my interest in a tract of land lying in Louisa County reputed to contain two hundred acres, and not far from the said limestone quarry.

I devise my house and lot or lots in the city of Washington to my beloved wife and her heirs—I give and bequeath my ownership in the Negroes and people of whom held by me, to my dear wife, but it is my desire that none of them should be sold without his or her consent, or in case of their misbehaviour, except that infant children may be sold with their parent who consents for them to be sold with him or her and who consents to be sold.

I give all my personal estate of every description, ornamental as well as useful, except as herein after other wise given, to my dear wife—And I also give to her all my manuscript papers, having entire confidence in her discreet and proper use of them, but subject to the qualification in the succeeding clause—

Considering the peculiarity and magnitude of the occasion which produced the Convention at Philadelphia in 1787, the characters who composed it, the Constitution which resulted from their deliberations, its effects during a trial of so many years on the prosperity of the people living under it, and the interest it has inspired among the friends of free government, it is not an unreasonable inference that a careful and extended report of the proceedings and decisions of that body, which were with closed doors, by a member who was constant in his attendance, will be particularly gratifying to the people of the United States, and to all who take an interest in the progress of political science and the cause of true liberty. It is my desire that the report as made by me should be published under her authority and direction, and as the publication may yield a considerable amount beyond the necessary expenses thereof. I give the net proceeds thereof to my wife, charged with the following legacies to be paid out of that fund only—first I give to Ralph Randolph Gurley, secretary of the American Colonization society, and to his executors and administrators the sum of two thousand dollars, in trust nevertheless that he shall appropriate the same to the use and purposes of the said society whether the same be incorporated by law or not.

I give fifteen hundred dollars to the University of Virginia, one thousand dollars to the College of Nassau Hall at Princeton, New-Jersey, and one thousand dollars to the College at Uniontown Pennsylvania, for the benefit of their respective libraries; And it is my will that if the said fund should not be sufficient to pay the whole of the three last legacies, that they abate in proportion—I further direct that there be paid out of the same fund to the guardian of the three sons of my deceased nephew, Robert S. Madison, the sum of three thousand dollars to be applied to their education in such proportions as their guardian may think right. I also give out of the same fund to my nephew, Ambrose Madison, two thousand dollars to be applied by him to the education of his sons in such proportions as he may think right; and I also give out of the same fund the sum of five hundred dollars to each of the daughters of my deceased niece, Nelly Baldwin, and if the said fund shall not be sufficient to pay the whole of the legacies for the education of my greatnephews as aforesaid, and the said legacies to my great nieces, then they are to abate in proportion.

I give to the University of Virginia, all that portion of my library of which it has not copies of the same editions, and which may be thought by the board of visitors not unworthy of a place in its library, reserving to my wife the right first to select such particular books and pamphlets as she shall choose, not exceeding three hundred volumes.

In consideration of particular and valuable aids received from my brother in law, John C. Payne, and the affection which I bear him, I devise to him and his heirs, two hundred and forty acres of land on which he lives, including the improvements, on some of which, he has bestowed considerable expense, to be laid off adjoining the lands of Reuben and James Newman in a convenient form for a farm so as to include woodland and by the said Mr. Newmans—

I bequeath to my stepson, John Payne Todd, the case of medals presented me by my friend, George W. Ewing, and the walking staff made from a timber of the frigate, Constitution, and presented me by Commodore Elliot, her present Commander.

I desire the gold mounted walking staff bequeathed to me by my late friend, Thomas Jefferson, be delivered to Thomas J. Randolph, as well in testimony of the estemm I have for him, as from the knowledge I have of the place he held in the affections of his grand-father.

To remove every doubt of what is meant by the terms of tract of land whereon I live, I here declare it to comprehend all land owned by me, and not herein otherwise devised away—

I hereby appoint my dear wife to be sole executrix of this my will, and desire that she may not be required to give security for the execution thereof, and that my estate be not appraised—

In testimony hereof, I have this fifteenth day of April, one thousand eight hundred and thirty five. Signed, Sealed, published and declared this to be my last will & testament—

James Madison (Seal)

We have signed
presence of the testator
and of each other
Robert Taylor
Reuben Newman Senr.
Reuben Newman Jun.
Sims Brockman

I, James Madison, do annex this codicil to my last will as above to be taken as part thereof—

It is my will that the nine thousand dollars to be paid by my wife and distributed among my nephews & nieces, may be paid into the bank of Virginia, or into the Circuit Superior Court of Chancery for Orange, within three years after my death.

I direct that the proceeds from the sale of my grist mill & the land annexed sold at the death of my wife, shall be paid to Ralph Randolph Gurley, secretary of the American Colonization society, and to his executors & administrators, in trust, and for the purposes of the said society, whether the same be incorporated by law or not—

This codicil is written wholly by and signed with my own hand, this nineteenth day of April, 1835.

James Madison

Notes on the Will of James Madison

WASHINGTON, JEFFERSON, AND MADISON ALL MARRIED WIDOWS. Dolley Madison, one of the most famous of Presidential wives, was 17 years younger than her husband. They had no children of their own, but Madison had such close ties to his nieces and nephews that his Will provides a division of his property between them and his wife.

The most interesting aspect of Madison's Will are the provisions dealing with the publication of his record of the proceedings of the Constitutional Convention. One of the first decisions of that body was that it should conduct its deliberations secretly, presenting the country with a final version agreed to by the delegates, but without revealing the process by which it had been reached.

Madison was one of the leaders of the Convention. He attended regularly and kept a detailed day-to-day record of the debate. Questions of interpretation of the new charter were often the subject of hard political debate in the early years of the Republic. Several others in attendance who had kept notes had published them, and Madison was urged at various times to publish his record of the proceedings. He consistently refused, stating that he would not authorize publication until death had put all of the participants in the Convention beyond the reach of criticism. Madison himself proved to be the last survivor.

While it is clear from the Will that Madison regarded publication of his *Notes of Debates in the Federal Convention of 1787* as a contribution to public understanding of government, he unquestionably thought of the Journal as his property and a source of legitimate potential revenue for his family and other legatees. After publication, it was evident that Madison's was the most complete and accurate record of any available; it is now described as "the standard authority for the proceedings of the Convention" (Max Farrand).

Madison's Will reflects some of the ambivalence felt at the time toward the black population of the young nation. Madison owned slaves. He left them to his wife, though imposing restrictions on their sale. Presumably he believed their labor was essential to the operation of his plantation, Montpellier, which he wanted his widow to be able to enjoy. At the same time, his Will includes a substantial contribution to an organization seeking to improve the lot of former slaves who had been freed only to find that society was not prepared to accept them fully. The American Colonization Society was formed in 1816 by a number of people, including Bushrod Washington, to assist former slaves who wished to resettle in Africa. Some emigration was produced by the efforts of the Society. This led to the establishment of the nation of Liberia, but the movement rapidly lost momentum under attacks on it from abolitionists and the indifference of freed blacks to an artificial "repatriation."

Some of the early Presidents were closely associated over a long period in a way which

Tomb of President James Madison at Montpellier, Virginia.

became rare as the population and geographic area of the country grew. The Wills of Jefferson and Madison reflect their friendship. Jefferson bequeathed a particular cane to Madison; here Madison passes it on to Jefferson's grandson. Both left their libraries to the University of Virginia, an institution created by Jefferson and a very important center of interest in his later life.

Madison's Will is the second in this series to include a codicil. A codicil is a written amendment, made at a date following the execution of the will, which modifies the will but does not completely revoke it. Well-drawn codicils define clearly their relationship to the previously executed Will. Where there is unexplained contradiction between the provisions of a will and those of a codicil the rule of testamentary writings is that the later in time controls.

Though Madison was a well-to-do planter, his provisions for the widow, who survived him for 13 years, ran afoul of her misplaced trust in Payne Todd, her son by her first marriage. He consistently mismanaged her affairs. Montpellier, the plantation home, was sold within a year or two of Madison's death. The effort to publish the record of the Convention failed. Then, in a letter to President Jackson, dated Nov. 15, 1836, Mrs. Madison offered it to the United States, and in March 1837 Congress enacted the legislation necessary to purchase it from her for $30,000. That sum was in its turn rapidly dissipated.

In her last years Dolley Madison returned to Washington to live in a house on the east side of Lafayette Square near the White House. She again became a grande dame of Washington society, though faced with financial difficulties until Congress purchased the rest of Madison's papers in 1848, this time taking the precaution of putting $20,000 of the sales proceeds into a trust for her. She died on July 12, 1849.

The head of the cane (mentioned in Madison's Will) that had been made from wood from the *U.S.S. Constitution* and presented to the President by Commodore J. D. Elliott.

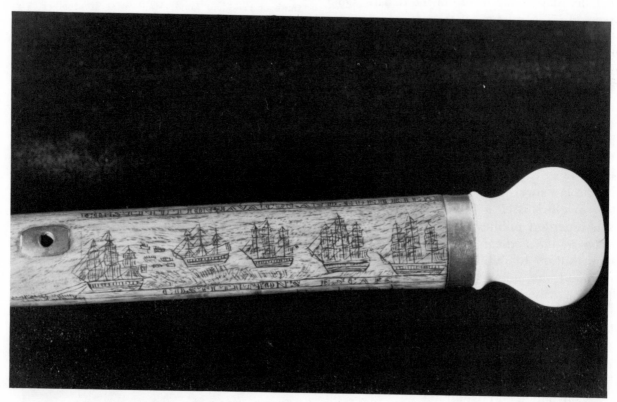

JAMES MONROE

J AMES MONROE, THE LAST OF THE SO-CALLED VIRGINIA DYNASTY, was born in Westmoreland County, Virginia, on April 28, 1758. His Scottish ancestors had come to America as early as 1650. Spence Monroe, his father, was a carpenter by trade; his mother, Elizabeth Jones Monroe, was the sister of a judge and delegate of Virginia to the Continental Congress.

Monroe's boyhood home, in an area noted for its patriotic fervor, was of the most primitive sort. His early schooling was from a field school operated by Parson Campbell. In the midst of the controversy with England, James Monroe at 16 entered the College of William and Mary, where he found resentment against Great Britain even higher than at home. Mon-

roe greatly admired Jefferson, under whom he later studied law; the two became great friends. At 17, Monroe raided the Governor's palace in Williamsburg to seize ammunition and at 18 he marched forth with other students and professors to join the Revolution. He was wounded at Trenton and was among those who wintered with Washington at Valley Forge.

After the war, Monroe returned to Virginia, where Jefferson was Governor, to become a member of the House of Delegates. He sat on the Governor's Council and also practiced law after being admitted to the bar in 1786. He aligned himself with the anti-Federalists in the Virginia convention which ratified the Constitution. In 1786 he married 17-year old Elizabeth Kortright, a New York belle who was the daughter of a wealthy merchant who had been a Tory during the Revolution.

In 1790, Monroe was elected to the U.S. Senate, but he resigned to serve as Minister to France, from 1794 to 1796. On a later mission to France he helped Minister Livingston negotiate the Louisiana Purchase for Jefferson. In 1811, under Madison, he became Secretary of State, residing in a house at 2017 I Street, N.W., Washington, D.C., which is still well preserved.

In 1816 James Monroe was elected President, the last of the Revolutionary era to occupy that office. His salary as President was $25,000 annually. His term in office coincided with the "Era of Good Feelings," a period of general prosperity following the War of 1812.

Monroe's first estate was Ash Lawn, which he advertised for sale with his slaves and 3,500 acres in 1825, having already sold 950 acres while in France. His most prestigious estate, however, was Oak Hill in Loudoun County, Virginia, which was designed by his friend Jefferson and completed in 1823. The lands of the estate Monroe inherited from Joseph Jones in 1806.

President Monroe was the first to occupy the White House after its renovation following its burning in 1814 by the British. Congress

Elizabeth Korthright Monroe

appropriated $20,000 for the purchase of furnishings. The Monroes sent to France for the new furniture in addition to selling the government much of their own. Entertainment in the Executive Mansion was lavish during the Monroe Administration—reportedly as much as $100 a night was spent on candles for the drawing room. Their daughter Maria became the first President's daughter to be married in the White House. The most notable visitor during the Monroe Administration was the Marquis de Lafayette in 1824.

In 1818 Congress appropriated an additional $30,000 for Executive Mansion furnishings. The funds were handled in a very careless fashion, however, for Monroe used his own furniture and diverted $6,000 of the money to his own use. This resulted in embarrassment to the President when Congress held him accountable for the money.

Monroe's popularity declined with the Panic of 1819 and it was with a sense of relief that the Monroes departed Washington for Oak Hill in March, 1825. Public service had cost Monroe dearly, and he spent part of his retirement at Oak Hill in a struggle to persuade Congress to give him some $53,000 he claimed was owed to him. His $9,000 salary as Minister to France, for instance, had been inadequate, as he had been expected to entertain lavishly; consequently he got into serious debt which only increased in time because of high interest charges. By the time he left the Presidency he was almost ruined, land values had fallen, and his Oak Hill estate alone was $75,000 in debt. When Congress finally agreed to honor his claim in 1826, it was for only $30,000—minus the interest he had demanded.

Mrs. Monroe died in 1830 and was buried in the garden on the estate. The next year Monroe found it necessary to sell Oak Hill. Ill and advanced in years, Monroe went to New York to live out the remainder of his life with his daughter, Maria Gouverneur. He died on July 4, 1831, at the age of 73. His funeral and burial were held in New York. His body was reinterred in 1858 in Hollywood Cemetery, Richmond, Virginia.

Text of the Will of James Monroe

Having given my estate called Ashfield to my daughter Elizabeth, which estate cost me about six thousand dollars, it is my will and intention to pay my daughter Maria that sum, to put them on an equality in the first instance; and then divide my property remaining after paying my just debts equally between them, my said daughters: with respect to the works in which I am engaged and leave behind, I commit the care and publication of them to my son in law Samuel L. Gouverneur, giving to him one third of the profits arising therefrom for his trouble in preparing them for publication, one third to my daughter Maria and one third to my daughter Elizabeth

I appoint and constitute my son in law Samuel L Gouvernieur my sole and exclusive executor of this my last will and testament, hereby revoking all others, giving him full powers to carry it into effect. I recommend my daughter E K Hay to the paternal care and protection of my son in law Samuel L Gouvernieur:

James Monroe (Seal)

Signed, Sealed, Published & Declared in   )
)
the presence of this sixteenth day of   )
)
May 1831.   )
    William M Price
Gouverneur S. Bibby -
Tench Ringgold
28 Beekman Street New
York   )
)
63 Prince St   )
)
City of Washington.   )

"Codicil recorded in Original Liber folio 515"
Codicil.

My very infirm & weak state of health, having rendered it altogether impossible for me to manage my own concerns in any one circumstance, I have committed them to Mr. Gouverneur. in whose integrity I have perfect confidence. This has been extended to the grant lately made me by Congress, which I have authorized him, to enter & dispose of, in his own name; well knowing that he will apply it in that way, with more advantage than if entered in mine - I mention this, as a particular & interesting example, with which I wish my family, as well as he & myself to be acquainted. The whole will be under the operation after my departure of my present testament. He will of course pay particular attention to my other debts, as well as to that which I owe to himself. And I further request Captain James Monroe & William M. Price, to adjust and settle any account between Mr. Gouverneur & myself—this request having been made at his suggestion

James Monroe. (Seal)

Signed sealed published and declared in   )
the presence of - this Seventeenth day of   )
June in the year of our Lord one thousand   )
eight hundred and thirty one   )

Charlotte Gobert
63 Prince Street
New York
Caroline Gobert
63 Prince Street
New York
Wm Grayson
43 Vesey St.
G W Bibby
31 Greenwich St.

I Frederick - A. Talmadge - Recorder of the City of New York, and a Justice of the Peace thereof, do hereby certify under my hand & seal, that A. H. Mickle was on the 6th day of Jany 1847 - Mayor of the City of New York, & as such a Justice of the Peace & authorized to administer the annexed oath of Gouveneur S. Bibby -
F A Tallmadge (L S)
Recorder of the City of New York
& a Justice of the Peace thereof

Be it remembered that on this Sixth day of January, in the year one thousand eight hundred & forty seven personally appeared before me Andrew H. Mickle Mayor of the City of New York, Gouverneur. S. Bibby a resident of the said City, who, being by me duly sworn, did depose & say, that he is a subscribing witness to the annexed instrument in writing, purporting to be the last Will & testament of James Monroe: that the said testator signed & published the said writing as his last will & testament; that he was of disposing mind and memory; that he the said Gouverneur- S- Bibby subscribed his name thereto in the presence of the testator, & at his request; and in the presence of the other subscribing witnesses thereto; that the signatures of the said Tench Ringgold & William, M. Price are in the hand writing of each respectively known to him, — that they signed the same at the request of the testator in his presence, in the presence of him the said Gouverneur - S - Bibby, and of each other, and that each of them the said Tench Ringgold, & the said William. M. Price have since departed this life.
Given under my hand and Seal the day and
year above
mentioned
A H. Mickle
Mayor of
the City of New York
(S E A L)

Notes on the Will of James Monroe

JAMES MONROE, LIKE HIS MENTOR JEFFERSON, suffered severe financial reverses near the end of his life. The Congressional action on his claim for reimbursement for expenses incurred on behalf of the Government was long delayed and niggardly. His Oak Hill estate had to be sold to pay debts, and he moved to New York to live with his younger daughter, Maria Gouverneur. The Will and "codicil" executed only a few days before his death reveal his weakened condition and dependence on his daughter and son-in-law at that stage.

The so-called codicil might more appropriately be described as an affidavit, since it purports to describe events which have already occurred—the transfer of assets to his son-in-law, Samuel Gouverneur, and creation of a broad authority in him to act for Monroe—rather than a disposition to be made in the future. Such an agency arrangement would terminate with the principal's death and the agent be required to account for funds expended and held. As the "codicil" states, the principal's funds would then pass under the terms of his

Will. The instrument may well have been prepared at Gouverneur's suggestion, since it reveals a sensitivity to the potential, in such a situation, for dispute or suspicion. The designation in the "codicil" of two named persons to settle the agent's account, an arrangement attributed to a suggestion made by Gouverneur, appears to have been designed to forestall any such problem.

Monroe's survivors felt no need to offer his Will for probate following his death, a circumstance which can be the product of either lack of assets in the estate or the assent or acquiescence of all interested parties, including creditors, to a form of distribution without administration. Apparently, it was later found necessary to establish the validity of the Will for some purpose, not necessarily connected with land or other assets located in New York, for an affidavit under oath was made in January 1847 by the sole surviving witness to the Will, who swore to facts which would establish that the formalities required for execution of a valid Will had been followed. This affidavit, plus proof that all creditors' claims had either been paid or were barred by the passage of time, could then be used with the Will in any state to establish passage of title to assets which Monroe owned at the time of his death.

Oak Hill, the James Monroe home.

JOHN QUINCY ADAMS

J OHN QUINCY ADAMS WAS THE SECOND OLD-
EST OF FIVE CHILDREN BORN TO JOHN AND
ABIGAIL ADAMS. The only President's son also
to become President, he was born on July 11,
1767 in Braintree (now Quincy), Massachusetts,
in the house next to his father's birthplace, and
he was rocked in the same cradle.

His first public service was at the age of
14, when he served as private secretary, to
Francis Dana, the American Minister to Russia
in St. Petersburg. In 1787 John Quincy Adams
graduated from Harvard, having earlier studied
in Paris and London. He was only 27 when he
was appointed U.S. Minister to the Netherlands in The Hague. In 1795 he was commissioned to assist in the exchange of ratifications
of the Jay Treaty with England.

While in England, young Adams again met
Louisa Catherine Johnson, the daughter of the
American consul in London. Louisa had been
born in London and had lived her entire childhood abroad; young Adams had first met her in
Paris when she was 4 and he was 12. They
were married in 1797. Their early married life
was spent in Berlin, where John Quincy Adams
was serving as Minister to Prussia.

When John Adams was defeated as President, John Quincy Adams returned to America
and was soon elected to the Massachusetts Senate and in 1803 to the U.S. Senate. In 1808
the Massachusetts Federalists forced him out of
the Senate and, now a Democrat-Republican,
he was appointed Minister to Russia in 1809
and, after the War of 1812, he became Madi-

son's Minister to Great Britain. When Monroe assumed office in 1817, he made Adams Secretary of State.

While he was Secretary of State, Adams regularly overspent his yearly salary of $3,500 by about $5,000. Luckily, he had lived quite frugally during his time as Minister to France and this helped to meet the deficits incurred as Secretary of State. In fact, under the management of his brother Thomas, his personal estate prospered. By the time he returned from abroad he was worth $100,000, a sum he invested in bank stock with a return of 6 per cent. From this private income he drew to support himself and his family while in office.

Despite his father's remark, "My son will never get a chance at the Presidency until the last Virginian is in his grave," John Quincy Adams was elected in 1824 as the consequence of a deal with Henry Clay, then Speaker of the House of Representatives. Since none of the candidates—Jackson, Clay, Adams, and Crawford—received a majority, the election was thrown into the House of Representatives, where Clay threw his support to Adams; in return, Adams appointed Clay Secretary of State. Jackson, who had received a popular plurality, was able to win in 1828.

Returning to his farm in Quincy for a life of relaxation and study, Adams suffered the tragic loss of his son. For two years he re-

mained in deep retirement. Then public life again beckoned, and at the age of 64 he returned to Washington to serve the Plymouth district in the House of Representatives. He was the first ex-President to serve in Congress, and refused to consider his legislative service as a demotion. The diaries he kept aided many historians in interpreting the political and social history of his times, and recognizing the importance of his library and papers, he left them to his son, Charles Francis Adams, with instructions to erect a fireproof building for their safekeeping. He also stipulated that they should always remain in the family and not be sold.

On February 21, 1848, Adams suffered a stroke in the House of Representatives; he died two days later. He was interred beside his father and mother in Quincy. Adams had accumulated properties in both Washington, D.C., and Massachusetts, although he was in financial difficulties when he left the Presidency, which paid him $25,000 annually. At his death his estate was valued at $60,000. Many of the objects enumerated in his will have been preserved. His ivory cane is now in the Smithsonian Institution, as is the Stuart portrait of his father, John Adams, and the other family portraits which he left his granddaughter, Mary Louisa Adams.

Louisa Catherine Adams (detail).

Text of the Will of John Quincy Adams

Know all men by these Presents, that I, John Quincy Adams, of Quincy in the County of Norfolk and Commonwealth of Massachusetts, Doctor of Laws, do make ordain, publish and declare this to be my last will and testament hereby revoking all wills by me heretofore made and particularly one made on or about the 30th day of October 1832, the last will made by me preceding the present, which has become mislaid among my papers so that I cannot find it; I therefore revoke and annul the same in all and every particular of the same; of which said will, as far as my memory retains it, Joseph Hall, Edward Cruft and James H. Foster were subscribing witnesses.

1st   I do hereby constitute and appoint my only surviving Son Charles Francis Adams of Boston, Esquire, my sole Executor for all my property in this Commonwealth or in the District of Columbia or elsewhere; and I direct him hereby to take out Letters of Administration as well in the County of Norfolk in this Commonwealth as or in the District of Columbia or elsewhere; and I direct him hereby to take out Letters of Administration as well in the County of Norfolk in this Commonwealth as in the County of Washington in the District of Columbia, and if necessary in the State of Pennsylvania, so that he may administer upon any property real, personal or mixed pertaining to me in any part of the United States at the time of my decease, and I hereby constitute my said son residuary Legatee of all property, real personal and mixed belonging to me, not otherwise disposed of by this will.

2nd   But in the event of the the decease of my said son, which God forbid, my beloved wife still surviving, I do hereby constitute her the sole Executrix of all my goods, estate and property not previously administered, with such assistant as she may name and as may be assented to by the Judge of Probate of the County wherein my said will may be proved and approved,

3rd   I give and bequeath to my beloved wife Louisa Catherine Adams my dwelling house and lot in the City of Washington number twenty two, square one hundred and seventy three, to Have and to Hold to her and her heirs and assigns forever, In fact, I gave it to her some years since, though no deed of conveyance of it to her has ever been executed.

4th   I give and bequeath to my said wife the dwelling house and farm of ninety acres of land, be the same more or less, being the farm situate at Quincy on which we reside to have and to hold during her natural life to her own use: the said farm including the lots of Salt Marsh heretofore leased in connexion therewith. I give to her the proceeds of the rents and profits accruing therefrom during her natural life, to her own use; and after her decease, I give and bequeath the said dwelling-house, farm and lots of Salt Marsh to my son Charles Francis Adams, to have and to hold to him and the heirs of his body forever,

5th   I give and bequeath to my said wife the dwellinghouses and land situated in F. Street in the City of Washington being the one in which we now reside and the adjoining one now occupied by Albion K Parris, together with the stable lot appertaining thereto to have and to hold during her natural life to her own use. I give to her the proceeds of the rents and profits accruing therefrom during her natural life.

6th I give to my said wife the furniture of the dwelling house at Quincy aforesaid in which we reside, with the exception of such articles as may be hereinafter specifically otherwise devised. I give to her also all my carriages and horses, china, plate and plated wares as well at Quincy as at Washington excepting such articles as are hereinafter otherwise devised, and all the wines in the cellars and closets in my dwelling houses in both places.

7th I give to my said wife in lieu and as a full equivalent for her right of dower in all the rent & residue of my real estate, whether in Massachusetts or at Washington or elsewhere, provided she consent to renounce the same, the sum of two thousand dollars per annum, to be paid to her by my Executor during her natural life; and I do hereby constitute the same a charge upon my estate, to be paid to her in each and every year that she may live,

8th I give to my son Charles Francis Adams all my shares and certificates of stocks in the Middlesex & Quincy Canals, Bramtree and Weymonth Turnpike, Banks Insurance Companies, Markets and Hotels; Also all my interest in the mortgages upon the Real Estate and City Stocks and generally all and singular the personal property of evert description of which I shall die possessed not otherwise herein devised, and subject to the charge of payment of all my debts to hold the same upon the following conditions and for the following purposes to wit:

That he shall during the natural life of my wife aforesaid, Louisa Catherine Adams, annually make account to the Judge of Probate, for the County in which this my said will shall be proved of all the rents and profits, dividends on income accruing upon all my said personal property—, and out of the net annual balance so accounted for, that he shall pay over to my said wife during her life one entire third part of such balance in each and every year; and of the remaining two thirds of said balance that he shall reserve to himself one half of the same to his own use and behoof, and of the other half, that he shall pay over to my daughter in law Mrs. Mary Catherine Adams, one moiety thereof during her natural life, and the remaining moiety to my grand daughter Mary Louisa Adams, being the daughter of my son John Adams deceased and of said Mary Catherine:

And,

Upon the decease of my said wife, Louisa Catharine Adams then and thereafter, it is my will that a division be made of all the principal of my personal property thus held by my said son and Executor, according to an appraisment made by persons regularly appointed by the Judge of the Probate Court for the time being in the County wherein this my will shall be proved, and one half of the same so appraised shall be set off and given to my said son Charles Francis Adams by the said Appraisers, subject to the approbation of the Judge; and of the other half of the same, it is my will that my said son shall stand seized for the purpose of paying over to the said

Mary Catherine Adams during her natural life, the sum of Six hundred dollars per Annum free of every charge out of the income and proceeds accruing from such half of my personal property: and all the remainder of said income and proceeds shall be paid over to my Grand daughter Mary Louisa Adams during the natural life of her said mother; and upon the decease of the said Mary Catherine Adams it is my will that the whole of said half part of said property, as well as all other personal property held in trust by my said Executor for the benefit of said Mary Louisa Adams, whether arising from sales of Real Estate as herein provided, or however otherwise, shall be settled upon her the said Mary Louisa Adams by my said Executor, in such form and manner, so far as the same may be practicable, as shall secure the principal sum thereof as well as the whole interest and income of the same to her own sole use and separate use, benefit advantage and behoof and wholly free and independent of all claim, right or title to the custody, control, interest, income or emolument thereof by any husband to whom she may then be or thereafter become married.

9th I give and bequeath to my son Charles Francis Adams my estate situate at Mount Wollaston in the town of Quincy consisting of three hundred and eighty seven acres, more or less, with the dwelling house and barns thereon situated and all the privileges and appurtenances thereto belonging: to have and to hold to him and after his decease to his eldest born male descendant, then surviving, and the heirs male of his body forever.

10th I give and bequeath to my son Charles Francis Adams and the heirs of his body all the rest and residue of my real estate, including all my wood lots, Quarry lands and Salt Marsh, of which I shall die seized within the limits of the towns of Quincy, Bramtree or Milton, to have and to hold to him and to his heirs and assigns forever; all of which lands to be ascertained by reference to the deeds and plans of the same now in the custody of my said son Charles Francis Adams:— Provided there by secured to be paid by the said Charles Francis Adams, the principal sum of twenty thousand dollars, which said sum shall be a Capital for the benefit of my Grand daughter Mary Louisa Adams; the interest accruing upon which shall be paid over semiannually to her during her life, and the principal at her decease shall be paid over to the heirs of her body if she shall leave any, and if not, it shall be subject to her disposition by devise in and by her last will and Testament.

11th I give and bequeath to my son Charles Francis Adams my estates situated in Tremont Street and in Court Street in the City of Boston and County of Suffolk; the latter having been conveyed to me by my father and the former having been purchased by me from John Lowell and Isaac P. Davis; to Have and to hold to him and the heirs of his body forever.

12th I give and bequeath to my grand daughter Mary Louisa Adams my estate in Beach Street in the City of Boston, and also the estate of which I now stand possessed under breach of condition of Mortgage in Curve Street in said Boston, should the same become mine, as is probable, by fore closure, in regular course of law; and also all the right title and interest which I have or may have in two Stores on the Eastern-railway Avenue in said Boston, numbered Thirty three & Thirty five and

Forty nine and Fifty-one, over and above the amounts for which they are respectively mortgaged to the estate of the late Thomas B. Johnson Esquire—to Have and to hold the abovementioned real estate to her and her heirs and assigns forever.

13th   I give and bequeath to my son Charles Francis Adams the estate, situated in Weston in this Commonwealth, bequeathed to me by my friend Ward Nicholas Boylston Esquire; and also the whole of my real estate situated in the City and County of Washington in the District of Columbia, consisting of my houses in F. Street and the land thereto appertaining, subject to the life estate already herein granted to my wife Louisa Catherine Adams; also my store and house situated on Pennsylvania Avenue, which I bought of Easton; also the estate known under the name of the Columbia Mills, which I bought of George Johnson; and also the square numbered Five Hundred and Ninety Two, and all other lands of which I may die seized and possessed in the District of Columbia to have and to hold to him the said Charles Francis Adams his heirs and assigns, In Trust, however, and for the following purposes, to wit: To pay the net income, rents and profits of the same and each and every of the same to my said grand daughter Mary Louisa Adams so long as any of the said estates shall remain unsold; but it is my will that my said Executor do make sale and pass deeds of each and every of the same, the consent of the said Mary Louisa Adams being first had and obtained, as soon after my deceased as he shall may deem expedient, and the proceeds of all such sales that he invest as speedily as may be in stocks bearing interest at the rate of six per cent per annum in the Commonwealth of Massachusetts, the same to be held by my said Executor in trust as aforesaid, paying the interest and income of the same to the said Mary Louisa semi-annually, and the principal to be settled upon the said Mary Louisa Adams upon the same event and subject to the same and each and every of the same conditions, directions, restrictions and limitations with regard to the rights of any future husband of the said Mary Louisa, as are expressed in the eighth article of this my will.

14th   And I do hereby constitute and create a charge upon all the various devises of real estate and of the equivalent for the real estate at Quincy herein made for the benefit of my said Grand daughter Mary Louisa Adams, that out of the annual proceeds rents or profits of the same there be paid during the life or the widowhood of her mother Mary Catherine Adams the sum of Six hundred dollars in each and every year to the said Mary Catherine Adams.

15th   I give and bequeath to Elizabeth C. Adams, Isaac H. Adams, John Quincy Adams and Joseph H. Adams, the surviving children of my brother the late Thomas B - Adams of Quincy the house and farm in Bramtree and the House and farm in Medford which were mortgaged to me by my said brother, and of which I have taken legal possession For breach of condition of said mortgage—to Have and to Hold to them and to the survivor of them in fee as joint tenants and not as tenants in common.

16th   I give and bequeath my Library of Books my Manuscript books and papers and those of my father and all my family pictures, except such as may be herein otherwise specifically devised to my son Charles Francis Adams, trusting that his mother shall at all times have the use of any of the books in the library at her discretion; and I recommend to my said son Charles Francis Adams, as soon as he shall find it suit his own convenience to cause a building to be erected, made fire proof in which to keep the said library, books, documents and manuscripts safe, but always to be subject to his convenience; and I especially recommend to his care the said library, manuscripts, books and papers, and that he will as far as may be in his power keep them together as one library to be transmitted to his eldest son as one property to remain in the family and not to be sold or disposed of as long as may be practicable, being always confided to the faithful custody of the person holding the legal property in the same.

17th   I give to my grand-daughter Mary Louisa Adams the Portrait of my father, painted by Stewart and all the other family portraits now in my house in F. Street which I occupy.

18th   I give and bequeath to the people of the United States of America an ivory cane presented to me by Julius Pratt of Meriden in Connecticut and by me deposited in the custody of the Commissioner of Patents at Washington to remain in his custody until called for by me. The said cane bears on it an inscription in honour of the repeal of the House of Representatives prohibiting the reception of petitions on the subject of Slavery, 3^d December 1844. being inserted therein as the date upon which the said rule was rescinded, according to the request of the donor—which said cane it is my desire should be kept in the Patent Office of the United States in future as it has been heretofore.

19th   I give and bequeath to my grandson John Quincy Adams son of my son Charles Francis Adams, a gold headed cane cut from the timbers of the frigate Constitution and presented to me by Minot Thayer, Samuel A. Turner Ebenezer T. Fogg Solomon Richards & Harvey Field, Committee April 1st 1837 on the head of which is engraved the members of the House of Representatives of Massachusetts from the several towns of my District in the year 1837, in token of their sense of my public services in defending in the Congress of the United States the right of petition of the people of the United States in that body; and I request my son to have the custody of this bequest until his said son John Quincy shall come of age.

20th   I give and bequeath to my grandson Charles Francis Adams second son of my son aforesaid a cane also cut from the timbers of the frigate Constitution, and given to me by its Commander Commodore Isaac Hull in the year 1836, which is marked upon a silver ring immediately under the head of said cane.

21st   I give to my grandson Henry Brooks Adams, third son of my son aforesaid a cane made of olive from Mount Olivet in Jerusalem, given to me by my nephew Joseph Harrod Adams by whom it was caused to be cut on the spot, he being personally there as an Officer of the United States.

22nd   I have given to my daughter A. B. Adams wife of my son Charles Francis Adams the port folio of Engravings of pictures of Colonel John Trumbull, presented to me by him. I now give to her a silver tankard which was my mothers, from her grandfather John Quincy—also the portrait of the said John Quincy at two years of age now in her house at Quincy, and that of his mother, being Anna Shepard, daughter of the celebrated Thomas Shepard, minister of the Gospel of Charlestown, by whom the estate at Mount Wollaston was bequeathed by will to the said John Quincy. These pictures were given to me by will of Norton Quincy, only son of the said John Quincy.

23rd   I give and bequeath to my friend the Reverend Dr. Nathaniel L. Frothingham, a seal with a devise of an oak acorn, and the motto "alteri seculo" as a suitable small token of my personal esteem and friendship for him.

24th   I give and bequeath to my friend Dr. George Parkman of Boston a seal enchased with the image of General George Washington as a small token of the esteem and affection which I bear to him.

25th   I give and bequeath to my grandson John Quincy Adams my Chronometer made by French, bearing his initial bearing the same as my own, to be kept by his father until he shall think proper to deliver it to him.

26th   I give to my grand daughter Mary Louisa Adams, my seal bearing a Lion engraved upon a Silesian stone, which I had engraved there at the time of my tour through that country: the gold medal presented to me by the Corporation of the City of New York struck on the opening of the grand Canal—the silver cup with the inscription "circes pocula nosti"—and the seal engraved on a Sardonyx—with my cipher on one side and the Boylston arms on the other. I give all other medals coins or presents of small value which I have received, a silver wafer box and pair of portable candlesticks—my own cushion, seal at arms on a cornelian and my seal with the devise of the Eagle and Lyre to my son Charles Francis Adams. Also a bronze medal given to me by Commodore Jesse D. Elliot struck by his order in honor of Thomas Cooper Esqr, and also another medal in Silver which he directed to be given to the historical society of Rhode Island, refused by that society shortly before his death and held by me subject to their order. Also the history of the Croton Aqueduct a present from the City of New York.

27th   I give to my daughters in law Mary Catherine Adams widow of my son John Adams and to Abigail Brown Adams, wife of my son Charles Francis Adams one hundred dollars each to purchase some permanent token of remembrance of me which they may leave to their daughters; and I further give to my said daughter Mary Catherine Adams the clock with the device of Penelope in my chamber at Washington.

28th   I give to my nephew and namesake John Quincy Adams my small seal with my cipher engraved upon a cornelian; and a pair of gold sleeve buttons with the motto "æquam memento servare mentem" which I wore when I was President of the United States.

29th   I give to each of my two grand daughters, Mary Louisa Adams, daughter of my son John Adams, deceased, and to Louisa Catherine Adams, daughter of my son Charles Francis Adams one half of the sums deposited in my name in the Institution for savings in the City of Boston; the said sums to remain on deposit there until the thirteenth day of August 1852. when the youngest of the two will, if living attains the age of twenty one years; as soon after which as may be the whole of the said deposite with the interest accumulated thereon, shall be paid in equal portions to each of my said grand daughters and in case of the decease of either of them before the said Louisa Catherine Adams shall come of age, then the whole shall be paid over to the survivor. And should it be the will of God that neither of them should so long live, then I give the said deposite to their mothers in equal portions, on the whole to either of them if one of them only shall live until the said thirteenth of August 1852.

30th   I also give to my son Charles Francis Adams and to his heirs and assigns the Pew numbered Fifty four in the Stone Meeting house at Quincy—also the Pew in the Gallery numbered Five and the family tomb in the grave yard opposite the said meeting house.

31st   I also give to my wife Louisa Catherine Adams the pew which I own in St. Johns church at Washington and also the pew which I own in Christ Church at Quincy.

32d   I give and devise to the Supervisors of the Adams Temple and School fund at Quincy all the remaining pews in the Stone Meeting house at Quincy of which I retain the property, to be by them held or sold as in their judgment shall be deemed best; and the proceeds of the same shall be applied to the erection of a stone school house over the cellar which was under the house formerly built by the Reverend John Hancock, conformably to the deed of gift of my deceased father John Adams, of the twenty fifth of July in the year eighteen hundred and twenty two to the Inhabitants of the Town of Quincy.

33rd   I give and bequeath to my cousin Louisa Catherine Smith the sum of fifty dollars per annum as an annuity to be paid by my Executor during her life and as a slight token of my regard for her.

In testimony whereof I have hereunto set my hand and seal at the City of Boston this Eighteenth day of January in the year of our Lord eighteen hundred and forty seven.

John Quincy Adams (Seal)

Signed, sealed, published and declared by   )
)
the above named John Quincy Adams as and)
for his last will and testament in our   )
)
presence, who in his presence and at his   )
)
request and in presence of each other have)
)
hereunto set our names as witnesses the day)
)
and year above written.   )
    James H. Foster
    Edward Brooks
    Allen C. Spooner

            Copy
             Attest
              J.

The cane, mentioned in the Will, had been presented to John Quincy Adams in 1844 by Julius Pratt & Co. of Meriden, Connecticut.

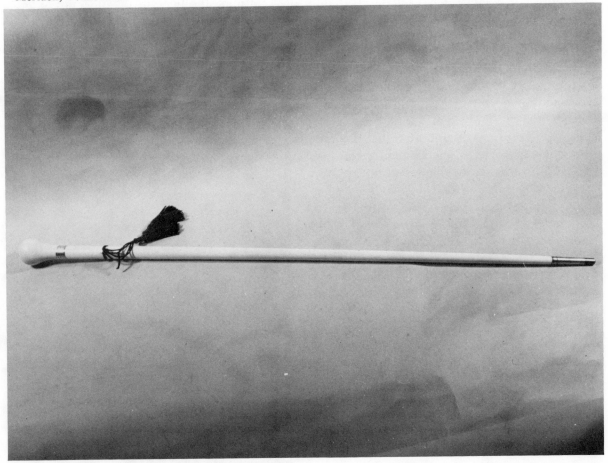

Notes on the Will of John Quincy Adams

THOUGH HIS WEALTH WAS NOT NEARLY AS GREAT AS WASHINGTON'S, John Quincy Adams' Will approaches his in length and complexity. Aside from the numerous bequests of specific mementoes, the immediate beneficiaries of the Presidential bounty were his widow, his sole surviving son, Charles Francis Adams, and the widow and daughter of his deceased son, John; but his eye was also on future generations of Adamses.

Thus, we find in the devises pieces of real estate to his son and to his granddaughter language referring to "the heirs of his (her) body" (paragraphs 4th and 10th), or in one instance "the heirs male of his body" (paragraph 9th). This phrasing denotes a fee tail interest, one more restricted than the complete ownership called a fee simple. The fee tail interest in land was created to limit future succession to real estate to lineal descendants. It was designed to keep property in the family permanently by restricting the power of the living member to transfer it away. Protection against transfer outside the family was not airtight. In fact, throughout history, as one branch of the legal profession works on techniques to tie up property in accordance with the owner's wishes, other lawyers are evolving sophisticated techniques by which these wishes and the interests sought to be created in future generations can be defeated. Successful or not, the use of the fee tail here suggests a vision of permanent relationship between the Adams family and particular property. It has a little of the flavor of European landed aristocracy without the title of nobility.

The fee tail form of title ·to land was brought to this country by the colonists as one component of a larger system of land law transplanted from England. Independence did not destroy the structure of English law on this side of the Atlantic. The body of that law was too large, too complex, and too useful to discard in toto. However, a pragmatic process of selective repeal and modification by statute and court decision began immediately—and has continued ever since. In this process, as elements of the law cease to be suited to the needs of the time and place they are discarded. One casualty in this process has been the fee tail estate in land which has now virtually disappeared in the United States. Curiously, Massachusetts is one of a very few states where any vestige at all can be said to persist, and there it does not seriously inhibit the desire of the current owner to do with property as he chooses.

Abolition of the fee tail interest in land has, of course, not destroyed the dynastic urge. The phenomenon is found in all generations in some of those who are able to combine a strong sense of family continuity with substantial wealth. Now the urge tends to manifest itself in the creation of trusts, as long-lived as the law permits, the benefits of which are to be enjoyed by a series of generations.

John Quincy Adams in the House of Representatives as he suffered the fatal stroke.

Oil painting of John Quincy Adams by Pieter van Huffel.

The provisions of the Will dealing with the library reveal some of the same motivations. John Adams left his papers to his son, John Quincy Adams. The body of papers was extensive, for John Adams kept a diary throughout his long life, saved the correspondence that he received, and retained copies of the correspondence that he sent as well as a variety of papers prepared for other purposes. This has proved a treasure trove for historians, but it represented a problem for John Quincy Adams when he came to write his Will, for to the papers of John Adams had then been added his own extensive diaries and the collected papers of a long life of public service.

His solution was to direct his son, Charles Francis, to create and maintain a library for these materials. This became the first Presidential library in the modern sense—though papers of other non-Presidential Adamses were added to it—but it was a purely family undertaking. For over 50 years following John Quincy Adams' death the library remained the responsibility solely of his descendants and under their control alone. When the sons of Charles Francis Adams decided to transfer the collected papers of all the Adamses to the Massachusetts Historical Society, they imposed a condition of nondisclosure for another 50 years. Thus, the Adams papers did not become available to historians and others with a legitimate interest until several years after most of Franklin D. Roosevelt's papers became available.

John Quincy Adams' desire to preserve and organize these collections was far-sighted indeed. Until the very recent past the Presidents showed little appreciation for the permanent interest and importance of their papers or for the necessity to take steps to preserve them as a single collection. However the implicit assumption that the Adams family alone should make decisions as to what should be made available, to whom, and when, was less wise. Fortunately this practice has been changing.

Sally, the White House doll. It was used by the Adams children during their father's Presidency.

ANDREW JACKSON

ANDREW JACKSON'S FATHER, ALSO NAMED ANDREW, was a linen weaver in Ireland prior to settling in the Carolina highland in 1765 to farm. He died in 1767, leaving two children and an expectant widow who gave birth to Andrew on March 15, 1767. Born near the border of North and South Carolina, Jackson was the first President to enter the world in the comparative poverty of a log cabin.

In 1780 Jackson was left alone, his mother having died of yellow fever while nursing wounded Revolutionary soldiers and his two brothers having died in that war too. He became an apprentice to a saddler, also attending an "old-field school" where he got a rudimentary education. When he was 18 he studied in the law office of Spruce McCay in Salisbury and in 1787 he was admitted to the bar of North Carolina.

Jackson's climb to success began when the Governor of North Carolina selected him state's attorney in the Cumberland settlements in western North Carolina, soon to become the state of Tennessee. When he first settled in Nashville in 1788, the community was a settlement for protection from the Indians. Later he went into partnership with his friend John Overton in a successful and prosperous law practice and in 1791 he married Rachel Donelson, the divorced wife of a Kentuckian named Lewis Roberts.

As a lawyer, Jackson began to speculate in land, so that his holdings soon ran into many thousands of acres. He bought a 330-acre tract from Rachel's brother in 1792 and established his farm, which he first called Poplar Grove. His business continued to flourish while he lived there and in 1796 he bought another tract of 640 acres in a different location, where he set up his new home, calling it Hunter's Hill. In addition to his farming and his law practice, he also operated a store for a time.

In 1796 he was selected to serve as Tennessee's first delegate to the House of Representatives. In the following year he was elected to the U.S. Senate. Dissatisfied with politics, he resigned from the Senate and, at age 32, accepted a seat on the Superior Court of Tennessee.

With the turn of the century, Jackson's personal fortunes dwindled, partly as a result of the national financial panic, but more because of overextension of investments and misplaced confidence. The Hunter's Hill estate was sold in 1804 to tide him over his financial crisis. Because of Rachel's love of the estate, however, he repurchased it after becoming President, selling it again in 1840 to a relative of his wife's.

Following the sale of Hunter's Hill, Jackson opened a store at Clover Bottom, settling there and building a group of log cabins. The farm prospered and he was able to build a more prestigious house—The Hermitage—by 1819, with additions in 1831 and 1834.

During the 1819 depression, Jackson was very hard-pressed for money to meet obligations incurred in Alabama speculations. Having loaned money freely, he was now forced to sue to retrieve his money. He brought suit against 129 people who owed him money on a single day.

Jackson's failure to win the Presidency in 1824 brought about a more determined campaign in 1828, which proved successful. However Rachel died before her husband was inaugurated. Racked with tuberculosis, Jackson returned in 1837 to The Hermitage, where he lived until his death on June 8, 1845. He left his entire Hermitage estate to his adopted son, Andrew Jackson, Jr.

An 1889 newspaper described the condition of the estate as follows:

"At the death of General Jackson he owed but two debts of any magnitude, one of them $15,000 to Frank Blair of Washington, the other to General Planchin of New Orleans. His estate consisted of The Hermitage, then containing about 1,200 acres, on which he had about 100 negroes besides stock of all kinds. Besides this he owned his plantation in Mississippi which the adopted son and heir afterward sold with the negroes then on it for $40,000. This left The Hermitage, with the negroes and all else on it, clear of debt, somewhere near $150,000." Even so, when Jackson died he was land-poor, that is, he had little actual cash. His salary as President had brought him $25,000 annually.

Of the objects enumerated in Jackson's will, many may be found in the museum at The Hermitage, including the sword presented by the state of Tennessee; the blade of the elegant sword presented by the Rifle Company of New Orleans; and the gold sword presented by the citizens of Philadelphia; also several of his pistols and many canes. Two of his pistols had been bequeathed to General Robert Armstrong for his bravery during the British and Indian war.

The Hermitage, the home of Andrew Jackson.

Text of the Will of Andrew Jackson

Hermitage
June 7th, 1843

In the name of God amen— I Andrew Jackson Sr., being of sound mind memory and understanding, and impressed with the great uncertainty of life, and the certainty of death, and being desirous to dispose of my temporal affairs so that after my death no contention may arise relative to the same; and whereas, since executing my will of the 30th of September, 1833, my estate has become greatly involved by my liabilities for the debts of my well-beloved and adopted son Andrew Jackson jnr which makes it necessary to alter the same: Therefore I, Andrew Jackson Sr., of the County of Davidson and State of Tennessee do make, ordain, publish and declare this my last will and testament, revoking all other wills by me heretofore made.

First I bequeath my body to the dust whence it comes, and my soul to God who gave it, hoping for a happy immortality through the atoning merits of our Lord Jesus Christ, the Saviour of the world. My desire is that my body be buried by the side of my dear departed wife, in the garden of the Hermitage, in the vault prepared in the garden, and all expenses paid by my executor hereafter named. *Secondly*, that all my just debts to be paid out of my personal and real estate by my executor; for which purpose to meet the debt my good friends, General J. B. Blanchin & Co., of New Orleans for the sum of six thousand dollars, with the interest accruing thereon, loaned to me to meet the debt due by A. Jackson Jr, for the purchase of the plantation from Hiram G. Runnels, lying on the east bank of the river Mississippi in the State of Mississippi; also, a debt due by me of ten thousand dollars, borrowed of my friends, Blair and Rives, of the city of Washington and District of Columbia, with the interest accruing thereon, being applied to the payment of the land bought of Hiram G. Runnels as aforesaid; and for the faithful payment of the aforesaid recited debts, I hereby bequeath all my real and personal estate. After these debts are fully paid, *Thirdly*, I give and bequeath to my adopted son, Andrew Jackson Jnr, the tract of land whereon I now live, known as the Hermitage tract, with its butts and boundaries, with all its appendages of the three lots of land bought of Samuel Donelson, Thomas J. Donelson and Alexander Donelson sons & heirs of Savern Donelson, deceased, all adjoining the Hermitage tract, agreeable to their butts and boundaries, with all the appurtenances thereto belonging or in any wise apertaining, with all my negroes that I may die possessed of, with the exceptions hereafter named, with all their increase after the before recited debts are fully paid, with all the household furniture, farming tools, stock of all kind, both on the Hermitage tract farm, as well as those on the Mississippi plantation, to him and his heirs, forever. The true intent and meaning of this my last will and testament is, that all my estate, real personal and mixed, are hereby first pledged for the payment of the above recited debts and interest, and when they are fully paid, the residue of all my estate, real personal and mixed are hereby bequeathed to my adopted son A. Jackson Jnr, with the exception hereafter named, to him and his heirs forever.

Fourth, Whereas I have heretofore by conveyance deposited with my beloved daughter, Sarah Jackson, wife of my adopted son A. Jackson jnr. given to my beloved granddaughter, Rachel Jackson, daughter of A. Jackson jnr., and Sarah his wife, several negroes therein described, which I hereby confirm. I give and bequesth to my beloved grandson, Andrew Jackson son of A. Jackson jnr and Sarah his wife a negro boy named Ned, son of Blacksmith Aaron and Hannah his wife, to him and his heirs forever. *Fifth*, I give and bequeath to my beloved little grandson, Samuel Jackson, son of A. Jackson jnr. and his much beloved wife Sarah, one negro boy, named Davy or George, son of Squire and his wife Giney, to him and his heirs forever.

Sixth, to my beloved and affactionate daughter, Sarah Jackson, wife of my adopted and well beloved son, A. Jackson, jnr, I hereby recognize by this bequest, the gift I made her on her marriage, of the negro girl Gracy, which I bought for her, and gave her to my daughter Sarah as her maid and seamstress with her increase, with my house-servant Hannah and her two daughters, namely Charlotte and Mary, to her and her heirs forever. This gift, and bequest is made for my great affection for her—as a memento of her uniform attention to me and kindness on all occasions, and particularly when worn down with sickness, pain and debility. She has been more than a daughter to me, and I hope she never will be disturbed in the enjoyment of this gift and bequest by any one.

Seventh, I bequeath to my well beloved nephew, Andrew J. Donelson, son of Samuel Donelson deceased, the elegant sword presented to me by the State of Tennessee, with this injunction, that he fail not to use it when necessary in support and protection of our glorious union, and for the protection of the constitutional rights of our beloved country, should they be assailed by foreign enemies or domestic traitors. This, from the great change in my worldly affairs of late, is, with my blessing, all I can bequeath him, doing justice to those creditors to whom I am responsible. This bequest is made as a memento of my high regard, affection and esteem I bear for him as a high-minded, honest and honorable man.

Eighth, To my Grand-nephew Andrew Jackson Coffee I bequeath the elegant sword presented to me by the Rifle Company of New Orleans, commanded by Captain Beal, as a memento of my regard, and to bring to his recollection the gallant services of his deceased father Genl John Coffee, in the late Indian and British war, under my command, and his gallant conduct in defense of New Orleans in 1814 and 1815, with this injunction: that he wield it in the protection of the rights secured to the American citizens under our glorious constitution, against all invaders, whether foreign foes, or intestine traitors.

I bequeath to my beloved grandson, Andrew Jackson, son of A. Jackson Junr & Sarah his wife, the sword presented to me by the citizens of Philadelphia, with this injunction: that he will always use it in defense of the constitution and our glorious union, and the perpetuation of our republican system: remembering the motto—"Draw me not without occasion, nor sheath me without honor."

The pistols of Genl Lafayette which was presented by him to Genl George

Washington, and by Col Wm Robertson presented to me, I bequeath to George Washington Lafayette, as a memento of the illustrious personages thru whose hands they have passed—his father, and the father of his country. The gold box presented to me by the corporation of the city of New York, the large silver vase presented to me by the ladies of Charllson, South Carolina, my native State, with the large picture representing the unfurling of the American banner, presented to me by the citizens of South Carolina, when it was refused to be accepted by the United States Senate, I leave in trust to my son A. Jackson Jnr, with directions that, should our happy country not be blessed with peace, an event not always to be expected, he will at the close of the war or end of the conflict, present each of said articles of inestimable value to that patriot residing in the city or state from which they were presented, who shall be adjuged by his countrymen or the ladies to have been the most valiant in defense of his country and our country's rights.

The pocket spy glass, which was used by Genl Washington during the revolutionary war, and presented to me by Mr. Custis, having been burned with my dwelling-house, the Hermitage, with many other invaluable relics, I can make no disposition of them.

As a memento of my high regard to Genl Robert Armstrong, as a gentlemen, patriot, and soldier, as well as for his meritoreous military services under my command during the late British and Indian war, and remembering the gallant bearing of him and his gallant little band at Enotochopco creek, when falling desperately wounded, he called out "My brave fellows, some may fall but save the cannon"—as a memento of all these things, I give and bequeath to him my case of pistols and sword worn by me throughout my military career, well satisfied that in his hands they will never be disgraced—that they will never be used or drawn without occasion, nor sheathed but with honor. *Lastly*, I leave to my beloved son all my walking-canes, and other relics, to be distributed amongst my young relatives —namesakes—first, to my much esteemed namesake, Andrew J. Donelson, son of my esteemed nephew, A. J. Donelson, his first choice, and then to be distributed as A. Jackson Jnr may think proper.

Lastly, I appoint my adopted son, Andrew Jackson Jnr my whole and sole executor to this my last will and testament, and direct that no security be required of him for the faithful execution and discharge of the trusts hereby reposed in him. In testimony whereof I have this 7th day of June, one thousand eight hundred & forty-three, hereunto set my hand and affixed my seal, hereby revoking all wills heretofore made by me, and in the presence of

Andrew Jackson (Seal)

Marion Adams   Richard Smith
Elizabeth D. Long   R. Armstrong.
Thos. J. Donelson

Notes on the Will of Andrew Jackson

WRITTEN WHEN JACKSON WAS 76, about two years before his death, the Will of Andrew Jackson seems entirely consistent with history's portrayal of him as an emotional, loyal, vigorous, and opinionated lawyer, soldier, political opponent, judge, U.S. Senator and President. Among the Wills in this book it is one of the most highly personal documents. The explicit avowal of religious faith, the repeated expressions of patriotic sentiments, and the warmth of its allusions to the members of his family are not unique in this book but are expressed with unusual fervor.

Though President and Mrs. Jackson had no children of their own, they were part of a large family through Mrs. Jackson's connection with the Donelson clan. She was one of 12 children, most of whom had settled in the central Tennessee area. In 1809 twins were born to the wife of her brother, Severn. The Jacksons were permitted to adopt one, the Andrew Jackson, Jr., named as principal beneficiary under the Will. Another nephew of Mrs. Jackson, Andrew Jackson Donelson (also named in the Will), was raised in the Jackson home and became Jackson's secretary during his Presidency.

Jackson's personal fortunes ebbed and flowed during his life, as the Will's reference to substantial debts suggests. His principal asset, The Hermitage estate at Nashville, was left to his adopted son, whose improvidence had plagued Jackson throughout his life. In little more than 10 years the son had lost the estate for payment of debts. Thereafter, a private, philanthropic organization, the Ladies' Hermitage Association, acquired the property and has preserved it as a museum.

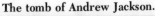

The tomb of Andrew Jackson.

MARTIN
VAN BUREN

MARTIN VAN BUREN, SON OF ABRAHAM VAN BUREN, a tavern keeper and farmer of Dutch descent, was born in Kinderhook, New York, on December 5, 1782. He learned the rudiments of English and Latin grammar in his native village. At the age of 14, he began to study law in the office of Francis Silvester and continued his law training in New York City, until he reached the age of 19. He was admitted to the bar in 1803. In 1807 he married his cousin, Hannah Hoes, who bore him four sons before her early death in 1819. In 1808 he was elected surrogate of his home county, a position he held for five years. In 1812, he achieved his first major success in politics with his election to the New York state senate.

He entered national politics as a U.S. Senator after establishing a secure base in New York. Following his term in the U.S. Senate, from 1821 to 1828, during which he was a stalwart Jacksonian Democrat, Van Buren progressed to Governor of New York, Secretary of State, and in 1832, Vice President of the United States with a salary of $5,000 annually. He supported Jackson in his struggle against the United States Bank and so established himself as Jackson's protégé and successor in 1837.

When Van Buren entered the White House he had been a widower for 18 years. Shortly after he became President, Dolley Madison introduced her cousin Angelica Singleton to the oldest son of the President, Major Abraham Van Buren, and the two were soon married. Miss Singleton was the well-educated daughter of a wealthy and socially prominent South Carolina planter. Van Buren himself, despite his humble background, had acquired luxurious tastes and cultural pretensions. He immediately proceeded to renovate the Executive Mansion. The sum of $27,000 was appropriated by Congress for the purpose, but this brought much adverse criticism from the public, who tagged his term the "gold and silver administration." His salary as President was $25,000 annually; he drew it in a $100,000 lump sum upon completion of his term.

To put himself on the proper footing with the earlier Presidents, Van Buren had purchased the 200-acre Van Ness estate on the Hudson River, which he named Lindenwald. The house had been built in 1797 on land that had once belonged to Van Buren's ancestors.

Van Buren's term began with a panic in which hundreds of banks and businesses failed, unemployment soared and the country was wracked by a depression. He lost the election of 1840 and returned to his estate at Lindenwald, where he lived the remainder of his life in retirement; his youngest son and his family added cheer to the household during his declining years. Once after his retirement, in 1848, he made another attempt to gain the Presidency on the Free Soil Party ticket, but again failed.

On July 24, 1862, Van Buren died at his home on the Hudson. He left an estate valued at $250,000. Shortly after his death, however, both the house and its furnishings were sold.

An 1842 portrait of Angelica Singleton Van Buren by Henry Inman, showing the Hiram Powers bust of Van Buren, as well as the bust itself mentioned in Van Buren's will, remain in the White House collections to this day. Also there is the silver pitcher presented to him by his old friend, Benjamin Butler.

Angelica Singleton Van Buren, President Van Buren's daughter-in-law and official hostess (detail). In the background of the portrait is the bust of Van Buren mentioned in his Will.

Text of the Will of Martin Van Buren

I, Martin Van Buren of the Town of Kinderhook, County of Columbia and State of New York, heretofore Governor of the State and more recently President of the United States but for the last and happiest years of my life, a Farmer in my native Town do make & declare the following to be my last Will and Testament.

First. I direct my Executors hereinafter named to pay, without delay, my funeral expenses & all outstanding bills, debts in the ordinary acceptation of that term I owe none & hope to leave none.

Secondly. I direct that no account shall be taken of advances by me heretofore made to either of my sons and that they shall be considered as settled, with the exceptions of a bond I hold against my son Abraham for two thousand Dollars and also a note against my son John for Four Thousand Eight hundred and fifteen dollars, which were agreed to be considered as business transactions strictly, the amount due on each at my death (the interest having been puntually paid to the present year) is to be charged to them respectively, and deducted from their shares of my Estate. The like charge and deduction shall be made in respect to any future payments by me or my Estate in cases where I have made myself liable as surety for either of my sons, but in which nothing has yet been paid by me.

Thirdly. In consideration of advances which I have made to my sons Abraham & John, whilst none have been made to my son Smith Thompson, I bequeath to the latter all my personal chattels & effects, excepting therefrom all the debts that may be due to me, and stocks that I may own at my death and also my wine & stock on my farm. My miscelaneous library is intended to be included in this bequest, but not my law library which I bequeath to my son John.

Fourthly. I give to my grand son Singleton Van Buren a gold snuff box, presented to me with the Freedom of the City, by the corporation of the City of New York, and to my Granson Martin son of Abraham the marble bust made of me by Powers, which I had previously presented to his mother & now transfer to the son by her direction. I give to my grandson Martin son of my son Smith Thomson a silver pitcher, presented to me some years since by my old & always sincere friend Benjamin F. Butler.

Fifthly. I direct my Executors to expend four hundred dollars, or so much thereof as may be necessary, in obtaining a copy of the bust of me by Powers, which copy I give to my Grandson Edward Livingston Van Buren.

Sixthly. I direct my executors to lay out five hundred Dollars for Keep Sakes for my grandson Francis Van Buren, and my grand daughters Anna, Ellen, Catherine & Eliza Van Buren.

Seventhly. I request my Executors to regard themselves as standing towards my best of sisters Dirike Van Buren if she shall survive me, in the relation I occupied when living, & to omit nothing in the way of pecuniary advances that may contribute to her comfort out of my Estate.

Eighthly. I direct my executors to pay to my niece Christina Cantine Two hundred dollars & to each of my nieces Lucretia Van Buren & Jane Ann Van Buren the sum of one hundred dollars; and I give and devise to my nephew Martin Van Buren son of my brother Lawrence & to his heirs and assigns forever, all my interest in a small dwelling with the lot on which it stands adjoining his fathers house, conveyed to me by the latter as security for money lent, but the latter devise is upon condition that his father relieves me or my Estate from my remaining securityship to the State of New York.

Ninthly. I hereby appoint my three sons Abraham, John & Smith Thompson Executors of my Last and only Will; and I do hereby authorize & empower them, or such of them as shall take upon themselves the execution thereof, and the survivors & survivor of them, to fulfill by the execution of conveyances & otherwise, as may be proper, any contracts for the sale of lands, made by me which shall be outstanding at the time of my death.

Lastly. I hereby give devise & bequeath to my three sons Abraham, John & Smith Thompson all the remainder & residue of my personal estate not required for the purposes of my Will under the provisions above made, & all my real estate wheresoever situated, to be equally devided between them, To Have and to Hold their respective shares thereof to them, their heirs & assigns forever, subject to the following conditions & reservations, Viz first that out of avails of the sale of Lindenwald there shall be reserved & paid over to my son Smith Thompson his heirs or assigns the sum of Seven Thousand five hundred dollars in full satisfaction for his advances towards the expenses incurred by the additions to and improvements upon the dwelling house & out buildings with the expectation that the Place would be devised to him upon terms that would be equitable in respect to his brothers, the payment to be without interest during my life time. Secondly, that upon the sale of Lindenwald the preference shall be offered in succession to my sons, beginning for the reason above assigned & no other, with the youngest, if the son accepting the same is willing to pay therefor as much as the place can be sold for in the market.

The three pieces of plate last presented to me by my deceased friend Benjamin F. Butler, I bequeath to my three sons Abraham, John and Smith Thompson to be equally divided between them.

In Witness Whereof I have to this instrument set my hand & seal this eighteenth day of Jany. in the year of our Lord one thousand Eight Hundred and Sixty.

M. Van Buren (Seal)

Subscribed, sealed, published and declared, by the said testator Martin Van Buren to be his Last Will & Testament in the presence of us the undersigned, who, at his request, & in his presence and in the presence of each other have hereunto subscribed our names as witnesses & affixed our respective places of residence this 18 day of Jany 1860.

John M. Pruyn M.D. of Kinderhook
Laura Collins of Albany

If my faithful James remains with me until my death I wish my Executors to make him a present of one hundred dollars.

M. Van Buren

The bust of Van Buren mentioned in his Will.

Notes on the Will of Martin Van Buren

SOME OF THE COMPLEXITIES OF WILL DRAFTING arise from decisions on whether and how to relate transactions between the testator and his beneficiaries during life to the distribution of his estate after his death. Much of Martin Van Buren's Will is devoted to setting out his answers to such questions.

Thus, he had made loans ("advances" is the term he used) to two sons. Were they to be forgiven and forgotten, to be treated as assets of the estate and collected, or to be charged against the borrower's share of the estate, a form of indirect collection? Similarly, what of amounts which Van Buren or his estate might have to pay in the future for loans made to a son by another on the strength of Van Buren's guarantee? The paragraph of the Will headed "Secondly" contains his answer: Some advances are to be forgotten, others taken strictly into account.

A similar question was that of whether to equalize gifts made to two sons but not to the third. There is no legal requirement that children be treated alike, let alone with precise equality, either in gifts during life or by will. Yet many parents strongly desire to do so, and the intestate statutes are so constructed. Where a testator is aware that he has made unequal gifts to his children during life, overall equality is achieved by creating an offsetting imbalance in the will. Van Buren did this in his treatment of significant loans to two of his sons, and in the paragraph headed "Thirdly" makes a comparable adjustment for gifts, including the loans converted to gifts by forgiveness.

Finally, his division of the residue of his estate in the paragraph headed "Lastly" neatly reconciles four separate objectives: (1) equal division among his three surviving sons; (2) recognition that one son, Smith Thompson, had invested substantial amounts (of money? effort?) in improvements to Van Buren's farm, Lindenwald; (3) the conclusion that Lindenwald should belong to one owner rather than three and, therefore, must be sold; and (4) a preference for a son as its future owner but only if the interest of his other sons would be protected by a sale for its full market value.

Van Buren's sensitivity to these equities arising out of transactions during his life produced a more equal treatment of his three sons than would a will simply leaving his estate to those sons in equal shares.

Pitcher mentioned by Martin Van Buren in his Will.

WILLIAM HENRY HARRISON

WILLIAM HENRY HARRISON WAS BORN THE YOUNGEST OF SEVEN CHILDREN AT BERKELEY, a Virginia plantation in Charles City County, on February 9, 1773. Benjamin Harrison, his father, was one of the signers of the Declaration of Independence and later Governor of Virginia. His paternal ancestor came to Virginia only 25 years after the first settlement at Jamestown and was prominent enough to become clerk of the Virginia Council. His grandmother was the daughter of Robert "King" Carter, one of the wealthiest men in the American colonies.

William Henry Harrison was educated at Hampden-Sydney College in Virginia, and continued his education with the study of medicine in Richmond and at the College of Physicians and Surgeons in Philadelphia. His father's death in 1791 and the accounts of the Indian outrages on the western frontier, combined with a distaste for a medical career, caused him to enter the Army at the age of 18 as an ensign; six years later he was made captain. He transferred his rights in his Virginia birthplace to his brother for a large tract of land in Kentucky and $1,500 in cash.

In 1795, the young officer met Anna Tuthill Symmes, the daughter of a judge who owned a huge tract in the Northwest Territory. The two were married in 1798 over the objection of her father and in two years settled on 160 acres of land at North Bend (near Cincinnati) which he purchased from his father-in-law for $450. Here they spent the first years of their married life in a log house.

Harrison resigned his commission in 1798 and was appointed secretary of the Northwest Territory by President John Adams at a salary of $1,200 a year. One year later he became the territory's first delegate to Congress. When Indiana Territory was separated from the Northwest Territory in 1800, Harrison, only 28 years of age, became its first Governor, a position he held for 12 years at a salary of $2,000 a year. During this time he resided at Grouseland in Vincennes, an estate of some 300 acres which later became known as the "White House of the West." The house was almost a copy of his birthplace, Berkeley.

As Governor, Harrison made several important treaties with the various Indian tribes, but Tecumseh, the Shawnee chief, challenged them as illegal. After several confrontations with the Indians under Tecumseh, Harrison won the Battle of Tippecanoe in 1811, but failed to quell the Indian raids. The battle, although not a complete victory, disrupted Tecumseh's confederation. It also brought Harrison a citation by President Madison. Harrison finally defeated Tecumseh in the Battle of the Thames in Ontario in 1813, emerging as a national hero and rising to the rank of major general.

By this time the Harrisons had had a family of 10 children, one of whom died in infancy. In 1813, Harrison left Grouseland and returned to North Bend. From here he served as U.S. Senator from 1825 to 1828 and briefly as Minister to Colombia. He devoted much of his time to the management of his Ohio farm but was nonetheless constantly in debt. The house itself was not extraordinary. One visitor described it thus: "The furniture of the parlor could not have drawn very largely on anyone's resources. The walls were ornamented with a few portraits, some in frames, some disembodied from a frame. The drawing room was fitted in more modern style; but the whole furniture and ornaments in these rooms might have cost $200 to $250." His income increased to about $10,000 a year after 1834, when he became a clerk of court in his home county.

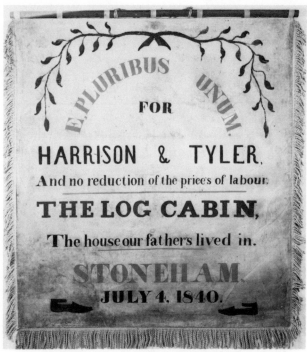

A Harrison and Tyler campaign banner.

Harrison was nominated for the Presidency in 1836, ran against Martin Van Buren, and lost the election, making a very poor showing. But in 1840, after the Depression of 1837, the country was so disaffected with the Democrats that the Whigs were able to mount a wild, exciting, and colorful campaign during which Harrison swept the country with a large majority.

Mrs. Harrison was ill at this time and did not accompany her husband to Washington for the inauguration. Harrison was 69 when he took his oath of office on a cold disagreeable day. He refused to dress properly for the weather and rode horseback, turning down the offer of carriages in the parade. Following the inauguration, Harrison fell ill, pneumonia developed, and within one month, on April 4, 1841, he was dead. He died in debt, his estate passing to his widow, who lived on to the age of 88. After Harrison's sudden death, Congress agreed to pay Mrs. Harrison a lump sum of $25,000 which was the presidential salary for one year. The house at North Bend later burned down, and with it most of the personal possessions and papers of the President. Only the house at Grouseland, where his son later lived, contains a few of his mementos.

Text of the Will of William Henry Harrison

I William H. Harrison of North Bend in the County of Hamilton & State of Ohio do hereby make this my last will & Testament *Viz*

In the first place I direct all my just debts to be paid and for this purpose I assign 1st all the lands I still hold in Green Township as well as that which has been assigned to me in the partition which was some time since made between Jacob Burnet (?) James Findlay and myself as the lots reserved and still held in copartnership with those gentlemen. 2ndly The lands which I hold in the State of Indiana and Illinios Viz A tract of about two hundred acres adjoining the lots of my addition to the town of Vincennes (in the said State of Indiana) & adjoining also to the old commons of said town— also three other tracts of land of 400 acres each in what is called the Donation in the vicinity of the said town of Vincennes being land granted to the persons who were heads of families at Vincennes at a certain period by the laws of the United States. also 150 acres lying on or near the Potoca River in the County of Gibson & State of Indiana & which 150 acres is part of a tract of 350 acres conveyed to me by William McIntosh. Also a tract of two   (acres) lying on the North West side of the Wabash in the State of Illinois fronting on the said river Wabash & nearly opposite to the steam mill which is a little above the town of Vincennes. I also appropriate the money which may be due to me at the time of my decease to this same object (Viz the payment of my just debts) & should the whole amount itself & the proceeds of the property above described not be sufficient for the object specified I hereby authorize my Executors to select as many of the lots which I hold in the said town of Vincennes (my addition) not exceeding the half as will answer the purpose & make up the deficiency

The tract of land lying on the Potoca in the County of Gibson above described contains 350 acres of first rate late. two hundred acres are to be taken off on either end of the tract it being   to satisfy the claim of Mrs. Cunningham she having my bond for $800 worth of land in the neighborhood of Vincennes. I   this as being the best land I had in that country.

I was not in law or equity indebted to Mr. Cunninghams Estate a   as the verbal bargain I made with him   his brother William acknowledged he heard John Ackman(?)   was that I should pay him in proportion to the success of his exertions to make money from the property entrusted to his management. But he never made any. The money which I paid his estate & the land here mentioned ought therefore to be considered as a gratuity.

I give my Executors full power over the property about described & authorize them or any two of them to dispose of it in any manner they may think best whether by private or public sale or by compact or compromise with my debtors.

I give to my dear wife my North Bend estate that is all that part of it which lies south of the State road running from the Big Miami through Cleves to Cincinnati with the exception of so much of that strip of land upon which Mr. & old Mr. lives as his hereinafter bequeathed. I give the said property to my wife during her natural life & all the rents issues & profits thereof & then to descend (?) in the manner herein after provided.

As I have already given to my dear deceased son Symmes his full proportion of my property I would be unjust toward the rest of my children to give his children a further But if my life should be spared I hope to be able to do something for them.

My beloved daughter Betsey Bassett(?) being will provided for requires nothing more of the goods of this world. I once gave to her husband Mr. Short the lands in Kentucky purchased of my brother Benjamin Harrison which cost me $5000 forty two years ago. He desired afterwards to relinguish them to my son William Henry. If however Mr. Short still wishes to retain them I hereby devise them to him the said John C. Short. They are the land held in copartnership with Steven & William Drew of Virginia & James House of Kentucky.

To my son William I give the farm he has had in possession for some time & for which I have given him a deed in fee simple. But as the deed is drawn in such a manner as to exclude him from the best part of the tract which I intended to give him. If I should be taken from this life before the error can be properly corrected I hereby declare my intention to be to give him three hundred acres of good land to be bounded Southwardly by the Ohio River Westward by a line to be run from such point on the said river as may be agreed upon by my son John Scott, my friend Judge John Matson & my said son William Henry. The commencing point of the said Western boundary being agreed upon the direction in which the line is to be run from said point to my northern boundary is to be determined by my said son John Scott & Judge Matson. The fourth or closing line of said tract is of course to be so run as to include the three hundred acres intended to be given & hereby given to my said son William Henry and to his heirs forever.

I had granted by deed to my son John Scott all that part of my North Bend property which lies north of the State road running through the town of Cleves. At his request I have agreed to exchange for this tract three hundred acres of my farm at the Mouth of the great Miami & I hereby confirm said exchange bequeathing to my said son John Scott three hundred acres bounded by the great Miami River, , the Ohio River, the land I lately sold to Abner(?) & I. Hayes & by a line to be run from points on the Ohio River as he may designated (nor higher up the said river than the hay press(?)) across to the land sold to the said Hayes on to my northern boundary line. But if the line so runs to include three hundred acres should be found to place either his tract or the one above it in an inconvenient shape my will is that my friends Judge Matson, George P. Torrence & Lewis Whiteman or any two of them shall determine the mode of running said line so as to do justice to all the parties concerned. My will is that the said described tract shall appertain to my said son Scott to him and his heirs forever as soon as he executes a release of the lands deeded to him beyond the state road leading through the town of Cleves.

After the   pains which I have taken to reclaim my son Benjamin from the habit of dissipation in which he has so long indulged finding that he still perseveres in that unhappy course and knowing that from that circumstance he is altogether incapable of taking care of any property I may give him I have considered it my duty as well in relation to him as to his son to limit his title to the property I shall give him to a life Estate.

I give him therefore all that part of the tract which I have heretofore deeded to my son John Scott which lies North of the following boundary Viz beginning where a small creek which crosses the road leading from Cleves to Taylors Creek crosses the West boundary of one of the out lots of the town of North Bend & which in the partition of the same was assigned to the heirs of Philip Stockton & which two lots are numbered 78 & 98 thence with the said creek across the said Taylors Creek road & across the second bottom of the Miami River to where the said run enters the first or low bottom of the Miami & thence by a due west line to the Miami river. The tract here described contains one hundred acres which I purchased of Mr.? C. Short as the attorney of his father a number of the out lots of the town of North Bend & the residue of a tract divided ? off to me as a partner of the firm of Burnet Findlay & Harrison. I give the use of the said described tract to my said son Benjamin during his natural life and at his death the one half thereof to his son Mr. Cleves Harrison & the other moiety to any other children he may have living at the time of his death which are legitimate & if he should have no such children then the whole of the said tract is   the property of the said John Cleves Harrison & if the said John Cleves Harrison should not survive his father & leaves no issue then the said tract of land shall go to the other legitimate children of said Benjamin & in entire default of issue of him the said Benjamin the said tract shall at his death revert to the mass of my estate to be devided amongst my heirs in equal portions. To my daughter Mary S. Thornton & to her heirs forever I give the farm on which her husband now lives also the part of the tract I own in section 9 of their township (& on which old Mr. Simon lives) which is included in the following boundaries Viz Beginning at the South East corner of said section No 9 thence north along the boundary line of said section No 9 & section No 3 to the land of Dr. Stephen Wood thence West along the boundary of said Woods land to the place when the pasture fence of John Cooper strikes the same being the North East corner of said parture & which said corner is about twenty rods to the East of said Coopers house thence in a direct line to the North West corner of a field upon the hill which has been for some years cultivated by the said Cooper & by John Neale &   thence along the Western boundary of said field & in the same direction across the lane in front of William Marklands house to the deviding line between my land & the said Marklands then East along the boundary of said Marklands land & McConnels land (late Schenks) to the place of beginning.

To my daughter Anna Tuttle I bequeath all the residue of the tract lately owned by my son John Scott & not herein bequeathed to my son Benjamin the said tract hereby bequeathed to my daughter Anna T being bounded as follows Viz Beginning on the state road running through the town of Cleves where the Sourth West corner of Dr. Woods land joins the same   along the middle of the said road to the Eastern boundary of the town of Cleves thence Northwardly along the same to the North Eastern corner of said town thence Westwardly along the Northern boundary of said town to the North Western corner of said town thence South along the Western boundary of said town to a point which shall be due East of the North eastern corner of the late William Putterhorns(?) land, thence due West to the Miam River thence up the same to the point where the Southern Boundary of the tract bequeathed to my son Benjamin strikes the same, thence Eastwardly along the said boundart to its outer section north the land of the heairs of Philip Stockton thence along the boundary of said Stocktons lots to their South East corner & thence North along the Western Boundary of Dr. S Woods land to the place of beginning.

My intention in relation to the above is perhaps better expressed by saying that I give to my said daughter Anna T all my land beyond (North) of the state road above mentioned, & West of Dr. Woods farm & east of the land before bequeathed to my son Benjamin with the Exception of my lots in the town of Cleves. I bequeath also to my daughter Anna Tea ten acres of land called the locust grove & lying North of Dr. Woods orchard the same being two five acre lots No 25 - No 26 in the old town of North Bend to her & her heirs forever. I also bequeath to my said daughter Anna T. at the death of her mother a tract of land which joins that first bequeathed to her & bounded as follows Viz on the said state road at the North East corner of that part of my North bend tract which goes the said road & which corner is between the house of Dr. S. Wood & the school house & the very point whereon the road leading from Northbend & which has been used for many years (but now stopped up) strikes the said state road thence Southwardly along the said old road & passing   a   log   house   or   cabin   (successively   occupied   by   Hardy Smith & now by John Keyser) to the foot of the hill (70 or 80 yeards below said house) thence westwardly through what is called the walnut grove pasture to a large Black locust tree which stands conspicuously on the top of the hill in said pasture & standing in that pasture thence still westwardly through a small gove of black locust trees to the place where the fence which now divides the field called the cold spring field from the field to the north of it, strikes the Western boundary of the B. Walnut grove pasture thence strike westwardly along the line of said fence to where it joins the lane leading from North Bend to Cleves thence Northwardly to the South West corner of the 40 acre tract lately laid off for Doct. Dudley thence Eastwardly to the South East corner of said tract thence Northwardly to the North East Corner of said tract, & thence East along the boundary of the first tract bequeathed to the said Anna T. & and lands of Dr. S Wood to the place of beginning . . .

The text of the Will of William Henry Harrison is the text of an eight-page undated fragment in the William Henry Harrison papers in the Library of Congress, series 1, folios 146-170.

Notes on the Will of William Henry Harrison

A MONG THE WILLS OF THE PRESIDENTS, that of William Henry Harrison is surely the crudest. It was not witnessed, it lacks a date, and the signature appears only in the opening line rather than at the end. It would be admitted to probate in few, if any, states today. The document simply lacks one or more of the formalities required by modern law as safeguards designed to assure that the decedent's expressed intent is accurately and completely known. In fact, it should not have been admitted to probate in Ohio. In 1840, the year before President Harrison died, the Ohio General Assembly enacted a statute clearly requiring all written wills to be signed at the end and in the presence of at least two witnesses.

Another shortcoming is its probable failure to dispose of all the testator's property. It speaks only of specific pieces of real estate. Any other real estate then owned or acquired before his death, and any property which he owned at his death other than real estate, is simply not disposed of by his Will, and would be divided between the widow and his lineal descendants under the applicable law rather than according to his expressed wish. Presumably President Harrison addressed himself in this Will to that property which he regarded as of significant interest or value, but he would have no assurance that his holdings would not change, that he would not acquire other property of value in the future or dispose of parcels he then held.

Customarily, the disposition of assets not otherwise mentioned in the will is handled through the use of a residuary clause. As the name implies, such a clause makes a gift of any assets left in the estate after payment of debts, taxes, etc., and after the other provisions of the will have been carried out. In its original usage such a clause was not ordinarily employed to make important gifts; it was included to dispose of assets too insignificant to mention specifically but which might not fall within the scope of those gifts expressed in general language. In short, it was used to insure that the Will would dispose completely of all property owned by the testator at his death. Today, typically, the residuary clause is used as the vehicle for disposing of a testator's principal wealth, and those clauses making gifts of amounts of money, or of particular assets, or of all of certain classes of property are used for comparatively unimportant purposes.

Like that of many early Presidents, Harrison held most of his wealth in real estate, and the Will does show a clear familiarity with those assets. He selected the pieces to be sold to pay debts. He provided that his widow should receive his home, North Bend, which overlooked the Ohio River near Cincinnati, though withholding part of the land comprising the whole estate. He designated particular pieces for each child and even restricted to a life estate the interest of the son who had disappointed him.

The manner of describing these properties is a point of some interest to a modern reader. These descriptions are typical of those found in early deeds or wills in sparsely settled communities where land is plentiful and precise boundaries are likely to be of minimal importance. Where disputes do arise, property descriptions such as these have often been found ambiguous because the landmarks used are not clearly identifiable ("a large black locust tree . . . on the top of the hill in said pasture") or are known to have shifted ("thence with said creek"), are contradictory (a parcel described as 300 acres in boundaries enclosing an area of much larger size), or are incomplete (the described boundaries fail to form a closed figure). Whether Harrison's descriptions in this Will caused any problems is not known, but they illustrate well the superiority of the modern surveyor's description proceeding in precise distances and directions from an established landmark.

JOHN TYLER

JOHN TYLER, THE FIRST VICE PRESIDENT TO ATTAIN THE OFFICE OF PRESIDENT THROUGH THE DEATH OF A CHIEF EXECUTIVE, was born at Greenway, in Charles City County, Virginia, on March 29, 1790. His home was near both Williamsburg and Richmond, two leading cultural centers of that era. Tyler was the sixth of eight children of John and Mary Armistead Tyler, and was the fourth generation of Tylers in America. His early education was in a small school kept by a sadistic teacher, John McMurdo. At the age of 11, Tyler led a rebellion against the teacher, tied him hand and foot, and locked him in the schoolhouse. At the age of 17 he graduated from William and Mary College; he took a law degree two years later.

Elected to the state legislature the same year his father became Governor of Virginia, young Tyler seemed destined for a brilliant political career. At the age of 23, Tyler married his first wife, Letitia Christian, also 23, the daughter of a wealthy Virginia planter. Tyler's tenure in the Virginia legislature was followed by four years in the U.S. House of Representatives and two terms as Governor of Virginia. In 1827 he was elected to the U.S. Senate and in 1840 he was chosen to run on the Whig ticket as Harrison's running mate under the slogan "Tippecanoe and Tyler too!"

Upon the death of President Harrison, Tyler immediately took over the office of President, thereby becoming the first Vice President to assume office upon the death of a President. Though elected as a Whig, Tyler aligned himself with the Democratic Party.

Mrs. Tyler was ill most of her stay in the White House and only attended two functions; her death in 1842, early in the second year, left Tyler with eight motherless children. In 1844, a gunship exploded while being inspected by the President, resulting in the death and injury of Government officials and crew. One of the victims was wealthy Senator Gardiner of Long Island, N.Y., whose 24-year-old daughter the President married three months later when he was 54. The second Mrs. Tyler assumed the duties of White House hostess, becoming one of the most colorful First Ladies. Tyler's second marriage produced seven more children. His first child was born in 1816 and his last died in 1947, a time span of 131 years.

Because of Tyler's unpopularity in Congress, they refused to grant him the usual sum needed for the upkeep of the White House, for such things as lights, fuel and other expenses. Although not a rich man, Tyler paid many expenses out of his own pocket to maintain the life-style of his old Virginia home. His salary was the same as Washington had received, $25,000 per annum to be paid quarterly.

During Tyler's term in the White House, he purchased a run-down 1,200-acre estate in Virginia for $12,000, which he named Sherwood Forest. It was located just a few miles from Greenway, his childhood home. Here he retired in 1845, after both the Whigs and Democrats had rejected him for another term.

For 17 years, Tyler enjoyed his retirement on his Virginia plantation. In 1861, on the eve of the Civil War, he was chosen as a member of the Peace Convention in Washington. Returning disillusioned to Richmond, he declared his belief that no settlement could be arranged and recommended secession. In May, 1861, he was elected a member of the provisional congress of the Confederate States. Five of his sons fought for the Confederacy.

John Tyler died on January 18, 1862. His body, draped by a Confederate flag, lay in state in the hall of the Confederate Congress, in Richmond, Virginia. A solemn train of 150 carriages stretching a quarter of a mile followed the hearse. No official notice of his death was taken in Washington, nor was he accorded the 30-day mourning period usually proclaimed to honor a former President. The provisions made in Tyler's will that his remains be buried at Sherwood Forest were not fulfilled; he was buried in Hollywood Cemetery, Richmond, Virginia, where until 1894 he lay in an unmarked grave; at that time Congress appropriated $10,000 to erect a monument on it.

Frightened and unsettled, his 41-year-old widow was left with seven children—one a mere babe in arms—faced with debts and a 1,600-acre plantation with 70 slaves to manage during a savage war. In 1882 Congress voted Julia Tyler an annual pension of $5,000. She died in 1889 and was buried next to her husband in Richmond.

John Tyler highly valued the papers of his Administration and made provisions in his will for their disposition. His public papers were entrusted to the care of his four sons and two sons-in-law, while his private papers were left in the custody of his wife. Some of the papers were taken to Richmond for safe-keeping during the war when Mrs. Tyler evacuated to New York. She and her son Lyon later attested to their having been consumed in the Richmond fire of April 2–3, 1865. It is reasonable to assume that the bulk were left in the house, which was ransacked on many occasions as the armies passed back and forth; many of the papers were carried off and destroyed. Lyon G. Tyler later collected letters from contemporaries to whom his father had written. These form the bulk of the remaining 1,410 Tyler papers which Lyon G. Tyler sold to the Library of Congress in 1919.

Text of the Will of John Tyler

My Will. 1. In the name of God Amen. This is my last will and testament, written wholly with my own hand, with my name subscribed thereto, this 10th day of October in the year of our Lord and Savior 1859, whereby I revoke and cancel all other wills and testaments heretofore made by me.

2. In the first place I empower my dear wife to make out my estate, suitable provision for my burial, which I wish to be accompanied with no unnecessary expense. Let the people of this County, whose fathers helped me on in my battle of life with a zeal and constancy rarely ever equaled, and never surpassed, be invited to attend my funeral obsequies, and let my body be consigned to the tomb in the earth of the County, wherein I was born, there to repose until the day of resurrection, my wife will select the spot on Sherwood Forest, and mark it by an uncostly monument of granite or marble. I desire also that the will cause a suitable memorial to be erected over the remains of my father and mother at Greenway, should it not be done in my life time inscriptions both for my own and their will be found in the paper enclosing this.

3. I have purchased a house and lot on Hampton River called the "Villa Margaret" out of certain monies which arose out of the sale of Kentucky Lands, in which lands the late Alexander Gardiner of New York, the brother of my wife, had an interest which amounted to ten thousand dollars, and which he bequeathed to his sister my wife, and deeming it proper and right that the investment aforesaid which was made at her request, should enure to her in fee simple. I give and bequeath to my wife Julia Gardiner Tyler, the said house and lot in absolute fee simple to her and her heirs forever. I have made two payments for said house and lot. The third and last falls due on or about the 16th day of July 1860, and I hereby charge and subject my whole estate real and personal to the payments of the same. I also subject my estate to the payment of any balances which may be clear of the said Ten Thousand Dollars, to my wife over and above the payments for said purchase and improvements made on said lot, it is my intention to leave behind me a statement of all the expenditures.

4. I Give and bequeath to my wife all my estate both real and personal so long as she may remain my widow. The great responsibility of rearing our children will desolve upon her, and I place therefore in her hands all that can arise in the shape of income from my estate to enable her not only to consult her own comfort but to acquit herself of the high responsibilities of a mother. At her marriage or death, I give the same to the survivors of my children by her as the means of starting them in life and of perfecting their education, my children of my first marriage will see in this, my estate being limited nothing more than an attempt and desire on any part to place these children on a footing of equality with them even as far as I am able and not proceeding from any want of devoted affection for them or the descendants of any of them— I have limited the bequeath in this clause to my wife during her widowhood not in restraint of marriage but purely in reference to our children who

while they will find all the nurture in a mother's love while she remains unmarried, yet I can have no trust of confidence in a stepfather who of course must be unknown to me, she will be restricted to her legal proportion of my estate in the event of her marriage.

5. I constitute and appoint my sons Robert, John and Tazewell Tyler, and my son David G. Tyler and my sons-in-law James Sample and William Waller, my Literacy Executors bequeathing to them for revision and publication if they shall think proper, all such of my papers as relate to my own times and relate either to my own Biography or to public affairs. My collection of autographs and all my private papers not relating to public affairs I give to my wife.

6. I give and bequeath to my wife all our horses and carriages along with my man Peter Hall as her Coachman and any one of the boys she may select as the footman or outrider and I direct that she shall use and enjoy all my property without liability for waste. I desire that she will return to court a full inventory of my personal property but without appraisement, and I invest her with the discretion and power to sell any portion of said personal estate either privately or publicly as she may deem best in order to pay my debts should she find it necessary to do so. I give to my dear daughter Julia on her marriage, should such event occur during her mother's life time and while she remain my widow, her choice of the Negro girls under her own age, as a maid servant, and I hope that my wife will upon each of our children (the boys) attaining the age of twenty one years, select for each a Negro boy as his own separate property. The execution of this request will be superseded by the marriage of my wife or her death. I desire also that my wife will take good care of my faithful servants William Short and Fanny Hall, so that their old age may be rendered comfortable, I fully acquite and discharge each and all of my children of my first marriage, the living and the dead from all sums appearing to be clear to me on my books or otherwise up to this day. Lastly I constitute and appoint my beloved wife Julia Gardiner Tyler my sole executor of this my last will and testament and desire that the court will permit her to qualify without giving security. In testimony whereof I have unto this my last will and testament written wholly in my own hand subscribed my name and affixed my seal this 10th day of October, 1859.

WITNESS
Junius Roane
Wm. H. Clopton

John Tyler   (SEAL)

Codicil. To this my last will and testament written this 13th day of March, 1860 in my own hand writing with my own proper seal annexed I bequeath along with the house and lot near Hampton all the furniture of every description which I purchased with the property as well as all that I have purchased from my quarters since for the establishment to my dear wife the pieces for the same being changed in abatement of the sum of money mentioned in the third item or clause of my will. 2. page—I invest her also with authority to sell and dispose of any slave or slaves who may prove refranctory, either reinvesting in other or after such manner as she may deem most conclusive to the interest of my estate should she die before the children shall have attained the age of twenty one years. I hope that their elder brothers

Robert Tyler or Tazewell Tyler or their uncle David L. Gardiner or someone of them will qualify as the guardian of such infants or infant. Subscrided in my own hand writing the day and year above stated as a codicil

WITNESS   John Tyler   (SEAL)
Junius Roane
Wm. H. Clopton

2. Codicil. To the above last will and testament written with my own and signed and sealed by me this 29th day of October in the year 1860 as circumstances may arise which may render the sale of my lands and personal property necessary and proper I invest my wife with full authority to sell and convey the same upon the concurrence in such opinion of my son Robert Tyler and brother-in-law David L. Gardiner to be employed in writing by them; such concurrence also to be given for the sale of either the real or personal property seperate and apart from the other and should either die before any such sale is made then I desire that the survivor of the two shall unite with him in judgment either of my other sons by my first marriage he may select. This power to sell is to continue only as long as my wife continues my widow.

WITNESS   John Tyler   (SEAL)
Junius Roane
Wm. H. Clopton

Julia Gardner Tyler (detail).

Notes on the Will of John Tyler

TYLER'S WILL reflects the need he felt to reconcile the claims of his widow, the needs of a large family of minor children, the oldest then only 13, and his affection for the adult children of his first marriage. The last proved to be the easiest to resolve, for those children were left only the explanation that Tyler hoped they would understand the naturalness of the priority he gave to the claims of others still dependent on him.

In a happy marriage, which Tyler's was, a husband will typically be content to trust to his widow the protection of their minor children unless he feels some doubts about her judgment or her experience in managing family finances. These do not appear to have been factors here, but Tyler seems to have been preoccupied with the possibility that his wife, still in her early 40's, might remarry. His Will exhibits a fear that their children's interests might be neglected in that event. Amateur analysts can speculate whether his concern was based on a belief that a future husband would acquire legal rights in his wife's property which could prejudice his children, a fear that his wife's normal concern for their children might be diluted by remarriage, or simply his distaste for that prospect. As it happened, the second Mrs. Tyler lived until her death on July 8, 1889, without remarrying.

Whatever the motivation, the Will illustrates three techniques which a husband who feels as Tyler felt can try. Aside from the Hampton River property which had been purchased with his wife's inheritance, Tyler restricted her interest in his property to the period of her *widowhood*, a status which would end with either death or remarriage. Second, though naming her Executrix of his Will, he limited her power to sell real estate by imposing a requirement of the assent of other family members to the sale. This would reduce the risk that fixed assets might be converted to cash, a much more easily dissipated form of property. Third, he named other adult members of the family, rather than their mother, as guardians of his minor children.

Parents are termed the natural guardians of their children, and, ordinarily, a surviving parent will be named if court appointment of a guardian should be necessary. Appointment of the parent is not required though and, in fact, will be avoided where past conduct or current life style suggest that the parent is plainly unsuitable—or where there may appear to be some special need to protect the financial interests of the minor against the risk of abuse by the parent. Similarly, it is customary for the husband's will to nominate his wife as guardian of their minor children in the belief that she can be relied upon to protect their financial interest fully. As Tyler's Will illustrates, where there may be some concern on that score, nomination of one other than the surviving parent to be guardian creates the additional protection of a second adult with an interest in the affairs of the minor children and with legal status to inquire into their handling.

Another point of interest in the Tyler Will is his designation of Literary Executors. Their responsibility is quite different from that of the Executor. As the adjective suggests, their task is literary, not financial—to review the testator's papers with a view to possible publication. Of course, any proceeds realized become assets of the estate to be administered and distributed under the terms of the Will.

Finally, Tyler's Will demonstrates how much a testator is dependent on the good will and diligence of the living to carry out his instructions. Tyler's first expressed wish in his Will was for burial on his own plantation, but he died in Richmond during the Civil War and was buried there. His body has never been moved. George Washington was somewhat more successful in this respect. His express direction for the construction of a new vault for family burial was carried out—more than 30 years after his death.

JAMES K. POLK

JAMES KNOX POLK WAS BORN IN MECKLEN-
BURG COUNTY, NORTH CAROLINA, ON
NOVEMBER 2, 1795. He was the oldest son of
Samuel Polk, a farmer and surveyor whose
great-grandfather emigrated to the United
States from Ireland, and Jane Knox, whose
father had been a captain in the Revolutionary
War. His family moved to Tennessee in 1806,
where his schooling was fragmentary. His ill
health forced him to leave school. Educated
under a private tutor, he was academically sufficiently prepared in 1815 to enter the University of North Carolina, from which he
graduated in 1818 with an impressive record.

Following his graduation and his admission
to the bar in 1820, Polk entered into law practice with Judge Felix Grundy, from whom he

later purchased his Nashville home, which he
called the Polk Place. During his legal career
he came to know Andrew Jackson, whose protégé he became. On January 1, 1824, Polk
married Sarah Childress, the accomplished
daughter of a prosperous Tennessee merchant.
Polk was at this time holding his first political
office, that of state legislator. In 1825 he was
elected to Congress from Tennessee, a position
he held for 14 years, the last four as Speaker of
the House. Andrew Jackson persuaded him to
run for Governor of Tennessee in 1839; he was
elected and served until 1841.

Polk was defeated for a second term as
Governor. His aspirations then turned to the
nomination for Vice President on the Democratic ticket in 1844; however, a deadlock among

Polk house at Columbia, Tennessee.

the contenders for the Presidential nomination made Polk the party's candidate against the Whig nominee, Henry Clay, a man who had sought the office since 1824. Polk, considered the first dark-horse candidate for the Presidency, had a hard campaign against his more seasoned opponent. His positions favoring the annexation of Texas and the acquisition of Oregon won him the election.

The White House left its mark on Polk; when he departed, in 1849, he was aged, silver-haired, and in poor health. He returned to the Polk Place at Nashville to live out a retirement that was to last only a few months.

He died on June 15, 1849, at the age of 53, and was buried at the Polk Place. After Mrs. Polk's death, the house was torn down and the graves on the property moved to the Capitol grounds. The only house remaining as a Polk shrine is that alluded to in his will as the house and lot in Columbia, Tennessee, occupied by his aged mother, Jane Polk. Most of the Polk memorabilia have been assembled in that house, which is operated by a private foundation. Thus, Polk's desire as expressed in his last will and testament was honored neither by the people nor by the state he loved. In 1893, when his carriage was exhibited at the Columbian Exposition, it was in such a dilapidated condition as to show little respect for a man who had held such high office.

For a lad who was frail at youth and on the verge of death, Polk had achieved much. His estate amounted to between $100,000 and $150,000 at his death; part of this he had saved from his $25,000 annual salary as President. Childless, Sarah Polk survived her husband by 42 years. In 1882 Congress gave her a $5,000-a-year widow's pension.

Text of the Will of James K. Polk

In the name of God Amen! I James K. Polk of the State of Tennessee, but residing during the term for which I was elected President of the United States, in the city Washington, considering the uncertainty of life and the certainty of death, do make, ordain and publish this may last Will and Testament, as follows,—that is to say—

It is my will and desire—and I do so direct, that all just debts which I may owe, at the period of my death, shall be paid out of my estate, by my executors hereinafter named.

I devise and bequeath to my brother William H. Polk and his heirs forever, the Remainder interest which I own, in the house and lot—lying and being in the town of Columbia Tennessee, at present occupied by my aged mother Jane Polk and in which she holds a life estate.

I devise and bequeath to my nephew Marshall T. Polk—now a Cadet at the Military Academy at West Point, and his heirs forever—all the lands which I own, lying in the State of Arkansas, which said land was presented to me by the United States; and as I have much gratitude for the future welfare and prosperity of my said nephew Marshall T. Polk, whose father and mother are both dead, and for whom I am guardian, it is my request that my beloved wife Sarah Polk, will from time to time, give him such further aid and assistance, out of the estate hereinafter devised and bequeathed to her, as in her discretion she may think right and proper, provided he shall in her judgement, prove to be worthy of such aid and assistance, and she shall be, in a situation to do so, without embarrassment or inconvenience to herself.

I devise and bequeath to my beloved wife Sarah Polk, to be held used and enjoyed by her, during the period of her natural life, the dwelling house and lots and all the grounds, with the appurtenances thereunto attached and belonging, situated, lying and being in the City of Nashville in the State of Tennessee, which said house, lots and premises, I purchased from the estate of Felix Grundy deceased, and exec. John M. Bass, and which on my return to Tennessee, I design to make my future residence. It is my will and desire, that my said wife Sarah Polk shall have the full right as long as she may live—to the exclusive possession, occupation and enjoyment of the said house, lots and premises, and to add to, alter or change the improvements thereon as she may think proper. And as my beloved wife Sarah Polk and myself have mutually agreed with each other, that at our respective deaths, it is desired by us, that our bodies may be interred on the said premises—which I have denominated the Polk Place, and as it is also our desire that the said house, lot, and premises should never pass into the hands of strangers who are not related to us by consanguinity, I do hereby, with a view to prevent such a contingency, devise, bequeath and give, the said house, lots and premises, and all the appurtenances thereunto belonging or apportioning, from and after the death of my said wife, to the State of Tennessee, but to be held by the said State of Tennessee in Trust for the following uses, objects and purposes, and none other, that is to say: the said State of Tennessee, through its Governor for the time being, of if he should decline to assume the execution of the Trust, then through such other person, as the Legislature of the said State, may from time to time impower and authorize for that purpose, shall permit the said house, lots and premises, to be occupied, used and enjoyed by such one of my blood relations, bearing the name of Polk, as may be designated by the said State, as its authorized agent, preferring always my nearest of kin of the name of Polk it there be such a person who shall be deemed worthy, and a proper person to occupy the house; but if at any time, there shall be no such blood relation bearing the name of Polk, then the said house, lots and premises, shall be occupied, used and enjoyed, by such other of my blood relations as may be designated by the said State to execute this Trust. Which same of my blood relations shall, after the death of my said beloved wife Sarah Polk, from time to time, use, occupy and enjoy, the said house, lots and premises, shall be required to keep the same in repair, so as to prevent them from delapidating or falling into decay, shall pay the public taxes thereon, and shall preserve and keep in repair the tomb, which may be placed or erected over the mortal remains of my beloved wife and myself, and shall not permit the same to be removed, nor shall any buildings or other improvements, be placed or erected over the spot, where the said tomb may be. I request the public authorities of the State of Tennessee, whose people I have so long served in various public stations, and to whom I am under so many obligations of gratitude, at the death of my beloved wife Sarah Polk to accept and execute the Trust specified in this devise.

I devise, bequeath and give to my beloved wife Sarah Polk and her heirs forever, all the balance of my estate, not herein before disposed of, where soever situated, including all my lands—and real estate, all my servants and personal property of description—in the States of Tennessee, Mississippi or elsewhere, and including also money and debts and securities, which may be due or owing to me, or held by me. I have entire confidence that my beloved wife Sarah Polk, who has been constantly identified with me in all her sympathies and affections, through all the vicissitudes of my public and private life, for more than twenty five years, and who by her prudence, care and economy, has aided and assisted me, in acquiring and preserving the property which I own, will at her death, make a proper and just disposition of what property she may then possess—between her relations and mine. This is left entirely to her sole discretion, but with a request, if she shall deem it proper, that it may be distributed as equally as practicable between such of her blood relations and my blood relations, whether they be the nearest of kin or not, as she may select and deem to be the most worthy recipients of it. Should I survive her, unless influenced by circumstances which I do not now foresee, it is my intention to emancipate all my slaves, and I have full confidence, that if at her death she shall deem it proper, she will emancipate them.

I do hereby nominate, constitute and appoint my beloved wife Sarah Polk Executrix, and my faithful and trusty friends, John Ambrose and Daniel Graham Executors to this my last Will and Testament.

In Witness whereof, I have hereunto subscribed my name, and affixed my seal this twenty eighth day of February in the year of our Lord one Thousand, eight hundred and forty nine.

James K. Polk

Signed, sealed and delivered
by the testator in our presence and
the presence of each other as his
last Will and Testament and witnessed
by us at his request.

    James   Thomas
    H. L. Tunney

Tomb of President and Mrs. James K. Polk.

Notes on the Will of James K. Polk

POLK'S WILL WAS EXECUTED LESS THAN A WEEK BEFORE THE END OF HIS TERM; his death followed less than four months later at the end of a triumphal tour of the South which he was making on his way home to Nashville. His widow survived him and made her home in the Polk Place mentioned in the Will, until her death on August 14, 1891.

The provisions made by Polk for the Polk Place are among the most interesting in any of these Wills. They demonstrate the extreme lengths to which the desire to keep a particular piece of property in one's family can go—and perhaps also the effect of the Presidency on a man's ego. President and Mrs. Polk had no children of their own, but Polk still sought to assure that his home would be occupied only by his relatives *forever*. Forever is a long time, so most people regard such a desire as slightly irrational. At most, they may try to tie up property for a limited time following their deaths.

More importantly, the law imposes restrictions on the length of time during which the wishes of the dead will be permitted to prevail over the judgment of the living. While it is more tolerant of plans to set property aside permanently for charitable (public) rather than for private purposes, President Polk's trust would not qualify for those more relaxed rules. The state of Tennessee is of course, a public institution representing all the citizens of the state, but its role here was to be limited to acting as a trustee for private beneficiaries, the relatives of the former President living at any particular time.

Many Presidential homes have been withheld or recovered from the mainstream of real estate transactions to be preserved permanently as special places of historic interest. Undoubtedly, this practice will and should continue for future Presidents, but under existing laws it can be done only by dedicating such property to a public rather than a private use—which is as it should be.

The Will leaves "the balance of my estate" to Mrs. Polk outright, but the President could not resist making "a request" as to the way in which she might dispose of any of it that still remained at her death. Language such as his, urging an equal division between her relatives and his, is termed precatory. It has often proved a fertile breeding ground for litigation between those who contend that such words are really gently expressed commands which must be obeyed and those who maintain that they are only suggestions which the recipient is free to observe or ignore. While the lay reader would probably feel that the language here cannot possibly be read as intended to impose a duty binding his widow, the decided cases have produced some surprising results in this respect. The moral is to use such language very cautiously, if at all, and when it is used to explain the legal effect intended by it.

Pocket wallet used by James K. Polk.

ZACHARY TAYLOR

T HE ANCESTORS OF ZACHARY TAYLOR MIGRATED TO AMERICA FROM ENGLAND IN 1692 and settled in eastern Virginia, where they intermarried with many of the families prominent in the social and political life of both that state and the nation. Richard Taylor, Zachary's father, had held a colonel's commission in the Revolution. Zachary Taylor was born in Orange County, Virginia, on November 24, 1784. When he was less than one year old, his father moved near the settlement of Louisville in Virginia's western county of Kentucky. The frontier settlement, afforded few opportunities for formal schooling. Taylor, however, developed an avid interest in things military which he discussed with his neighbors, many of whom were veterans of the Revolu-

tion. At 24 he applied for a commission in the Army and was appointed a first lieutenant.

Two years later, in 1810, Taylor married Margaret Smith of Calvert County, Maryland, who accompanied him to New Orleans and to frontier army posts throughout his long military career. The daughter of Walter Smith, a Maryland planter, she had only a home education and little social ambition.

Taylor served as captain at the beginning of the War of 1812. His brave defense of Fort Harrison gained him promotion to the rank of major. The reorganization of the Army after the war brought about a reduction in rank, whereupon Taylor resigned to become a farmer. The Black Hawk War in 1832 brought Taylor back into service with the rank of colonel. In 1836 he gained an important victory over the Seminole Indians at Okeechobee, and was promoted to brigadier general. During the Mexican War, he won brilliant victories and rose to the rank of major general. He emerged from the Mexican War as a hero, with the nickname "Old Rough and Ready."

Before the Mexican War, Taylor had acquired a home at Baton Rouge, Louisiana, and a 1,923-acre cotton plantation with 81 slaves on the Mississippi River. He had hoped to become a farmer again following his retirement from the military. Known as Cypress Grove Plantation, it had cost Taylor $35,000 in notes and $60,000 in cash. The four-room house at Baton Rouge to which he retired after the war he nicknamed The Spanish Cottage.

In 1848 the Whigs found in Taylor the man they thought would win the Presidential election for them. His military achievements would appeal to the North while his rural farm background and homespun touch would surely win the South, so ran the theory. Taylor was totally unaccustomed to the turmoil of politics. He had never held public office either by appointment or election, had never even voted in an election. He was the first regular Army man to become President, the others having been citizen soldiers.

President Taylor's stay in the White House ended when, on July 4, 1850, while attending dedication services at the Washington Monument, he fell ill and died five days later. Following obsequies in the capital, his body was taken to Kentucky for burial in a family plot in Springfield.

By the time of his death, Taylor had amassed an estate of approximately $142,000 in real estate, stocks, and cash, which he left to his wife and three surviving children. Mrs. Taylor died two years after her husband. His son Richard served the Confederacy as a lieutenant general.

Sketch of Zachary Taylor (detail) made a few days before the President's death.

Text of the Will of Zachary Taylor

Testamentary Paper
No. 3
dated July 20, 1846.

Life being at all times uncertain; and, more especially, as regards one in my situation, therefore in the event of my being cut off by the hand of the enemy, disease or in any other way before joining my family, I wish the following disposition made of my property.

I give to my excellent wife Maragret Taylor, all my real estate in the city of Louisville, State of Kentucky, consisting of three large store or ware-houses on Wall Street, and one small lot, or part of a lot I purchased of Mr. William C. Galt, I believe on Jefferson Street, with my stock in the Louisville Bank and Bank of Louisville, consisting of one hundred shares, and my stock in the Northern Bank of Kentuchky, consisting of five shares, with the following servants, slaves for life, Charles Porter, Tom, Dicy, Jane and her two children William and Caroline, with all the household furniture of every kind I may die possessed of, forever, to dispose of when and as she may think best or proper.

I give to my son Richard twenty-one thousand dollars to be paid him on the first day of January next 1847, out of any money then in the hands of my merchants in New Orleans, Messrs. Mannsel (?) White & Co. with the plantation I recent cultivated in the Parish of West Feliciana and State of Louisiana, and in the County of Wilkinson, State of Mississippi, now rented out, asjoining the lands of Capt. John Sims, John Wiker,(?) Esq. & others, forever, to dispose of as whenever he may think proper to do so.

I give to my daughter Mary Elizabeth, eleven thousand dollars, to be paid her on the first day of January next 1847, out of my money which may be in the hands of my merchants as aforesaid, after paying my son Richard the legacy previously stated and out of the proceeds of my present years crop, with the servant woman Mary, a slave for life, I purchased of Capt. N. L. Macrae, and her four children, forever to dispose of as she may think proper. But should the money in the hands of my merchants not be sufficient, in addition to the proceeds of my present crop, after paying the first named legacy, then the eleven thousand dollars be be mad good to her, out of the first money arising out of the net proceeds of my crop, with ten per cent interest until paid.

I leave to my daughter Ann M. Wood, sixteen shares of stock in the Louisville Gas Bank, and whatever money may be due me at the time of my death, as well as any money that may be in the hands of my merchants at that time, after the disposal of my present years crop and the payment of the legacies referred to, as well as to make up to her, in addition to what she may receive, ten thousand dollars with interest on the same at ten per cent per annum until paid out of the net proceeds of my plantation.

I wish my plantation and servants kept together for ten years, and after paying the several legacies referred to, the net proceeds of my crops to be equally divided between my two daughters, Ann M. Wood and Mary Elizabeth until they receive the sum of twenty thousand dollars including that has been previously left them, after which the net proceeds of the crops to be equally divided between the three Ann, Mary E. and Richard, until the end of the said ten years, when the property to be equally divided among the three as above named.

I wish my debts paid, there being only one of about a thousand dollars, due on account of security for the late Thos. H. Chew (?) in which Judge Edward McGehee of Wilkinson, Mississippi, is concerned, who had the management of the same, I having paid a portion of it.

I wish the servants only moderately worked and kindly treated, and the old one taken good care of an made comfortable, which I hope my children will have attended to.

I leave my friend, Judge Edward McGehee of Wilkinson County & state of Mississippi, my Executor to see my wishes carried into effect, which I hope he will not hesitate in doing.

(signed) Z. Taylor

Matamoros,   Mexico
    July 20th, 1846

Note. There is now in the hands of my merchants, Messrs, Mannsel White & Co. about twenty thousands dollars at interest; due me from Capt. Allison. I think about seven hundred, and a thousand or more from others, with interest on bank stock say seven hundred dollars, and rent of houses one thousand (more?) which in addition to my crop of the present years, which might be near 12 or 14 thousand, ought to amount to about seven(teen) thousand dollars, and no doubt will do so on the first day of January next and particularly when the crop is all disposed of.

/signed/ Z. Taylor

Notes on the Will of Zachary Taylor

WHEN ZACHARY TAYLOR PREPARED THIS WILL, he was in the middle of his campaign in the Mexican War, and therefore its obviously stop-gap character is perfectly understandable. The failure to revise it during the next four years is less excusable, but the phenomenon of the temporary will allowed to become permanent by default is common—as is that of the notes on a will to be executed in the future, written by one who dies intestate.

The temporary character of this Will is visible in many ways. One is its seemingly conditional character set out in the opening sentence, ". . . therefore *in the event of my being cut off . . . before joining my family*, I wish the following disposition made of my property. . . ." Of course, Taylor later did rejoin his family so that a completely literal reading of this language would render the provisions which follow it ineffective since they rest on a condition (being cut off. . . . before. . . .) which never occurred. However, in cases where this kind of question has been raised, courts have been much more inclined to treat such language as a statement of motive for writing the Will than as a condition which must be met for the provisions of the Will to be given effect. Since this Will was admitted to probate the language here was clearly interpreted in that way.

Another indication of the temporary nature of the document is the memorandum listing Taylor's assets then in the hands of his agent plus amounts which he expected the agent to be receiving in the near future. The legacies to his son, Richard, and to his daughter, Mary Elizabeth, are specified to be payable from that particular source on a named date, January 1, 1847—which Taylor himself survived for more than three years.

Gifts of money expressed in this fashion raise potentially difficult questions of interpretation. If the date specified for payment has passed, or the anticipated source of payment no longer exists, is the legacy defeated or has the intended legatee a claim for a like amount from some other source? Either is possible; the answer depends upon the testator's "intent." That intent is a useful standard where the question to be decided has been anticipated in preparing the Will and clearly answered one way or the other. Where the question has either not been foreseen or the answer is left in doubt, the effort to determine "intent" becomes an attempt to construct one from reasonable inferences drawn from other provisions of the will that may seem to have some bearing on the question. Where the rest of the will offers inadequate evidence of the testator's probable intent, legal rules of construction are invoked to supply needed answers. Since these rules sometimes turn on accidents of phrasing, the result produced may or may not conform to the testator's probable preference, and may or may not satisfy the survivors as just. This procedure provides answers when answers are needed and are not otherwise available. It also provides a clear lesson on the importance of foreseeing the questions which may have to be answered and answering them clearly according to the testator's wishes.

The Zachary Taylor home in Baton Rouge (as illustrated in *Harper's New Monthly Magazine*, November, 1854).

MILLARD
FILLMORE

MILLARD FILLMORE, THE SON OF NATHANIEL AND PHOEBE MILLARD FILLMORE, was born in a cabin in Locke (now Summerhill), Cayuga County, New York, on January 7, 1800. His parents, impoverished frontier farmers from New England, had settled on poor land in upstate New York. Even the title to their land was defective and their closest neighbor was four miles away. His father's library consisted of two books, the Bible and a book of hymns, and young Millard did not own a dictionary until he was 18.

Nathaniel Fillmore, discouraged with farming, was determined that his son learn a trade; and so at the age of 14 Millard was apprenticed to a cloth maker at a salary of $55 a year. Millard received a skimpy education at this time in a one-room country school. His teacher there was a red-haired girl named Abigail Powers of Stillwater, New York, the daughter of a Baptist minister and two years Fillmore's senior, whom he was to wed 12 years later.

In 1822, Millard Fillmore moved with his parents to East Aurora, New York, 18 miles from Buffalo, where he began teaching and later clerked with a law firm. From 1823 to 1830 he practiced law in East Aurora before going to Buffalo to join in partnership with Joseph Clary, a prosperous lawyer in that city. He never went to college.

Fillmore's first elected public office was that of representative from Erie County to the state legislature in 1828. During his three terms there he won acclaim for his ability, integrity, and honesty and was elected to the U.S. House of Representatives for four terms. The election of 1848 pushed Fillmore from the office of comptroller of New York to that of Vice President, at a salary of $5,000. The death of Zachary Taylor on July 9, 1850, suddenly thrust Fillmore into the office of President with a $20,000 increase in his salary. He was inaugurated immediately in a ceremony without fanfare or parade. The Fillmores, with their daughter, Mary Abigail, and son, Millard Powers, moved into the Executive Mansion.

In 1852, the Whig party passed Fillmore over in favor of General Winfield Scott, who lost the election to the Democrat Franklin Pierce. While preparing to leave Washington for Buffalo, Mrs. Fillmore fell ill and four weeks later she died. The President, then 53, retired to Buffalo with his family. In less than one year he suffered another blow in the death of his only daughter. Millard Fillmore went to Europe to overcome his bereavement and, while in Rome, he was nominated for the Presidency by the Know-Nothing Party; in the election he received only one electoral vote.

In 1858, a wealthy 44-year-old widow, Mrs. Caroline Carmichael McIntosh, married the ex-President. By the terms of the marriage

Silver coffee urn; part of a silver service purchased by Millard Fillmore from proceeds derived from the sale of Mrs. Fillmore's carriage.

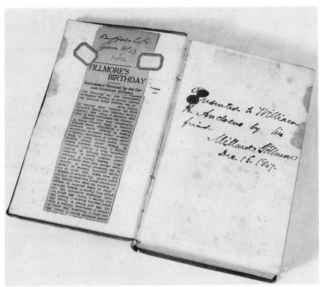

A book from Millard Fillmore's library.

contract, Fillmore had complete control of her fortune. He bought a large mansion in Buffalo, where the Fillmores lived in splendor; his guests included Presidents Lincoln and Johnson. Fillmore also became a philanthropist, devoting himself to numerous worthy causes until his death on March 8, 1874.

In his will, Millard Fillmore left all his property, excepting monies left his brothers and sisters, to his wife and his son, who auctioned off most of his father's possessions; both of the ex-President's houses were soon torn down. Fillmore had carefully preserved his papers in his Buffalo home and had remarked: "In those cases can be found every important letter and document which I received during my Administration, and which will enable the future historian or biographer to prepare an authentic account of that period of our country's history." His son did not value the importance of the papers; in his will he directed that all the valuable letters and documents of his father's Administration be destroyed in 1889. It is evident that the administration of the son's estate did not comply fully with the will, as several groups of the papers have since appeared and remain in the Buffalo Historical Society.

Text of the Will of Millard Fillmore

I Millard Fillmore of the City of Buffalo in the State of New York, do make publish and declare this my last Will and Testament in manner following, that is to say: Believing that the Laws of the State of New York have provided for as equitable a distribution of the little property which I am likely to leave at my decease, as I could make by will, except that in a few particular cases it is therefore my desire to leave its distribution and descent to the operation of law and the antenuptial contract existing between me and my beloved wife Caroline C. except as hereinafter expressed.

First: I feel it a duty and a pleasure to record my dying testimony to the noble qualities of my beloved wife Caroline C. who has ever proved a Kind affectionate and devoted wife and I hereby ratify and confirm the antenuptial contract between us and wish my executors and heirs to see it fully and faithfully carried out and executed and if she and my son Millard Powers shall both survive me, I hope and trust that they may love each other as I have loved them as they will both be orphans, indeed, I hope also that they will mutually render to each other other every assistance due from a most affectionate parent to a beloved child, and from a most affectionate and dutiful child to a beloved parent; and with this I shall rest in peace.

Secondly: I hereby release and bequeath unto each of my brothers, Cyrus Fillmore and Calvin T. Fillmore all claims of every name and nature which at my decease I may have against them or either of them or their heirs or legal representatives; and I hereby authorize my executors or either of them to acknowledge the same satisfied.

Thirdly: I give and bequeath unto each of my sisters Olive A. Johnson and Julia Harris an annual annuity of four hundred dollars ($400) per annum during her natural life to be paid to each of them quarter yearly, for her sole use and benefit free from all claim or control of her husband.

Fourthly: I give and bequeath to my brother Calvin T. Fillmore and his wife Miranda, and the survivors of them and to his or her heirs and assigns the farm of one hundred acres, now occupied by him in the town of Scio Washtenaw County Michigan being the Northern quarter of section number twenty three (23) in township number two South of Range number five east excepting the east sixty acres.

Fifthly: I give one thousand dollars to the Buffalo Orphans Asylum; to be securely invested on Bind and Mortgage for the use of said Asylum.

Sixthly: I leave all the rest and residue of my estate, real and personal to the operation of the said antenuptial contract, which fixes and settles the rights and claims of my said wife in and to my estate in lieu of all other claims, and the remainder of said estate, I leave to be inherited and distributed according to the laws of the State of New York, except as herein otherwise directed. But as the objects nearest my heart are my dear wife and son, I will and desire that during their joint lives they share equally in the net income of my estate, and if after the payment of all charges thereon including said bequests, annuities and the third due my said wife by the antenuptial contract—my son's share thereof shall be more than said third, then my will and desire are that the surplus be equally divided between them, and in case my wife shall survive my son thereafter his death I will and desire that she shall during her natural life recieve one half of the net income of my estate without deducting from such half any part of the annuities herein granted instead of the third as provided in said antinuptial contract and I hereby appoint my said wife Caroline C. and my said son Millard P. and my friend Nathan K. Hall executrix and executors of this my last Will and Testament hereby revoking all former wills by me made.

In witness whereof I have hereunto set my hand and seal at Buffalo this eighth day of December eighteen hundred and sixty five (1865)

Millard Fillmore

The above instrument consisting of one sheet of parchment was at the date thereof signed published and declared by the above signed Millard Fillmore to us well known, to be his last Will and Testament in presence of us who at his request and in his presence have and in the presence of each other subscribed our names as witnesses thereto.

Wm Ketchum Buffalo New York
O. H. Marshall Buffalo New York

I Millard Fillmore of the City of Buffalo in the State of New York do make this my first codicil to my last Will in words following:

Whereas in and by my last Will and Testament dated on or about the eighth day of December 1865 (executed on Parchment in Duplicate) I did by the third item bequeath unto each of my sisters Olive A. Johnson and Julia Harris an annuity of four hundred dollars during her natural life, to be paid and vested at the times and in the manner therein expressed.

And whereas also since the making of said will the expenses of living have greatly increased, and the advancing age of the Legatees may render a large bequest prudent if not absolutely necessary I therefore hereby increase said annuity to each of them from four to six hundred dollars, to be paid at the times and vested in the manner expressed in said Will.

In Witness whereof I have hereunto set my hand and seal this 19th day of September 1868.

Millard Fillmore

The above instrument in writing consisting of one sheet of parchment was at the date thereof signed published and declared by the above named Millard Fillmore to us well known to be his Codicil to his last Will and Testament in presence of us who at his request and in his presence and in the presence of each other have subscribed our names as witnesses thereto.

Cyrus P. Lee Buffalo Erie County New York
Wm Ketchum Buffalo Erie County New York

I Millard Fillmore of the City of Buffalo in the State of New York do make this my second Codicil to my last Will in words following:

Whereas in and by my will bearing date the eighth day of December 1865 and hereto annexed I devised to my brother Calvin T. Fillmore a certain farm therein described situate in the town of Scio in the State of Michigan which has since been sold, and taking into consideration his feeble health and small amount of property, I give and bequeath unto him an annuity of five hundred dollars ($500) per annum during his natural life to be paid to him quarter yearly.

And whereas also, it is my desire as well as my duty to provide for the comfortable maintenance and support of my said wife and as far as I am able to provide against all contingencies and having by said bequest to my relatives and the Orphan Asylum discharged my duty in that behalf, and feeling and rejoicing that my son and only child Millard P. Fillmore is quite able to provide for himself (at least during the life of my said wife) I therefore do hereby will and direct that after the payment of my funeral expenses, and all just debts and the bequest to the Orphan Asylum, that all my personal property as soon as conveniently may be, be invested in United States or New York Stae bonds or bonds of the New York Central and Hudson River Rail Road, and out of the interest accruing thereon the said annuities shall first be paid and all taxes and assessments upon my real and personal estate whether occupied or possessed by my said wife or not, and the balance I hereby bequeath to my said wife and direct the same to be paid to her during her natural life; and at her decease if any of the said life annuitants shall then be living that the then present value of his or her annuity at the rate of six percent shall be paid off, and the residue of my estate descend to my heirs and next of Kin according to the Laws of the State of New York.

In witness Whereof I have hereunto set my hand and seal this 28th day of April, 1873 in duplicate.

Millard Fillmore

The above instrument in writing of one sheet of parchment was at the date thereof, signed and published and declared by the above named Millard Fillmore to us well known to be his second Codicil to his last Will and Testament in presence of us who at his request and in his presence and in the presence of each other have subscribed our names as witnesses thereto.

Cyrus P. Lee Buffalo
Chas. D. Marshall of Buffalo Erie County N.Y.

Notes on the Will of Millard Fillmore

T HE WILL AND CODICILS OF MILLARD FILLMORE were executed many years after he had left office, and they reflect his life and situation in that later period. He had married a second time. The second Mrs. Fillmore was a widow and wealthy in her own right. Before they were married the two entered into an agreement governing their interests in each other's property. Such an agreement, if based on a fair disclosure of the assets and debts of the parties, will replace the provisions made by law for the protection of a surviving husband or wife. The terms of their agreement are not visible in Fillmore's Will, but the fact of its existence and his recognition of its binding effect on him is evident. However, his second codicil shows that he did not believe that the agreement precluded him from making more generous provision for his widow than its terms would have required.

An antenuptial contract can be a useful tool in defining the claims which those who are about to be married will be able to make on the wealth of the other after marriage; it can be used either to expand or to contract the rights

The silver snuff box which Millard Fillmore presented to his second wife.

which the law would otherwise attach to the marital status. For example, it works well in the case of second marriages between persons of some means who agree that the families of their respective first marriages should have a primary claim to assets in the distribution of their estates. However, these contracts must be handled with care, for their effect is to inhibit the usual freedom of a property owner to revise his will in response to changed circumstances.

Another interesting aspect of Fillmore's Will is its explicit reliance on the provisions of the intestate statute of the state of New York as the sole standard for disposition of some of his assets (paragraph 6th). Used as he did, to describe those who are to take assets at his death, the provisions are redundant since the statute would operate anyway on assets not otherwise disposed of by the Will.

Such terminology can be useful to identify those who are to take at a time other than testator's death, but it can raise difficult problems of interpretation if not handled with care. For example, the last paragraph of the second codicil provides that income from certain assets be paid to Mrs. Fillmore for life, then "descend to my heirs and next of kin according to the laws of the state of New York." President Fillmore died in 1874, his widow in 1881. Were the "heirs and next of kin" then entitled to take the property to be determined from among those who were living in 1874 or only those alive in 1881?

The point is a subtle one, turning on the meaning of "heirs and next of kin." Does it mean only one's closest relatives, using the intestate statute as the standard of closeness, at the time of one's death, or can it refer to relationships viewed at another time? There is no required answer. A testator is free to give these terms meanings of his choosing but must do so explicitly if the potential for argument is to be avoided. The draftsmen of other wills in this series have handled this particular problem more successfully than did the draftsman of this one. (See, for example, the Wills of Franklin D. Roosevelt and John F. Kennedy.)

FRANKLIN PIERCE

FRANKLIN PIERCE, BORN ON NOVEMBER 23, 1804, IN HILLSBOROUGH, NEW HAMPSHIRE, was the sixth of eight children of Benjamin and Anna Kendrick Pierce. His father had distinguished himself during the Revolution, was self-educated, and was active in the politics of his state. His home—which doubled as a tavern—became the focal point of gatherings at which Franklin was first exposed to political discussions.

Franklin attended a brick schoolhouse a mile and a half from his home and later an academy in Hancock. He then enrolled at Francestown Academy and Phillips Exeter Academy, and in 1820 he entered Bowdoin College, whose president was a friend of his father's; his classmates included Henry Wadsworth

Longfellow and Nathaniel Hawthorne, the latter of whom became a lifelong friend. He was no great scholar at first (by his junior year he was at the bottom of his class), but he finished third in his class by the time of his graduation in 1824. He began to study law, was admitted to the bar in 1827—in the same year his father became Governor of New Hampshire—and at the age of 24 he was elected to the state legislature, becoming Speaker two years later.

While at Bowdoin, Pierce had met Jane Means Appleton, daughter of a former president of the college. In 1834, they were married. By this time he had been elected to Congress, and after his second term, in 1837, he was elected U.S. Senator. But the loss of two sons in infancy so afflicted his wife that Pierce gave up a promising political career in 1842 to return to Concord, where he resumed his law practice. In 1845 he declined the offer to fill the unexpired Senate seat of Levi Woodbury as well as several other political appointments, giving as his reason the fixed purpose "never again to be voluntarily separated from my family for any considerable time, except at the call of my country in time of war."

This call came in 1846, when Pierce joined the ranks as a private in a volunteer company in the Mexican War. He soon rose to the rank of colonel and on March 3, 1847, was commissioned brigadier general by President Polk and participated in the capture of Mexico City.

The 1852 Democratic convention was unable to agree on a Presidential candidate, and on the 35th ballot the Virginia delegation proposed the name of Franklin Pierce. He carried the convention on the 49th ballot. Mrs. Pierce was opposed, as was their 11-year-old son Benjamin, who said he hoped his father would lose. Pierce himself was said to have expected to lose to his opponent, General Winfield Scott, but he won overwhelmingly.

Just prior to his inauguration, the family was returning from a funeral in Lawrence, Massachusetts, when the axle of the train in which they were riding broke, killing Benjamin, their only surviving son. Mrs. Pierce never recovered from the loss. Pierce was inaugurated on March 4, 1853; Mrs. Pierce was unable to attend the ceremony. No President ever entered the office under more personal sorrow. Mrs. Pierce wore black during the entire Administration and social activities were greatly curtailed. When he left the White House in 1857, President Pierce took his wife on a tour of Europe, hoping that her health would improve as a result; but nothing could assuage her grief, and she died in 1863 of consumption. Six years later, on October 8, 1869, Franklin Pierce died.

Having no children left, Pierce willed his estate of $70,000 to relatives, mostly nieces and nephews. Two houses where he lived both as a child and adult have been preserved. The papers of the President were left with "all of the rest and residue of my Estate of every kind & description" to his nephew, whose family sold the bulk of them to the Library of Congress after 1903.

Mrs. Franklin Pierce and her son Benny (detail).

Text of the Will of Franklin Pierce

I, Franklin Pierce of Concord in the County of Merrimack and State of New Hampshire with profound thankfulness to God for prolonged life and many mercies, do make and ordain this to be my last will and testament hereby revoking and annuling all wills by me heretofore made.

1st. I give and bequeath to my Brother Henry D. Pierce seven thousand dollars. From this sum my Executor will deduct whatever sums of money my Brother may owe me at the time of my decease.

2nd. I give and bequeath to Susan T. Pierce, wife of my Brother, three thousand dollars to be held in her own right and at her sole disposal forever.

3d. I give and bequeath to my Nephew Kirk D. Pierce ten thousand dollars.

4th. I give and bequeath to my Sister-in-law, Mary M. Aiken, one thousand dollars from this sum my Executor will deduct two advancements of one hundred dollars each. The dates of these advancements my dear Sister will know.

5th. I give and bequeath to my Nieces Anna K. Parker, I. Jane Henshaw and Jeanie A. Aiken three hundred dollars each.

6th. I give and bequeath to Harriet Bond and Frank P. Bond children of my niece—to Jane Appleton George and Anna George, daughters of John H. George and to Georgia Ray and Bella Ray, daughters of Frederick Ray of Andover Mass. two hundred dollars each.

7th. To my Nieces Ann Wentworth, Fanny Potter, Charlotte J. Bond and to my Nephew Solomon McNeil I give and bequeath two hundred dollars each, as a token of affectionate rememberance.

8th. To Una Hawthorne, Julian Hawthorne, and Rose Hawthorne, children of my dear friend, I give and bequeath five hundred dollars each.

9th. To Prof. Charles A. Aiken of Princeton, N.J. I give & bequeath five hundred dollars.

10th. I give and bequeath to my Nephew John McNeil one thousand dollars and to each of his daughters Anna and Fanny, three hundred dollars.

11th. I give and bequeath to Josiah Minot one thousand dollars. Also the picture of the grand Plaza Cathedral in the City of Mexico by Gonldi and the bone cane which once belonged to General Lafayette. I also give and bequeath to his three daughters Isabella, Grace and Fanny *Each* two hundred dollars.

12th. I give and bequeath to Benjamin Pierce Moore of Hillsborough five hundred dollars and to Benjamin Pierce George, son of John H. George one thousand dollars.

13th. I give and bequeath to Grace A. Williams daughter of Willard Williams five hundred dollars.

14th. I give and bequeath to Joseph Robinson of Concord five hundred dollars.

15th. To Mrs. Sarah A. Williams wife of Willard Williams I give and bequeath eighteen hundred dollars, to be held in her own right and at her own disposal forever, and also a small picture (Mother and child) hanging in the parlour and a small Japanese box in my chamber.

16th. To the City of Concord I give and bequeath in trust for the "Concord Public Library" one thousand dollars. The interest of said sum to be expended annually in the purchase of books and the principal to remain as a perpetual fund for the object indicated.

17th. I make the following specific bequests

The sword presented to me by the Ladies of Concord in 1847 I give to my Nephew Kirk Dearborn Pierce. The sword presented to me by the State of New Hampshire after my return from Mexico, I give to my Nephew Frank Hawthorne Pierce, with the hope that should occasion arise for their use, in repelling foreign aggression, in vindicating the rights of American citizens the world over, or in the faithful upholding of the sacred Constitution framed and adopted by the fathers of the Revolution, the weapons may not be dishonored in their hands.

To Colo. Thomas J. Whipple the case of pistols and all other articles now in his possission which were used by me during the war with Mexico, and also my silver mounted Mexican saddle. To Colo. Thos. P. Pierce my steel Scabbard and service sword and the holster pistols which I used through the Campaign in which he so faithfully and gallantly served.

To Colo. Thomas H. Seymour of Ct. a cane made from the flag staff of the Castle of Chepultepec which was cut down by his own sword. To Colo. J. H. George the best horse I may own at my decease, to be selected by himself, with a special request that he be not kept a day simply because he is a gift from me. I also give to Colo. George the neatly mounted hickory cane cut at Jamestown Va. My name in Roman letters on the Knots of the stick. To Hon. Clement March the hickory cane now in his possession. To the eldest son of the late Charles S. Davies of Portland the badge of the society of the Cincinnati presented by his father to mine and worn by Genl. Lafayette when he visited the United States in 1825. This badge is now in the possession of Dr. Davies. I give to my Brother Henry D. Pierce my badge of the Cincinnati Society. To Hon. J. G. Abbott of Boston a cane presented by his relative William Fletcher of Chelmsford long since deceased, to my father. And to his son Franklin Pierce Abbott a framed picture of "the Penitent" which I purchased in

Italy and which now hangs in the parlour. To James Langdon of Plymouth I give a cane with this inscription. "Presented to Franklin Pierce Jany. 1, 1855. To Charles D. Norton I give the best carriage and sleigh to be selected by himself which I may own at my decease. To Andrew Peirce Jr. of Boston two pictures octagonal in form. One Hager her infant and the Angel the other the destruction of Sodom. To Thomas W. Peirce of Topsfield a cane, now in his possession made from a plank of old Ironsides and also the picture of Judith and Holifernes. To Richard S. Spofford of Newburyport a large framed picture of our Savior in the Hall of Judgment before Philate. To Sidney Webster I give a very large picture (original) of our Saviour, Peter and the tribute money considered when I purchased it in Florence a work of rare merit. To Mrs. Ray wife of Frederick Ray of Andover Mass. on oil painting of the harbor of Venice and surroundings which she particularly admired when here long ago, also a small toilet case of rose wood & ivory she may have noticed it on the commodi at the cottage last summer; and to *her* her daughter Georgia a pretty sketch by her mother of a scene in North Hampton.

18th. All the rest and residue of my estate of every kind & description whether real personal or mixed, I give devise and bequeath to my Nephew Frank H. Pierce.

19th. Should any person to whom a bequest is made in this will die prior to my decease such bequest will lapse and be taken to be and treated as mull & void.

20th. I hereby constitute and appoint Josiah Minot of Concord sole Executor of this my last will and testament. In witness whereof I hereunto set my hand and seal this 22nd. day of January, A.D. 1868.

FRANKLIN PIERCE (LS)

Signed, sealed, and declared as and for his
last Will and Testament, by Franklin Pierce
in the presence of us, who at his request and
in his presence, have subscribed our names as
witnesses thereto.

BENJA. GROVER
CHS. MINOT
JA. MINOT

Notes on the Will of Franklin Pierce

ALTHOUGH HE WAS ELECTED TO HIS COUNTRY'S HIGHEST OFFICE, Franklin Pierce was a tragic figure at the time he wrote his Will. Yet his Will, written when he was a childless widower, has no hint of pathos. It begins with an expression of gratitude for long life and past blessings, then proceeds in a simple, straightforward way to make gifts of money, art objects, relics with patriotic associations, and other property to 51 different people, an unusually large circle of family and friends for a testator to wish to remember. The choice of individual items for particular people reflects care and thoughtfulness—as does the specific request that the testator's best horse, one to be selected by the donee for himself, not be re-

tained as much as an extra day because it had once belonged to the testator.

Pierce thought of his gifts in personal terms. If one of those named in the Will died before he did, he did not want that person's relatives to be substituted to receive his gift. The provisions of Paragraph 19th assure that result. Had that paragraph not been included, a statute (called the Anti-Lapse Statute) would save the gift in certain situations for members of the family of the deceased donee. With it included, the gift to any such person would fail and be added to the gift of the residue to Pierce's nephew.

Pierce did not, however, seek to project his wishes into the future beyond his death. Apart from the contribution to an endowment for his hometown library, all his gifts were made outright in form, leaving each donee completely free to do with the gift as he or she might choose.

Facsimile of a section of the last page of the Will of President Pierce.

JAMES
BUCHANAN

JAMES BUCHANAN WAS BORN ON APRIL 23, 1791, near Mercersburg, Pennsylvania. His father, also named James, had come to America from northern Ireland eight years earlier and settled in eastern Pennsylvania. When James was 16 years of age his father enrolled him in Dickinson College in Carlisle, where he studied Latin, Greek, mathematics, geography, logic, history, literature and philosophy. In 1808 he was expelled from college for misconduct but was allowed to return to the school in the winter of 1808, graduating the following year. Thereafter he studied law under James Hopkins in Lancaster, was admitted to the bar in 1812, and set up a law practice there. He was a Federalist member of the Pennsylvania legislature from 1814 to 1816.

The romance of Buchanan's youth ended in grief. He was deeply in love with Ann Coleman, the daughter of a millionaire ironmaster of Lancaster, who objected to her engagement to Buchanan. She died before an understanding could be effected; Buchanan remained a bachelor all his life. His niece, Harriet Lane, who had been orphaned at nine and had chosen her uncle as her guardian, was trained to become the head of his household. She accompanied him on his political appointments both in Washington and abroad, and was his official hostess in the White House.

Buchanan was an accomplished lawyer and by the time he was 29 he made as much as $8,000 a year. He entered politics as a Federalist but shifted his allegiance to the

Democrats. Elected to the U.S. House of Representatives in 1820, he remained in the House 10 years, serving as chairman of its Judiciary Committee.

In 1831, Buchanan had decided to retire to private life but was persuaded by President Jackson to become Minister to Russia. He remained in St. Petersburg until 1834, then resumed the practice of law in Lancaster. Within a few months he was elected to the U.S. Senate, an office he had always wanted; he took his seat on December 15, 1834, and served for more than a decade.

After the election of James K. Polk as President in 1844, Buchanan was selected as his Secretary of State, a post which he eagerly accepted. In 1848 Buchanan sought the Democratic Presidential nomination, but it went to Lewis Cass. In any case a Whig, Zachary Taylor, was elected President in 1848; Buchanan retired from office and bought an estate of 22 acres, known as Wheatland, in Lancaster. For four years he devoted more time to correspondence and following politics than he did to his law practice. In 1852 Buchanan was again a candidate for the Democratic nomination for President, only to lose to Franklin Pierce. Soon afterward, however, Pierce appointed him Minister to England, a post which kept him in the limelight until 1856, when the Democratic national convention in Cincinnati nominated him its candidate for the Presidency. Buchanan's unsuccessful opponent was John C. Frémont, the first Republican Presidential candidate.

By 1860 the Democratic Party had split into northern and southern factions and the split party with two separate candidates—with Buchanan not a contender—brought a sure victory for the Republicans with the election of Abraham Lincoln.

Social life in the White House during the Buchanan Administration was enhanced by the presence of Harriet Lane, who gained experience during her uncle's tenure at the Court of St. James's. Perhaps second only to Dolley Madison in charm and her command of the social graces, she entertained elegantly in her

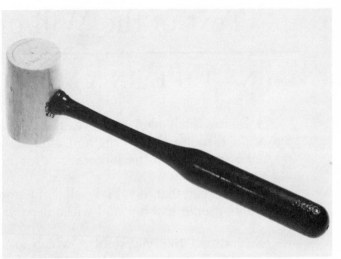

Gavel used at the Democratic national convention to nominate James Buchanan as the Presidential candidate.

role as mistress of the White House. With her uncle's approval she married Henry Johnston of Baltimore in 1866.

Leaving the White House in 1861, Buchanan turned to Lincoln, his successor, and said, "If you are as happy my dear sir on entering this house as I am on leaving it and returning home, you are the happiest man in the country." He died at home in Pennsylvania on June 1, 1868, having occupied his last years with study, writing, and politics.

His will bespeaks his dedication to his friends and family. He gave much to the Presbyterian Church, to the city of Lancaster, and to his servants; the remainder of the estate he divided among the 11 surviving descendants of his father's family. Less than two years before his death, Buchanan summed up his total wealth as $310,000—$205,600 in stocks and bonds, $41,190 in personal loans, $46,560 in real estate and $16,650 owed by family members. His salary of $25,000 as President could have accounted for little of his estate. Harriet Lane Johnston gave many of the family mementoes to the Smithsonian Institution. The remainder are to be found at Wheatland, which is now operated by a private foundation.

Text of the Will of James Buchanan

IN THE NAME OF GOD, AMEN.

I James Buchanan, late President of the United States, in the humble hope of Salvation through the merits and atonement of my Lord and Saviour, Jesus Christ, do make and publish the following as my last will and testament.

1. I direct that my body shall be interred in the Woodward Cemetery, in a plain and simple manner and without parade.

2. I direct that my debts, (which are small) and my funeral expenses shall be paid by my Executors out of my personal estate not herein specifically bequeathed.

3. I give and bequeath to my niece Harriet Lane Johnston, wife of Henry E. Johnston, my brother Rev. Edward Y. Buchanan, and my nephew J. Buchanan Henry, all the books, plate, beds and bedding and all the house hold and kitchen furniture belonging to me and in my dwelling house at Wheatland at the time of my decease, to be equally divided between by themselves; they allowing Esther Parker two hundred dollars worth of the same free of charge; and it is my will that no inventory or appraisement be made of these articles.

4. I give and bequeath to my brother Edward Y. Buchanan, all my wearing apparel, my gold watch, watch chain, and seals.

5. I give and bequeath to my valued friend, Esther Parker, who has long been a faithful and useful member of my family the sum of Five Thousand Dollars, which with Two Thousand Dollars already given to her she well deserved, and I commend her to the kindness of all my relatives after my decease.

6. I give and bequeath to the City of Lancaster, my two certificates of Loan Nos. 42 & 43 from the said City, for One Thousand Dollars each, or in case I shall dispose of them in my life time, then the sum of Two Thousand Dollars instead thereof in trust to employ the annual interest of the same in purchasing fuel for the use of the poor and indigent females of the City of Lancaster, during the winter season. This bequest is to be incorporated with the fund of Four Thousand Dollars provided by me some years ago for the same purpose and is to be administered in the same manner by the City Authorities.

7. I give and bequeath to the Presbyterian Church of the City of Lancaster, of which I am a member the sum of One Thousand Dollars.

8. I direct that all the real estate of which I may die seized shall be sold by my Executors, either at public or private sale, when in their opinion this will best promote the interest of my residuary Legatees and conveyed by them or the survivor of them to the purchaser or purchasers in fee simple.

9. It is my will that the proceeds of the sales of my real estate with the rents issues and profits whereof together with the whole of my remaining personal estate, of whatever nature or kind, this may be, shall be divided and distributed among my relatives, in the following proportions, to wit: I give and bequeath the one fourth part of the same to my niece Harriet Lane Johnston, the daughter of my deceased sister, Jane B. Lane; and I give and bequeath another fourth part thereof to my brother Edward Y. Buchanan, and it is my will that neither of these shall be charged with the considerable advancements I have made to each in my lifetime. I give and bequeath the one fifth part of the same to my nephew J. Buchanan Henry, the surviving child of my deceased sister, Harriet B. Henry. It is my will that the remaining portion of this my estate shall be divided into three equal parts, the first part thereof, I give and bequeath to John N. Lane, James B. Lane, Elliott E. Lane, minor sons of my deceased nephew, James B. Lane, and to the survivors or survivor of them;-another equal third part thereof; I give and bequeath to my niece Mary E. Dunham, the daughter of my deceased sister, Maria T. Yates; and the remaining third part thereof, I give and bequeath to Maria B. Weaver, Jessie Magaw, formerly Jessie Weaver, James B. Weaver and John Bless Weaver, minor children of my deceased niece Jessie Magaw Weaver and the grand children of my deceased sister, Maria, by her first husband Dr. Jesse Magaw, and to the survivors or survivor of them.

And it is my will that my executors shall retain in their own hands the amount of the legacy of the three minor sons of James B. Lane, with its accumulations, and as each of them shall severally attain the age of twenty-one, pay over to him the share to which he may then be entitled, and it is also my will that my executors shall retain in their hands the amount of the Legacy to the four minor children of my niece Jessie Magaw Weaver, with its accumulations and as each of them shall severally attain the age of twenty-one pay over to him or her the share to which he or she may be then entitled. Should my Executors deem it necessary for the maintenance and education of the two younger of these children to wit:- James B. Weaver and John Bless Weaver, they may apply the interest and even a portion of the principal of their respective shares for this purpose but under their own immediate directions.

Whilst feeling full confidence both in the integrity and eminent business capacity of Edward E. Johnston, the husband of my niece, Harriet Lane Johnston, I yet deem it prudent to secure to her a maintenance against the unforseen contigencies of future years. For this purpose I appoint my hereinafter named Executors Hiram B. Swarr and Edward Y. Buchanan, or the survivor of them, trustees or trustee, and direct them to retain in their hands, and invest and manage to the best advantage free and discharged from the debts and control of her said husband, the two thirds of the amount bequeathed to her as one of my residuary legatees under this my will, in trust that they or the survivor of them, shall pay to her annually or semi-annually the interest accruing thereupon for her sole and separate use during the life of her said husband, and her separate receipts for the same shall be sufficient acquittance.

And on these further trusts, that should the Harriet Lane Johnston survive her said husband, then to pay to her the principal of the fund thus created. Should she die in his lifetime, having a child or children, then in trust to pay to such child or children or the survivor or survivors of them, or their lawfully appointed Guardians for their use and their property, the whole of the said fund. But should the said Harriet Lane Johnston, die in the lifetime of her said husband, without leaving a child or children then it is my will that the said Trustees or the survivor of them shall pay the whole of the said fund to the children of my brother Edward Y. Buchanan, and to my nephew J. Buchanan Henry, and to the survivors or survivor of them all, share and share alike to whom I give and bequeath the same.

And finally I appoint my brother Edward Y. Buchanan and my trusty friend Hiram B. Swarr, to be the Executors and Executor of this my last Will and Testament.

Given under my hand and seal, at Wheatland in the County of Lancaster this twenty-seventh day of January, one thousand eight hundred and sixty-six.

JAMES BUCHANAN (SEAL)

Declared and published by the testator to be his last will and Testament in the presence of us.

W. W. Brown   J. W. F. Swift

I, James Buchanan, do hereby add this codicil to my last will and testament dated on the 27th January 1866, Viz:-

I direct that my executors shall apply towards the payment of the residuary Legacy left to my nephew, J. Buchanan Henry, by my last will and testament, the principal and interest due upon the bond from him to me, dated on the 15th June, 1866, for the sum of Fourteen thousand six hundred and fifty dollars ($14,650.00)

ITEM:- I give and bequeath to Martha J. Lane, the widow of my deceased nephew James B. Lane, a legacy of Two Thousand Dollars.

Given under my hand and seal at Wheatland this twenty-ninth day of April one thousand eight hundred and sixty-seven

JAMES BUCHANAN (SEAL)

This is a codicil to be added to and taken as a part of the last will and testament of me James Buchanan.

I hereby direct my Executors named in my last will and testament to place all the papers, correspondence and private and public documents connected with my public life in the hands of my friend, William B. Reed, who having shown to me in my retirement great kindness and in whom I have entire confidence to enable him to prepare such a biographical work I desire. With this view I direct my Executors to pay to the order of William B. Reed, such sums in the aggregate not exceeding one thousand dollars, as may be necessary in his opinion to secure the proper publication of such biographical work, and in case it or any part of it is not so used it shall go into the remainder of my estate.

As some compensation for the work which Mr. Reed has undertaken to perform I give and bequeath to his wife, Mrs. Mary L. Reed, the sum of Five Thousand Dollars which I direct to be a legacy for her seperate use and benefit, and in case of her death for her children, said amount to be paid to her on the completion of the work, or in the event of her death, before that then to ther children.

I give and bequeath to Peter Hillyer, Mary Smithgall and Lizzie Stoner, domestics now with me, or lately in my employ, each the sum of one hundred dollars.

In witness whereof I have hereunto set my hand and seal at Wheatland this twenty-ninth day of August, A.D. one thousand eight hundred and sixty-seven (1867)

JAMES BUCHANAN (seal)

Signed, sealed and declared by the said James Buchanan, as and for a codicil to his last will and in the presence of us.

J. B. Baker   Eliza Guest.

I declare the following to be a codicil TO MY LAST WILL AND TESTAMENT, dated the 27th day of January, 1867.

I give and devise unto Hariet Lane Johnston, the wife of Henry E. Johnston, and to her heirs and assigns my dwelling house at Wheatland, and the tract of land connected therewith, containing about twenty-two acres with the appurtenances; and I charge her for the same the sum of Twelve Thousand Dollars. In the settlement of my estate she is to account to my Executors for this sum of money and it is to be deducted from the residuary share of my estate bequeathed to her under my will.

Given under my hand and seal at Wheatland, in the County of Lancaster this thirty-first day of August, one thousand eight hundred and sixty-seven.

JAMES BUCHANAN (seal)

$140. U.S.S. attached

Notes on the Will of James Buchanan

JAMES BUCHANAN WAS NEARLY 66 WHEN HE ASSUMED OFFICE AS PRESIDENT. Among the Presidents, only William Henry Harrison was older. When he came to write his Will and codicils he had been living in comparative obscurity for a number of years and was then in his mid-70's.

Buchanan was the only President never to have married, so, like his immediate predecessor, Pierce, he had neither widow nor children to whom to leave his property. He divided it principally among his collateral relatives—a brother, nieces, a nephew, and their children. (One of the nieces, Harriet Lane Johnston, served as his official hostess in the White House, marrying only in 1866.) He also made provisions for charity and for servants or employees. His final testamentary act, the codicil dated January 27, 1867, was concerned with the disposition of his papers to a prospective, presumably sympathetic, biographer. Like many other Presidents, Buchanan, nearing the end of his life, showed concern for the preservation of the record of his career in public life, perhaps hoping for vindication in the longer view.

The Will contains the first illustration in this series of provisions intended to solve certain common problems of estate planning and administration. Seven of the legatees named were minors, at least as of the date of writing the Will. A gift to a minor introduces special problems for the executor. He will have to deal with the minor, at a minimum, to obtain the minor's assent to the distribution made to the minor. However, transactions resting on the assent of a minor are vulnerable because the law permits minors, on reaching majority, to disavow transactions to which consent had previously been given. This privilege rests on the assumption that it is necessary for the protection of minors who, by hypothesis, are too im-

mature and inexperienced to protect themselves in dealings with the adult world. This element of uncertainty may be avoided by one wishing to enter a transaction involving a minor's interest by requiring that it be carried out through a guardian appointed by an appropriate court. Guardianship, like estate administration, has its own drawbacks though, in cost, legal paperwork, and limitations on the kinds of action permitted. Dissatisfaction with these disadvantages has led to efforts to find other ways of handling a minor's property that will avoid the necessity to appoint a guardian.

Buchanan's Will illustrates one such technique, the use of a trust for minors. Trust terminology is not used in his Will, but the direction to the Executors to retain the legacies to minors, to accumulate the earnings, and to distribute both to them only as each should reach majority, created a trust. New responsibilities were thus added to those of simply winding up the affairs of the deceased and, depending on the ages of the minors, a potentially much longer period of administration was involved. Though not called trustees, the Executors would be treated as such.

Bible on which James Buchanan took the oath of office.

Wheatland, home of James Buchanan.

One of the problems raised by minors' ownership of property is its availability to meet a minor's needs during minority. This is more complex than it might appear on its face. One's natural reaction might be that, of course, a minor's property, like an adult's, ought to be available to meet current needs. However, the effect of making it readily available during minority is to reduce the amount of property which the legatee will actually receive at majority and, thereby, the amounts which his wishes will control. Moreover, there may be an overlap with the parents' duty to provide support for the minor from their assets and, as a result, a potential conflict with their ideas on the best way to handle those assets.

Buchanan's Will shows a recognition of these problems. Except as to two named "younger" children the Executors (trustees) are given no authority at all to spend or pay out funds to minors until their majority. As to those two, funds may be applied for their education and support during minority but only under "immediate direction" of the Executors, suggesting a certain wariness of parental decisions. Later wills in this series provide somewhat different solutions to these problems.

Another point of interest is the testator's di-rection to the Executors to sell his real estate. Under traditional theory, now changing in some states, title to real estate passes immediately at death to devisees (where it is disposed of by will), or to heirs (in the case of intestacy). They take title, though this title is subject to a power of sale either given to the Executors in the will or created by a necessity to find cash to pay debts, taxes, or expenses of administration.

Buchanan's real estate was included in the residue of his estate. His Will divided the residue among 11 named persons in a complicated scheme involving fractions as large as one-fourth and as small as one-thirtieth. Seven of the eleven were minors. Co-ownership of individual pieces of real estate in this form usually proves impractical. It can work smoothly where it is foreseeable that all those interested will be content to continue the investment and enjoy their share of the property by receiving an appropriate fraction of the cash income it produces. Buchanan, as an experienced lawyer, would have known the snarls which co-ownership often creates. By directing, not simply empowering, the Executors to sell his real estate, he eliminated that potential for future problems.

ABRAHAM
LINCOLN

A BRAHAM LINCOLN WAS BORN IN A ONE-
ROOM DIRT-FLOOR LOG CABIN ON THE
NOLIN RIVER, THREE MILES SOUTH OF
HODGENVILLE, KENTUCKY. Lincoln wrote in
his autobiography: "I was born Feb. 12, 1809,
in Hardin [now Larue] County, Kentucky. My
parents were both born in Virginia. My
mother, who died in my tenth year, was of a
family of the name of Hanks. My father, at the
death of his father, was but six years of age;
and he grew up literally without education. He
removed from Kentucky to what is now
Spencer County, Indiana, in my eighth year.
We reached our new home about the time the
state came into the Union. It was a wild re-
gion, with many bears and other wild animals
still in the woods. There I grew up. There

were some schools, so called; there was absolutely nothing to excite ambition for education.
Of course when I came of age I did not know
much. Still somehow, I could read, write and
cipher to the Rule of Three; but that was all.
The little advance I now have upon this store
of education, I have picked up from time to
time under the pressure of necessity.

"At twenty-one I came to Illinois, and
passed the first year in Macon County. Then I got
to New Salem, at that time in Sangamon, now
in Menard County, where I remained a year as
sort of a clerk in a store. Then came the Black
Hawk War; and I was elected a captain of the
Volunteers, a success which gave me more pleasure than any I have had since. I went
through the campaign, was elated, ran for the

legislature the same year [1832] and was beaten—the only time I have been beaten by the people. The next and three succeeding biennial elections, I was elected to the legislature. I was not a candidate afterwards. During this legislative period I had studied law, and removed to Springfield to practice it. In 1846 I was once elected to the lower House of Congress. Was not a candidate for reelection. From 1849 to 1854, both inclusive, practiced law more assiduously than ever before. Always a Whig in politics, and generally on the Whig electoral tickets, making active canvasses. I was losing interest in politics, when the repeal of the Missouri Compromise aroused me again. What I have done since then is pretty well known.

"If any personal description of me is thought desirable, it may be said, I am, in height, six feet four inches, nearly; lean in flesh, weighing on the average, one hundred and eighty pounds, dark complexion, with coarse black hair, and grey eyes—no other marks or brands recollected."

He met Mary Todd at a ball and awkwardly approached her, saying, "Miss Todd, I want to dance with you the worst way"—which he did, being a very awkward dancer. In 1842 he was married to Mary Todd. Shortly thereafter he purchased the house in Springfield, Illinois, the only home the Lincolns ever owned. It was purchased at a cost of $1,500 from the minister who had performed their marriage.

In 1846, he won a seat in the U.S. House of Representatives and served until 1849, when he returned to the Illinois law circuit. At the convention of 1858, following his speech—"A house divided against itself cannot stand; I believe this government cannot endure permanently half slave and half free"—he was nominated for the U.S. Senate. Although the race for Senate proved unsuccessful, the loss was mitigated by two accomplishments which later aided him in the Presidential race. First, it gave him his first opportunity to campaign for a high office. Secondly, his debate with Stephen A. Douglas on the issue of slavery and seces-

sion attracted nationwide attention, making him a national figure.

In 1860, Lincoln was chosen on the third ballot as the Presidential candidate at the Republican national convention in Chicago. In his speech at New Haven on March 8, 1860, Lincoln said, "I am not ashamed to confess that 25 years ago I was a hired laborer, hauling rails, at work on a flatboat—just what might happen to any poor man's son. I want every man to have a chance." Lincoln won the election of 1860 and when he departed Springfield for Washington, D.C., he sold his household furnishings and rented his house. His Administration was to become the most eventful in American history.

Mrs. Lincoln suffered much during these turbulent years. She was rejected as disloyal by many of both the North and South and her immediate family fought on both sides. Despite this she maintained the courage to keep the White House on schedule. Personal tragedy befell the Lincolns for the first time at the White House in 1862 when their second son, William Wallace Lincoln, died suddenly. (Eddie had died in infancy.) Both the President and Mrs. Lincoln were deeply grieved and the social life was curtailed for a while. The family had only two sons left. Tad, their favorite, was a lovable youngster whose company his father greatly enjoyed.

The election of 1864 brought only two Republican candidates into the political arena, Abraham Lincoln and John C. Frémont: Frémont withdrew and Lincoln was promptly nominated. His Democratic opponent was a famed Northern general, George B. McClellan, who led a group of followers declaring the war a failure. In this election, soldiers voted in great numbers on the battlefield for the first time; despite the unrest and disunity in support of Lincoln, he carried the election and he was inaugurated in March 1865.

Shortly thereafter the war came to a close, the nation once more restored, and life seemed to take on a more normal aspect for the First Family. On April 14, 1865, as they sought relaxation in attending a play entitled *Our Ameri-*

can Cousin at Ford's Theatre near the White House, John Wilkes Booth fired a shot which ended Lincoln's life. He was carried across the street to a rooming house where he died a few hours later. Mrs. Lincoln never recovered from the death of her husband and remained in the White House almost a month after his death.

Although the Lincolns were not a wealthy family and despite Mrs. Lincoln's liking for fine clothes and inclination to periodic lavish spending, they managed to accumulate over $100,000 by the time of the President's death. His salary as President brought him only $25,000 annually. He left no will and the estate was settled by David Davis, Supreme Court Justice, who was appointed administrator. The President had left a net estate of $83,343, which Davis as ad-

ministrator increased to $110,974. At the settlement of cash payments from President Lincoln's estate Nov. 13, 1867, this amount was divided three ways: $36,765.60 went to Mrs. Lincoln, an equal sum each to Robert Todd Lincoln and to Thomas "Tad" Lincoln.

Congress also voted Mary Lincoln a $25,000 lump sum as well as a pension first of $3,000 and later of $5,000.

Tad died as a boy. Only one son, Robert Todd Lincoln, grew to manhood. He had a full and successful life, and became Secretary of War. Before his death in 1926 he donated his father's papers to the Library of Congress and dedicated the Lincoln Memorial in Washington, D.C.

For "Notes on Dying Without a Will" see page 281.

Top hat worn by President Lincoln to Ford's theatre.

ANDREW JOHNSON

ANDREW JOHNSON WAS BORN ON DE-
CEMBER 29, 1808, IN RALEIGH, NORTH
CAROLINA. His father, Jacob, was a sexton,
porter and constable; his mother, Mary
McDonough, did weaving for the inn where
her husband worked. Three years after Andrew's birth, his father died while rescuing two
friends from drowning. The widow was left
with two children, Andrew and William.

At the age of 10 his mother apprenticed
young Andrew to a tailor, James J. Selby. The
family moved to Greeneville, Tennessee, when
Andrew was 18. There he got work as a jour-
neyman tailor, and a year later he set up his
own shop. In 1827 he married Eliza McCardle,
a woman of some education, who taught him to
read and write.

Andrew Johnson's first elective office,
which he won by 500 votes, was that of alderman for the town of Greeneville. He was
reelected in 1829 and 1830 and advanced to
the office of mayor, which he held three years.
His interest in local politics continued, and in
1835 he was elected to the state house of representatives and, after two terms, to the state
senate. He soon felt he had outgrown local and
state politics and in 1843 he was elected to the
U.S. House of Representatives, where he
served for 10 years. He then served as Governor for two terms before being elected to the
U.S. Senate.

In 1851, while serving his fourth term in
the U.S. House of Representatives, Andrew
Johnson bought a new brick home on Main

Street in Greeneville for $950 and his old house. This was to be his permanent home and the one to which he would return to live out the remainder of his life.

While Johnson was serving in the Senate—the only Senator from a Confederate state to remain loyal to the Union—President Lincoln selected him to become the military Governor of Tennessee. He was still Governor when he was nominated for Vice President in 1864.

Thrust into the Presidency by the sudden death of Abraham Lincoln, Johnson, a Democrat, soon became a prime target for the radical Republicans who opposed his views on states' rights and his conciliatory treatment of the South. Because he dismissed Edwin M. Stanton as Secretary of War, President Johnson was impeached and subjected to trial in May 1868. The Senate acquitted him by one vote, however, and 60 years later the U.S. Supreme Court upheld Johnson's position by declaring the Tenure of Office Act invalid.

Mrs. Johnson appeared at only three functions during her stay at the White House. Owing to a long illness, weak and emaciated, she delegated her official role to her daughter, Martha Johnson Patterson. Congress had appropriated $30,000 to set the executive mansion in order; the President drew a salary of $25,000. Life in the White House was simple and plain; they enjoyed a family life much the same as they had lived it in Tennessee.

Soon after assuming office, a group of New York bankers and merchants purchased by subscription a new carriage complete with a span of horses and harness and presented it to the President. The President, maintaining that his ethics would not let him accept large gifts, declined, retaining only the parchment conveying the sentiments. His integrity drew wide praise.

In 1869, following his term as President, Andrew Johnson returned to his home in Greeneville. Unwilling to give up politics, he ran for the Senate in 1872 but was defeated. In 1875, however, he was elected to his old Senate seat in Washington, the only President ever subsequently to become Senator. While on a visit to Greeneville at the adjournment of the regular session, Johnson suffered a stroke and died on July 31, 1875.

Although born quite poor, Johnson managed to accumulate a sizable fortune through thrift and prudent investments. He was worth about $150,000 by 1869, when he returned to Greeneville after the Presidency. He improved his property there and bought a large brick business building. It was thought he intended it either for a bank or a large tailoring business. He suffered a reverse during the Panic of 1873 when he lost $73,000 with the collapse of the First National Bank of Washington.

Johnson's son, Andrew Johnson, Jr., continued to live in the house at Greeneville until his death in 1879. At that time an inventory of the estate of President Johnson was prepared and the estate was finally settled by Thomas Maloney, a grandson-in-law, and Andrew Johnson Patterson, a grandson, in 1883. The home, with most of its original furnishings, is now maintained by the National Park Service along with his original tailor shop.

The Johnson Presidential papers were sold to the Library of Congress by the family. His library is still owned by a descendant.

For "Notes on Dying Without a Will" see page 281.

Three books from President Andrew Johnson's library.

ULYSSES S. GRANT

DESCENDED FROM ENGLISH ANCESTORS WHO HAD SETTLED IN NEW ENGLAND IN THE 17TH CENTURY, Grant was born in a small frame cottage at Point Pleasant, Ohio, on April 27, 1822, the oldest son of Jesse Grant, a farmer and tanner. Shortly after his birth the family moved to nearby Georgetown, Ohio, where his father attracted much attention by building a two-story brick house in the middle of western frontier lands.

Grant's earlier years were spent helping his father on the farm, working and playing hard and attending the village school and nearby academies during the winter months. Young Grant was christened Hiram, with Ulysses as his middle name. When he was appointed to the United States Military Academy

in 1839, the Congressman recommending him erroneously submitted his name as Ulysses Simpson Grant, the middle name being his mother's maiden name. Grant never bothered to change the mistake.

Grant was the best horseman in his class but in his academic studies ranked only 21st in his graduating class of 39. His sloppiness of dress and his roll-call tardiness brought him numerous demerits.

Graduating from West Point at the age of 21, Grant was assigned to Jefferson Barracks, St. Louis, Missouri. Here he met Julia Dent, the daughter of Colonel Frederick Dent, a slave-owning farmer with a large nearby estate. Within a year the couple became engaged, though the Mexican War deferred the marriage until 1848. After the war he remained in the service despite frequent transfers to distant posts away from his wife and the two sons born within four years.

In 1854, Grant resigned from the Army and spent the next six years on a farm, which he named Hardscrabble, carved out of the Dent holdings at St. Louis. Unsuccessful at farming and real estate ventures, he moved to Galena, Illinois, in 1860. There he lived in a log cabin, was employed as a clerk in his father's leather store at $800 a year, and was considered by many to be a failure.

When the Civil War broke out, he offered to drill a company of Galena volunteers. Within three years he rose from colonel to commander of all the Union forces with the rank of lieutenant general. His wartime feats earned him the reputation as savior of the Union.

Three houses were offered Grant as tokens of appreciation for his military service. The one he chose was the house at Galena built in 1857 by Jackson Davis. Galena also presented him with a sword which is today in the Smithsonian Institution. He refused a house in Philadelphia that the Union Club had bought and furnished for $30,000, but later accepted the house at 205 I Street on Minnesota Row in Washington, D.C., moving east to occupy it for Christmas of 1865. It had formerly been the residence of Vice President John C. Breckinridge. A group of New Yorkers also presented him with $100,000, and a group of men from Boston with a $75,000 library.

Grant was promoted to full general in 1866 and in 1867 replaced Secretary Stanton in the Cabinet as interim Secretary of War until Congress reinstated Stanton the following year. His interest in politics grew, following a confrontation with President Johnson. When the Republican convention met in Chicago in 1868, war-hero Grant was nominated for President on the first ballot. His popularity as a soldier won him a sweeping victory.

Grant had little experience in politics or the functioning of government. He had never cast a vote until 1856, when he voted for James Buchanan. The Democrats as late as 1866 had

hoped to make him their candidate.

Grant's salary during his first term as President was $25,000, which was about the same as he had made as general. However in 1873, in his second term, the President's salary was increased to $50,000 a year. The family at that time consisted of four children, three sons and one daughter. Perhaps the most spectacular event in the White House was the marriage of Nellie Grant, the daughter, to Algernon Frederick Sartoris, a young Englishman. Her wedding gown cost $5,000 and the gifts on display at the wedding totaled more than $75,000.

When the Grants left the White House in 1877 they decided to take a tour around the world. They were entertained lavishly in every country and showered with gifts. After three years, they returned to Galena, where the President accepted the offer to have his name placed in the 1880 Republican nomination. He lost to James A. Garfield; embittered, he blamed his friends for having advised him poorly.

After this he gave up politics and moved to New York, where a fund of $95,000 had been raised by Hamilton Fish, Joseph Drexel, George Childs, and J. P. Morgan to buy a house at 3 East 66th Street (now demolished). From 1881 to 1884 he devoted his interest and funds to a banking firm that was systematically looted by his son's partner, Ferdinand Ward.

When the bank was obviously failing, Grant went to a friend, William H. Vanderbilt, to borrow $150,000 for one day to keep the firm going. The check was turned over to Ward, who absconded, and Grant was informed the next day that the firm had failed. Several friends contributed $1,000 each so that Grant would have money to buy food and other necessities.

Vanderbilt was willing to cancel his debt but the Grants insisted on turning over everything they owned to meet the obligations, including the deeds to the properties in Washington, Philadelphia, Galena, and St. Louis as well as their household furnishings. The Grants reluctantly accepted pay from Vanderbilt for the general's war souvenirs, but

Mrs. Grant had them sent to the Smithsonian Institution.

The result of the Vanderbilt episode, together with Congressional efforts to help the former President in his emergency, appear in the following letter sent by President Chester A. Arthur:

Executive Mansion, February 3, 1885
To the Senate and House of Representatives:

I take especial pleasure in laying before Congress the generous offer made by Mrs. Grant to give to the Government, in personal trust, the swords and military (and civil) testimonials lately belonging to General Grant. A copy of the deed of trust and of a letter addressed to me by Mr. William H. Vanderbilt, which I transmit herewith, will explain the nature and motives of this offer.

Appreciation of General Grant's achievements and recognition of his just fame have in part taken the shape of numerous mementoes and gifts which, while dear to him, possess for the nation an exceptional interest. These relics, of great historical value, have passed into the hands of another, whose considerate action has restored the collection to Mrs. Grant as a life trust, on the condition that, at the death of General Grant, or sooner, at Mrs. Grant's option, it should become the property of the Government, as set forth in the accompanying papers. In the exercise of the option thus given her, Mrs. Grant elects that the trust shall forthwith determine, and asks that the Government designate a suitable place of deposit and a responsible custodian for the collection.

The nature of this gift and value of the relics which the generosity of a private citizen, joined to the high sense of public regard which animates Mrs. Grant, have thus placed at the disposal of the Government, demand full and signal recognition on behalf of the nation at the hands of its representatives. I therefore ask Congress to take suitable action to accept the trust and to provide for its secure custody, at the same time recording the appreciative gratitude of the people of the United States to the donors.

In this connection I may patiently advert to the pending legislation of the Senate and House of Representatives looking to a national recognition of General Grant's eminent services by providing the means for his restoration to the Army on the retired list. That Congress, by taking such action, will give expression to the almost universal desire of the people of this nation is evident, and I earnestly urge the passage of an act similar to Senate Bill No. 2530, which, while not interfering with the constitutional prerogative of appointment, will enable the President in his discretion to nominate General Grant as general upon the retired list.

Chester A. Arthur

Following receipt of a pension granted by Congress in 1885, Grant moved to a cottage at Mt. McGregor, New York, owned by a friend who loaned it furnished to the Grant family. There he spent the last five weeks of his life on his deathbed, stricken with throat cancer as he managed to complete his memoirs. He finished them four days prior to his death on July 23, 1885. Including his Long Branch cottage, Grant had accumulated $200,000 in real estate, with an annual income of $15,000 a year from trust funds, but had lost it all in the 1884 bank failure. He had only $80 in his pocket and $130 in the house when Vanderbilt made the offer mentioned in President Arthur's message. When Grant died, there was no record of a will or even an inventory of his estate, since there was no estate left.

Following Grant's death, Mark Twain published the memoirs. Their success in great measure secured Mrs. Grant's financial future, with royalties of about $500,000.

An act was also approved by Congress to pay the expenses of a state funeral.

For "Notes on Dying Without a Will" see page 281.

RUTHERFORD B. HAYES

RUTHERFORD B. HAYES WAS BORN IN DELAWARE, OHIO, ON OCTOBER 4, 1822, the youngest of three surviving children of Rutherford and Sophia Birchard Hayes. His father, originally from Vermont, had been a storekeeper until his death three months prior to Rutherford's birth. The youngster was raised by his uncle Sardis Birchard in a house which, together with some 25 acres, he was to inherit in 1873 when Birchard died.

At an early age Rutherford was sent to an academy at Norwalk, Ohio; then in 1837 to a boarding school run by Isaac Webb in Middletown, Connecticut. In the autumn of the following year, 16 years of age, he entered Kenyon College at Gambier, Ohio, where he excelled in logic, philosophy, mathematics, and literature, graduating valedictorian of his class in 1842. After a 10-month stint with a Columbus law firm he entered Harvard Law School in 1843. Following his graduation in 1845, he practiced law for five years in Lower Sandusky (now Fremont), Ohio. In 1849 he moved to Cincinnati, where he met Lucy Webb, a student at Wesleyan Female College and the two were married in 1852 following her graduation.

At the outbreak of the Civil War in 1861, Hayes enlisted and was made a major of the Ohio volunteer infantry; wounded four times, he was eventually promoted to major general. While on the battlefield he was nominated and elected to Congress, though he remained in service until Lee's surrender.

In December, 1865, he took his seat in

the House of Representatives as a staunch Republican supporter of radical reconstruction; he was admired for his honesty and efficiency. Two years later he resigned from Congress and was elected Governor of Ohio.

When the Republicans met for their national convention in Cincinnati in 1876, Hayes seemed a likely candidate. Thanks to his hard-money position Hayes won the nomination on the seventh ballot over the better-known James G. Blaine. His opponent in the election was Democrat and former Governor of New York Samuel J. Tilden, a reformer. The campaign was heated, fiercely disputed, and the outcome contested. Although Hayes received a minority of the popular votes, a partisan election commission declared him the winner by one electoral vote two days prior to the inauguration.

Soon after the Hayes family moved into the White House, Mrs. Hayes announced that she would serve no liquors or wines at any social functions. The Women's Christian Temperance Union applauded her decision, raised money to have her portrait painted, and presented it to the White House. A disgruntled public, though, began referring to the First Lady as "Lemonade Lucy." In any case, she was devoted to her husband. The Hayes family was a happy one. Three sons, Birchard, Webb, and Rutherford, were born in the first years of their marriage and were in college when the other children, Fanny and Scott Russell, were still barely of school age. Hayes' Presidential salary was $50,000 a year.

Hayes's pledge not to run in 1880 led to his retirement in 1881 to Spiegel Grove, his estate in Fremont, where he spent the remaining 12 years of his life. He devoted his last years to philanthropic works. Prior to his death on January 17, 1893, he had designed the monument that would serve as the memorial for him and his wife, who had died four years earlier. Shortly before his death he remarked he had "rather die at Spiegel Grove than live anywhere else."

Spiegel Grove is now owned by the state of Ohio, and the nearby museum and library

Lucy Webb Hayes

may well be considered the progenitor of the present Presidential libraries. Influenced by the Centennial of 1876, Hayes became quite history-conscious and saved nearly everything, including a section of the plank from the platform on which he stood to take his oath of office. All of these items are in the museum.

Text of the Will of Rutherford B. Hayes

In the name of the Benevolent Father of all: I, Rutherford B. Hayes of Spiegal Grove, Fremont Ohio, do make and publish this my last will.

1. I wish all my just debts to be fully paid.

2. I give and bequeath the house place known as Spiegel Grove, and all the personal property connected therewith to Birchard A., Webb C., Rutherford P., Fanny and Scott R. Hayes to be by them held in common without sale or division of the same until all parties or the survivors of them agree to the sale or division, but in case of sale or division the same to belong equally to my said children or their heirs

3. The residue of my estate real and personal I give and bequeath equally to my five children, provided that my son Birchard A. is to be charged Twenty five thousand ($25000.) Dollars the amount heretofore advanced to him

4. The interest of my daughter Fanny in said estate is to be held by my son Birchard A. in trust for her benefit and support and all payments by him are to be directly to her on her personal receipt or for her benefit.

5. I appoint my sons Birchard A., Webb C., and Rutherford P. Hayes executors of this my last will and testament

6. The said executors are to have full power to sell and convey said property both real and personal and to execute deeds and contracts relating thereto and to carry out existing contracts

It is my desire that my said executors be not required to file and inventory or to give any bond.

I hereby revoke all wills and codicils heretofore by me made

In testimony whereof I have hereunto set my hand and seal this twelfth day of April 1890

Rutherford B. Hayes

Signed sealed and published and declared by Rutherford B. Hayes the above named testator as and for his last will and testament in our presence, who at his request and in his presence and in the presence of each other have subscribed our names as witnesses thereto.

J. H. Wilson
Irvin Fangboner

Notes on the Will of Rutherford B. Hayes

THERE IS LITTLE THAT IS REMARKABLE about the Will of President Hayes. His wife had already died when he prepared it; five grown children were living. He provided that they should each receive an equal share of his property, taking into account $25,000 already advanced to Birchard, the oldest son. The children are named in the Will in the order of their births, but it does not reveal the spread in ages of nearly 18 years. This spread may be reflected, rather indirectly, in the fact that he named only his three older sons, all in their 30's, as his Executors.

The Will is more striking for what it fails to say than for what it does say. Hayes had an active law practice in Cincinnati in the 1850's, but his Will provides only very limited powers for the Executors, and it fails to nominate a guardian for his son, Scott, although he was nearly two years short of his majority when it was written. Paragraph 4th, creating a trust of the interest of his one daughter, is exceptionally sketchy. Many easily foreseeable questions about the trustee's responsibilities and the beneficiary's rights are not covered at all. This is in sharp contrast to the abundant and minute detail on such subjects provided in wills written in the middle of the 20th century.

The provision governing the family home, Spiegel Grove, is interesting. Though left to the five children equally, each is given a power of veto over its sale or division. Ultimately, Hayes's descendants transferred Spiegel Grove to the state of Ohio to be a museum of Hayes's Presidency, reserving only a right in his descendants to occupy an upper floor from time to time.

Desk presented to Rutherford B. Hayes by Queen Victoria.

JAMES A. GARFIELD

JAMES ABRAM GARFIELD WAS BORN IN ORANGE, OHIO, ON NOVEMBER 19, 1831, the son of a frontier farmer. His father, Abram Garfield, was a native of New York descended from an English Puritan who settled in Watertown, Massachusetts, in 1630. James Garfield's mother, Eliza Ballou Garfield, was a descendant of French Huguenots who had come to America in 1685. The youngest of five children, James was only two when his father died.

James's first schooling began at the age of three when he began to read. At the age of 10 he began to work at home and on adjoining farms to help out his mother; he continued his education in the village school during the winters. He also worked as a canal driver and as a schoolteacher.

At 20, Garfield entered a college in Hiram, Ohio, and three years later he transferred to Williams College in Massachusetts from which he graduated in 1856. Returning to Ohio, he married his boyhood sweetheart, Lucretia Rudolph, the daughter of the leading merchant in Hiram, whom he had met at college. Settling in Hiram he rose to a professorship of Greek and Latin at the local college (since 1867 called Hiram College) and, at the age of 26, was made its president. He also found time to study law, and was eventually admitted to the bar, and he served as lay preacher in the Disciples of Christ church.

Garfield's first interest shown in politics was in 1856 when he voted for John C. Frémont, the first Republican candidate. He became an effective speaker and conducted himself well in political debates. As a result, Garfield was elected to the Ohio state senate in 1859. When the Civil War began he became a lieutenant colonel of Ohio volunteers. His brilliant performance gained him the rank of brigadier general within a year; he was the youngest of that rank in the Army. During his tour of duty in the military he was elected to the House of Representatives in 1862. Although he was a major general in September 1863, he resigned at President Lincoln's request three months later to take his seat in Congress, where he served for 17 years.

In 1880 Ohio elected him U.S. Senator, an office he held in name only. That year, at the Republican national convention in Chicago, Garfield nominated John Sherman of Ohio for President in an effort to prevent Grant from winning a third term, which he believed would break all traditions and would not be in the best interest of the country. The 33rd ballot showed 306 votes for Grant and 400 divided between three other candidates. The 34th ballot startled the hall with the announcement of 36 votes for Garfield. He won on the 36th ballot, receiving 399 votes. He chose as his running mate Chester A. Arthur, of a rival Republican faction.

The election of 1880 was close in terms of the popular vote, but Garfield defeated the Democratic candidate, General Winfield Hancock, by an electoral vote of 214 to 155.

Garfield's term of office was brief—only 200 days. On July 2, 1881, as Garfield and Secretary of State Blaine were at the railroad depot in Washington about to depart for a Williams College reunion, a frustrated office-seeker, Charles J. Guiteau, fired two shots from a revolver which sent the President to the floor. Garfield lingered on until September 19, 1881, when he died at Elberon, New Jersey. The body was brought to Washington, where it lay in state in the Capitol. Twenty days after his death was finally laid to rest in Cleveland, Ohio.

In 1876 Garfield had purchased a farm at Mentor, Ohio, 23 miles from Cleveland. Although the acreage contained a small farm house, he enlarged the building into a 26-room house and named it Lawnfield. He paid $115 an acre for the farmland on which the house stood. Here he had lived, in the years before he was President, with his wife, four sons, one daughter and his mother. Now, after the solemn ceremonies were ended, Mrs. Garfield, in her early 40's, returned to Lawnfield to live for most of the remainder of her life (she died in 1918) and witness the many memorials erected in her husband's memory. Having served less than a year, Garfield did not live to collect his full year's salary of $50,000. However, Congress, the year following his death, awarded his widow the sum of $50,000 and a $5,000-a-year pension. She was also the beneficiary of a $25,000 insurance policy her husband had providentially taken out in 1881.

Garfield left no will. An inventory of the estate was prepared by Joseph Rudolph, administrator, and filed in the Probate Court, Lake County, Ohio, May 1, 1882. It listed assets with a value of $61,733.06 to be divided among the heirs. Lawnfield is now owned by the Western Reserve Historical Society and maintained by the Lake County Historical Society as an historic house.

President Garfield lies mortally wounded. (From a sketch made at the bedside of the President by W. A. Rogers.)

CHESTER A. ARTHUR

C HESTER ALAN ARTHUR WAS BORN ON OC-
TOBER 5, 1830, IN FAIRFIELD, VERMONT.
His father, William Arthur, was born in northern Ireland in 1796, possessed a degree from
Queen's College in Belfast, had emigrated to
Canada (where he was a teacher), and later
studied law in Burlington, Vermont. A Baptist
revival meeting he attended strongly influenced him to become a minister in 1827. He
met Malvina Stone, the daughter of a New
Hampshire pioneer, in Canada, where they
were married in 1821. Chester Alan Arthur was
the fifth child and oldest son of this union.

Young Arthur's education began in a small
academy run by James I. Lourie in Union Village, New York, where he moved with his parents at the age of nine. In 1844 his father

moved his pastorate to Schenectady, where
Chester enrolled in Union College to study
classics. This institution had an enrollment of
250 students and was then one of the
best-known Eastern colleges. He taught school
between years to finance his education and
graduated Phi Beta Kappa in 1848. He taught
school in North Pownal, Vermont until age 20,
then studied law in New York City, and was
admitted to practice in 1854. His specialty was
the defense of Negroes' rights. His interest in
politics began more or less as a hobby, but by
1852 he had cast his first vote for Winfield
Scott and in 1854 he participated in the first
convention under Republican auspices in New
York State in Saratoga. In 1859 he married Ellen Lewis Herndon, the daughter of a Virginia

136

Fishing reel used by Chester A. Arthur.

naval officer.

After the outbreak of the Civil War, Arthur was appointed by a Republican Governor as quartermaster general of New York State, charged with provisioning the militia. He was replaced when a Democrat became Governor, and in 1863 he returned to active law practice until 1872. During this time he remained active in New York politics and was a staunch supporter of Grant, who, in turn, appointed Arthur collector of customs for the Port of New York, a post that provided an annual income close to that of the President. The customs house had long been noted for abuses, which were condoned by Arthur. Although Arthur himself was not corrupt, he had allowed New York politicians the customary patronage. President Hayes removed him in 1878.

In 1880 Arthur and Roscoe Conkling, the state Republican leader, went to the Republican convention to nominate Grant for a third term. Instead Garfield was nominated for President and, to pacify Conkling, Arthur was nominated—and elected—Vice President.

During his short term as Vice President, Arthur remained loyal to the Republican machine, but when Garfield was assassinated and Arthur became President in 1881, his outlook changed and he made an effort to modify the practice of political patronage.

Arthur took his oath of office as President on September 19, 1881, at his house at 125 Lexington Avenue, New York City. Here his first child had been born, a son who died in infancy. Several years later another boy, Alan, and a girl, Ellen, were born to the couple. Mrs. Arthur died of pneumonia on January 12, 1880. Upon entering the White House, Arthur chose his widowed sister to assume the duties as official hostess.

Immediately upon assuming office, he began redecorating the White House and 24 wagonloads of the household goods of previous Presidents were hauled off to the auction block, where they were sold for $3,000. He hired Louis Comfort Tiffany to refurbish the rooms of the White House complete with stained glass. Among the other changes which Arthur made to the White House was the installation of the first elevator and tiled bathroom. He employed a French chef and steward from New York experienced in gourmet cooking. Also on the staff was the President's old family cook, Bridget Smith, who returned with him to New York after his term of office and received a small bequest in his will as "my faithful and devoted servant."

President Arthur's name was presented at the Republican national convention at Chicago in 1884, but lost on the fourth ballot to James G. Blaine. Twenty months after leaving office, Arthur died suddenly on November 18, 1886, of apoplexy; he is buried near his wife at Albany's Rural Cemetery. Though he spent most of his $50,000 annual salary while in office and though there was then no Presidential pension, Arthur was well off. He owned stocks, a number of inherited valuable pieces of property in New York City and in Long Branch, New Jersey, and several thousand dollars in cash on hand. His total worth was around $161,000.

Text of the Will of Chester A. Arthur

In the name of God, Amen!

I Chester A. Arthur of the City of New York, do make, publish and declare this my last Will and Testament in words and figures following, to wit:

First I direct my Executors hereinafter named to pay all my just debts and funeral expenses.

Second I give and bequeath to my faithful and devoted servant Bridget Smith the sum of Five hundred (500) dollars.

Third I give, devise and bequeath all my estate, real and personal to my said Executors or such of them as shall qualify and take upon themselves the execution of this my Will and the surviro of them to have and to hold upon the following uses and trusts and for the purposes following, to wit: In trust to divide the same into two equal parts or shares and to collect the income, rents, issues and profits of each of such shares and after payment of all legal and necessary expenses to apply the income of one of such shares to the use of my son Chester Alan Arthur until he shall attain the age of Thirty (30) years and when he shall attain such age of Thirty years then to assign, transfer, convey, pay over and deliver said last mentioned share to my said son. If my said son die before me or before attaining such age of thirty years then and in either of such events I give, devise and bequeath said share to his issue living at his death and in default of such issue to my daughter Ellen Herndon Arthur.

And upon the further trust to apply the net income of the other of said shares to the use of my daughter Ellen Herndon Arthur until she shall attain the age of Twenty three (23) years and when she shall attain such age of Twenty three (23) years then to assign, transfer, convey, pay over and deliver said last mentioned share to my said daughter. If my said daughter die before me or before attaining such age of Twnety three (23) years then and in other of such events I give, devise and bequeath said share to her issue living at her death in default of such issue to my son Chester Alan Arthur.

Fourth I authorize and empower my Executors to continue any investments made by me in my lifetime and to invest any moneys of my estate in Bond secured by mortgage or unencumbered real estate or in United States or New York State or City Stocks or securities or in bonds of any incorporated Rail Road Company which for five years prior to such investment have had a continuous market value of par or upwards and have not defaulted in the payment of interest.

Fifth I authorize and empower my said Executors for the purpose of partition or division of my estate or the payment of debts or any of the purposes of this my will to sell and convey any of my real estate wheresoever situate and good deeds or instruments of conveyance thereof to make, execute and deliver.

Sixth I nominate, constitute and *appoint* my sister Mary E. McElroy *Guardian* of the person and estate of my daughter during her minority and my friends *Charles E. Miller, Daniel G. Rollins* and *Seth B. French* all of the City of New York, *Executors* of this my last Will and Testament hereby revoking all former and other Wills by me at any time made.

In Witness whereof I have hereunto set my hand and seal the Eighth day of March in the year of our Lord One thousand eight hundred and eighty six.

Chester A. Arthur

Signed, Sealed, Published and Declared by Chester A. Arthur the within named testator as and for his last Will and Testament in the presence of use who thereupon at the request of said Testaor and in his presence and in the presence of each other have hereunto subscribed our names as Witnesses.

Rastus S. Ransom   336 W 5   St. New York
James C. Read   22 East 41 St NY.
Jas. Alex. Briggs,   32 Nassau St. New York

President Arthur (with rod and reel) bass fishing at Alexandria Bay, New York.

Notes on the Will of Chester A. Arthur

PRESIDENT ARTHUR WAS WIDOWED WITHIN THE YEAR BEFORE HIS SURPRISE NOMINATION TO THE VICE PRESIDENCY. He was left with a teenage son and a daughter seven years younger. Six years later when he wrote his Will his daughter had become the teenager; his son had just attained majority. The provisions for distribution to the son at age 30 and the daughter at age 23, on the surface, could seem to suggest less confidence in the son's judgment than in his daughter's. More probably, they are designed to achieve distribution of the one-half share of each in the estate in the same year, 1894.

The hand of the professional legal draftsman is clearly seen in this Will. No layman would indulge in verbal overkill such as, "to assign, transfer, convey, pay over and deliver," or "I nominate, constitute and appoint . . ." Nor would it occur to one to use the term "issue" when the word "children" would serve equally well. ("Issue," meaning lineal descendants, is a useful word where there is a possibility that those entitled to take under it may be of different generations, but there was no such potential here.)

Another, more valuable attribute of the professional draftsman's work is the coverage of unlikely contingencies. President Arthur's basic scheme was a simple division between his two children in equal shares. The draftsman asks, suppose a child should not live to the time prescribed for distribution, and receives the answer, the child's issue shall take the share instead. The draftsman asks, suppose the deceased child has no issue, and receives the answer, then the other child shall take both shares. The draftsman asks, suppose the other child is not alive then either, and receives the answer, then the other child's issue shall take both shares.

This kind of coverage of progressively more unlikely combinations of events can continue until the patience of the client or draftsman ends, or a so-called "end disposition" is made which is thought to cover all conceivable circumstances. This could be a gift to an institution, thereby eliminating, as far as humanly possible, the risk of mortality of one's chosen donees. Where the client wishes property kept in the family in all events, the end disposition may be to the closest relative (heir or next of kin) then living of the testator, or of someone else who will have to have died to bring the provisions into play. (The notes to the Will of President Fillmore discuss some of the potential for ambiguity in this solution.)

Establishment of trusts for his children created a responsibility in the Executors (trustees) to make the property productive, i.e., to see that it was invested in income-producing forms. In paragraph 4th the testator identified particular kinds of investment which he believed suitable for this purpose, and authorized the Executors to invest in them. Such provisions were typical of wills drawn in that era, often confining investment choices more narrowly than here, sometimes even limiting investment to a single, specific kind.

Experience has shown that provisions which spell out too specifically the testator's investment preferences are not really satisfactory. Whatever the testator's own experience may have been, the selection of investments in the light of up-to-date information is more likely to be successful than that based upon anyone's long-range prediction of investment quality in the future. Moreover, language authorizing, or even directing, particular investments or classes of investments can be a trap for the fiduciary. It does not always protect him against liability if he relies on its apparent authority and the investment sours. He must constantly monitor the safety and productivity of investments and dispose of them if current experience dictates—even though they were once the testator's favorites. Conversely, if the fiduciary believes he has found a better investment than those authorized in the will, he faces the question whether the will requires him to ignore his better judgment.

GROVER CLEVELAND

S TEPHEN GROVER CLEVELAND (he later dropped his first name) was born in Caldwell, New Jersey, on March 18, 1837, of English and northern Irish descent. His father, Richard F. Cleveland, was an ordained Presbyterian minister, and Grover was born in the Presbyterian parsonage once occupied by Rev. Stephen Grover, for whom the boy was named. The fifth child in a family of nine, Grover grew up in an atmosphere combining discipline and play. By the time Grover was four his father accepted a pastorate at Fayetteville, New York, where Grover attended an academy and clerked in a country store.

In 1850 the family moved to Clinton, New York, where his father died in 1853. After working several years as a teacher and book-keeper for the New York Institute for the Blind in New York City, Grover set out for the West, but stopped in Buffalo en route and stayed there to work for his uncle, Lewis W. Allen. In 1855 he became a clerk in the Buffalo law firm of Rogers, Bowen and Rogers; four years later, when he was already paid a salary of $600 per year, he was admitted to the bar, though he had not attended college.

During the Civil War, when Grover Cleveland was drafted, he chose to remain at home to support his mother, while his brothers were in uniform; he paid a substitute, as the law allowed, and continued to practice his profession. In 1863 he was appointed assistant district attorney in Erie County, a post he held for three years. In 1870 he was elected the

141

Democratic sheriff of Erie County. He was nominated by the Democratic Party in 1881 for mayor of Buffalo, and elected. Because of his outstanding performance, in 1882 he was elected Governor of New York, a post he held until nominated for the Presidency in 1884. Out of power since the Civil War, the Democrats were victorious by an electoral margin of 219 to 182.

At 47, the second bachelor to enter the White House, Cleveland initially selected his sister, Rose Cleveland, to serve as official hostess. Rose Cleveland's stay was short, for two years later the President married Mary Frances Folsom, the daughter of his former law partner. He was the first President to be married in the White House. Then 21 years old, Mrs. Cleveland became the youngest First Lady ever to occupy the White House and the first wife of a President to give birth to a child— Esther Cleveland, 1893—in the White House. The couple had five children in all.

Upon leaving the White House in 1889, Mrs. Cleveland prophetically remarked that she wanted everything left just as it was for her return in four years. Cleveland, instead of returning to Buffalo, bought a home at 816 Madison Avenue in New York City. For their summer home, the Clevelands purchased a house on Buzzards Bay at Cape Cod which they named Gray Gables.

Leaving his law practice for a second time, Cleveland accepted the Democratic nomination for President in 1892. President Harrison, his opponent, whose wife had just died in the White House, was in deep mourning and Cleveland, suffering from the gout, stayed at home and did little campaigning. Cleveland became the only President to serve two non-consecutive terms.

One of his last official acts was to deliver an address at the sesquicentennial celebration at Princeton University; there he announced he had purchased a house in the town of Princeton, where he planned to retire. He bought the house through Charles Francis Adams for a sum of $30,915; it was named Westland, and had been built in 1854 by Commodore Robert F. Stockton. The Clevelands added to the house and also installed a billiard room. They continued to keep Gray Gables as their summer home until 1904, when their daughter Ruth died at Gray Gables. To escape the memories, they purchased Intermont near Tamworth, New Hampshire.

Cleveland died on June 24, 1908, and he was buried in the Princeton Cemetery. In 1913, the Cleveland Memorial Tower in Princeton was dedicated in his memory. Cleveland as President earned $50,000 a year and left an estate of $250,000.

President and Mrs. Grover Cleveland's wedding cake box.

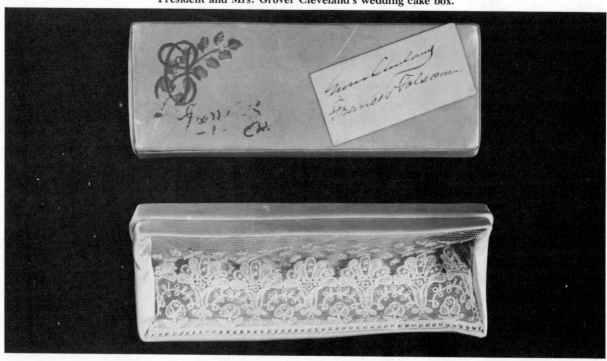

Text of the Will of Grover Cleveland

I Grover Cleveland of the Borough of Princeton in the State of New Jersey, do make, publish and declare this my last will and testament-hereby expressly revoking all previous wills by me made.

First. I hereby direct, that after the payment of all my debts and funeral expenses, an appropriate monument with brief inscription, and only moderately expensive, be erected at my grave and paid for out of my estate. I desire to be buried wherever I may reside at the time of my death, and that my body shall always remain where it shall be at first buried—subject to its removal only if it shall be absolutely necessary in order that it shall repose by the side of my wife and in accordance with her desire.

Second. I give to my niece Mary Hastings daughter of my Sister Anna Hastings, the sum of three thousand dollars to be paid to her as soon as practicable after my death.

Third. I give to my friend Richard Watson Gilder, the watch given to me in 1893 by the said Gilder and E. C. Benedict and J. J. Sinclair—and also the chain attached to the same when last worn by me.

Fourth. I give to each of the four daughters of my nephew Richard Hastings, now or lately living with my sister Anna Hastings, the sum of two thousand dollars each.

Fifth. I give to Frank S. Hastings, my good friend and Executor of this will, as the most personal memento I can leave to him, the seal ring I have worn for many years, which was given to me by my dear wife, and with whose hearty concurrence this gift is made.

Sixth. I give to my two daughters Esther and Marion, and to my two sons Richard F. and Francis G. the sum of ten thousand dollars ($10,000) each, to be paid *to be paid* to them respectively as they each shall arrive at the age of twenty-one years. Until these legacies are paid, or shall lapse, they shall be kept invested, and the income derived therefrom shall be paid to my wife; and the aggregate of said income, shall be applied to her to the support, maintenance and education of said children in such manner and in such proportions as she shall deem best, without any liability to any of said children on account thereof. If however either of my said daughters, shall before her legacy becomes payable, cease for any reason to reside with her mother, then and from that time, the income arising from the investment of her legacy, shall be paid to said daughter. In case either of my said children shall die before his or her legacy shall be actually paid, leaving a child or children then said legacy shall be paid to said child or children; but otherwise the said legacy shall lapse and become a part of the residuary estate disposed of by this instrument.

Seventh. All the rest and residue of my estate and property of which I may die seized or possessed, of every kind and nature, and wheresoever the same may be situated, I give, devise and bequeath to my dear wife Frances F. Cleveland and to her heirs and assigns forever; and I hereby appoint her guardian of all my children during their minority.

Eighth. I hereby appoint my wife Frances F. Cleveland Executrix and Frank S. Hastings Executor of this my last will and testament.

Witness my hand and seal at Princeton N. J. this 21st day of February One thousand nine hundred and six. (1906).

Grover Cleveland (L.S.)

The foregoing instrument was, on the day it bears date, signed by Grover Cleveland the testator therein named, in the presence of each of us, and we both being present at the same time. And the said testator did then and there acknowledge and declare, to us and each of us, that said instrument was his last will and testament; and thereupon we did in the presence of each other and of said testator, and at his request, subscribe our names hereto as attesting witnesses.

Andrew F. West Princeton N.J.
John H. Finley, New York City, N.Y.

Book of trout flies used by President Grover Cleveland.

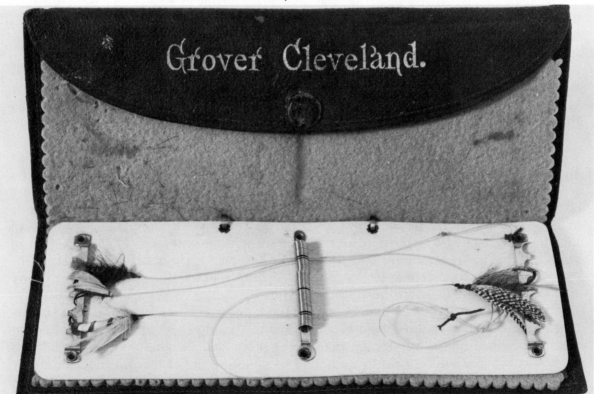

Notes on the Will of Grover Cleveland

WHEN HE ASSUMED OFFICE THE FIRST TIME Grover Cleveland was a bachelor, but within 15 months he became the second President to marry in office. He and John Tyler both married women many years their junior; both had several children by that marriage. When it came to will writing, both faced the necessity to weigh the claims on them of those minor children and of a widow in early middle age. Their Wills demonstrate that they did not see the problem in the same light.

Cleveland's Will exhibits almost none of the concern shown in Tyler's for the possibility that his wife's remarriage might adversely affect the interests of his children. Cleveland left $10,000, payable at age 21, to each of his four children, who, at the time of his death, ranged in age from 14 to 4; but the bulk of his estate was left to his widow outright. The interest given to Mrs. Cleveland, unlike Mrs. Tyler's, could not be affected in any way by her remarriage. Of course, enactment of the Married Women's Property Acts (see Notes on the Will of Thomas Jefferson), establishing for married women the recognition of power to own property in their own right, could account for the difference between Tyler's and Cleveland's Wills in this respect. This is not probable, however, for Tyler could have avoided a second husband's control over his wife's property simply by putting Mrs. Tyler's interest into trust. One can only speculate whether the difference in their interests ultimately influenced the widows' subsequent lives. Mrs. Cleveland did, in fact, remarry; Mrs. Tyler never did.

With respect to the $10,000 left to each child, Cleveland also displayed confidence in his wife's judgment. During their minority the income from their funds was made payable to her, though only to use for their "support, maintenance and education" rather than for her own benefit. However, he authorized her to determine both the particular use to be made of the income and the proportions in which it would be spread among the children. Strict equality was not to be a concern. She was relieved of any duty to account for her expenditures and was named guardian of the children in spite of the theoretical potential conflict between their interests and hers.

Such flexibility in the handling of children's property is almost always preferable when one can start from a base of confidence in the spouse's judgment and shared good will towards the common children. The risks of overreaching by a parent or blatant favoritism for one minor child over another are usually less significant than the costs of creating machinery to prevent those possibilities. Where a child or children of a prior marriage are involved, attitudes are likely to be less predictable and machinery to protect the interests of a minor more clearly justified.

Spectacles and case owned by President Cleveland.

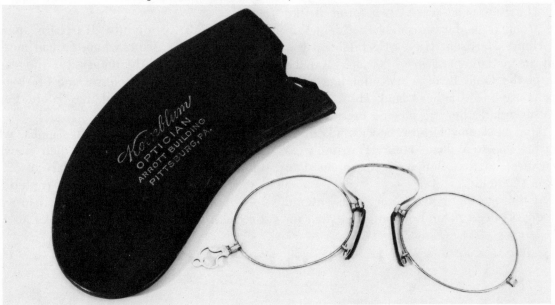

BENJAMIN HARRISON

B ENJAMIN HARRISON, THE ONLY GRANDSON OF A PRESIDENT TO ALSO BECOME PRESI-DENT, was born in North Bend, Ohio, on August 20, 1833. He was the third son of John Scott Harrison, who served two terms in the U. S. Congress and was a son of President William Henry Harrison. His early childhood was spent on his father's farm of 600 acres on the bank of the Ohio River while attending a log schoolhouse on his father's land. He was seven when his grandfather was elected President. By this time the family fortune had dwindled appreciably due to William Henry Harrison's extravagance, so that Benjamin was obliged to work in the fields.

At the age of 15, the young man entered Farmer's College (later Belmont) near Cincin-nati, and two years later he transferred to Miami University at Oxford, Ohio. Graduating at age 19, Harrison went to Cincinnati, where he was admitted to the bar after two years of studying law.

In 1853, Benjamin Harrison married Caroline Lavinia Scott, whom he had met several years before at the university. She was the daughter of a Miami professor and Presbyterian minister who had founded the Oxford Female Institute, a school for girls.

Harrison's first job in Indianapolis, where the young couple moved after their marriage, was that of a court crier at a salary of $2.50 a day. Their first residence was a rented one-story frame house; later they moved to a two-story house with attic and porch. An able, industrious lawyer, Harrison progressed rapidly in his career. Two children were born to the couple, a son, Russell, and a daughter, Mary, who later married James R. McKee, a prosperous merchant of Indianapolis. Harrison became reporter to the U.S. Supreme Court in 1860 and moved into a large home where he lived until after the Civil War.

During the second year of the Civil War his career was interrupted when the Governor of Indiana granted him a commission as second lieutenant. He rose to colonel of the Indiana volunteer infantry, participated in General William T. Sherman's march on Atlanta in 1864, and earned a brevet as brigadier general. Returning to Indiana after the war, Harrison entered politics, running unsuccessfully for Governor, but in 1881 he won a term in the U.S. Senate. Defeated for reelection, in 1887 he returned to Indiana, convinced that his political career was over.

In 1888, the Republican Party named him its candidate for President against Democratic incumbent, Grover Cleveland. Harrison won the election. Life in the White House during his Administration was uneventful. Mrs. Harrison was a gracious hostess, quite religious and most sympathetic to the needy. She was the first president-general of the Daughters of the American Revolution and started the White House china collection. The last months of the Administration were saddened by her eight-month illness and death on October 24, 1892.

Harrison, still in deep mourning in 1892, did little active campaigning and Cleveland won the election. Harrison returned to the 16-room house on Delaware Street in Indianapolis which he had purchased before becoming President. The house had been built in 1874 at a cost of over $21,000. He resumed his successful law practice in Indianapolis, and in 1898 he represented Venezuela in a boundary dispute with Great Britain.

Four years after the death of his first wife, Harrison married her niece, Mary Scott Lord Dimmick, who had been a White House secretary. Neither of his children attended the wedding and the event estranged Harrison from his family. The second Mrs. Harrison bore the former President a daughter.

The practice of law had brought success to Benjamin Harrison, who left an estate of $375,000. The larger portion of the estate was left to his widow, who survived until 1948. His last residence, in which he died on March 13, 1901, and which he left to his widow, is now an historic house filled with family treasures and mementoes. The enumeration of these articles in his will emphasizes his great awareness of their historical importance, an awareness more characteristic of earlier Presidents than of his immediate predecessors.

Caroline Scott Harrison (detail).

Text of the Will of Benjamin Harrison

I, Benjamin Harrison—of the city of Indianapolis in the State of Indiana, do make, ordain and publish this my last will and testament, hereby revoking all wills heretofore made by me.

Item One: As a first charge upon my estate, after the payment of my debts, I give and bequeath to the Union Trust Company of Indianapolis, as Trustee, if my wife shall survive me, the sum of One hundred thousand dollars ($100,000) upon the condition and for the uses and purposes following to wit: Said sum shall be invested with the greatest prudence, at the best rate of interest consistent with security, and the interest and income of the fund shall be paid semi-annually to my dear wife Mary Lord Harrison, during the term of her natural life. It the principal sum of this bequest should be impaired by any loss before the full distribution of the residue of my estate, such loss shall be made good from the residuary estate. At the death of my said wife, any earned interest or income not paid over to her shall be paid to her legal representative and the principal of the fund shall become part of my residuary estate and be distributed as hereinafter provided, my said trustee shall have the right to take over for this fund any bonds, stocks, notes or other interest or dividend paying securities that may belong to me at my death, at the price paid by me therefor.

Item Two: I further give, devise and bequeath to my said wife the sum of Fifteen Thousand Dollars: This bequest is absolute and without any trust or condition whatever.

Item Three: I give and bequeath to my dear little daughter Elizabeth Harrison, in addition to other bequests hereinafter mentioned, the sum of Ten Thousand Dollars ($10,000.). This legacy shall be paid by my Executor to my wife, as trustee and shall be used at the discretion of said trustee for the benefit of said Elizabeth, when she becomes of age or marries any unexpended balance shall be paid over to her; but if she should die before receiving it, any such unused balance of the sum shall become the absolute property of her mother, my wife. Said trustee shall not be required to give any bond.

Item Four: I give and bequeath to the Union Trust Company of Indianapolis, the sum of ten thousand dollars upon the following trusts and conditions to - wit: Said sum shall be safely invested and the income thereof reinvested and accumulated until my dear Grandson and namesake Benjamin Harrison McKee shall attain the full age of twenty-one years when the said principal sum and all the increase thereof shall be paid over to him. If however the circumstances of my said Grandson should at any time become such that the sum of the interest on this legacy is necessary for his comfortable support or the completion of his education it may be so applied by the trustee. If my said Grandson should die before attaining his majority, the principal of said fund with the accumulations thereof shall be paid to my executor and become a part of my residuary estate to be divided as hereinafter provided.

Item Five: I give and bequeath to my dear grandchildren Mary Lodge McKee, Marthena Harrison and William Henry Harrison each the sum of Twenty-five hundred dollars in addition to other gifts herein mentioned.

Item Six: I give, devise and bequeath to my sisters Sarah H. Devin and Anna H. Morris and to my sister-in-law Elizabeth Scott Parker each the sum of Five Hundred Dollars.

Item Seven: I give and bequeath to my sister Bettie H. Eaton an annuity of six hundred dollars to be paid to her by my executor each year during her natural life in quarterly payments.

Item Eight: I give and bequeath to my nephew and name sake Benjamin Harrison Jr.,—son of my brother John—the sum of Five Hundred dollars.

Item Nine: I give and bequeath to the Indianapolis Orphan Asylum the sum of Five Hundred dollars; to the Eleanor Homr or Childrens Hospital located on the old Gresham Homestead on North Capital Avenue the sum of Five hundred dollars, and to Summer Mission for sick children of which I have been President the sum of One Hundred Dollars.

Item Ten: I give and bequeath to my faithful Secretary E. Frank Tibbott the sum of Five Hundred Dollars.

Item Eleven: I have already delivered to my children Russell B. Harrison and Mary Scott Harrison the jewelry and many other things that belonged to their mother, and now have packed and ready for delivery to them most of the other things that belonged to their mother; these and any remaining china, vases or pictures painted by their mother and all vases, pictures, bric-a-brac lamps and any articles of furniture or ornament that were presented to her and that may be in the house at my death I give to said Russell and Mary to be equally divided between them. This gift is not to be taken to include articles of furniture purchased by their mother for the house and paid for by me.

Item Twelve: Confirming to my wife Mary Lord Harrison all of the gifts she has received I hereby give and bequeath to her absolutely all the silverware, plate cutlery, pictures, vases, bric-a-brac, lamps, furniture, china, table linen, piano and all other house-furnishings and appurtenances, and all books, that were purchased and brought into use within six months before our marriage, and all that have been or may be purchased by me or by her since that time; Also the case of silverware purchased by me before of Harris and Shaffer of Washington D.C. I also give and bequeath to my said wife for and during her natural life all the residue of the furniture, house furnishings, pictures, bric-a-brac, books and all other articles of household use or ornament that were owned by me at a period earlier than said six months, and that may be in my house at my death, except such articles as are disposed of by Item Eleven, or, by other special provisions of this will. I also give to my said wife absolutely all horses, vehicles, harness, robes and stable furnishings that I may be possessed of at my death.

Item Thirteen: As to so much of the personal property mentioned in the next preceeding Item as is given to my wife for life only I direct that at her death the same shall be equally divided between my surviving children and the issue of any that may have died—such issue taking the parents share. My wife shall not be required to file any inventory of this property, nor to give any bond for its safe keeping, nor be liable for any loss or injury happening to the same.

Item Fourteen: I give devise and bequeath also my wife Mary Lord Harrison, for and during the full term of her natural life my homestead on North Delaware Street, in the city of Indianapolis, being now street number twelve hundred and fourteen (1214) and consisting of two lots of ground; as I now remember twenty four and twenty-five of Martindales addition, with the brick dwelling house, stable and all other improvements thereon. And I direct that all taxes, general and special, that my accrue or be assessed against said homestead and all repairs that may be necessary to keep the house and premises in good order shall be paid and made out of the residuary estate by my Executor and also the cost of keeping said property insured.

Item Fifteen: I further give, devise and bequeath to my said wife Mary Lord Harrison and to her heirs and assigns forever in fee simple, the six lots purchased by me of Dr. Seward Webb, and situated in Herkimer County, State of New York on the Fulton Chain of Lakes, at the junction of First and Second Lakes of said chain being my summer home, called Berkeley Lodge, together with all the improvements thereon, all the furniture, fixtures and other personal property of every sort in or used with said Lodge, including boats. My wife has helped me to create this little place and we have spent many happy days there.

Item Sixteen: If another child should be born to me of my present marriage, I give and bequeath to such child the sum of ten thousand dollars. If a boy shall be born to me he shall bear my name and my sword and sash shall be given to him instead of to my son Russell.

Item Seventeen: All debts of every nature owing to me by my son Russell are hereby remitted and my executor is directed to cancel any evidences of indebtedness he may find among my papers.

Item Eighteen: In the event of the death of my wife before me or before our little daughter Elizabeth shall attain her majority, I direct that my wifes sister Elizabeth Scott Parker shall be the guardian of the person of my said daughter and the Union Trust Company of Indianapolis the Guardian of her estate. And as the death of my wife during our childs minority would deprive the latter of the Home I have provided for them and the life provision for my wife would lapse I deem it right that a special additional provision should be made to enable the guardian of her person to give her a suitable home. In the event then of the death of my wife before me or before our daughter Elizabeth has attained her majority I direct that a sum sufficient to produce an assessed net annual income of Two Thousand dollars shall be retained by the said Union Trust Compnay out of my general estate, or out of the said sum of One Hundred thousand dollars set apart for my wife by item one of this will, if she shall survive me and die before our daughter attains her majority—

that the sum so set apart shall be invested and of the proceeds two thousand dollars shall be paid annually to the Guardian of the person of my said daughter Elizabeth until she attains her majority. This provision is in addition to all others made for said Elizabeth.

Item Nineteen: I have had it in mind to make a collection of the papers, manuscripts, autographs, badges, medals and other such things belonging to me that might have a public interest and to present it to a Historical Society where it might be kept safely and together—instead of dividing them between my wife and children—but no suitable place or organization being now available here I make the following disposition of the more important of these articles. None of them shall be taken or sold by my Executor, but all that are not specifically given to particular persons by this will shall remain in the custody and use of my wife during her natural life as a part of the household effects and at her death shall be divided share and share alike between my surviving children and the issue of any that may have died—the issue of any child taking the parents share. (a.) I give and bequeath to my wife Mary Lord Harrison absolutely, the Crayon Portrait of me by Ferris, and all other portraits and photographs of me that may be about my house: my library table and the ink stands and other things I have used with it; My cuff-buttons—(except the pair given to Elizabeth, and the pair given to my brother John), my shirt studs and all other personal trinkets not otherwise disposed of; the watch seal given to me by her mother (the portrait of her Aunt contained in it she shall have re-set and give it to Mary Lodge McKee): my grand Army cane that I have used so long, to be kept for Elizabeth, and all other canes belonging to me to keep or to bestow upon my friends as she shall choose; the gold menu card of the banquet given to me by the citizens of San Francisco; the Utah Silver Salver; the medal presented to me by the New Jersey Historical Society: I also give and bequeath to her all of my letters, papers, memoranda, manuscripts, scrap books and all prints or printed or written matter of every kind relating to my private or public life or to the lives of my ancestors and all my correspondence and papers of any kind. (b.) I give to my son Russell B. Harrison the portrait of his mother by Ferris, one of the engravings of William Henry Harrison with the small picture of North Bend at the bottom; the gold medal voted by Congress to Genl. Wm. H. Harrison in commemoration of the battle of the Thames: the parchment certificate of the election of my Grandfather to the Presidency: My sword and sash (unless a son should be born to me of my present marriage, in which case it shall go to him): The gold badge with Washington on one side and Harrison and Marton on the other: the invitation on gold plate of the Society of California Pioneers: the gold card presenting the freedom of the city of San Francisco, the invitation to the lunch at the Lawyers Club, New York enclosed in a silver envelope; the silver log cabin given to me in Baltimore and the Silver Card given to me in commemoration of the Memorial Palace at Pueblo, Colorado. (c.) I give to my daughter Mary Harrison McKee the small portrait of her mother painted in Vienna and the small pencil sketch of her by Ferris of Philadelphia: the portrait of my Grandfather Harrison painted by Lyon of Louisville, which is now hanging in my Library—but was formerly hung in the front hall: the medal presented by Brazil and the gold card of invitation to the reception of the Union League of San Francisco, the medal presented by the city of Sacramento: the address of the civil, industrial and commercial bodies of New York with the silver case enclosing it: the silver plate or card, from the Citizens of San Jose and the silver card of invitation to the inspection and drill of the First California Light Battery.

(d.) I give and bequeath to my daughter Elizabeth Harrison, my long gold watch chain; my silver toilet set; all of my souvenier spoons; the miniature of her mother; the portraits of my Grandfather Harrison and of my grandmother Harrison, the former by Beard. I have marked it for identification; the water-color of my Great Grandfather Benjamin Harrison; the large picture of North Bend; the small portrait of me on wood, my cuff buttons of silver (or platinum) and gold bands; the Columbian Gold Medal presented by Spai; my grand Army and Society of the Cincinnati badges; the Gold Medal Commemoration of the First inauguration of President Washington, the Bennington Medal, presented in connection with the dedication of the monument there; the card of Greeting from Monterey, California; the silver plate presenting the freedom of Glenwood Springs, Colorado; the card or place of invitation of the Union League of Los Angeles, Cal; the silver statuette of Riggin of the U.S.S. Baltimore; the case of small badges and medals that hangs in my library, and the horn chair in my library, made for me by a friend in Texas.

(e) I give to my grandson, Benjamin Harrison McKee my watch and chain with the trinkets attached (If he shall die before me these shall go to my daughter Elizabeth) Also my Lefever shot gun—the Daily shot gun and the rifle shall be treated as part of the out fit of my Aderondack camp. (f) I give my brother Carter my loyal Legion badge and a cane to be selected by my wife and to my brother John my gold sleeve buttons marked "H" and a cane to be selected by my wife.

Item Twenty: If my son Russell or my daughter Mary should die before me the articles given to them respectively by Items eleven (11) and nineteen (19) of this will shall go to their respective children in equal shares. Should my wife die before my all of the things given to her absolutely by Items twelve (12) and nineteen (19) of this will, except the papers, memoranda and manuscripts relating to my public life and any addresses or lectures prepared by me, shall go to and become the absolute property of my daughter Elizabeth. The papers described in the foregoing exception shall in such case to to my friends John H. Holliday and Rev. M. L. Harris in trust to determine after consultation with Hon. W. H. H. Miller and other friends what if any public use shall be made of them, and afterwards to select some Historical Society to whose care they may be committed. In case my daughter Elizabeth should die before me, and no other child of my present marriage should survive me all of the things given to said Elizabeth by Item Nineteen (19) of this will shall go to and be the absolute property of my wife, Mary Lord Harrison, except the portraits of my grand-father Grand-mother and Great grand-father and the picture of North Bend. These shall go—the portraits of my Grand-father and Great Grand-father to my Grandson Benjamin Harrison McKee. The portrait of my Grand-mother to Mary Lodge McKee and the picture of North Bend to my grandson William Henry Harrison. Should however another child be born to me then all of the things given in said Item to Elizabeth shall go to such child. And I do further will and direct that if said Elizabeth shall die before me and another child of my present marriage shall survive me that all of the provisions of item eighteen (18) of this will shall be taken to apply to such child precisely as if its name were written therein in place of the name of Elizabeth.

Item Twenty-one: The provisions made in this will for my wife Mary Lord Harrison and in lieu of all her interest and rights at law in my estate as my widow.

Item Twenty-two: All the rest and residue of my estate I give devise and bequeath as follows: Said estate shall be divided into as many equal shares as I shall leave children surviving me, and one additional share for the issue of any child that may have died leaving issue surviving me. One such share I give, devise and bequeath to my son Russell B. Harrison in trust for his children Marthena Harrison and William Henry Harrison and any other child or children that may hereafter be born to him, to be applied and used for the support and education of such children or the survivor or survivors of them. Such portion of each childs share as may not have been before expended for its benefit shall on the coming of age of such child, or its marriage be paid over to it, and in the event of the death of one of my said grandchildren before its share is distributed to it, such share shall go equally to the survivors under the same trust and conditions. If said Russell shall die before me, or before he has executed this trust or shall resign, his wife Mary Saunders Harrison is hereby appointed trustee of this trust. Said trustees shall neither of them be required to give any bond.

Second I give, devise and bequeath one equal share of this residuary estate absolutely and in fee simple to my daughter Mary Harrison McKee if she shall survive me. Should she die before me leaving a child or children who survive me then this share shall go to them in equal parts—but shall be paid over to and held by the Union Trust Company of Indianapolis as trustees for them; the income shall from time to time be paid to their legal guardian or guardians, and as each shall arrive at majority or shall marry the principal sum due to each shall be paid to him or her by the trustee should any of said children die before the principal of said trust fund is paid over to it or them, the share of such child shall go to the survivor or survivors in equal shares and should all of said children die before becoming entitled to receive the principal of said trust fund then said fund shall be treated and divided as a part of my residuary estate among the other beneficiaries thereof in the proportions and under the conditions mentioned as to each.

Third: I give, devise and bequeath absolutely and in fee simple to my daughter Elizabeth Harrison one full equal share of this my residuary estate.

Fourth: If another child or other children should be born to me of my present marriage and should survive me each such child shall take and have one full equal share of this my residuary estate which is hereby devised and bequeathed to them in addition to all other provisions made for them in this will. The residuary devises and bequests are all to be taken as in addition to my specific legacies or bequests. In case no child of my present marriage shall survive me then my wife Mary Lord Harrison is hereby given the option, to be exercised within one year after my death to renounce and surrender by suitable deeds or other writings delivered to my executor the provision made for her in Item One of this will, of a trust fund of One Hundred thousand dollars, and the life estate in my homestead given to her by Item fourteen of this will, and the life estate in certain furniture given to her by Item twelve of this will. If she shall elect to and shall surrender these provisions then I hereby give, devise and bequeth to her in lieu thereof that one full share of this my residuary estate that would have gone under this will to our daughter Elizabeth, if she had survived me and no other child of my present marriage had so survived me— that is the total number of shares as provided in this item shall be increased, in the case provided for here, by one and that share shall go to my said wife. The surrender and renunciation above provided for, if given, shall not in any way affect or abate any other provisions or legacies made or given to my wife by this will but they and each of them shall have full effect and be executed as if no renunciation had been made.

The word "unavoidable" in Item one of this will was erased and the following words interlined by me before signing: the words "or may be" in Item twelve; "me" in paragraph (d) of item nineteen; "brother Carter my" in paragraph (b) of Item nineteen and "Item to" in Item twenty.

Item Twenty-three: I hereby mominate and appoint The Union Trust Company of Indianapolis, Indiana, to be the Executor of this my last Will and Testament.

In witness whereof I have hereunto set my hand and seal at Indianapolis, in the State of Indiana, this twentieth (20th) day of April A.D. Eighteen hundred and ninety-nine (1899)

Benj. Harrison (seal)

The foregoing will was signed, sealed and acknowledged by the said Benjamin Harrison in our presence and was declared by him to be his last will and testament and at his request and in his presence and in the presence of each other we now subscribe our names hereto as witnesses, this twentieth (20) day of April A.D. 1899.

W. H. H. Miller (seal)
Harry J. Milligan (seal)
Howard Cole (seal)

I, Benjamin Harrison do make, ordain and publish as a part of my foregoing last will and testament by way of codicil the following provisions to-wit: First. In view of the fact that my estate has been increased since the making of the foregoing will and of the further fact that the net income that can now be realized from safe investments is so small and of my desire that my wife may be better able to maintain a suitable household for herself and our little daughter. I do hereby will and devise it that the trust fund set apart by Item One of my foregoing will shall be increased from One Hundred Thousand dollars to the sum of One hundred and twenty-five thousand dollars.

Second: On re-reading item fourteen of my foregoing will I have thought it well to declare for greater clearness that my Executor shall continue to pay out of the feneral funds of my estate all taxes and assessments and the cost of all repairs and insurance upon and for my said homestead during the whole period of the life tenantcy of my wife therein.

Third: If I should die before making a subscription to the building fund of the First Presbyterian Church of Indianapolis I give and bequeath to the Trustees and said church the sum of One thousand dollars to be used for that purpose. If before my death I have made a subscription for the purpose named of any amount it shall be taken to cancel this legacy.

Fourth: No gifts that I have given or may hereafter give during my life shall be a charge against any of the legacies or bequests given by my will save as in the preceding paragraph mentioned.

In Witness whereof I have hereunto set my hand and seal at Indianapolis, Indiana, this (13th) Thirteenth day of February A.D. 1901.

Benj. Harrison (seal)

The foregoing will was signed, sealed and acknowledged by the said Benjamin Harrison in our presence and declared by him to be his will, and at his request and in his presence and in the presence of each other we now subscribe our names as witnesses this thirteenth day of February A.D. 1901.

W. H. H. Miller (seal)
John B. Elaine (seal)
Lou A. Robertson (seal)

Plate from the official Benjamin Harrison White House china.

Notes on the Will of Benjamin Harrison

Benjamin Harrison's first wife died when he was 59, near the end of his Presidency. Three and one-half years later he married again. When he came to write his Will, Harrison was faced with a delicate family situation. His new bride was a widow younger than either the son or daughter of his first marriage. She was a niece of the first Mrs. Harrison, and had been the latter's secretary in the White House following the death of her first husband. Harrison's marriage to a woman who was their contemporary was resented by his children who, as a result, became permanently estranged from their father, but it rewarded him with a new daughter born ten months later.

The product is a long and complex instrument containing explicit instructions which would not ordinarily be required in a more harmonious situation where the testator can rely on the mutual affection and concern of family members for each other. Harrison felt obliged to spell out in detail just which furnishings of his home and which mementoes of his career should pass to his adult children or their families—and which should not (Items 11, 12, 19). More important, knowledge of probable animosities, spoken or unspoken, must have complicated the construction of a framework for dividing assets between his wife and the children of two marriages.

Clearly, the adult children were subordinated here to the widow and minor child. Unless an estate is very large, this will usually be the case because it reflects the primary financial obligations of the testator at that time. However, Harrison did not ignore the claims of his older children, despite their reaction to his remarriage; nor did he leave them to be satisfied by his widow in her will as he might have done had she been their parent too. Broadly speaking, the pattern he used was to give outright to his wife and minor child a comparatively small proportion of his total wealth (Items 2, 3, 12, and 15), plus the use of, or income from, much more substantial assets for his widow's life (Items 1, 14, and codicil). Having first made these provisions for them, the Will then divides the residue into equal shares, one for each child living at the time of his death and, covering the contingencies, one for the descendants collectively of any child who might die before him leaving descendants living at the time of his death. The share of his son was left to him only as trustee for the son's children, suggesting either that the son was affluent and, therefore did not need assets or that his father was more disappointed in him than in his sister.

One hundred thousand dollars—raised in the codicil to $125,000—was specified as the amount to be set aside in trust for his widow for her life (Item 1 and codicil). She was also given the use of his Indianapolis home for life (Item 14). The rest, aside from property which was made the subject of specific bequests or required to pay legacies, appears to go into the residue to be divided among the children. However, seemingly insignificant or technical provisions here could seriously reduce the portion of the residue available for distribution during the widow's life. Their effect indirectly increases the size of her trust. Thus, the provisions requiring the Executor to pay the taxes, insurance, and cost of repairs on the Indianapolis home (Item 14 and codicil) would require the holding back of substantial amounts of the residue to meet these liabilities of an indeterminate amount. (A natural reluctance to avoid surcharge leads executors to take no chances of holding back too little.) Creating even more uncertainty is the third sentence of Item 1, which provides that any losses in value of trust assets which occur before the full distribution of the residue are to be made good from the residuary estate. The residue would not be fully distributed as long as the widow lived and the obligation to meet the costs of the house continued. Should the Executor then treat this provision as another contingency requiring that funds be retained to cover such losses? If so, how much? In sum, President Harrison may have given his two adult children considerably less than he thought, particularly since his widow did not die until 1948, when she was 90 years old.

The Notes on the Will of Chester Arthur pointed out that coverage of possible contingencies, likely and unlikely, is one of the hallmarks of professional will-drafting. This becomes progressively more complicated as the number of people involved increases and the period of time for distribution of the property lengthens. This is illustrated in Harrison's Will by provisions which, among other things, cover the possibility that, before Harrison's death, (a) additional children would be born, or (b) his minor child would die, or (c) one or both of his adult children would die, or (d) his wife would die, or (e) combinations of the foregoing would occur. Since some of his estate was not to be distributed until both he and his wife had died, the draftsman has also provided for additional events which could occur following his death but before hers. The provisions creating shares of the residue payable to the children of Harrison's son present similar problems.

Only one combination of these alternative sequences of events can actually occur. In varying degrees it may be possible to predict which combination is most likely, but the professional draftsman is not apt to be satisfied or comfortable with an instrument which deals only with that sequence, or even with a few combinations, which respond to the contingencies most likely to occur. The goal is to prepare an instrument which will supply clear answers to whatever happens. One result is to increase the length and complexity of any but the very simplest of wills and trusts. This reduces the readability of many instruments to satisfy a need that will actually arise in only a comparative handful of situations. In those situations, however, the protection that full coverage

supplies, against the cost and inconvenience of going to court to obtain a needed answer, fully justifies the cost imposed on all.

Complete coverage is not easy to obtain. The draftsman must bring to the task sufficient imagination to anticipate the possible questions and the patience, thoroughness, and clarity of thought needed to express clear answers. As in other human undertakings requiring a high degree of skill, the results are mixed.

The guardianship provisions (Item 18) deserve special comment. These deal with the possibility that both he and his wife would die before their daughter reached her majority. They make a distinction between the guardian of the estate and the guardian of the person. Though one person can serve in both capacities, and in the case of a parent as guardian usually does, the dual titles reflect the fact that there are two quite different functions to be performed. The guardian of the estate has property management duties; the guardian of the person is charged with the responsibility to see that the minor is, within his or her means, suitably clothed, housed, fed, educated, etc.

Harrison chose the bank, which was also named Executor, as guardian of the estate. He named his wife's sister as guardian of the person. He apparently anticipated that she would take the child into her own home, because the Will provides an annual income of $2,000 to be paid to the guardian during the period of minority. This provision would obviate any need for the guardian to establish, to a court's satisfaction, which household expenditures should be paid from the minor's funds. It is a desirable and thoughtful provision, but one seen infrequently.

This is the first Will in this series to name a corporation, an Indianapolis trust company, as Executor. It was a wise choice. The terms of the Will created duties to be performed for the life of a comparatively young woman, and the presence of potential family discord called for a disinterested fiduciary.

WILLIAM McKINLEY

WILLIAM MCKINLEY WAS BORN IN NILES, OHIO, ON JANUARY 29, 1843, the seventh of nine children. His paternal ancestors came from England and northern Ireland to America 100 years before his birth. His mother's family was of English, Scottish, and German descent. William McKinley, Sr., was a small-scale iron manufacturer. The family moved to Mahoning County, Ohio, where William studied for eight years in Union Seminary before entering Allegheny College in Meadville, Pennsylvania. William sought a teaching position in the public schools and later as a clerk in the local post office; he never graduated from college. At age 18, he enlisted in the Union Army as a private, was promoted to second lieutenant, and at the end of the war was a breveted major.

Following the war, McKinley studied law and was admitted to the bar in Ohio in 1867. While practicing law in Canton he met Ida Saxton, the daughter of a leading local banker; they were married on January 25, 1871.

McKinley's first political office was that of a Republican member of Congress in 1876 at the age of 33. Within three years he was appointed to the Ways and Means Committee, later becoming chairman of that committee. During his 14 years in the House he became a leader in the Republican Party, presiding over the 1884 Ohio Republican state convention and being elected a delegate-at-large to the national convention. In 1891, a year after he lost his seat in Congress, he was elected Governor of Ohio, and he was reelected in 1893. In 1896 he was nominated for President at the Republican national convention.

In 1876, the McKinleys sold the house on North Market Street in Canton, which had been given to them as a wedding present by the bride's father, and took up residence in the Ebbett House in Washington, D.C. McKinley's savings when he entered Congress were $10,000, part of which he had invested in an office building in Canton. Strapped for money, he borrowed funds to finance his early campaigns for reelection. As Governor, McKinley received $8,000 a year. The couple lived at the Chittenden Hotel in Columbus and later in nearby Neil House after the first hotel had burned down. When they returned to Canton, they rented the former home which they had sold 20 years before.

The campaign of 1896 had dynamic personalities as well as issues. This campaign produced a great campaign manager, Mark Hanna, who advised McKinley simply to stay home and conduct a front-porch campaign. The Republican Party sent delegations numbering in the hundreds to Canton to hear McKinley hold forth from his porch. McKinley won the election.

McKinley's Vice President, Garret A. Hobart, died on November 21, 1899, and when the Republican national convention met in 1900 to renominate McKinley, Theodore Roosevelt relinquished the governorship of New York to become his Vice President. McKinley and Roosevelt won the election.

Mrs. McKinley suffered from phlebitis and deep depressions and epileptic fits. Grieved from the death in infancy of her two daughters, and in chronic ill health, she spent most of her married life as a feeble, frail woman confined to her chair. During the second Administration her condition grew worse and a rolling chair was obtained for her use. She recovered sufficiently to accompany her husband to Buffalo to attend the Pan-American Exposition but she stayed at the nearby home of the president of the exposition, awaiting her husband's return from a reception on the exposition grounds. As one of the guests filed past the President he

fired two shots from a pistol concealed in a handkerchief. The President staggered into the arms of his secretary. He was rushed to an emergency hospital on the grounds, where a quick operation was performed before the President was taken to the house where his wife was waiting. He died eight days later, on September 14, 1901.

In 1899 the McKinleys had rebought the house in Canton for $14,500, and here Mrs. McKinley lived the remainder of her life among her husband's mementos. She died in 1907. The house fell into disrepair and by 1934, about to collapse, was abandoned. It was disassembled to move to the World's Fair of 1939 but was never moved or rebuilt. Mrs. McKinley's family home does remain in Canton and a few of the McKinley mementoes have been collected by the Stark County Historical Society.

McKinley had loaned a boyhood friend, Robert L. Walker, $17,000 to help him out of a financial crisis. Walker went broke and McKinley was bankrupted trying to repay notes he had endorsed for his friend, losing his entire savings as well as his wife's $100,000 fortune. Mark Hanna, his political colleague, had to raise another $100,000 among McKinley's many friends to fully repay the obligation. Three years later, in 1896, the erstwhile bankrupt was elected President. His salary as President was $50,000 a year tax-free, which afforded him a gracious life-style. He still saved a portion each year, which was invested. At the time of his death his estate was valued at $215,000.

Cup and saucer from which President William McKinley last drank in Buffalo, New York.

Text of the Will of William McKinley

EXECUTIVE MANSION, WASHINGTON

I publish the following as my latest will and testament, hereby revoking all former wills.

To my beloved wife Ida S McKinley I bequeathe all of my real estate wherever situate, and the income of any personal property of which I may be possessed at death, during her natural life.

I make the following charge upon all of my property both real and personal, to pay my mother during her life one thousand dollars a year, and at her death said sum to be paid to my sister Helen McKinley.

If the income from property be insufficient to keep my wife in great comfort and pay the annuity above provided, then I direct that such of my property be sold so as to make a sum adequate for both purposes.

Whatever property remains at the death of my wife I give to my brothers and sisters share and share alike. My chief concern is that my wife from my estate shall have all she requires for her comfort and pleasure and that my mother shall be provided with whatever money she requires to make her old age comfortable and happy.

Witness my hand and seal this 22nd day of October 1897. To my last will and testament made at the City of Washington Dist. of Columbia.

William McKinley (seal)

The foregoing will was witnessed by us this 22nd day of Octover 1897, at the request of the testator, and his name signed thereto in our presence, and our signatures hereto in his presence

G. B. Cortelyou
Charles Loeffler

Notes on the Will of William McKinley

T HE WILL OF PRESIDENT McKINLEY is one of the simplest in the book. The two McKinley children had died young; his wife was an invalid. Though he did not leave her his property outright, the solicitous concern which he had shown her for many years is reflected in the Will's provisions. Her needs and those of his mother were clearly intended to be paramount to the provisions for his brothers and sisters.

While the reader may be attracted to its relative simplicity, the Will is open to criticism. It fails to name an Executor, though it is obvious that his wife was not expected to administer the estate herself. The uncertainty which this omission creates is enhanced by the generality with which the standard for his wife's support is expressed (all she requires for her "comfort and pleasure"). Thus, an unidentified fiduciary to be named by a court is left with extremely broad discretion on how to achieve the testator's primary goal.

There is also possible ambiguity in the provision for his mother. Is she entitled to $1,000 per year or to "whatever money she requires to make her old age comfortable and happy"? Both standards are stated in these brief paragraphs; the two are not necessarily the same.

Headlines announce the shooting of McKinley.

The New York Press

NEW JERSEY EDITION.

LARGEST REPUBLICAN CIRCULATION BY MANY THOUSANDS OF COPIES A DAY.

VOL. XIV.—WHOLE NO. 5,029.   NEW YORK, SATURDAY MORNING, SEPTEMBER 7, 1901.—TWELVE PAGES.   PRICE [ONE CENT in Greater New York, Newark and Jersey City. TWO CENTS everywhere else.]

PRESIDENT McKINLEY SHOT DOWN; WOUNDED TWICE BY AN ANARCHIST

Nation's Executive Still Alive and It Is Hoped He Will Recover from His Wounds.

ONE BULLET EXTRACTED, BUT THE OTHER REMAINS

Assassin Advanced Under the Guise of Friendship; Then Fired from a Concealed Weapon.

B UFFALO, Sept. 6.—Just a brief twenty-four hours ago the newspapers of the city blazoned forth in all the pomp of headline type, "The Proudest Day in Buffalo's History." To-day in sackcloth and ashes, in sombre type, surrounded by grewsome borders of black, the same newspapers are telling in funereal tones to a horrified populace the deplorable details of "The Blackest Day in the History of Buffalo."

President McKinley, the idol of the American people, the Nation's Chief Executive and the city's honored guest, lies prostrate, suffering the pangs inflicted by the bullets of a cowardly assassin, while his life hangs in the balance.

Out in Delaware avenue, in the home of John G. Milburn, President of the Pan-American Exhibition, with tearful face and heart torn by conflicting hopes and fears, sits the faithful wife, whose devotion is known to all the Nation.

SECRET SERVICE WAS WARNED A YEAR AGO

Told of a General Plot to Kill After Bresci Assassinated Humbert.

TWO REDS WERE ARRESTED

THE DISCOVERY OF LETTERS

Would-Be Murderer Came from Cleveland with Plan Arranged for the Crime.

WOUNDS, THOUGH GRAVE, MAY NOT PROVE FATAL

Cabinet Members Hurrying to Buffalo to Join Their Chief and Give All Aid Possible.

BUFFALO, Sept. 6.—The following bulletin was issued by the President's physician at 10.40 p. m.:

"The President is rallying satisfactorily and is resting comfortably. Temperature 100.4 degrees, pulse 124, respiration 24."

This was signed by Drs. P. M. Rixey, M. B. Mann, R. E. Parke, H. Mynter and Eugene Wanbin, and also by Secretary Cortelyou.

The police have learned that the would-be assassin is Leon Czolgosz. He was born in Detroit, came here from Cleveland.

THEODORE ROOSEVELT

T HEODORE ROOSEVELT WAS BORN ON OC-
TOBER 27, 1858, IN NEW YORK CITY. His
ancestors, of Dutch extraction, had been na-
tives of New York since the early 17th century.
He was born into the wealthiest circumstances
of any President up to that time. Theodore was
the second of four children. His father, also
named Theodore, was a merchant. His mother,
Martha Bulloch Roosevelt, had an aristocratic
Southern background.

Young Theodore's boyhood was spent in
New York City, where he received his early
schooling from tutors and struggled to overcome
his asthma and general physical frailty. His sum-
mers were spent in resorts at Madison, New Jersey, in the Adirondacks, or at the family's summer
house in Oyster Bay. By the time he entered

Harvard in 1876 he had developed into a robust
young man. While in his senior year, he started
writing his first book, which was on the War of
1812. During his entire life he wrote some 40
books, using the earnings of his books to supplement his income.

At the death of his father, young Theodore
inherited $125,000. Upon graduation in 1880 he
purchased 155 hilltop acres at Oyster Bay for
$30,000 and with $16,975 he built the 23-room
Oyster Bay home which he later named Sagamore
Hill. Soon after his graduation in 1880 he married
19-year-old Alice Hathaway Lee of Boston and the
two took a honeymoon trip to Europe.

Following a brief study of law at Columbia
Law School at the close of 1881, Roosevelt became a member of the New York Assembly; he

was the youngest member of that body, and was twice reelected.

Roosevelt's political career was abruptly interrupted by the sudden death of his wife and mother on the same day in 1884. The double blow plunged him into great despondency and he went to the Dakotas for two years to assuage his grief in vigorous outdoor life. While there he entered into a cattle venture which resulted in a $50,000 loss.

In 1886, he returned East and unsuccessfully ran for mayor of New York. He turned to writing for the next two years, producing a book each year. President Benjamin Harrison appointed him a member of the United States Civil Service Commission in 1889, a post in which he won a good deal of recognition. From 1895 to 1897 he was police commissioner of New York City. In 1897, he accepted the post of assistant secretary of the Navy, which he held for one year, leaving to organize the Rough Riders to fight in the Spanish-American War. As a result of his reputation in the war he was elected Governor of New York in the fall of 1898.

Two years later Roosevelt was named on the Republican ticket as McKinley's second Vice President. With the sudden death of McKinley on September 14, 1901, Theodore Roosevelt at the age of 42 was the youngest man yet to become President of the United States. In 1905 he became President in his own right. In 1906 he received the Nobel Peace Prize for arranging the negotiations between Russia and Japan that ended the war between those two nations. He also was largely responsible for the Second International Peace Conference at The Hague in 1907 in a vain effort to end all wars.

In 1886, two years after the death of his first wife, Roosevelt married wealthy Edith Kermit Carow, a childhood friend. By his second marriage Roosevelt had four boys and one girl; which, including Alice by his first marriage, made a total of six children. Mrs. Roosevelt, during her seven years as First Lady, gave more private entertainments than any of her predecessors. The most significant event was perhaps the marriage of the President's daughter Alice, who became the 10th White House bride when she married Representative Nicholas Longworth on February 17, 1906.

Roosevelt declined to run again in 1908. He chose as his successor William Howard Taft, whose conservatism in office so displeased Roosevelt that he ran against Taft on a Progressive Party ("Bull Moose") ticket in 1912. Woodrow Wilson, the Democratic candidate, won the three-way election. On January 6, 1919, Roosevelt died unexpectedly in his sleep and was buried in a cemetery at Oyster Bay.

Mrs. Roosevelt survived him by 28 years. Following her death in 1948, Sagamore Hill and the Theodore Roosevelt birthplace in New York City, at 28 East 20th Street, became national sites housing most of the mementoes and books, and some of his numerous papers. His estate at the time of his death was valued at $811,000, one of the largest of any President up to this time.

When Roosevelt returned to private life he took with him the papers representing the seven years as Chief Executive. Two years before his death, he and Mrs. Roosevelt jointly decided the papers should go to the Library of Congress with the proviso that no one except him or those designated by him could see them during his lifetime. Six large boxes were shipped on December 22, 1918. A few days following his death three additional packing cases were shipped, later followed by four more large cases which were found in the hayloft of the barn at Oyster Bay. In 1958 Alice Longworth donated seven volumes of her father's diaries to the Library of Congress, making a total of 250,000 items.

Miniature book from the political campaign of Theodore Roosevelt in 1904.

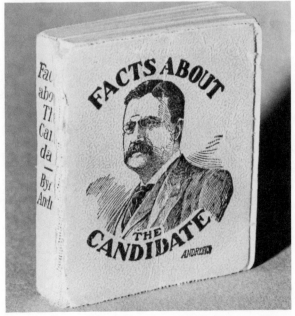

Text of the Will of Theodore Roosevelt

I, Theodore Roosevelt, of Oyster Bay, County of Nassau, and State of New York, hereby make and do publish and declare this to be my *Last Will and Testament*, revoking all former *wills* by me made.—

FIRST: As I have given to my daughter *Alice* all the silver given as wedding presents on my marriage with her mother. I give my other silver, plate, and plated ware to my other children to be divided as equally between them according to value as may be possible.-

SECOND: I direct my Executors who shall qualify or take upon them the execution of my will to divide the trust fund of Sixty Thousand dollars given by the third clause of my Father's will to his Executors *in Trust* for my benefit into as many shares of equal value as I shall have children who or issue of whom are living at my decease, and *I devise* and *bequeath* one of such shares to each one of my surviving children, and one to the issue, collectively and according to their stocks, of each of my children who may die before me leaving such issue respectively.

THIRD: All the rest, residue and remainder of my estate, both real and personal, wheresoever and whatsoever, including any legacies which may lapse and all other property which I have power to appoint and dispose of by will, *I devise and bequeath* to my *Executors* who shall qualify, the survivor of them and their successors *in trust*:—

I. To collect and receive the rents, profits, interest and income, and apply them to the use of my wife, *Edith Kermit Roosevelt*, during her life.—

II. I authorize and empower my wife by last *Will and Testament* published and executed after my decease, to dispose of the principal of this trust to and among any one or more of my issue in such shares and portions, and either absolutely or upon any trust or limitation, respectively, as she shall declare.—

III. In default of any such testamentary dispostion by my wife after my decease, *I devise and bequeath* all said *rest, residue* and *remainder* of my estate both real and personal, wheresoever and whatsoever, including any legacies which may lapse and all other property which I have power to appoint or dispose of by will to my children who survive my wife, and to the issue surviving her of any deceased child of mine, according to their stocks.—

FOURTH: I *direct* my *Executors* to hold each share of my estate which any infant legatee or devisee may be or become entitled to aboslutely under this will until such infant attains the age of twenty-one years, and that, in the mean time, they collect and receive the income of each share so held respectively and apply them to the use of the infant legatee.—

FIFTH: I direct that my *Executors* shall not be required to file any inventory of my estate or give security for the same or any part thereof. *I authorize and empower* my *Executors and Trustees*, the survivor of them and their successors, to sell and partition my real and personal estate all at one time or different parcels from time to time, and to consent to the sale or partition of any real estate in which I may be interested. *Such* sales may be either public or private, and they are authorized to execute all proper instruments for carrying such sales and partition into effect. I also authorize them to personally appraise my real and personal property and divide and allot the same to the various trusts and among the several legatees and devisees in accordance with such appraisement which shall be final and conclusive beyond any dispute or appeal. *I* also *authorize* them to retain and hold, at the risk of the share to which the same may be allotted, as an investment for any trust hereby created or for any infant legatee any investment, real or personal, which I may leave; and *I authorize* them to invest and reinvest the whole or any part of the proceeds of real and personal property sold, and all money or personal property held or received by them as *Trustees* or for any infant legatee in and upon real estate, or bond secured by mortgage on railroads, or on real estate, or the bonds, stocks, or obligations of corporations, in in such other stocks, evidences of debt, or property, real or personal, whether of or situated in the United States or any other country, as in their own personal judgment may seem best; and, from time to time, to sell any real or personal property held or purchased by them, and to change the investments as and whenever they please; and they shall not be responsible for any losses arising therefrom.—

SIXTH: I further authorize my *Executors and Trustees* out of the income of each share held *in trust* and of each share held during the minority of a legatee or devisee respectively, to pay all taxes, assessments and expenses for repairs or insurance thereon; also, from time to time, in their discretion, to make leases of the real estate forming any part thereof upon such terms and conditions, not however exceeding twenty-one years, as to them may seem disirable; also to build upon, alter or improve any such real estate, expending for the purpose any of the other principal of such share, as in their own personal judgment may seem wise.—

SEVENTH: I name and appoint my wife, *Edith Kermit Roosevelt* and my son *Theodore Roosevelt Jr*, and *George Emlen Roosevelt, Executrix and Executors* of and *Trustees* under this my will. *In* case any of them or any one who may be from time to time appointed *Executor and Trustee* pursuant to this clause of my will, shall fail to qualify or cease to act from any cause, *I direct* that the trusts and powers herein contained shall vest in and may be fully executed by the one or ones who shall be qualified or acting, and *I authorize* my duly qualified and acting *Executors or Trustees*, and the survivor of them, by an instrument in writing duly acknowledged to appoint a new *Executor and Trustee* to fill each vacancy as it may occur, and the person so appointed shall thereupon become vested with all the estate and powers of an *Executor and Trustee* herunder, the same as if named by me herein as such.—

IN WITNESS WHEREOF, I have hereunto subscribed my name and set my seal this 13th day of December, in the year of our Lord one thousand nine hundred and twelve. —

Theodore Roosevelt

Subscribed, sealed, published, acknowledged, and declared by the *Testator, Theodore Roosevelt*, as, for, and to be his *Last Will and Testament* in our sight and presence, whereupon, *at his request* and in his sight and presence, and in the sight and presence of each other, *we and each* of us do *sign our names* as attesting witnesses the day and year last above written.

Frank Harper
George Douglas Wardrop.

Leather chaps worn by Theodore Roosevelt.

Theodore Roosevelt campaigning for the Presidency.

Notes on the Will of Theodore Roosevelt

THE WILL OF THEODORE ROOSEVELT is the first in this series to illustrate two elements common to wills that are part of complex modern estate plans. One of these is the power of appointment. Though the power of appointment is not a modern creation, it has come into extensive use in the United States only in comparatively recent times.

The essence of a power of appointment is that it offers a technique for accomplishing a transfer of property in two stages. The first is the creation of the power by the owner of property (called the donor). The second is the exercise of the power by the person in whom it has been created (called the donee). The principal advantage of the power of appointment is its flexibility. It permits the creator of the power to define the terms of the transfer to the extent he wishes, yet to leave elements of it open to be completed by the holder of the power in the future.

Paragraph 3rd of this Will is a good example of one of its common uses. Roosevelt placed the residue of his estate in trust. His widow was made the only beneficiary as long as she lived. At her death he wished the property to pass to his descendants. He could not know who would then be alive, or what their needs or circumstances might be, but his widow would. He trusted her judgment and brought it into play in disposing of his property by giving her a power of appointment—but only within the limited class of his descendants. However, within that class, she could, in her will, designate those to receive, fix their shares, and decide whether or not to put them in trust.

These choices, of course, are also available to a widow whose husband leaves her his estate outright. That is a common course where the estate is modest and should be made completely available to meet the surviving spouse's needs. Where it is large and those needs can be met with a gift of the income from the property, the power of appointment can have significant advantages over the gift outright. It can, though it need not, limit the area of the donee's discretion. It can also save the cost and inconvenience of a second estate administration; it can reduce taxes depending on the scope of the power conferred. (Roosevelt lived before the era when death tax considerations bulked as large as they do now, so that was hardly his motivation.) There are other, less significant advantages as well.

The creation of a power of appointment does not assure that it will be used. In fact, there are circumstances in which it is anticipated that it will not be. Either way, a well-drawn will contains an alternative gift to go into effect if the power should not be exercised—another example of the draftsman covering various contingencies. Here subparagraph III of paragraph 3rd deals with precisely this possibility.

A second modern characteristic of this Will is the development of provisions dealing with questions of administration of the property as distinguished from those which define who is to receive it. These problems were becoming more visible to draftsmen in the early part of the 20th century as growing use of the trust device raised them in concrete form for trustees, beneficiaries, and courts. Since the creator of a trust has very broad power to define its terms, legal draftsmen began to include many more provisions to create rules of administration applicable to the particular trust or estate. Roosevelt's Will represents this tendency only in an embryonic form, as comparison with some of the later wills in this volume will make evident.

WILLIAM H. TAFT

WILLIAM HOWARD TAFT WAS BORN IN CINCINNATI, OHIO, ON SEPTEMBER 15, 1857. His father was an able lawyer and judge, Alphonso Taft, who later served as Secretary of War and Attorney General under President Grant and as Minister to Austria and Russia under President Arthur. William attended public schools in Cincinnati and at the age of 17 graduated from Woodward High School. At Yale University he finished second in a class of 121 students. Two years after his graduation from Yale in 1878, he completed law study at the University of Cincinnati.

Admitted to the bar in Ohio, Taft became assistant prosecuting attorney for Hamilton County. In 1882 President Arthur appointed Taft an internal revenue collector at a salary of $10,000 a year. He resigned within the year out of disgust with the spoils system which his job entailed and returned to practicing law in Cincinnati.

Taft's ambition was to sit on the Supreme Court. His first judicial post was an appointment as judge of the superior court of Ohio in 1887. In 1890, at the age of 33, he accepted the office of U.S. Solicitor General at a salary of $7,000 a year. Two years later he was named a Federal circuit court judge. In 1900 President McKinley appointed Taft head of the newly formed Philippine Commission. Taft was next appointed Secretary of War in February 1904, by Theodore Roosevelt.

Hand-picked by Roosevelt as his successor, Taft was nominated as President at the

Republican national convention in 1908. The Democratic candidate, William Jennings Bryan, was making his third attempt at the Presidency. Roosevelt campaigned vigorously for Taft, confident that his successor would continue his progressive policies. Taft won a smashing victory.

By Taft's Administration Congress had appropriated $25,000 a year for transportation expenses and the President's salary was raised to $75,000 a year, the first increase since Grant's Administration.

In 1886 Taft, 29 years of age, had married Helen Herron, three years his junior, the daughter of John V. Herron, who was at one time a law partner of President Hayes. The couple had three children. Mrs. Taft was well prepared to be First Lady. She brought with her education, travel experience, strong character, individuality, and social graces that won her high praise. She was economical in running social affairs and helped her husband save $100,000 of his salary. In May of the second year of his Administration she was suddenly paralyzed from a stroke, which resulted in her confinement in the White House for months.

Following his unsuccessful bid for a second term in 1912, Taft accepted the Kent Professorship of Law at Yale University. In 1913 he was also elected president of the American Bar Association. President Wilson appointed him co-chairman of the National War Labor Board in 1918. Taft's support of Warren Harding in 1920 was rewarded when on June 30, 1921, at the death of Chief Justice White, Harding appointed Taft Chief Justice of the United States, making him the only man ever to serve successively as President and Chief Justice. Taft served until 1930, when ill health forced his retirement.

During his lifetime Taft occupied many houses. His birthplace in Cincinnati has been restored and houses many of his mementoes. When the Tafts were first married, Taft took his bride to The Quarry, a house on East McMillan Street in Cincinnati, where the first of their three children was born. In 1890, when they moved to Washington, D.C., they rented a small house at 5 Dupont Circle for $100 a month. In 1892, Taft bought a rambling shingled cottage at Murray Bay outside of Quebec, Canada. As Chief Justice Taft, lived at Wyoming Avenue and 23rd Street in Washington, D.C., in a house he bought for $75,000. He died there on March 8, 1930, and was the first President to be buried in Arlington National Cemetery. At the time of his death his estate totaled $475,000. Mrs. Taft survived him for 13 years, dying on May 22, 1943.

William Howard Taft in his official White House automobile, a White Steamer.

Text of the Will of William H. Taft

I, William H. Taft, do make this my last will and testament:

I.

I hereby revoke all former wills.

II.

I give to Yale University the sum of ten thousand dollars ($10,000) to be added to the principal of the alumni university fund and credited to the class anniversary fund of the Academic Class of 1878.

III.

I give and bequeath the following legacies:

To my secretary, Wendell W. Mischler, five thousand dollars ($5,000);

To Margaret McNamara, one thousand dollars ($1,000);

To Annie McNamara, seven hundred fifty dollars ($750);

To Thomas Halpin, seven hundred fifty dollars ($750).

IV.

All my papers, manuscripts, correspondence, addresses and copyrights, in my custody, in the Library of Congress or elsewhere, I give to my three children, hereinafter named, for such use as they may deem it wise, after consultation with my wife, to make of them.

V.

All of the rest, residue and remainder of my estate, real, personal or mixed, in the United States of America, the Dominion of Canada or elsewhere, of which I may die seized and possessed, or to which I may be entitled or in which I may have any interest at the time of my death, I give, devise and bequeath to my dear wife, Helen H. Taft, absolutely.

Should my wife die before I do, or should we die together under circumstances making it doubtful which one of us dies first, then it is my will that all of said residue of my estate shall be divided among my children, as follows:

One-fourth (¼) to go to my son Robert Alphonse, and in case of his death before mine, to his children; one-half (½) to my daughter, Helen Taft Manning, and in case of her death before mine, to her children; and one-fourth (¼) to my son, Charles Phelps, and in case of his death before mine, to his children.

VI.

I hereby appoint my wife as executrix, and if permissible under the law, request that she be required neither to give bond nor to file an inventory. Should my wife not survive me, I appoint my son, Robert, my executor, with a similar request.

In testimony whereof I have hereunto set my hand and affixed my seal this 3rd day of June, A.D., Nineteen Hundred and Twenty-five.

William H. Taft (seal)

Signed, sealed and published and declared by William H. Taft, the above named testator, as and for his last will and testament, in the presence of us, who, at his request and in his presence, and in the presence of one another, have subscribed our names as attesting witnesses thereto on the day and date of said will:

John S. Flannery, Hibbs Building, Washington, D.C.
Anna Connell, Clinton, Conn.
Edwin O. Burke, 1,518 Kingman Place, Washington, D.C.

FIRST CODICIL
to
LAST WILL AND TESTAMENT
of
WILLIAM H. TAFT.

I, WILLIAM H. TAFT, do make, publish and declare this First Codicil to my Last Will and Testament executed on, to-wit, June 3, 1925:

I. In my said Will, I have given to YALE UNIVERSITY a legacy of TEN THOUSAND DOLLARS ($10,000), to be added to the principal of the Alumni University Fund and credited to the Class Anniversary Fund of the Academic Class of 1878. As I have recently made a subscription to the ENDOWMENT FUND of $20,000,000, now being raised for said UNIVERSITY, of the sum of TEN THOUSAND DOLLARS ($10,000), payable in five annual installments of TWO THOUSAND DOLLARS ($2,000) each, I direct that any payments which I may make in my lifetime on account of said subscription shall be deducted from the amount of the aforesaid legacy and whatever may remain unpaid on account of said subscription at the time of my death shall be paid in full satisfaction of said legacy.

II. I give and bequeath a legacy of FIVE THOUSAND DOLLARS ($5,000) to the FOUNDATION OF THE TAFT SCHOOL, at Watertown, Connecticut, established by my brother, Horace D. Taft, and I direct that the total amount of any gifts or contributions which I may make to said FOUNDATION in my lifetime shall be deducted from the amount of said legacy and the balance paid over in full satisfaction thereof.

III. I hereby ratify and confirm my said Last Will and Testament in all other respects, save as modified by this Codicil.

IN TESTIMONY WHEREOF, I have hereunto set my hand and affixed my seal this 27th day of April, A. D. 1927.

William H. Taft

Signed, sealed, published and declared by WILLIAM H. TAFT, the above named testator, as and for a Codicil to his Last Will and Testament, in the presence of us, who, at his request and in his presence and in the presence of one another, have subscribed our names as attesting witnesses thereto on the day and date of said Codicil.

Geo. Pauly Way   31 Hillhouse Ave., New Haven, Conn.
William Winston Crossley   2227-20 St., N.W. Washington, D.C.
Edwin O. Burke   Mitchellville, P.O. Md.

CODICIL
to
LAST WILL AND TESTAMENT
of
WILLIAM H. TAFT.

I. WILLIAM H. TAFT, do make, publish and declare this Codicil to my Last Will and Testament executed on, to-wit, June 3, 1925:

I. In my said Will, I have given to YALE UNIVERSITY a legacy of TEN THOUSAND DOLLARS ($10,000), to be added to the principal of the Alumni University Fund and credited to the Class Anniversary Fund of the Academic Class of 1878. As I have recently made a subscription to the ENDOWMENT FUND of $20,000,000, now being raised for said UNIVERSITY, of the sum of TEN THOUSAND DOLLARS ($10,000), payable in five annual installments of TWO THOUSAND DOLLARS ($2,000) each, I direct that any payments which I may make in my lifetime on account of said subscription shall be deducted from the amount of the aforesaid legacy and whatever may remain unpaid on account of said subscription at the time of my death shall be paid in full satisfaction of said legacy.

II. I give and bequeath a legacy of TWENTY-FIVE HUNDRED DOLLARS ($2500) to the FOUNDATION OF THE TAFT SCHOOL, at Watertown, Connecticut, established by my brother, Horace D. Taft, and I direct that the total amount of any gifts or contributions which I may make to said FOUNDATION in my lifetime shall be deducted from the amount of said legacy and the balance paid over in full satisfaction thereof.

III. I give and bequeath a legacy of TWENTY-FIVE HUNDRED DOLLARS ($2500) to the ALL SOULS UNITARIAN CHURCH, of Washington, D. C.

IV. I hereby ratify and confirm my said Last Will and Testament in all other respects, save as modified by this Codicil.

IN TESTIMONY WHEREOF, I have hereunto set my hand and affixed my seal this 1st day of June, A. D. 1927.

William H. Taft

Signed, sealed, published and declared by WILLIAM H. TAFT, the above named testator, as and for a Codicil to his Last Will and Testament, in the presence of us, who, at his request and in his presence and in the presence of one another, have subscribed our names as attesting witnesses thereto on the day and date of said Codicil.

William W. Crossley   2227-20th St., N.W., Washington, D.C.
Mary Hanson   3214-11-Pl S.E. Washington, D.C.
Edwin O. Burke   Mitchellville, P.O. Md.

Notes on the Will of William H. Taft

PRESIDENT TAFT'S WIFE AND THREE CHIL- DREN OUTLIVED HIM. Thus, the first paragraph of Article V, leaving the residue of his estate to his wife, took effect, and the second paragraph, making an alternative gift to his three children, did not. Nevertheless, that paragraph is interesting for the way in which it draws the line between the operation of the two methods of disposing of his property.

Although the subject is not peculiar to the 20th century, modern methods of transportation and the disastrous accidents that they sometimes produce have made the public more conscious of the possibility of simultaneous, or near simultaneous, deaths. In preparing a will, consciousness of this potential raises several questions. Should a condition of survival for some stated period of time beyond the testator's death be attached to gifts made in the will? Failure to do so can mean that a legatee who outlives a testator briefly will be treated as having been the owner of property left him by the testator, even though there was never any opportunity to enjoy it. Such treatment can have serious disadvantages, among them inclusion of the property as an asset of a second estate for purposes of its administration. If then a condition requiring survival for a period of the time beyond the testator's death seems desirable, what should be the period? Thirty days? Six months? Something else? The longer the period, the longer the intended recipient's enjoyment will be postponed which may be inconsistent with the testator's wish to provide the legatee with the benefits as quickly as possible. A layman might think the problem easily solved by requiring survival until the asset actually becomes available, but no longer; for example, by writing—if he shall survive until the administration of my Estate has been completed. Unfortunately, this flexible formula contains serious disadvantages, tax and otherwise, so that it is avoided.

President Taft attached no condition that would be contingent upon his wife's survival to some time beyond his death. Under the Will his children take only "should my wife die before I do." So stated, the condition contains a potential problem in its operation if there should be uncertainty about the order in which persons die. This is, essentially, a question of fact. If the order of deaths is known, provisions that turn on survival or non-survival are perfectly workable whether the deaths occurred within a short period of each other or not. However, if the sequence cannot be determined, such provisions break down, and the question of who shall take the property must be resolved by a rule applicable to this specific situation. The problem has been presented often enough so that a statute, the Uniform Simultaneous Death Act, has been enacted in virtually every state to provide answers where the instrument does not.

That statute provides solutions which a testator need not accept. Each testator has the power to make his own rule for this situation, and this President Taft did by specifying that his children should take the residue of his estate "should we [he and his wife] die together under circumstances making it doubtful which one of us dies first." This solution will save the cost and inconvenience of double estate administration of the same property and is ordinarily to be preferred. However, there are situations in which, to minimize taxes, an opposite result will be preferable in the case of gifts to a surviving spouse.

Article IV of the Will disposes of the papers of the former President by dividing them among his three children "for such use as they may deem it wise." This is entirely consistent with the belief demonstrated both by his predecessors and his successors that the papers were his property to be disposed of as he saw fit. The gift to his three children effectively shifted to them the difficult responsibility of determining how best to balance the private and public interests in these documents. Recent Presidents have been encouraged by Congress, to make these decisions themselves.

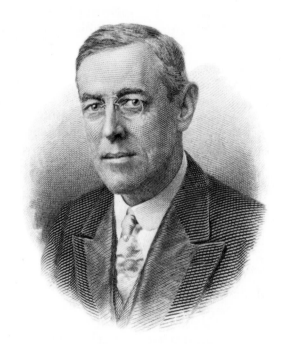

WOODROW
WILSON

THOMAS WOODROW WILSON (his full name), the son of a Presbyterian minister, was born on December 28, 1856, in Staunton, Virginia. His paternal grandfather, James Wilson, came to America from northern Ireland in 1807. His mother's forebears were Scottish. Woodrow entered Davidson College in North Carolina at 17, but transferred to Princeton the following year. After graduating from Princeton in 1879, he briefly attended the University of Virginia Law School, but left because of poor health.

In 1882, Wilson began the practice of law in Atlanta, but he abandoned the profession a year later to enter Johns Hopkins University, where he earned his doctor's degree in government and history; his thesis, *Congressional Government*, won him wide acclaim. He also began teaching, first at Bryn Mawr, then at Wesleyan University, and finally at his alma mater, Princeton. There he became professor of jurisprudence and, in 1902, president of the university.

At 28, Wilson had married Ellen Axson, a Presbyterian minister's daughter, a person of sweet temper and sound judgment who had a great influence on her husband. They had three daughters—Margaret, Eleanor, and Jessie.

Wilson first rented a house on campus and later bought the lot next to that house. His writings were bringing him an income of between $1,500 and $4,000 a year, from which he built his own home in Tudor style, which he named Library Place. After he became president of Princeton, he moved into the official president's residence. Wilson's ambitious attempts to reorganize the curriculum and the eating clubs soon made him unpopular with the university establishment, however, so when he was offered the chance to run for Governor of New Jersey by conservative Democrats in 1910, he accepted and won the election. When the Democratic national convention met in Baltimore on June 25, 1912, Wilson was placed as a favored-son candidate, and won on the 46th ballot. The election was a contest of personalities. Roosevelt had bucked the Republican convention, which nominated Taft, and formed the Progressive Party. By splitting the opposition, Roosevelt ensured Wilson's victory.

On August 6, 1914, at the age of 54, Mrs. Wilson died of Bright's disease in the White House; Wilson tried to overcome his sorrow by concentrating on official business. Within a year he met Mrs. Edith Bolling Galt, the widow of a Washington jeweler, and the two were married on December 18, 1915. The bride was the daughter of Judge William H. Bolling of Virginia. The honeymoon cost $2,739. When the public questioned Wilson's short period of mourning for his first wife, the latter's brother came forth with a defense of the President.

Woodrow Wilson was renominated by the Democratic national convention without opposition. Throughout his second term, Wilson worked long hours, drafting his speeches on his own typewriter into the late hours of the night. On April 12, 1917, he asked Congress for a declaration of war; the following year he presented Congress with his 14 points outlining America's war aims, the last of which involved his plan for the League of Nations.

In November 1918, Wilson went to Paris for the Peace Conference, becoming the first American President to visit Europe while in office. But when he presented the Versailles Treaty to the Senate, the Republican majority refused to ratify it. Wilson's determination to sell his idea led him on a speaking tour of the nation against his doctor's orders. While on the

tour he suffered a stroke on September 25, 1919, and his wife became both nurse and executive secretary to the invalid during the remainder of his term of office.

A sick man, Wilson left the White House in 1921 and moved to a commodious residence he had purchased at 2340 S Street, where he lived the remaining three years of his life. He died on February 3, 1924, and became the first and only President buried inside the National Cathedral in Washington, D.C.

Wilson's salary at Bryn Mawr College was $1,500 a year, which he supplemented by writing a college textbook, *The State*, and delivering lectures at Johns Hopkins. At Princeton, he was the highest-paid professor of his day. His salary as President was $75,000 annually with $25,000 for traveling expenses. The Wilsons were frugal while in the White House; they received many gifts, especially on their European trip, which they took with them when they left the White House. The President managed to save a good deal of his earnings—a wise policy, as there was no Presidential pension until 1958. His list of publications from 1885 to 1924 is extensive and probably accounts for a large part of his savings. In addition, the second Mrs. Wilson was wealthy in her own right.

While in the White House, Wilson accepted $10,000 from each of 10 of his friends to make possible his purchase of the $150,000 residence on S Street. One of the 10, Bernard Baruch, also purchased the lot next to the house to keep anyone from building on it and to afford the President privacy. At his death, Wilson's estate was estimated to be $600,000.

The President's widow continued to live in the S Street house surrounded by the Wilson mementoes until her death in 1961. She gave his library and Presidential papers to the Library of Congress and at her death their house was left to the National Trust for Historical Preservation. The personal effects were divided between the National Trust and the Smithsonian Institution, with objects associated with the first Mrs. Wilson going either to the family or to the birthplace at Staunton, which is maintained as an historic site.

Text of the Will of Woodrow Wilson

I, Woodrow Wilson, being of sound and disposing mind and in every respect in full vigour of mind and body, do declare the following to be my last will and testament:

I will and devise all my property, of whatever kind, real and personal, after the payment of any just debts that may constitute a claim upon it at the time of my death, to my beloved wife Edith for her lifetime, with the request that she distribute among my daughters such articles of clothing, jewelry, personal ornament, or art material as may have been the personal belongings of their mother, and with the direction that my daughter Margaret shall receive out of the income of my estate, so long as she remains unmarried, the sum of twenty-five hundred dollars annually, unless that amount should at any time exceed one-third of the entire annual income of my estate; in which case I direct that she shall receive one-third of that income annually.

Upon the death of my beloved wife Edith, it is my will and direction, should she die without issue, that the whole of my estate, real and personal, or so much of it as shall remain unexpended or undispersed, shall revert to my children, share and share alike; and that, should she die leaving issue, her child or children shall inherit, share and share alike, with my daughters living at the time of the execution of this instrument.

I do hereby also name and appoint my beloved wife Edith sole executor and administrator of this my last will and testament.

Duly signed and acknowledged in the City of Washington, in the District of Columbia, on the thirty-first of May, in the year of our Lord one thousand nine hundred and seventeen, in the presence of the witnesses whose signatures are below inscribed.

Woodrow Wilson

In the Presence of:

Helen Woodrow Bowes
I. H. Hoover.
Ralph M. Rogers.

Notes on the Will of Woodrow Wilson

T HE BRIEF PARAGRAPHS OF PRESIDENT WILSON'S ONE-PAGE WILL contain little to distinguish it from many others filed in the office of the Register of Wills of the District of Columbia in 1924. His first wife died early in his first term of office. He remarried about 16 months later, and at the time of his death was survived by his widow and the three adult daughters of his first marriage. His Will provides that, except for a share of income for an unmarried daughter, his widow should enjoy his entire property for her life; at her death it is to be divided among his children—and her issue, if any, then living. The last is a rather unusual provision in its generality, since it would include children Mrs. Wilson might have by any marriage, past, present, or future. In fact, she and the President had no children; she did not remarry after his death in 1924, but lived as a widow for almost 38 years.

The introductory clause in a will serves to identify the testator and his purpose. The language here describing his state of mind and physical health is frequently found in wills. It has a pleasant ring; it does no harm but neither does it add anything. Capacity to make a will is

Edith Bolling Wilson.

indeed an essential element, but a testator's declaration that he has it does not help one who is trying to prove that fact, nor hinder one seeking to prove the contrary. In those—fortunately rare—situations in which a will is contested for lack of capacity, the evidence presented will be almost entirely concerned with facts not visible on the document itself.

It is interesting that the testator identified himself here as Woodrow Wilson. His given name was actually Thomas Woodrow Wilson, but he dropped his first name when he began to write for scholarly publications. Perhaps he thought that Woodrow Wilson would be more easily remembered than the more common Thomas Wilson. The use of his name as altered in this way has no effect whatsoever upon the validity of the Will.

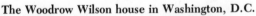

The Woodrow Wilson house in Washington, D.C.

WARREN G. HARDING

ARREN GAMALIEL HARDING, the son of a country doctor, was born on a farm just outside the little town of Blooming Grove, Ohio, on November 2, 1865. He was the oldest of eight children. The Puritan forebears of his father had landed at Plymouth and migrated to Ohio in 1820.

After study at local schools, Harding at 14 entered Ohio Central College at Iberia, graduating three years later. In 1882, after his family moved to Marion, Ohio, he began to read law, sold insurance, and eventually turned to journalism. He soon became editor and part owner of the Marion *Star*, a failing newspaper that circulated in a town of 4,000 population, bought for a mere $300 by the elder Harding and two others. The town grew and so did the

newspaper and its printing plant. Harding entered local politics, and was elected a state senator and became lieutenant governor.

In 1891, at the age of 25, Harding had married Florence Kling De Wolfe, a divorcee five years his senior, and the daughter of the town's richest banker. By her previous marriage she had one son, Marshall Eugene De Wolfe, whose two children were mentioned in Harding's will. Mrs. Harding's influence was a major factor in his political success. She believed in him and encouraged him constantly. When Harding became ill shortly after their marriage, Mrs. Harding took an active role in rescuing his newspaper.

In 1910 Harding was nominated as the Republican candidate for Governor of Ohio, and suffered his first political defeat. Discouraged, he considered withdrawing from politics, but in 1912 Harding was picked to nominate William Howard Taft at the Republican national convention, and two years later he ran for U.S. Senator against his good friend Joseph Foraker, defeating him but retaining his friendship. When the Republican national convention met in 1916, Harding went as a delegate-at-large from Ohio, and was chosen its permanent chairman.

The head of the Republican Party in Ohio, Harry M. Daugherty, saw Presidential timber in Harding. He was not the immediate favorite; others at the Republican national convention in Chicago in 1920 were much better known. The balloting was in a stalemate until, on the 10th ballot, Daugherty nominated his protégé after conferences in a "smoke-filled room." His campaign, with "normalcy" the watchword, was conducted from his front porch in Marion. He won by a record landslide majority.

The President found relaxation in camping trips with his important friends, such as Harvey Firestone, Henry Ford, and Thomas Edison. He also played golf and attended baseball games, but his greatest pastime was poker, which he played nearly every night. Both President and Mrs. Harding liked to meet people. They enjoyed entertaining and were noted for their huge garden parties. Although Prohibition eliminated wine and liquor from the formal dinners and parties, it was available to the President's card-playing cronies.

Harding did not live to face the Teapot Dome scandal that disgraced his Administration. As criticism of his associates grew, in the summer of 1923, he set out on a speaking tour which extended to Alaska. Wearied from the journey, he was stricken with pneumonia in San Francisco. The news of his death on August 2, 1923, swept swiftly and unexpectedly through the country and the bitterness against his Administration was temporarily forgotten. After his remains made the five-day journey to Washington, he received a state funeral, then was taken back to Marion, Ohio, for interment.

The Harding house on Mount Vernon Av-

enue in Marion, containing most of his mementoes and souvenirs, was opened to the public in 1926. The rest of the memorabilia were given to the Smithsonian Institution. President Harding left an estate worth $930,444.54. He owned stocks in the Marion Baseball Company, the Chautauqua Company, and various enterprises in engineering, oil, gas, and iron, as well as the Harding Publishing Company. Six weeks before his death he had sold his interest in the Marion *Star* to Louis H. Brush and Roy D. Moore for $550,000. President Harding also made a new will six weeks before his death.

Mrs. Harding took all of her husband's correspondence with her when she left the White House. During the year and a half that remained of her life she destroyed some of his papers. However, 325,000 documents were left to the Harding Memorial Association, which in 1963 deposited them in the Ohio Historical Society.

President Woodrow Wilson and President-elect Warren G. Harding riding to the Inauguration in 1921.

Text of the Will of Warren G. Harding.

IN THE NAME OF THE BENEVOLENT FATHER OF ALL:

I, WARREN G. HARDING, of the City of Marion, County of Marion, and State of Ohio, do make and publish this my last will and testament.

First: My will is that all just debts and funeral expenses be paid out of my estate, as soon after my decease as may be found convenient.

Second: I give, devise and bequeath to my wife, Florence Kling Harding, the East half of the East half of lot No. 221, in the City of Marion, Ohio, (it being at this time the East half of the Star Office Building), and lot No. 929, in Barnhart's Addition, in the City of Marion, Ohio, (it being our residence on Mount Vernon Avenue), to have and to hold all of said real estate in fee simple.

Third: I further give, devise and bequeath to my said wife, during her natural life, the income, dividends, interest or earnings on One Hundred Thousand Dollars, per value, of government bonds or other government securities, that I may own at the time of my death, and also to my said wife, I give and devise any and all dividends that may accrue from and be paid on my entire stock holdings at the time of my death in what is now known as the Harding Publishing Company, or any successor corporation or reorganization of said Harding Publishing Company. To accomplish the carrying out of the foregoing bequest to my said wife, Florence Kling Harding, my said executor is hereby authorized and directed to hold as trustee One Hundred thousand Dollars in the above referred to government securities and the stock of the Harding Publishing Company and pay the income therefrom semi-annually to my said wife during the period of her natural life. At her death the principal involved in this bequest shall be divided share and share alike among my brother, George Tryon Harding, Jr. and my sisters, Charity M. Remsberg, Abigail V. Harding and Carolyn Votaw. In case my brother or any of my sisters should not survive me, but should leave children, such child or children shall receive their parent's share. In case there arises a time during the herein created trust when it becomes necessary or advisable to change any of the securities or stock therein, the trustee may, with the approval of the Probate Court, effect such change. If my brother or any of my sisters precede me in death without children then the share in such trust of such decedent shall be divided share and share alike among the survivors included in this bequest, or their heirs.

Fourth: I give, devise and bequeath to my father, George Tryon Harding, during the period of his natural life, the income, interest or other return from Fifty Thousand Dollars of government bonds or other government securities that I may possess at the time of my death, and my said executor is hereby authorized and directed to hold as trustee Fifty Thousand Dollars in such securities and pay the income therefrom semi-annually to my said father. If, for any reason, there are not adequate government securities in my possession at the time of my death the sum lacking shall be made good from dividend-paying stocks or other securities of which I am possessed at the time of my death. At the death of my father the proceeds of this trust shall be divided share and share alike among my brother and sisters, as provided in the foregoing paragraph, providing for the distribution of the trust set up in favor of my wife, Florence Kling Harding.

Fifth: I also give, devise and bequeath to my said wife all the personal property contained in our home, absolutely and forever, but I request her to give a finger ring and a watch to each of the three sons of my brother, George Tryon Harding, Jr., and leave to her judgment the bestowal of gifts, souvenirs, mementoes and any articles of historical value to any society, organization or person as she may see fit.

Sixth: I further give, devise and bequeath to my father, George Tryon Harding, the use of the residence property he occupies at the time of this writing, upon the condition that upon his death the title, in fee simple, shall pass to my sisters who may be then living.

Seventh: I give, devise and bequeath to each and every one of my nephews and nieces at the time of my death, Ten Thousand Dollars.

Eighth: I give, devise and bequeath to Jean DeWolfe and George DeWolfe, grandchildren of my wife, who may be living at the time of my death, Two Thousand Dollars each.

Ninth: I give, devise and bequeath to George H. Van Fleet Two Thousand Dollars; to Henry R. Schaffner One Thousand Dollars and to James C. Woods One Thousand Dollars, as a mark of my appreciation of the faithful service rendered to me in the conduct of the Marion Star.

Tenth: I give, devise and bequeath to Trinity Baptist Church of Marion, Ohio, Two Thousand Dollars, and to St. Paul's Episcopal Church, of Marion, Ohio, One Thousand Dollars.

Eleventh: I give, devise and bequeath to the Marion Park Commission, of Marion, Ohio, Twenty-Five Thousand Dollars to be applied in the creation of some permanent improvement, to be determined by the Commission, in any one of the three city parks of Marion, Ohio.

Twelfth: I give, devise and bequeath all the residue of my property, real and personal, to my brother and sisters then living, in fee simple and absolutely, to be divided among them share and share alike. In the event that my brother or any of my sisters should not survive me but should leave children, such child or children shall receive their parent's share.

Thirteenth: I request that no part of my estate shall be expended for a monument other than a simple marker at my grave.

Fourteenth: I hereby nominate and appoint Charles D. Schaffner, of Marion, Ohio, my executor and trustee for the purpose of carrying out the provisions and bequests of this my last will and testament, and request the Probate Court, of Marion County, Ohio, to confer upon him as such executor and trustee all authority under the laws of the State of Ohio and under the provisions of this will.

And I further request the Probate Court of Marion County, Ohio, to make such allowances by way of compensation for the execution of the trust herein created and for his services as executor as may be considered fair and reasonable.

Fifteenth: I hereby revoke all other wills by me heretofore made.

IN TESTIMONY WHEREOF, I hereunto subscribe my name at Washington, District of Columbia, this twentieth day of June, in the year of our Lord, One Thousand Nine Hundred and Twenty-Three.

Warren G. Harding

The foregoing instrument was signed at the end thereof, by the said WARREN G. HARDING, in our presence, and we heard him acknowledge the same as his last will and testament, and at his request and in his presence and in the presence of each other we hereunto respectively subscribe our names as attesting witnesses, at Washington, District of Columbia, this twentieth day of June, A. D. 1923.

Geo. B. Christrace Jr resides at Marion, Ohio.
Charles E. Heard resides at Portsmouth, Ohio.
H. W. Daugherty resides at Columbus, Ohio.

Harding's Tomb, Marion, Ohio.

Notes on the Will of Warren G. Harding

PRESIDENT HARDING AND HIS WIFE, who survived him by only a little more than a year, had no children. He was the owner of a local publishing company in Marion, Ohio, which had prospered through their joint efforts. His estate was large enough so that he felt able to care generously for his wife and, at the same time, make provision for his brothers and sisters and other relatives, employees, and friends. The principal vehicle used, as in many other Presidential wills, was the creation of a trust.

Probably the most interesting element of this Will is that which appears in the second to last sentence of paragraph 3rd. The comments following Theodore Roosevelt's Will noted that in the early part of the century draftsmen began to include in wills and trust instruments provisions dealing specifically with problems of administration. It was also noted that these typically released the fiduciary from rules of law to which he would otherwise be subject.

This provision in Harding's Will goes to the opposite extreme. Should the trustee believe that it is necessary or advisable to change investments, he must submit the question to the Probate Court and obtain its approval. Presumably this reflects the principal kinds of investment that Harding expected the trust to hold. These included stock in his publishing company and government notes or bonds. While it might seem quite natural to rely upon the trustee to select from among the many issues in the latter category, it is understandable that Harding would not want the shares in his closely held company to be given up by the trustee without some review of that decision. It is not at all certain, at least in the case of ordinary testators, that the Probate Court would accept the responsibility sought to be imposed. Though resolving disputes between trustees and beneficiaries or between co-trustees, courts typically have proved unwilling to assume a general advisory role to fiduciaries.

Many of the Presidential wills have reflected the religious beliefs of the testator, usually at the very beginning. Harding's is the last example of that practice—which is certainly not to say that he was the last President to hold such beliefs.

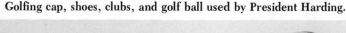

Golfing cap, shoes, clubs, and golf ball used by President Harding.

CALVIN COOLIDGE

JOHN CALVIN COOLIDGE (his full name) was born of English stock on July 4, 1872, in Plymouth, Vermont. His ancestor, John Coolidge, had settled in Watertown, Massachusetts, in 1630. Calvin's father was an important man in his community, serving as farmer, storekeeper, deputy sheriff, representative, and senator in the Vermont legislature. He was to inherit many of his father's traits—thrift, shrewdness and a laconic temper.

In 1895 Coolidge graduated from Amherst College. He then read law in Northampton, Massachusetts, and opened his own office there after being admitted to the bar. Within two years he was elected a member of the city council, followed by city solicitor, representative in the state legislature, city mayor, and

state senator. Early in this active political career, in 1905, he married Grace Goodhue, the daughter of an engineer.

In 1915 Coolidge ran for his first statewide office as lieutenant governor, which he won, serving for three years. A conservative, he was elected Governor in 1918, 20 years after he opened his law office in Northampton. His belief in the economy of time, effort and money had won him the confidence of the people of the state of Massachusetts. His handling of the Boston police strike in 1919, in which he called out the state guard to assure public safety, won him national recognition. When the deadlock in the Republican national convention of 1920 was broken by the nomination of Harding, Calvin Coolidge became his running mate.

In the summer of 1923, Vice President Coolidge went to his father's home in Plymouth, Vermont, to spend a vacation. Awakened on the night of August 2 with news of the sudden death of President Harding, he calmly took the oath of office from his father, who was a notary public.

Coolidge's popularity was so great that even his Democratic opponents were unable to make the Harding scandals damaging to his successor's Administration; in 1924 Coolidge, with the slogan "Keep Cool and Keep Coolidge," was elected to the Presidency in his own right. His chance of being reelected in 1928 would have been promising had he not sent forth the message "I do not choose to run."

After the Coolidges left the White House in 1929, they returned to the Northampton house at 21 Massasoit Street which they had rented for 24 years before and after their stay in the White House. In 1930, wanting more privacy, they purchased a secluded estate, The Beeches, from Dr. Henry Noble MacCracken, president of Vassar College, for $45,000. Here they lived out the remainder of their lives. Death came to Calvin Coolidge on January 5, 1933, of a thrombosis. He was buried in the family graveyard in his hometown of Plymouth, Vermont. Mrs. Coolidge lived until July 8, 1957.

Coolidge entered the White House with investments of at least $200,000. He also came to own considerable property in Vermont through inheritance from his father. His thrifty nature made him save about $50,000 of his $75,000-a-year Presidential salary and he made wise investments as one of the House of Morgan's preferred buyers, who was able to buy stocks at reduced price before they were offered to the public. His main source of income after he left office was from writing. His newspaper column earned more than $200,000 a year. The estimated worth of his estate at the time of his death was $500,000.

Grace Goodhue Coolidge (detail).

Text of the Will of Calvin Coolidge

"The White House"
    Washington
Will of Calvin Coolidge of Northampton,
    Hampshire County, Massachusetts

Not unmindful of my son John, I give all my estate both real and personal to my wife Grace Coolidge, in fee simple—Home at Washington, District of Columbia this twentieth day December, A.D. nineteen hundred and twenty six.

Calvin Coolidge

Signed by me on the date above in the presence of the testator and of each other as witnesses to said will and the signature thereof.

Everett Sanders
Edward T. Clark
Erwin C. Geisser

Calvin Coolidge Homestead.

Notes on the Will of Calvin Coolidge

THE WILL OF PRESIDENT COOLIDGE, the shortest and simplest of any in this book, supports the testator's general reputation for taciturnity and succinct expression. At President Coolidge's death on January 5, 1933, it was legally effective to transfer all of his estate to his wife, who survived him and lived until July 8, 1957. The phrase referring to his son John served the purpose of barring any claim by him—or on his behalf—for the share given by statute to a pretermitted heir (i.e., one not mentioned in the Will and inferred to have been simply overlooked, rather than intentionally disinherited). By specifically naming John, the President demonstrated conclusively that he had not overlooked him and did, in fact, intend to leave his entire estate to his wife to the exclusion of his son.

Though the one-sentence Will was effective to carry out the testator's main objective, a modern draftsman would criticize its omission of provisions which (1) could have been useful to Mrs. Coolidge in administering the estate, and (2) would have expressed the testator's wishes in the event that he survived Mrs. Coolidge, or, more importantly, that he survived both Mrs. Coolidge and their son. The former would have included, at a minimum, appointment of Mrs. Coolidge as Executrix and guardian of their son, a waiver of any requirements that she give bond beyond what might be needed to protect creditors, and a grant of powers appropriate to the office. It might also have included a provision nominating someone else to be Executor and guardian if Mrs. Coolidge should be unable or unwilling to perform.

Future contingencies which might be covered in a will can be very extensive, a potential amply illustrated by other wills in this book. The detailed coverage in such Wills as those of Presidents Lyndon Johnson, Truman, Hoover, Kennedy, and Eisenhower is hardly mandatory, but this one goes too far in the other direction. For purposes of will-drafting, brevity is rarely the soul of wit.

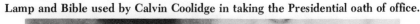

Lamp and Bible used by Calvin Coolidge in taking the Presidential oath of office.

HERBERT C. HOOVER

H ERBERT HOOVER WAS BORN IN WEST BRANCH, IOWA, ON AUGUST 10, 1874, the first President to be born west of the Mississippi River. He was the second of three children born to Jesse Clark and Huldah Minthorn Hoover. His father, a village blacksmith, died when Herbert was six and by the time he was eight his mother, a Quaker preacher, also died. Their orphaned children were taken in by various relatives.

After graduation in 1895 from Stanford University, he launched his career as a mining engineer, working in California, New Mexico, Nevada, and Colorado. In 1897 he accepted a job as general manager in Western Australia of a British gold mining firm at a salary of $600 a month.

In 1899 he returned to California and married Lou Henry, a girl he had met while attending Stanford University and with whom he was to have two sons. The newlyweds took off for China, where he had accepted a job as chief engineer of the Chinese Imperial Bureau of Mines at a salary of $20,000 a year.

From China Hoover traveled in many parts of the world from 1902 to 1908, circling the globe five times. In 1908 he went in business for himself and in 1909 published a book *Principles of Mining*. By the time he was 40 he had a worldwide chain of offices, and with the start of World War I in 1914 he shifted his occupation from a salaried job of $100,000 a year to organizing the American Relief Committee for the starving in Belgium. With the entry of the United States into the war, President Wilson appointed Hoover chief of the United States Food Administration. A Quaker and a humanitarian, Hoover achieved national and international recognition for his work during the war period.

Following the Armistice, Hoover was put in charge of shipping food to the starving millions in Europe and in 1921 the program was extended to include Russia.

When Warren Harding assumed the Presidency in 1921 he appointed Hoover as Secretary of Commerce. Hoover took up residence at 2300 S Street, leaving the adobe-styled house he had built in 1919 on land leased from Stanford University. Hoover reorganized the department and when President Harding died in 1923, incoming President Coolidge retained Hoover as Secretary of Commerce until August, 1928. Hoover became the Republican Party's leading contender for the nomination in 1928 and won on the first ballot at the national convention in Kansas City. The Democrats nominated the colorful "happy warrior" and Catholic Al Smith. Hoover, by now a multimillionaire, won the election in one of the greatest landslide victories, carrying 40 of the 48 states. Less than a year later the country plunged into a financial crisis as the stock markets crashed and the banks closed.

The Hoovers completely changed everything in the White House and when government officials refused to disburse money for certain requests, it was paid for by the President himself.

As might be expected, Hoover was made scapegoat for the Depression by the Democrats. His own party renominated him as their candidate in 1932, but Hoover was defeated by Franklin Delano Roosevelt.

Both Truman and Eisenhower appointed Hoover to chair committees to reorganize the Executive Branch. In 1947 he was asked to reorganize the food supply of Germany and to head a campaign which grew into the United Nations International Children's Emergency Fund. Hoover also served as a trustee of Stanford University for 40 years and was chairman of the Boys' Clubs of America for 20. He founded the Stanford Union, the School of Business Administration, and the Hoover Institute and Library on War, Revolution and Peace, the latter of which he endowed.

At the death of Mrs. Hoover in January 7, 1944, the house at Palo Alto was given to Stanford University for use as a residence for the president of the university. The former President lived the remainder of his life in his suite at the Waldorf Towers in Manhattan, which he acquired in 1934. He devoted much time to writing books and articles before his death on October 20, 1964, at the age of 90. He had served in 35 different posts under five Presidents during his lifetime. Between 1909 and the time of his death he published more than 43 of his works.

Development of the Herbert Hoover Memorial Park at West Branch began in 1935 when Allan Hoover, the President's son, acquired the birthplace cottage. In 1954 the Herbert Hoover Birthplace Foundation, Inc., was formed. The Herbert Hoover Presidential Library at West Branch was dedicated on August 10, 1962. The latter houses all of the papers and related historical materials enumerated in his will. The log cabins used as the White House retreat on the Rapidan River in Virginia were given by him to the Shenandoah National Park. Much of President Hoover's money was given to charity. His salary as President was $75,000 per year, and after 1958 he received a pension of $25,000 per year.

Hoover's remains were removed to the Capitol to lie in state for two days, after which he was buried near his cottage in West Branch.

President Hoover fishing on the Rappadan River.

Text of the Will of Herbert C. Hoover

I, *HERBERT HOOVER*, a resident of the City, County and State of New York, hereby make, publish and declare this as and for my Last Will and Testament, hereby revoking all former wills and codicils heretofore made by me.

FIRST

I give and bequeath to *COSTA BORIS*, if he shall survive me, and to *LORETTA CAMP*, if she shall survive me, the sum of Ten thousand dollars ($10,000) each.

SECOND

I give and bequeath to *HERBERT HOOVER, JR., ALLAN HOOVER* and *NORTHCUT ELY*, as Trustees, the sum of Fifty thousand dollars ($50,000), to deposit the same in an interest-bearing bank or savings account and to dispose of the principal and interest thereof as follows:

1. To pay the net income thereof to *BERNICE MILLER* during the trust term.

2. To transfer and pay over to *BERNICE MILLER* annually the sum of Five thousand dollars ($5,000) out of principal.

3. Upon the termination of the Trust, to transfer and pay over the principal then remaining to my Executors to be added to and disposed of as part of my residuary estate.

4. This Trust shall terminate upon the death of *BERNICE MILLER* or upon the payment to her of all the funds held in trust, whichever shall first occur.

THIRD

I give and bequeath the sum of Thirty thousand dollars ($30,000) to each of the following persons who shall survive me:

ELIZABETH DEMPSEY
MAOMI YEAGER

I give and bequeath to *HUGO MEIER*, if he shall survive me, the sum of Five thousand dollars ($5,000).

I give and bequeath to *EVELYN MARSHALL*, if she shall survive me, and be employed by me at the time of my death, the sum of Ten thousand dollars ($10,000), and I direct my Executors to pay this legacy in three equal annual installments. In the event of her death before the payment of any or all of the said installments, I direct that the balance shall be added to and become a part of my residuary estate.

I give and bequeath to any members of my secretarial staff, other than those named above, who shall survive me, who are employed by me at the time of my death and who have served more than nine (9) months in such employment, the sum of Three thousand dollars ($3,000) each.

I give and bequeath to my Executors, hereinafter named, the sum of One thousand five hundred dollars ($1,500), and without imposing any legal obligation upon them, I would like them to know that I desire, but do not direct, that they distribute this legacy among the Waldorf-Astoria Hotel servants in such proportions as they shall, in their absolute discretion, determine.

FOURTH

As evidence of my affection, I give and bequeath to my son, *HERBERT HOOVER, JR.*, if he shall survive me, my painting of the Desert Scene by Groll and my painting of the Boy and the Tigers which he already has in his home, the portrait of myself by Peacock now hanging in the Hoover Institution on War, Revolution, and Peace, and the print of the Lincoln Cabinet now in my apartment at the Waldorf-Astoria Hotel, and the painting of Benjamin Franklin. And, I also give and bequeath to my son, *HERBERT HOOVER, JR.*, if he shall survive me, and to his wife, *MARGARET W. HOOVER*, if she shall survive me, the sum of Five thousand dollars ($5,000) each.

I give and bequeath to my son, *ALLAN HOOVER*, if he shall survive me, the portrait of Mrs. Hoover by Delaslo and the painting of the Flemish Girl.

All my other paintings hanging in my apartment at the Waldorf-Astoria Hotel I give and bequeath to my sons *HERBERT HOOVER, JR.* and *ALLAN HOOVER*, to be divided among them in such manner as they may agree upon, or, if they do not agree within ninety (90) days after my death, by my Executor, *NORTHCUT ELY*, in as nearly equal shares as he shall deem practicable.

I give and bequeath to *THE HERBERT HOOVER PRESIDENTIAL LIBRARY*, at West Branch, Iowa, all of my medals, wherever located.

I give and bequeath all my personal belongings and other tangible personal property not otherwise disposed of in this my Will, to my daughters-in-law, *MARGARET W. HOOVER*, and *MARGARET C. HOOVER*, if they shall survive me, or if only one shall survive me, all to such survivor, to be divided among them in such manner as they may agree upon, or, if they do not agree within nineth (90) days after my death, by my Executors in as nearly equal shares as they shall deem practicable.

FIFTH

I give and bequeath to *THE HOOVER FOUNDATION, INC.*, of New York, all of my memorabilia, documents, personal papers and books, which may be in storage in the State of California, and those located in my apartment in New York City and elsewhere.

Without imposing any legal obligation on the directors or officers of *THE HOOVER FOUNDATION, INC.*, I would like them to know that:

1. I desire, but do not direct, that all my papers relating to relief to overseas peoples be given by *THE HOOVER FOUNDATION, INC.*, to *THE HOOVER INSTITUTION ON WAR, REVOLUTION, AND PEACE* at Stanford University, under such conditions as *THE HOOVER FOUNDATION, INC.*, may impose.

2. I desire, but do not direct, that all my books and papers and memorabilia other than the above should be given by *THE HOOVER FOUNDATION, INC.*, to *THE HERBERT HOOVER PRESIDENTIAL LIBRARY* at West Branch, Iowa, as provided in my letter of donation to the United States of December 15, 1960, subject to the conditions mentioned therein in Annex A attached to that letter, and subject to such other conditions as *THE HOOVER FOUNDATION, INC.*, may determine.

SIXTH

ALL THE REST, RESIDUE AND REMAINDER of my property, real and personal, of whatsoever kind and nature and wheresoever situated, including any property to which I may in any way be entitled (excepting, however, any property over which I may have a power of appointment by will), hereinafter referred to as my "residuary estate", I give, devise and bequeath as follows:

(a) One-third thereof to *THE NATIONAL BANK & TRUST COMPANY OF FAIRFIELD COUNTY* as trustee under a certain Trust Agreement made by me dated the 17th day of October, 1961, for the benefit of Allan Hoover, Jr., and others, to be added to the principal of said trust and to be disposed of in accordance with the terms of said Trust Agreement.

(b) One-third thereof to *THE NATIONAL BANK & TRUST COMPANY OF FAIRFIELD COUNTY* as trustee under a certain Trust Agreement made by me dated the 17th day of October, 1961, for the benefit of Andrew Hoover, and others, to be added to the principal of said trust and to be disposed of in accordance with the terms of said Trust Agreement.

(c) The remaining one-third thereof to *THE NATIONAL BANK & TRUST COMPANY OF FAIRFIELD COUNTY* as trustee under a certain Trust Agreement made by me dated the 17th day of October, 1961, for the benefit of Lou Henry Hoover, and others, to be added to the principal of said trust and to be disposed of in accordance with the terms of said Trust Agreement.

If for any reason the foregoing disposition of my said residuary estate or any part thereof is ineffective or invalid, then and in that event only, I do hereby give, devise and bequeath any such undisposed of portion of my said residuary estate to my son, *ALLAN HOOVER*, or if he shall not survive me, then to such of his descendants as shall survive me, in equal shares, *per stirpes*.

SEVENTH

I direct that I be buried in the grounds of my birthplace at West Branch, Iowa, and I wish the remains of my wife to be moved there.

EIGHTH

I appoint my sons *HERBERT HOOVER, JR.* and *ALLAN HOOVER*, and my friend, *NORTHCUT ELY*, of Washington, D.C., Executors of and Trustees under this my Will.

I direct that my Executors and Trustees, whether originally named herein or acting under subsequent appointment, shall not be required to file any inventory of their respective estates or to render their accounts annually or at any other stated periods that may otherwise be provided for by law, or to give any bond or undertaking for the faithful performance of their respective duties, and if notwithstanding this express direction any such bond shall be required by any law, statute or rule of court, no sureties shall be required thereon.

In addition to the powers conferred upon executors and trustees by law, I give my said Executors and Trustees with respect to any and all property, whether real or personal, belonging to me at the time of my death or which may at any time be held hereunder, whether constituting principal or accumulated income, the following powers, exercisable in their absolute and uncontrolled discretion, and without authorization by any court:

To retain such property; to sell, mortgage, lease or otherwise dispose of the whole or any part of any real or personal property belonging to me at the time of my death, or at any time held by him hereunder, at either public or private sale, on any terms (for cash or on credit); to invest and reinvest the same in any securities or other property, real or personal, domestic or foreign, income or non-income producing, including preferred and common stocks and interests in investment trusts, irrespective of whether any such investments are of the class permitted by law for fiduciaries; to manage, maintain, alter, improve, develop, lease, exchange or abandon such property, and to grant options for the purchase thereof; to consent to the modification or extension of any note, extend the time of payment of any bond, mortgage, open account indebtedness, claim or other obligation in favor of or against my estate and to compromise, settle or submit the same to arbitration on such terms as they may deem advisable; to borrow money, and to pledge or mortgage any such property for the payment of taxes or for any purpose which, in their judgment, will facilitate the administration of my estate; to exercise all conversion, subscription, voting and other rights of whatsoever nature, including (but not by way of limitation) stock options relating to any of my aforesaid property; to grant proxies, discretionary or otherwise, in respect thereto; to make any distributions in kind or in money, or partly in each; to assent to, participate in or oppose any type of reorganization, readjustment, recapitalization, consolidation, merger, combination, dissolution or any other action with respect to any corporation and to take any action in connection therewith; to carry on any business owned by me or in which I may be engaged at the time of my death for any period of time and to invest additional moneys in or make loans to any such business or partnership or to sell or liquidate the same; to employ and pay the compensation of accountants, custodians, legal or investment counsel and other agents; to exercise any options or elections available to my Executors pursuant to any of the income, estate or gift tax provisions of the United States Internal Revenue Code applicable to me or my estate; to hold property in the name of my Executors and Trustees without designation of any fiduciary capacity or in the name of a nominee or unregistered; to form corporations and to transfer any property thereto; to pay any expenses in connection with any of the foregoing; to make any division or distribution of property in kind or otherwise and to allot any property or an undivided interest therein to any part, fund or share under this my Will; and generally to do all such further acts and things and to exercise all such further powers as, in their opinion, may be or become necessary or desirable in the control, management, preservation and distribution of my estate and property.

NINTH

I direct that all inheritance, estate, transfer, succession, legacy and death taxes or duties upon property required to be included in my taxable estate whether or not passing under this Will, and any interest and penalties thereon, shall be paid out of my residuary estate disposed of under Article *SIXTH* hereof.

IN WITNESS WHEREOF, I have hereunto set my hand and seal this 31st day of August, 1964.

Herbert Hoover

THE FOREGOING INSTRUMENT was, on the day of the date thereof, signed, sealed, published and declared by *HERBERT HOOVER*, the Testator therein named, as and for his *LAST WILL AND TESTAMENT*, in the presence of us, who, at his request, in his presence and in the presence of each other, have hereunto subscribed our names as witnesses.

Henry S. Ziegler
150 East 73rd Street
New York, New York
Thomas P. Ford
131 E 66th St
New York, N.Y.

Notes on the Will of Herbert C. Hoover

HERBERT HOOVER DIED IN 1964 AT THE AGE OF 90. He lived for more than 31 years after leaving office, longer than any other President. Only John Adams, among the Presidents, was older when he died.

His Will, executed near the end of his life, exemplifies a number of aspects of modern will drafting. One of these is the use of a so-called pourover provision. Article Sixth, disposing of the residue of his estate, makes a gift in equal thirds to the trustee of three existing trusts identified with precision in the Will. In each case the terms of the gift are described simply "to be added to the principal of said trust and to be disposed of in accordance with the terms of said Trust Agreement." The reader of the Will is left in the dark on the disposition to be made of this property. One must have access to the trust agreements to know who is to receive it—and when and how.

The pourover provision receives its name from the testator's use of an existing trust as a receptable to which the will simply adds ("pours over") additional property. It has become a very commonly used technique in estate planning and drafting, because it coordinates efficiently the administration of assets transferred in two different ways by one individual. Either this coordination, or the privacy of disposition achieved, or both, may have been the motivating factor for its use here, and also in Article Seventh of President Eisenhower's Will. It is impossible to tell from the documents themselves.

Although the advantages of a pourover will for a testator who creates a trust during his life are evident, there was for a time some question about the validity of the provision. The terms of the trust instrument ultimately controlled the disposition of assets of the probate estate, but it was neither executed with the formalities required for a will nor intended to operate as a will. Thus, some feared that, though the *will* was executed with those formalities and that intent, the gift which it made in this form might not comply with the provisions of the statute defining the way in which a will must be executed. These doubts have been dispelled by the widespread enactment of a statute with the cumbersome name, the Uniform Testamentary Additions to Trusts Act.

The notes on the Will of Theodore Roosevelt discussed the usefulness of a power of appointment as a two-stage transfer of property. Since the second stage requires affirmative action by the donee of such a power to exercise it, one must examine the donee's will (or other writings) to determine whether the power has or has not been exercised. The donee's will may explicitly answer that question—which is to be desired—but it may not. If it does not, but contains a general residuary clause disposing of all otherwise undisposed of property, then the legal authorities are divided on whether or not such a clause shall be interpreted as showing an intent to exercise any such powers available.

The donee of a power need not know of its existence to exercise it. Moreover, the power need not even be in existence when the donee's will exercising the power is executed, though it must be by the time the donee dies and his will becomes effective. Thus, the draftsman of a will may feel it important to consider what it should say about the testator's action with respect to powers of appointment—even though neither the testator nor the draftsman know of any existing powers, or of any powers which another family member might be planning to create.

To provide the maximum property possible for the objects of his affection and bounty, a testator may wish to exercise any and all powers which he may have at the time of his death. This is known as a "blind exercise" of powers, and it is illustrated by Article Seventh of President Truman's Will. On the other hand, the exercise of powers of appointment may have serious undesirable effects; if so, a provision like the parenthetical exception in the first sentence of Article Sixth of President Hoover's Will is inserted to avoid any possible interpretation of the general language of the clause as showing an intent to exercise powers of appointment, known or unknown.

Article Eighth of President Hoover's Will illustrates another aspect of modern will and trust draftsmanship. In appointing Executors and trustees, the Article explicitly relieves them of procedures which would otherwise be required of them as Executors. These include: (1) a bond to guarantee proper conduct of their office; (2) the filing with the court at an early stage of an inventory listing the assets known to exist and thereafter to be accounted for; and (3) the periodic filing of accounts to report in detail what they have done. Article Eighth also confers on the fiduciaries, in addition to all the powers which they would have under law, a long list of powers which they would not have but for the explicit grant. These authorize them to do things which they would either clearly not be permitted to do, or as to which there might be serious doubt.

One example is the grant of powers with respect to investment, usually a trustee's most important responsibility. Blanket authority is given here to the Executors and Trustees to retain indefinitely property owned by the testator at his death (which would include his investments) and to make new investments in any kind of property whether or not it is of the class permitted by law for fiduciaries. The law of trust administration contains well-established criteria for measuring the suitability of investments held for trust purposes, but President Hoover and his draftsman chose to disregard

this conventional wisdom preferring instead to rely solely on the judgment of the fiduciaries uninhibited by customary legal restraints.

Broad grants of authority, such as these, are now common rather than unusual. They are included routinely by many legal draftsmen, a practice implying serious criticism of the law of estate and trust administration. They reveal a belief that procedures and restrictions on fiduciary action developed over centuries to protect those with an interest in an estate or trust against possible mismanagement actually have a negative value. Since each testator may, within limits, create rules for his particular estate or trust, the response to such a belief is to insert a set of rules of the sort illustrated here. A testator who does so is not indifferent to protection of the interests of those for whom he is making provision. He simply feels that those interests will be better protected in this way than through the application of the traditional rules.

The needs and preferences of an individual testator can be met by tailor-making his particular will or trust. The broader problem of reconsideration of a system that produces this response more frequently than not is the responsibility of the professions affected and of state legislatures. In recent years these considerations have been under intensive study which has borne fruit in the form of model statutes such as the Uniform Probate Code and the Uniform Trustee's Powers Act. These statutes, or others similar to them, have been enacted, in whole or in part, in a number of states, but the process of reform is far from complete.

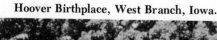

Hoover Birthplace, West Branch, Iowa.

FRANKLIN D. ROOSEVELT

F RANKLIN DELANO ROOSEVELT, the scion of
an aristocratic Dutch family that came to
America around 1636, was born at Hyde Park,
New York, on January 30, 1882. His father,
James Roosevelt, a millionaire country gentleman and railroad executive, was 53 years old
when Franklin was born; his mother Sarah Delano Roosevelt, was only 27. He was a fifth
cousin of Theodore Roosevelt, who became
President when Franklin was 19 years old.

After graduating from Groton, Franklin
entered Harvard in 1900, becoming president
of the college newspaper. He was also elected
to many of the student clubs. He had a keen,
alert mind and had finished Groton, a six-year
school, in four years, an ardent student of history and world affairs. Following graduation

from Harvard, Franklin attended Columbia
Law School and was admitted to the bar in
1907.

While at Harvard the 21-year-old
Roosevelt fell in love with his sixth cousin,
Anna Eleanor Roosevelt, whom he had known
since both were children. Both of her parents
had died by the time she was 10 and she had
been raised by her grandmother. When
Eleanor and Franklin were married in 1905,
the bride was given away by her uncle, President Theodore Roosevelt. In 1910 Roosevelt
was elected a state senator as a Democrat in
Republican Dutchess County, and soon
evinced extraordinary adroitness as a politician.

President Wilson appointed Roosevelt as
assistant secretary of the Navy and by 1920 he

197

Franklin D. Roosevelt in his Plymouth phaeton at Warm Springs, Georgia in 1933.

was so well known that he was chosen to run for Vice President by the Democratic convention; the Cox-Roosevelt ticket lost by a landslide. In the summer of 1921, at the age of 39, he was stricken with polio. Remaining active in politics during his recovery, Roosevelt campaigned on crutches for Governor of New York, and with the support of Al Smith won the election in 1928. Proving himself a strong Governor for four years, Roosevelt left the governorship in 1932 during the great Depression to run against Herbert Hoover. Roosevelt won the confidence of the disheartened people and was elected.

By 1914 six children had been born to Franklin and Eleanor. All were grown by the time they moved into the White House except one who died in infancy. Eleanor Roosevelt became an active First Lady, serving as a wife, mother, writer, and humanitarian. She was constantly traveling, lecturing, writing, teaching, speaking her mind, and working for causes she believed in.

When the Democrats held their convention in 1936, Roosevelt was still their most popular candidate. The Republicans chose Alfred M. Landon, who had been a successful Governor of Kansas; he carried only Maine and Vermont. Breaking all precedents and traditions, Roosevelt was elected to a third term in 1940 against Wendell Willkie, the Republican choice. In 1944 Roosevelt won a fourth term, this time defeating New York's Governor Thomas E. Dewey. His running mate was Harry S. Truman.

Roosevelt's fourth term was cut short by his death on April 12, 1945, of a cerebral hemorrhage in the Little White House at Warm Springs, Georgia.

Roosevelt directed in his will that his body be buried in the Rose Garden at Hyde Park after he learned that someone had suggested he be buried in the Washington National Cathedral. He also requested in his will that a simple stone be erected over his grave; both requests were carried out.

In 1939 he had deeded Hyde Park to the nation as a National Historic Site and a year later he dedicated the library adjacent to the house. Here he left his papers and personal mementoes. When the Roosevelt family waived their rights to life tenancy to Hyde Park on November 21, 1945, the house and library were opened to the public. Shortly after Franklin and Eleanor Roosevelt were married, Mrs. James Roosevelt built a home for her son and his wife adjoining hers at 49 East 65th Street in New York City.

Across the road from Hyde Park on a hill overlooking the Hudson River, Roosevelt built an informal house of stone and clapboard to serve as a cozy retreat, naming it Top Cottage. Here Mrs. Roosevelt spent much of her time after his death. Also used as a retreat was the family estate at Campobello, a small island in New Brunswick, Canada, 70 miles northeast of Mount Desert, Maine. A large rambling house built on four acres of land by Roosevelt's father, the place had served as a summer resort since Franklin's childhood days. Another Roosevelt retreat was a six-room cottage in Warm Springs, a Georgia spa with healing qualities in the water, where Franklin Roosevelt found relief from his illness. Early in 1927 the Georgia Warm Springs Foundation was incorporated as a non-profitmaking institution. Roosevelt invested half a million dollars, two thirds of his personal fortune, in the Foundation.

Most of Roosevelt's fortune was inherited from family holdings in a sugar refinery, banking, and railroads. His salary as state senator and as assistant Navy secretary would have been insufficient to support either his growing family or his prohibitively high personal medical expenses. Luckily, Eleanor Roosevelt had a private income of $7,500 a year and Franklin inherited $100,000 from his father and his step-brother. His mother left him $920,000 and the 600-acre estate at Hyde Park, which he in turn left to his wife. Roosevelt liked to invest in speculative investments, with indifferent results. He fared better with his stamp collection, a hobby he began in early childhood; following his death it fetched $250,000 at a public auction. All told, his estate amounted to $1,940,999 by the time of his death. Eleanor Roosevelt, who pursued an active career after the President's death, died on November 7, 1962, in her 78th year and was buried beside her husband at Hyde Park.

Facsimile of a segment of the Will.

EIGHTEENTH: The word "Trustees" wherever used in this Will shall be deemed to refer to the Trustees herein named or the survivors or survivor of them, or their successor or successors, and any bank or trust company which my Trustees may appoint pursuant to the provisions of Article FIFTEENTH hereof.————————

IN WITNESS WHEREOF, I have hereunto set my hand and seal and initialed each of the preceding nineteen pages hereof this /2 day of November, 1941.————————

Text of the Will of Franklin D. Roosevelt

I, FRANKLIN D. ROOSEVELT, residing in the Town of Hyde Park, County of Dutchess, State of New York, do hereby make, publish and declare this to be my Last Will and Testament, hereby revoking all other wills and codicils at any time heretofore made by me.

FIRST: I direct my Executors hereinafter named to pay and discharge all my just debts and funeral expenses as soon after my death as may be practicable.

SECOND: I direct that all transfer, estate and inheritance taxes and death duties and demands applicable to or payable on account of all gifts, devises and bequests made in and by the terms of this my Last Will and Testament be held chargeable to and payable out of the assets of my residuary estate and not chargeable to or payable by or collectible from the persons to whom or for whose benefit such gifts, devises and bequests are made.

THIRD: I direct that my Executors hereinafter named erect a simple stone over the grave of my wife and myself to be located in the garden of my property in the Town of Hyde Park, County of Dutchess and State of New York, preferably in accordance with directions left by me in a separate memorandum, the cost thereof to be paid by my Executors out of my residuary estate.

FOURTH: I give and bequeath to the RECTOR, WARDENS and VESTRY of ST. JAMES CHURCH, Hyde Park, Dutchess County, New York, of which I am Senior Warden, the sum of Five Thousand Dollars ($5,000.00) to be added to the Cemetery Fund and used for the upkeep of the Roosevelt family burial lots, the grave of my wife and myself, and for general cemetery upkeep purposes.

FIFTH: I give, devise and bequeath to GEORGIA WARM SPRINGS FOUNDATION, a New York membership corporation, all of the real estate located in Meriwether County, State of Georgia, owned by me at the time of my death, with all the buildings and improvements thereon, together with all personal property located thereon or therein or appurtenant thereto.

SIXTH: I give and bequeath to each of the persons who are my employees or servants at the time of my death and whose salaries or wages are at that time being paid by me personally the sum of One Hundred Dollars ($100.00).

SEVENTH: (A) If my wife, ANNA ELEANOR ROOSEVELT shall survive me, I direct that she shall have the right to use during her lifetime, at such place or places as she may wish, all or any part of the jewelry, books, paintings, pictures, works of art, statuary, silver, plate, china, glass, ornaments, rugs, tapestry, automobiles and boats and their equipment, household furniture and equipment and other tangible personal property of a similar kind or nature which I may own at the time of my death and wherever located, except such personal property bequeathed to Georgia Warm Springs Foundation under Article FIFTH of this Will; PRO-VIDED, HOWEVER, that my said wife shall select the articles of personal property to be used by her as aforesaid and shall notify my Executors in writing of the articles so selected by her within six (6) months after my death. Upon the receipt of such written notification by my Executors, my said wife may take possession of the arti-cles of personal property so selected by her, and my Executors shall have no further obligation or responsibility with respect to the personal property so selected, and I give and bequeath the remainder interest therein to my Trustees hereinafter named to dispose of in the manner hereinafter provided in Paragraph (F) of this Article SEVENTH.

No bond or other security shall be required of my said wife with respect to the personal property so selected or the use thereof by her, and my Trustees shall not be responsible or accountable for the proper use or preservation of such property.

(B) The articles of personal property not selected by my said wife as aforesaid, or, if my said wife shall not survive me, then all of said personal property described in Paragraph (A) of this Article SEVENTH may be selected by my children living at the time of my death and by my Executors for the issue than living of any deceased child or children of mine in the manner, shares and proportions hereinafter provided in Paragraph (C) of this Article SEVENTH, and I give and bequeath to my said children and, subject to the provisions of Paragraph (C) of this Article SEVENTH, to the said issue of any deceased child or children of mine all of the personal property so selected.

(C) Each child of mine and my Executors for the issue collectively of each de-ceased child of mine, if any, shall have the right to select any or all of the personal property hereinabove referred to in Paragraph (B) of this Article SEVENTH, pro-vided, however, that the aggregate value of the articles of personal property selected by each such child and the aggregate value of the articles of personal property selected by my Executors for the issue collectively of each deceased child of mine shall not exceed one fifth (1/5th) of the total value of the personal property hereinabove referred to in Paragraph (B) of this Article SEVENTH as appraised for the purpose of fixing the New York State estate tax.

Such selections shall be made by the unanimous agreement of my children, or, if there be any deceased child or children of mine leaving issue surviving, then by the unanimous agreement of my children and my Executors within three (3) months after my death, if my said wife shall not survive me, or, in case my wife shall sur-vive me, within three (3) months after the expiration of the time within which my said wife is to make her selection as provided in Paragraph (A) of this Article SEVENTH, or within three (3) months after notification by my Executors by regis-tered mail that such selection by my said wife has been made, whichever period shall first expire.

My Executors are hereby authorized to enter into such agreement as aforesaid with my children for and on behalf of the issue of any deceased child or children of mine, and in making such agreement my Executors shall represent such issue and stand in their place and stead for all purposes germane hereto, whether such issue or any of them be under or over the age of twenty-one (21) years, and such agreement shall be absolutely and irrevocably binding upon all such issue; but no right or title in or to any such personal property shall vest in any of such issue whether or not such issue or any of them be under or over the age of twenty-one (21) years unless and until said Executors shall have made the division and delivery thereof provided for in the next to the last paragraph of this Paragraph (C).

If my children, or if there be any deceased child or children of mine leaving issue surviving, then if my children and Executors cannot within the period of time herein provided reach a unanimous agreement as to the articles of said personal property to be selected as aforesaid, then such selections shall be made by my children and by my Executors for the issue collectively of any deceased child or children of mine in the order of the seniority of my children, starting with the oldest child, the issue collectively of any deceased child of mine to take the place of his, her or their parent in the order of selection. Such selection shall be made by my oldest child, or, if such child shall not be then surviving but shall leave issue then surviving, then by my Executors for the issue collectively of such child within three (3) months after my death, if my said wife shall not survive me, or, in case my wife shall survive me, within three (3) months after the expiration of the time within which my said wife is to make her selection as provided in Paragraph (A) of this Article SEVENTH, or within three (3) months after notification by my Executors by registered mail that such selection by my said wife has been made, whichever period shall first expire, and thereafter each child or my Executors for the issue collectively of any deceased child shall have a similar three-months' period within which to select after the expiration of the time allowed such next older child, or notification by my Executors by registered mail that the selection shall have been made by the next older child, whichever date is earlier.

No selection of personal property hereunder by any child of mine shall be deemed to be properly made unless the same be in writing, clearly identifying the property selected, and mailed or delivered to my Executors within the period specified herein for the making of such selection. Upon the receipt by my Executors or any of them of such written notification as aforesaid and the determination by my Executors, in their sole discretion, that the total value of the personal property so selected has not exceeded the share of the appraised value permitted to be selected by such child, the person making such selection shall be permitted to take possession of the personal property so selected and my Executors shall have no further responsibility or obligation with respect thereto.

In making selections for the issue of any deceased child or children of mine, the judgment of my Executors concerning the articles to be selected, the propriety thereof and the relative value thereof shall be binding and conclusive upon all persons interested in my estate, and no right or title in or to any of my said personal property so selected by my Executors shall vest in any of such issue, whether or not such issue or any of them are over or under the age of twenty-one (21) years, unless and until said Executors shall have made the division and delivery thereof provided for in the paragraph immediately following.

My Executors shall divide among the issue of any deceased child, whether or not such issue or any of them are over or under the age of twenty-one (21) years, for whom selections have been made hereunder by agreement or otherwise, the personal property so selected, and their judgment in making such division shall be final and binding on all persons interested in my estate; PROVIDED, HOWEVER, that my Executors may hold, during the minority of any person or persons for whom selections have been made hereunder by agreement or otherwise, the personal property so selected and shall deliver said property to such person or persons when he, she or they respectively attain the age of twenty-one (21) years; or my Executors may, if they so elect, deliver such property to a parent or any legally appointed guardian of the property of such minor or minors, and upon making such delivery my Executors may obtain from such parent or guardian a receipt for such property and they shall thereupon be relieved from all responsibility or obligation in regard to such property and shall not be accountable for the application that the parent or guardian may make thereof.

Whenever under this Paragraph (C) my Executors are permitted or required to give any notice, they shall not, when acting for the issue of any deceased child or children of mine in the manner herein provided, be required to give said notice to any of the issue of said deceased child or children whether or not such issue or any of them are over or under the age of twenty-one (21) years.

(D) I request my children and if there be any deceased child or children of mine leaving issue surviving, then also my Executors, to select only such articles of personal property as my children and the issue of any deceased child or children of mine may be in a position to use personally in their own homes. I further request my said wife, children, Executors and issue of deceased children, if any, that upon the occupancy of the main house at Hyde Park, Dutchess County, New York, by the Government of the United States, the greater part of the personal property situate therein or used in connection therewith be given to the Government so that the general character of the house be not altered, but this request shall not be construed as a restriction or limitation on the right of my said wife, children and Executors to select, as hereinabove in this Article SEVENTH provided, such of the personal property as my said wife, children and/or issue of any deceased child or children of mine may wish for personal use in their own homes.

(E) All of the said personal property not so selected by my said wife, my children and my Executors for the issue of any deceased child or children of mine, as hereinabove in this Article SEVENTH provided, shall be offered by my Executors as a gift to the Government of the United States for display at the Franklin D. Roosevelt Library or at the Roosevelt main house at Hyde Park, Dutchess County, New York; provided, however, that my Executors shall have the right, in their sole discretion, to fix the time within which the Government of the United States shall elect to accept all or any part of the said personal property. All of the said personal property not selected by my said wife, my children and my Executors for the issue of any deceased child or children of mine, and/or accepted by the Government of the United States as hereinabove in this Article SEVENTH provided, may be sold by my Executors in whole or in part at public or private sale or sales, at such time or times and upon such terms and conditions as they, in their sole discretion, may deem advisable.

(F) If my said wife shall survive me and shall select personal property as hereinabove provided in Paragraph (A) of this Article SEVENTH, then I direct that upon her death my Trustees shall dispose of the articles of personal property selected by her, as aforesaid, in the same manner, shares and proportions and upon the same terms and conditions as set forth above in Paragraphs (C) and (E) of this Article SEVENTH for the disposition of the personal property not selected by my said wife, except that the period within which selections shall be made shall be measured from the date of death of my said wife and the value to be used for such personal property shall be the value thereof as of the date of death of my said wife as my Trustees shall in their sole discretion determine. My Trustees shall have and possess, with respect to the disposition of such personal property, all of the discretion, rights, powers, privileges and immunities granted to my Executors by such Paragraphs (C) and (E) of this Article SEVENTH. As to this property, I make the same requests as are set forth in Paragraph (D) of this Article SEVENTH.

(G) If, in selecting articles of personal property as hereinabove provided, any disputes or disagreements shall arise among or between my said children or any of them or between any child or children of mine and my Executors or Trustees, as the case may be, acting for and on behalf of the issue of any deceased child or children of mine, with respect to any of the said personal property or their respective rights thereto or the manner or method of selecting the same, then my Executors or Trustees, as the case may be, shall have the sole and final right to adjudge all said disputes or disagreements, and their decision in such case or cases shall be final and binding on all persons having any interest in my estate, and for the purpose of carrying out any such adjudication my Executors or Trustees, as the case may be, shall have the right to divide and/or distribute the property subject to any said disputes or disagreements to such children or issue of deceased children in such manner, shares and proportions as my Executors or Trustees, in their sole discretion, shall determine.

EIGHTH: All of the rest, residue and remainder of my estate, both real and personal, of whatsoever kind, nature and description, and wheresoever situate, of which I shall die seized or possessed, or to which I may be legally or equitably entitled at the time of my death, or over which I shall have any power of appointment (hereinafter, and heretofore in Articles SECOND and THIRD of this Will, referred to as "my residuary estate"), I give, devise and bequeath to my son, JAMES ROOSEVELT, and my friends, BASIL O'CONNOR, Esq., of 120 Broadway, New York, N. Y., and HENRY T. HACKETT, Esq., of Poughkeepsie, N. Y., IN TRUST, NEVERTHELESS, to hold, manage, sell, exchange, invest and reinvest the same, and every part thereof, and to collect, recover and receive the rents, issues, profits, interest and income thereof (hereinafter referred to as "income"), and, after deducting the commissions of the Trustees and the proper and necessary expenses in connection with the administration of the trust, to apply the balance of the income and distribute the principal of the trust fund, after deducting the Trustees' commissions thereon, in the amounts and manner hereinafter in this Article EIGHTH provided.

(A) If my said wife shall survive me, the Trustees shall first pay to her one half (1/2) of the net income of the trust fund, in quarterly instalments, and they shall also pay to her annually the balance, if any, of the net income of the trust fund remaining after making the payments provided for in Paragraph (B) of this Article EIGHTH, for and during the term of her natural life.

(B) During the lifetime of my said wife, if she shall survive me, the Trustees shall pay out of the remaining one half (1/2) of the net income of the trust fund to or for the account of my friend, MARGUERITE A. LE HAND, such sum or sums, at such time or times and in such manner as my Trustees, in their sole discretion, shall deem necessary and reasonable to discharge expenses incurred or which may be incurred by or for the said Marguerite A. Le Hand for medical attention, care and treatment during her lifetime. The Trustees are also authorized, but not directed, to pay out of the said remaining one half (1/2) of the net income of the trust fund to or for the account of the said Marguerite A. Le Hand, during the lifetime of my said wife, such sum or sums not exceeding a total of One Thousand Dollars ($1,000.00) per annum, at such time or times and in such manner as my Trustees, in their sole discretion, shall determine for maintenance and living expenses of the said Marguerite A. Le Hand. If the said Marguerite A. Le Hand shall survive both my said wife and myself, then upon the death of my said wife, or upon my death if my said wife shall not have survived me, the Trustees shall set apart from the principal of the trust fund such amount as they, in their sole discretion, shall deem necessary to carry out the provisions of this Paragraph and shall hold such principal upon a separate and independent trust and pay out the income and/or the principal thereof to or for the account of the said Marguerite A. Le Hand in the amounts and at the time or times and in the manner and for the purposes hereinabove in this Paragraph provided. Upon the death of the said Marguerite A. Le Hand, the Trustees shall assign, convey, transfer, pay over and distribute any principal then remaining in such trust fund, together with any income thereon, in equal shares to my children then living and the issue then living of any deceased children of mine, such issue to take *per stirpes* and not *per capita*.

(C) If my said wife shall survive me, the Trustees shall permit her to use during her lifetime, without cost or obligation except as hereinafter provided, the parcels or tracts of land which I may own at the time of my death situate on Campobello Island, New Brunswick, Canada, with the buildings and improvements thereon; provided, however, that she shall notify the Trustees in writing within six (6) months after my death of her intention to use such property, and provided further that she shall, at her own expense, keep the property in good repair; pay all taxes and assessments levied against or with respect to such property after my death; pay all costs of maintenance of the property; and continue to pay the same during her lifetime. No bond or other security shall be required of my said wife with respect to such property or the use thereof by her.

(D) Upon the death of my said wife, or if she shall not have survived me, then upon my death, the Trustees shall assign, convey, transfer, pay over and distribute one half (1/2) of the principal then remaining in the trust fund, together with all accumulations of income, if any, after making provision for the said Marguerite A. Le Hand as hereinabove in this Article EIGHTH provided, in equal shares to my children then living and the issue then living of any deceased children of mine, such issue to take *per stirpes* and not *per capita*.

The Trustees shall divide the remaining one half (1/2) of the principal of the trust fund into as many equal shares as there shall be children of mine then living and/or children of mine who shall then be deceased leaving issue then surviving, and shall set apart one share for the benefit of each such child then living and one share for the benefit of the issue collectively of each such deceased child.

The Trustees shall hold each such share set apart for the benefit of each child of mine then living upon a separate and independent trust, and shall manage, sell, invest and reinvest the same and every part thereof and collect, recover and receive the rents, issues, interest, income and profits thereof (hereinafter called "income"), and after deducting the commissions of the Trustees and the proper and necessary expenses in connection with the administration of the trust, shall pay the net income in quarterly instalments to such child for and during the term of such child's natural life.

Upon the death of each such child for whom a separate and independent trust has thus been established, the trust in respect of his or her share shall terminate and the Trustees shall assign, convey, transfer, pay over and distribute the principal of such trust fund, together with all accumulations of income, if any, to the then surviving issue of such child, in equal shares *per stirpes* and not *per capita*, and in default of such issue the Trustees shall assign, convey, transfer, pay over and distribute the said principal and accumulations of income, if any, as if the same were my personal property and I were then to die intestate and resident in the State of New York,

The Trustees shall hold each such share set apart for the benefit of the issue collectively of each such deceased child of mine upon a separate and independent trust during the lifetime of the person who shall be the youngest of the issue for whom such share has been set apart and who shall have been living at the time of my death, and shall manage, sell, invest and reinvest the same and every part thereof and collect, recover and receive the rents, issues, interest, income and profits thereof (hereinafter called "income"), and after deducting the commissions of the Trustees and the proper and necessary expenses in connection with the administration of the trust, shall pay the net income in quarterly instalments and in equal shares to such issue *per stirpes*; provided, however, that as to each of such issue who is under the age of twenty-one (21) years, the Trustees shall apply his or her portion of the net income of the trust fund, or such part thereof as the Trustees, in their sole discretion, may deem proper, for the support, maintenance and education of such minor, accumulating the balance, if any, until such minor shall attain the age of twenty-one (21) years, and thereupon the Trustees shall pay to such person the accumulations of income. Upon the death of such person who shall have been the youngest of such issue as aforesaid and who shall have been living at the time of my death, the trust for such issue shall terminate and the Trustees shall assign, convey, transfer, pay over and distribute the principal of such trust fund, together with all accumulations of income, if any, to such issue, in equal shares, *per stirpes*.

If the share for the benefit of the issue collectively of a deceased child of mine shall have been set apart, as hereinabove provided, upon the death of my said wife after my death, and if none of the issue then living of such deceased child shall have been living at the time of my death, then no trust of such share shall be created and the Trustees shall assign, convey, transfer, pay over and distribute such share to such issue, in equal shares, *per stirpes*.

(E) If, at the termination of any of the trusts herein in this Article EIGHTH created, or at the time any payments shall be made under Paragraph (D) of this Article EIGHTH, any portion of the principal of such trust fund or any portion of a share for the benefit of the issue collectively of a deceased child of mine, as the case may be, shall be payable to a minor, the Trustees are empowered to continue to hold such portion of the principal or share so payable in trust during the minority of such person and in such event shall manage, invest and reinvest the same and apply so much of the net income thereof as in their absolute judgment and discretion they may deem necessary for the maintenance, support and education of such minor, and shall accumulate the unexpended balance thereof until such minor attains the age of twenty-one (21) years, when the Trustees shall convey, assign, transfer and pay over the principal, together with all accumulations of net income thereon, absolutely to such person; or the Trustees may, if they so elect, pay such principal or income, or both, to a parent or any legally appointed guardian of the property of such minor entitled to the same, and upon making such payment the Trustees may obtain from such parent or guardian receipts for such principal or income, or both, as the case may be, and the Trustees shall thereupon be relieved from all responsibility in regard to such principal and income and shall not be accountable for the application that the parent or guardian may make thereof. The foregoing authority shall be construed as a power only and shall not operate to suspend the absolute ownership of such property by such minor or to prevent the absolute vesting thereof in him or her.

NINTH: The provisions herein contained for the benefit of my wife, Anna Eleanor Roosevelt, are and shall be in lieu of dower and of all other right, title and interest of any kind whatsoever in and to my estate.

TENTH: I authorize and empower my Executors and Trustees as follows:

I. To sell at public or private sale or sales and to lease, mortgage or exchange all or any part of my estate, wheresoever situate, at such times and upon such terms and conditions as they, in their sole discretion, may deem advisable, and to execute and deliver proper conveyances and transfers thereof.

II. At the risk of my estate and without responsibility to my Executors, to retain and in their sole discretion to turn over to my Trustees in the erection of the trust herein created, any property, stocks, bonds or other investments in which at the time of my death all or any portion of my estate shall be invested.

III. At the risk of the trust funds and without responsibility to my Trustees, to retain all or any part of the property, stocks, bonds or other investments in which, at the time of my death, any portion of my estate shall be invested and which shall be turned over by my Executors to my Trustees in the erection of the trust herein created, although not of the character authorized by law for trust investments, and, in their sole discretion, to sell, dispose of, call in or change the property and investments comprising the trust funds or any part thereof, and to invest and reinvest the same and the proceeds of the sale thereof or any uninvested funds, in such stocks, bonds or other securities as my Trustees, in their sole discretion, may deem proper, and in making such investments and reinvestments my Trustees shall not be limited to securities of the character authorized by law for trust investments. No purchaser upon any sale by my Trustees shall be bound to see to the application of the purchase money arising therefrom or to inquire into the validity, expediency or propriety of any such sale.

IV. To vote or consent in person or by proxy upon all stocks, bonds or other securities held by my Executors and/or Trustees; to exchange the securities of any entity for other securities issued by the same or by any other entity, at such times and upon such terms and conditions as they may deem proper; to deposit said securities with any protective or other representative committee; to consent to the reorganization, consolidation or merger of any entity, or to the sale or lease of its property, or any portion thereof, to any person or entity, or to the lease by any person or entity of his or its property, or any portion thereof, to such entity, and upon such reorganization, consolidation, merger, sale or lease, to exchange the securities held by them for the securities issued in connection therewith; to pay all assessments, subscriptions and other sums of money as they may deem expedient for the protection of their interests as holders of any stocks, bonds or other securities, and to exercise any option contained in any stocks, bonds or other securities for the conversion of the same into other securities, or to take advantage of any rights to subscribe for additional stock, bonds or other securities, and to make any and all necessary payments therefor, and generally to exercise in respect of all stocks, bonds or other investments or property held by them all rights, powers and privileges as are or may be lawfully exercised by any person owning similar property in his own right.

V. In their sole discretion, to cause the securities which may from time to time comprise my estate, or any part thereof, or the trust funds hereby created, or any part thereof, to be registered in their names as Executors or Trustees hereunder, as the case may be, or in their own names, or in the name of their respective nominee, or to take and keep the same unregistered, or to retain them, or any part thereof, in such condition that they will pass by delivery.

VI. To compromise and adjust any claims of whatsoever nature which may be made against, or in favor of, my estate, or the trust hereby created, upon such terms and in such manner as my Executors or Trustees, as the case may be, in their sole discretion, may deem advisable.

ELEVENTH: In dividing my estate, or any portion thereof, or the principal of the trust funds or any accumulated net income, or any portion thereof, into parts or shares, or in distributing the same, I authorize and empower my Executors or Trustees, as the case may be, in their sole discretion, to make such division or distribution in kind, or partly in kind and partly in money, and for the purpose of such division or distribution the judgment of my Executors or Trustees, as the case may be, concerning the propriety thereof and the relative value of properties allotted for such purpose shall be binding and conclusive upon all persons interested in my estate.

TWELFTH: I authorize and empower my Executors, in their sole discretion, to borrow any moneys which they may deem proper or convenient for the payment of any cash legacies and/or any taxes which, under Article SECOND of this Will, my Executors are directed to pay, and to secure such loans by the mortgage, pledge or hypothecation of any property in my residuary estate; and no person making any such loan to my Executors shall be bound to inquire into the expediency or propriety thereof, and the judgment of my Executors as to the necessity or propriety of any such loan shall be final and conclusive upon all persons interested in my estate.

THIRTEENTH: The Trustees are authorized and empowered in their uncontrolled discretion to purchase or receive any bonds, notes, shares of stock, or other securities for the trust funds at a premium or at a price in excess of the call or redemption price or the amount payable at maturity or on liquidation, as the case may be, and in any such case the Trustees shall not use any part of the income thereof to amortize or otherwise restore to principal such premium or excess, however large.

FOURTEENTH: Any dividend regularly payable in the stock of the corporation or association declaring or authorizing the same in respect of any stock held by the Trustees shall be considered income and may be sold by the Trustees, and all such stock dividends or proceeds from any sale thereof shall be distributed as income. Any occasional or irregular dividend payable in the stock of the corporation or association declaring or authorizing the same in respect of any stock held by the Trustees shall not be distributed as income but shall be retained by the Trustees as part of the principal of the trust funds. All cash dividends of any kind and nature whatsoever, excepting liquidating dividends, received by the Trustees on any shares of stock held hereunder shall be treated as income.

FIFTEENTH: I hereby nominate, constitute and appoint my son, JAMES ROOSEVELT, and my friends, BASIL O'CONNOR, Esq., and HENRY T. HAKKETT, Esq., as Executors of this my Last Will and Testament, and as Trustees of the trusts herein created.

If any of said persons named as Executors shall not survive me or shall fail to qualify, or, having qualified, shall resign, die or become incapacitated, as Executor hereunder, then I nominate, constitute and appoint as a co-Executor hereunder such bank or trust company having a principal office for the transaction of business in the City and State of New York as the remaining Executors or Executor herein named, or their successor or successors, shall, in their sole discretion, appoint.

If any of said persons named as Trustees shall not survive me or shall fail to qualify, or, having qualified, shall resign, die or become incapacitated, as Trustee hereunder, then I nominate, constitute and appoint as a co-Trustee hereunder such bank or trust company having a principal office for the transaction of business in the City and State of New York as the remaining Trustees or Trustee named herein, or their successor or successors, shall, in their sole discretion, appoint.

SIXTEENTH: I hereby expressly direct that no bond or other security shall be required of said Executors or Trustees, or any of them, in this or in any other jurisdiction, to secure the performance of their respective duties as such.

SEVENTEENTH: The word "Executors" wherever used in this Will shall be deemed to refer to the Executors herein named or the survivors or survivor of them, or their successor or successors, or any administrator c.t.a., and any bank or trust company which my Executors may appoint pursuant to the provisions of Article FIFTEENTH hereof.

EIGHTEENTH: The word "Trustees" wherever used in this Will shall be deemed to refer to the Trustees herein named or the survivors or survivor of them, or their successor or successors, and any bank or trust company which my Trustees may appoint pursuant to the provisions of Article FIFTEENTH hereof.

IN WITNESS WHEREOF, I have hereunto set my hand and seal and initialed each of the preceding nineteen pages hereof this 12th day of November, 1941.

FRANKLIN D. ROOSEVELT   (L.S.)

The foregoing instrument, contained on this and the preceding nineteen pages, was signed, sealed, published and declared by FRANKLIN D. ROOSEVELT as and for his Last Will and Testament, in the presence of us, the undersigned, who, in his presence and at his request, and in the presence of one another, have hereunto subscribed our names and addresses as attesting witnesses this 12th day of November, 1941.

Grace G. Tully   residing at 3000 Connecticut Ave., Wash., D.C.
Thomas J. Qualters   residing at 2036 B Fort Davis St., S.E.
                                              Washington, D.C.
William F. Snyder   residing at 173 Mayflower Ave., New Rochelle, N.Y.

Notes on the Will of Franklin D. Roosevelt

PRESIDENT ROOSEVELT'S WILL WAS EXE-CUTED IN NOVEMBER 1941, shortly before the outbreak of World War II. He died three years and a few months later, survived by his wife and five adult children. Mrs. Roosevelt died in 1962.

Article Seventh, disposing of his tangible personal property, is one of the more interesting aspects of this Will. President Roosevelt's basic thought here was simple. He did not wish to try to select items for particular individuals. He wanted Mrs. Roosevelt to be able to use any of these things which she might wish to have, imposing only the requirement that she identify them within a reasonable period. He wanted his children to have an opportunity too, either at his death or Mrs. Roosevelt's, to take those items which they would enjoy having in their own homes, and he wanted them to have an equal opportunity to share in these things. If a child of his should have died before having had that opportunity, he wanted the children of that child to take instead. All the rest of this kind of property was to be offered to the United States Government for library or museum purposes.

Yet seven of the 20 pages of the Will are devoted to this subject. It is an excellent example of drafting to cover all contingencies. Here these include various possible sequences of death, minority, disputes over particular items or over the value to attach to them, etc. Though none of the provisions here are redundant, many are addressed to events not likely to occur. The question of whether to cover all of these is one of preference of the individual testator and his draftsman. Perhaps President Roosevelt anticipated some problems on this subject. Many testators with comparable family situations prefer to avoid the problem by leaving all such items to one person with a request that they be shared with other family members. Others simply leave them to the family in defined fractional shares and trust to the good sense and good will of the parties to divide them without rancor or dispute.

Article Eighth disposes of the residue of the estate and creates Roosevelt's basic scheme of distribution of his property. This employed the use of trusts to provide the income to Mrs. Roosevelt for life (with a piece of half of the income carved out to provide, within limits, for his secretary, Miss Le Hand, in case of need.) At the death of Mrs. Roosevelt, the trust assets were to be divided into halves, one half being split up immediately among the children, the other half split into trusts, one for each child. The income from each trust is payable to the respective child for life. At his or her death, that trust is to be terminated and its assets paid out to the descendants of that child. Again, the draftsman has provided for all the possible contingencies. Probably it is more important to do so with respect to the residue than in disposing of one's personal property. Certainly, this kind of drafting is often seen at this place in wills.

This pattern of disposition of property has some definite advantages. It assures the testator that the income beneficiaries, usually those closest to him, will receive a gift which will be enjoyed as long as they live, and it permits him to make another gift of the property when they die. In the case of the property put into trust for each child, Roosevelt, in effect, made gifts of the same property to his wife, his children, and his grandchildren in that sequence. The trust device, of course, creates a framework for making such gifts and assures professional management of the property until the final gift becomes effective. An income beneficiary may feel, correctly, that the right to the income from property is considerably less than complete ownership of it. On the other hand, if one is temperamentally uncomfortable with invading principal, the difference is more theoretical than real.

An additional reason for using this pattern of distribution is found in the tax law. Unless an income beneficiary is given a general power of appointment, as that term is defined in the tax law, the death of that beneficiary is not treated as effecting a transfer of the property subjecting it to death taxes—even though another person then actually begins to enjoy the property. Here, as to the property allocated to the trust for each child, only the death of Roosevelt himself exposed the property to death taxes. As to that property, neither the death of his widow nor that of the child would be a taxable event. This is in contrast to a series of transfers outright, first to the widow, then by her to the children, then by them to the grandchildren. At each step in such a sequence, the property would be subject to tax. This difference, sometimes described as "saving the second tax," offers a large incentive for the creation of trusts with these characteristics. It is a frequently criticized feature of the tax law which could, of course, be changed, but which so far has demonstrated great vitality.

The Notes on the Will of John Adams refer to the difficulties of describing the method of division of property among takers who are, or could be, members of different generations. Roosevelt's use of trusts to last for the life of his wife, then for the life of a child, with property distributed finally only among the descendants of the child, presented this drafting problem. The fourth paragraph of Part (D) of Article Eighth illustrates one possible solution as expressed by a modern draftsman. The terms *per stirpes* (by stocks) and *per capita* (by the head) are part of the will draftsman's standard vocabulary though they are probably understood by few of the testators who sign the instruments containing them. They are used in spite of that because their meaning is precise and would be difficult to convert into English which is any more easily understood.

Perhaps the most interesting provision of Franklin Roosevelt's Will is one which was not included. He was the first President to see the desirability of arrangements under which the papers of a President, as well as some of the mementoes of his term in office, would be kept together in a special library and museum owned and operated for the public. Though the legislation which is now the basis for the crea-

tion of Presidential Libraries was not then in force, he took steps in his second term to establish such a library and transferred to it during his life a large volume of papers and other items.

However, at the time of his death, many papers were still in his possession. Traditional theory, acted upon by Washington and all his successors, was that a President's papers belonged to him. When Roosevelt died, his Will controlled the disposition of all of the property which he owned at his death, and his Will was silent on the subject of his papers.

The matter was resolved by a suit, apparently friendly, to determine whether or not he owned these papers at the time of his death or had given them away during life though retaining possession of them. In *Roosevelt's Will*, 73 N.Y.S.2d 821(1947), the court held the latter. Though both intent and delivery are required to make an effective gift, the court found that both elements are present. It held that the requirements were met by a constructive delivery coupled with an obvious intent to treat these papers like those already transferred. This uncertainty, and the suit needed to dispel it, would have been unnecessary had the draftsman of the Will foreseen the problem—and made the obvious provision for it. Compare, in this respect, the Wills of Presidents Truman, Hoover, Eisenhower, and Lyndon Johnson, all of which were drawn with the benefit of the Roosevelt experience.

Laprobe used by Franklin D. Roosevelt when riding in his automobile.

HARRY S. TRUMAN

Harry S. Truman was born in Lamar, Missouri, on May 8, 1884, the oldest of three children of John Anderson Truman, a livestock dealer and mule trader, and Martha Ellen Young Truman. The house in which he was born had been bought two years earlier for $685. Because of a family controversy as to whether his middle name should be Solomon or Shippe (the names of his two grandfathers), a compromise left him with an initial that could stand for either.

When Harry was a boy of five, his parents moved into a $4,000 house in Independence, Missouri, where he grew to manhood. His first job was that of bank clerk. He had been rejected by West Point because of poor vision, and he never went to college. He left his job to return to the 600-acre family farm at Grandview 20 miles from Independence, where he spent 12 years as a farmer until he was 33.

In World War I, Truman, a member of the National Guard, helped recruit a unit of the Missouri artillery. He was promoted to first lieutenant and saw action in France. He left the military with the rank of captain.

On June 28, 1919, Truman married his childhood sweetheart, Elizabeth (Bess) Wallace, whose father owned a prosperous flour mill. Following a short honeymoon, the Trumans returned to live with Bess's mother at 219 North Delaware Street in Independence, in the very house they would someday inherit and live in the remainder of their life. Except for a brief time when they rented an apartment for $125 a month in Washington, D.C., while Truman was Senator and Vice President, and their residence in the White House and Blair House in the Presidential years, this was their only home.

After his marriage, Truman opened a haberdashery in Kansas City, Missouri, with an old army comrade. The business failed in 1922, leaving him deeply in debt. He refused to declare bankruptcy, however, and insisted on paying off all his debts.

That same year Truman was elected to his first political office, one of three administrators of Jackson County (which includes Kansas City), with the aid of the political machine of Tom Pendergast, Democratic boss of Kansas City. At this time he began to attend the Kansas City School of Law. His next elected office was in 1926 when he was chosen presiding judge (administrator) of Jackson County; he was reelected for two additional terms, suffering only one defeat before 1934, when he was elected U.S. Senator. He was reelected in 1940, and in 1944 President Franklin D. Roosevelt picked Truman as his running mate. Inaugurated in January, 1945, the President died less than three months later without ever having briefed his Vice President on the major issues confronting the nation. Truman soon set about initiating his own policies.

As Senator, Truman had lived frugally, with his wife serving as his secretary. Nonetheless, in 1940 he had been forced to borrow $3,000 against his life-insurance policy to finance his reelection campaign for the Senate. That same year the mortgage was foreclosed on his 81-year-old mother's farm. When Truman assumed the office of President his salary increased from $30,000 plus a tax-free $10,000 expense account to $75,000 with a $20,000 tax-free expense account. This was raised by Congress on January 19, 1949, to $100,000 in salary and $50,000 as expense account. (In 1951 the expense account became subject to income tax.)

In 1948, the Republicans, scenting victory, nominated New York Governor Thomas E. Dewey as their candidate. The Democrats,

somewhat reluctantly, chose Truman to be their standard-bearer. Undaunted, Truman conducted a "whistle-stop" campaign, traveling 31,700 miles for 35 days. The Republicans were confident of victory; the Chicago *Tribune* even printed its morning edition with headlines "DEWEY DEFEATS TRUMAN," and on the eve of the returns many radio announcers excitedly proclaimed a Dewey victory. But Truman won the election.

Following the war and the death of President Roosevelt, the White House was closed to official entertaining until November 1946. Mrs. Truman took a businesslike approach to running the White House and never accepted the formal role as First Lady, preferring a quiet, private life. The First Family spent the second Truman Administration across the street in Blair House, while the White House underwent a complete renovation costing $5,761,000 and lasting three years. At Blair House, they entertained on a limited scale, renting Prospect House in nearby Georgetown, D.C., as the official guest house of the President. In 1952, nine months before he left office, the Trumans moved back into the rebuilt White House.

Truman had no regrets about leaving the White House on January 20, 1953, for Independence. During his retirement he witnessed the marriage of his only daughter, Margaret, to E. Clifton Daniel, a journalist. He received a pension of $25,000 a year plus $50,000 for office expenses under an act of Congress passed in the fall of 1958. A project particularly close to his heart became the planning of the Harry S. Truman Library and Museum. According to the Truman Library, the Truman papers comprise an estimated 5.5 million documents. The library was dedicated in 1957, built with money, part of which (the final million dollars) was raised on a speaking schedule conducted by Truman. He also found time to publish his memoirs before his death on December 26, 1972. He was buried on the grounds of the Library, one of few Presidents not brought back to the nation's capital to lie in state. His funeral was confined strictly to his hometown of Independence as he had wished.

Text of the Will of Harry S. Truman

I, HARRY S. TRUMAN, of Independence, Missouri, do hereby make, publish and declare this to be my Last Will and Testament.

FIRST: I revoke all wills and codicils heretofore made by me.

SECOND: I request that my debts and my funeral and administration expenses be paid as promptly as shall be practicable.

THIRD: A. I have from time to time during my life given and transferred to the United States of America all of my right, title and interest in, and possession of, certain papers, historical materials and other property, to be kept in the Harry S. Truman Library in Independence, Missouri, on certain conditions enumerated in correspondence between me and the Administrator of General Services of the United States and the Archivist of the United States.

B. I hereby bequeath to the United States of America all of my right, title and interest in, and possession of, the following property:

I. All of my remaining papers as United States Senator, as Vice-President of the United States and as President of the United States, other than those thereof (a) which shall contain a label or other indication showing a reservation of title in me, or (b) which shall be determined by my Executors in their sole and absolute discretion to be related in whole or in part to the business or personal affairs of myself or any of the members of my family (which shall, for the purposes of this Will, include my wife, daughter, brother, sister, nephews and nieces).

II. All of my remaining historical materials, which shall, for the purposes of this Will, include all cartoons, books, portraits, statues, objets d'art, models, pictures and miscellaneous objects or materials having historical or commemorative values, other than those thereof (a) which shall be located at the time of my death in my private residence in Independence, Missouri or in any other private residence which I or my daughter may have at such time, or (b) which shall contain a label or other indication showing a reservation of title in me, or (c) which shall be determined by my Executors in their sole and absolute discretion to be related in whole or in part to the business or personal affairs of myself or any of the members of my family.

C. The bequest made in part B of this Article THIRD is made subject to the following conditions:

I. That all papers and historical materials so bequeathed shall be kept permanently in the said Harry S. Truman Library, subject, however, to the right of the Archivist of the United States in his sole and absolute discretion (a) to make temporary loans thereof to such persons, organizations or institutions as he shall so determine, (b) to dispose, by sale, exchange, gift or otherwise, of any such papers or historical materials which he in his sole and absolute discretion shall determine in writing to have no permanent value or historical interest or to be surplus to the needs of the said Harry S. Truman Library, or (c) to remove from the said Harry S. Truman Library any and all such papers or historical materials which he in his sole and absolute discretion shall determine to be necessary to preserve them from threatened destruction.

II. That all papers and historical materials so bequeathed shall be fully accessible to my wife, daughter and the members of the committee created by the provisions of Article FIFTH hereof.

FOURTH: A. It is my purpose to make the papers and historical materials bequeathed pursuant to the provisions of part B of Article THIRD hereof available for the purpose of study and research as soon as possible and to the fullest possible extent. "However, since the President and the Vice-President of the United States are the recipients of many confidences from others, and since the inviolability of such confidences is essential to the functioning of the constitutional offices of the Presidency and the Vice-Presidency, it will be necessary to withhold from public scrutiny certain papers and historical materials and classes of papers and historical materials for varying periods of time." Therefore, for the time being, as a condition of said bequest, the following classes of papers and historical materials shall be withheld from inspection by, and their contents shall be kept confidential and shall not be divulged to, anyone (including public officials), other than (i) regular employees of the National Archives and Records Service performing normal archival services on such papers and historical materials under the general supervision of the Archivist of the United States, and (ii) my wife, daughter and the members of the committee created by the provisions of Article FIFTH hereof:

I. Papers and historical materials that are classified as to secrecy and security pursuant to law, which classification shall be reviewed from time to time.

II. Papers and historical materials containing statements which may in any manner injure, embarrass or harass any living person or the living members of the family of any deceased person.

III. Papers and historical materials which may in any manner be prejudicial to the conduct of foreign relations with any government.

IV. Papers and historical materials containing statements made by or to me in confidence in any official capacity.

B. Subject to the approval of the committee created pursuant to the provisions of Article FIFTH hereof, the employees of the National Archives and Records Service may perform the classification services necessary pursuant to the provisions of part A of this Article FOURTH and may place any withheld papers and historical materials in special files where, for the time being, they shall be available only to my wife, daughter and the members of said committee.

C. All papers and historical materials withheld pursuant to the provisions of this Article FOURTH shall be reexamined from time to time by employees of the National Archives and Records Service under the direction of the Archivist of the United States, and, subject to the approval of the committee created pursuant to the provisions of Article FIFTH hereof, shall be opened to general use as soon as the passage of time or other circumstances have in the sole and absolute discretion of said committee removed the conditions that justify their being temporarily withheld.

D. It is my wish, subject to such rules and regulations as the Archivist of the United States shall prescribe, that *all competent private persons* interested in using the papers and historical materials bequeathed pursuant to the provisions of part B of Article THIRD hereof for *purposes of serious scholarly research* shall be granted equal access to those of such papers and historical materials not withheld pursuant to the provisions of this Article FOURTH.

FIFTH: The committee referred to in Articles THIRD and FOURTH hereof shall consist of the first named three persons from the following list who shall survive me:

A. Charles S. Murphy, formerly my special counsel.
B. David D. Lloyd, formerly of the White House staff.
C. Admiral Robert Dennison, formerly my naval aide.
D. Admiral Sidney Souers, formerly one of my assistants.
E. Samuel I. Rosenman, formerly my special counsel and now my lawyer.
F. Matthew Connelly, formerly my secretary.

In the event that any member of said committee shall die after me, he shall be replaced by the next named survivor.

SIXTH: I bequeath all of my papers and historical materials not bequeathed to the United States of America pursuant to the provisions of part B of Article THIRD hereof (a) to my wife and my daughter, in equal shares, if they shall both survive me, or (b) if only one of my wife and daughter shall survive me, to that one, or (c) if neither my wife nor my daughter shall survive me, to the issue of my daughter who shall survive me, in equal shares per stirpes, or (d) if none of my wife, my daughter and the issue of my daughter shall survive me, to the United States of America to be treated by the United States of America in the same manner as the papers and historical materials bequeathed to the United States of America pursuant to the provisions of said part B.

SEVENTH: All of the rest, residue and remainder of my property, real, personal and mixed, of whatsoever kind and nature and wheresoever situated, of which

I shall die seized or possessed, and all property in which I shall have any interest, and all property over or with respect to which I shall have any power of appointment, remaining after provision for the payment of my debts and my funeral and administration expenses and after provision for the distribution of those which shall become effective of the bequests provided for in part B of Article THIRD hereof and in Article SIXTH hereof, is hereinafter referred to as "my Remaining Estate".

EIGHTH: If my wife shall survive me, and if any (or all) of my daughter and her issue shall also survive me, I devise and bequeath to my Trustees hereunder property having a value equal to the aggregate value at the time of my death of all assets not hereby disposed of which "passed" (within the meaning of Section 2056(a) of the Internal Revenue Code of 1954), whether or not by reason of my death, from me to my wife and with respect to which a deduction will be allowed in determining the value of my "taxable estate" (as defined in Section 2051 of said Internal Revenue Code), in trust nevertheless, to add the same to my Residuary Estate, and to dispose of the same, with my Residuary Estate, in the manner provided in Article FOURTEENTH hereof. I direct that the devise and the bequest to my Trustees hereinbefore in this Article EIGHTH provided for shall be distributed out of that portion of my Remaining Estate remaining after setting apart the property described in parts A to D, inclusive, or Article TENTH hereof and in Article ELEVENTH hereof.

NINTH: All of the rest, residue and remainder of my Remaining Estate, remaining after provision, if my wife shall survive me and if any (or all) of my daughter and her issue shall also survive me, for the distribution of the devise and the bequest provided for in Article EIGHTH hereof, is hereinafter referred to as the "Balance of my Remaining Estate".

TENTH: If my wife shall survive me, and if any (or all) of my daughter and her issue shall also survive me, I devise and bequeath to my wife one-half of the Balance of my Remaining Estate. I direct that said one-half of the Balance of my Remaining Estate shall include the following property:

A. All of my jewelry, clothing and personal effects.

B. Any automobiles which I shall own at the time of my death.

C. All of the household furniture, furnishings and equipment, rugs, silverware, plated ware, china, glassware, linens, books, paintings, pictures and objets d'art which I shall own at the time of my death, other than the property referred to in part B of Article THIRD hereof and in Article SIXTH hereof.

D. All farm machinery and equipment, gardeners', mechanics' and other tools and domestic animals which I shall own at the time of my death.

ELEVENTH: I devise to Grandview Lodge No. 618, A. F. & A.M., as a site for a Lodge Hall, the southerly one hundred and ten feet of Lots 9 and 10 in Sheltons Addition to Grandview, Missouri.

TWELFTH: I direct that all estate, transfer, inheritance, legacy, succession and similar taxes upon or in respect of all property, or interest. therein, other than the property referred to in part B of Article THIRD hereof or any interest therein, which shall be included, under the laws of any or all of the United States, the State of Missouri and all other governments and governmental subdivisions, in my gross estate for the purpose of the determination of the amount of any such taxes, whether or not all of such property, or interest therein, is hereby disposed of, shall be paid out of that portion of the Balance of my Remaining Estate remaining after provision for the distribution of those which shall become effective of the devises and the bequest provided for in Articles TENTH and ELEVENTH hereof, and I direct that, to the extent that the devises and the bequests provided for in Articles SIXTH and EIGHTH hereof and in said Articles TENTH and ELEVENTH shall become effective, the property thereby disposed of shall be distributed to the respective persons entitled thereto (including my Trustees) free of all such taxes, that, if my wife shall survive me and if any (or all) of my daughter and her issue shall also survive me, the trust created by the provisions of said Article EIGHTH shall be established, and the income therefrom and the principal thereof paid to the respective persons entitled thereto, free of all such taxes, and that all property included in my gross estate for the purpose of any such determination and not hereby disposed of shall be paid to and held by the respective persons entitled thereto free of all such taxes.

THIRTEENTH: All of the rest, residue and remainder of the Balance of my Remaining Estate, remaining after provision for the distribution of those which shall become effective of the devises and the bequest provided for in Articles TENTH and ELEVENTH hereof and after provision for the payment of the taxes directed to be paid by the provisions of Article TWELFTH hereof, is herein referred to as "my Residuary Estate".

FOURTEENTH: If my wife shall survive me, and if any (or all) of my daughter and her issue shall also survive me, I devise and bequeath my Residuary Estate to my Trustees hereunder, in trust nevertheless, to hold the same, and also the property devised and bequeathed to them by the provisions of Article EIGHTH hereof and added to my Residuary Estate pursuant to the provisions of said Article EIGHTH, and to invest and reinvest all thereof, and to receive and collect the income therefrom, and to dispose of the net income therefrom and the principal thereof as follows:

A. During the life of my wife, my Trustees shall pay the net income from said trust to her. Said payments of said net income shall accrue to her from the date of my death.

B. My Trustees shall also at any time and from time to time, if my Trustees, other than my wife, in their sole and absolute discretion shall so determine, pay to my wife such portion or portions (including all) of the principal of said trust as my Trustees, other than my wife, shall so determine. I direct (i) that, in making any determination of whether or not any principal of said trust shall so be paid to my wife, and, if any such principal shall so be paid, of the amount thereof, my Trustees, other than my wife, shall consider only the interest of my wife and shall not consider the interest of any person entitled to receive the principal of said trust upon the death of my wife, (ii) that each such determination made by said Trustees shall be binding and conclusive upon my wife and upon the person or persons entitled to receive the principal of said trust upon the death of my wife, and (iii) that said Trustees shall not be under any liability to my wife or to any person or persons entitled to receive the principal of said trust upon the death of my wife either for failing to make or for making any such payment.

C. Upon the death of my wife, my Trustees shall pay over and distribute the principal of said trust then held by them (1) to my daughter, if she shall survive my wife, or (2) if my daughter shall not survive my wife, to and among the issue of my daughter who shall survive my wife, in equal shares per stirpes.

D. If my daughter and her issue shall all predecease my wife, then, notwithstanding the foregoing provisions of this Article FOURTEENTH, my Trustees shall, upon the death of the last survivor of my daughter and her issue, pay over and distribute the principal of said trust then held by them to my wife.

FIFTEENTH: If my wife shall survive me, and if neither my daughter nor any of her issue shall survive me, I devise and bequeath my Residuary Estate to my wife.

SIXTEENTH: If my wife shall not survive me, I devise and bequeath my Residuary Estate (1) to my daughter, if she shall survive me, or (2) if my daughter shall not survive me, to the issue of my daughter who shall survive me, in equal shares per stirpes.

SEVENTEENTH: The provisions herein made for my wife shall be in lieu of dower, homestead and all statutory marital rights she may have in my estate except such rights as she may have for maintenance at any time during the administration of my estate.

EIGHTEENTH: A. I direct that the word "issue", whenever used herein with respect to my daughter, shall be construed to mean (1) all of the legitimate blood descendants of my daughter and all of the legitimate blood descendants of each adopted person referred to in this part A and (2) all persons who shall have been adopted by my daughter or by any such legitimate blood descendant or by any person so adopted.

B. I authorize and empower my Executors to distribute and turn over to the respective devisees and legatees hereunder, including my Trustees, and I authorize my Trustees to accept and to continue to hold as principal of the trust hereby created, any or all real property and/or any or all personal property, tangible and intangible, held by my Executors at the time of such distribution. I authorize and empower my Trustees, upon the termination or earlier distribution, in whole or in part, of said trust, to make the payment and distribution of the principal thereof, or any portion thereof, in such property, real and personal, tangible and intangible, then held as such principal as my Trustees in their sole and absolute discretion shall determine. To the extent permitted by law, such distribution by my Executors and my Trustees shall be binding upon all persons interested in my estate and/or in the trust hereby created.

C. I hereby authorize my Executors and my Trustees, in the disposition of my estate and of the principal of the trust hereby created, if and to the extent that my Executors or my Trustees, as the case may be, in their sole and absolute discretion shall so determine and to the extent permitted by law:

I. To make the payment and distribution of any portion of my estate or of any such principal to which any infant shall be entitled to the parent of such infant, whether or not such parent shall be the legally appointed guardian of such infant.

II. Notwithstanding any direction herein contained to distribute any portion of my estate or of any such principal to any infant, to retain custody of all or any part thereof, and all or any of the income therefrom, until said infant shall attain his or her majority, and with respect thereto, to exercise all of the powers, and have all of the privileges and immunities, set forth in part B of this Article EIGHTEENTH, in this part C and in Articles TWENTIETH and TWENTY-FIRST hereof, and also at any time and from time to time, to pay to and/or apply to the care, education, maintenance and support and otherwise for the benefit of such infant all or any part of any such property and/or any such income therefrom then held by them, but I specifically direct that the interest of such infant in all property the custody of which is so retained, and all income therefrom, shall vest, only the right to possession thereof being postponed.

I direct that the written receipt of any parent referred to in division I of this part C for any money or other property paid or distributed pursuant to the provisions of said division I shall constitute a complete release to my Executors or my Trustees, as the case may be, for such money or other property.

D. I. If I and one or more of the persons entitled, under any of the provisions hereof, in the event that she or he or they shall survive me, to receive all or any part of my estate, or of the income from or the principal of the trust hereby created, shall die at or about the same time in or as a result of a common accident, catastrophe or other like cause, then, subject to the provisions of division III of this part D, I direct that, whether or not I shall actually have survived any such person or persons so dying, it shall be conclusively presumed for all purposes hereof that I have survived each such person so dying.

II. If, at any time while my wife shall be entitled to receive income from the trust hereby created, my wife and one or more of the other persons entitled, in the event that such other person or persons shall survive my wife, to receive all or any part of the principal of such trust shall die at or about the same time in or as a result of a common accident, catastrophe or other like cause, then, subject to the provisions of division III of this part D, I direct that, whether or not my wife shall actually have survived any such other person or persons so dying, it shall be conclusively presumed for all purposes hereof that my wife has survived each such other person so dying.

III. In the event that the application of any of the provisions of divisions I and II of this part D would result in invalidating in whole or in part the disposition, pursuant to any of the provisions hereof, of all or any part of my estate, or of all or any part of the income from or the principal of the trust hereby created, I direct that the provisions of said divisions I and II of this part D shall be applicable only to the extent, if any, that the application thereof shall not result in invalidating in whole or in part any such disposition of any part of my estate, or of the income from or the principal of the trust hereby created.

NINETEENTH: A. I nominate, constitute and appoint my wife, my daughter and The City National Bank and Trust Company of Kansas City (Kansas City, Missouri) as my Executors hereof and my Trustees hereunder.

B. I direct that, in the event of the death or resignation of either or both of my wife and my daughter or the failure or refusal of either or both of them to act as Executors hereof and/or Trustees hereunder, no alternate or successor Executors hereof and/or Trustees hereunder shall be designated.

C. In the event that at any time there shall be three Executors or three Trustees acting hereunder and authorized to act upon any matter in connection with or incident to the administration of my estate or the trust hereby created and they shall fail to agree upon such matter, the decision of a majority of such Executors or Trustees, as the case may be, authorized to act upon such matter shall be controlling.

D. In the event that at any time my daughter and said The City National Bank and Trust Company of Kansas City shall be acting as Trustees hereunder and they shall fail to agree upon whether or not the power granted to them by the provisions of part B of Article FOURTEENTH hereof shall be exercised and/or, if exercised, the extent and manner thereof, the decision of my daughter upon such exercise, and the extent to which and the manner in which the same shall be exercised, shall be controlling.

E. Whenever there shall be more than one Executor or more than one Trustee acting hereunder, such Executors and such Trustees may respectively at any time and from time to time, by a written instrument executed by both or all of them then acting, (1) designate one or more of them, severally or jointly, on behalf of both or all of them to execute all documents and other instruments, including, but not limited to, checks, drafts, notes, endorsements and instructions, and to have access to safe deposit boxes, and (2) change or revoke any such designation theretofore made.

F. I direct that, except to the extent required by law, no bond or other security shall at any time be required in any jurisdiction of any of my wife, my daughter and said The City National Bank and Trust Company of Kansas City for the faithful performance of their respective duties as Executors or Trustees.

TWENTIETH: I authorize my Executors, in the administration of my estate, and my Trustees, in the administration of the trust hereby created, in their sole and absolute discretion, to the extent permitted by law:

A. To hold and to continue to hold any or all real property and/or any or all personal property, tangible and intangible, owned by me at the time of my death, and, in the case of my Trustees, any or all such property, whether or not owned by me at the time of my death, received by them from my Executors, for such period or periods of time as they in their sole and absolute discretion shall determine, whether or not the same shall be income yielding, and whether or not the same shall constitute investments then authorized for fiduciaries by the laws of the State of Missouri or any other State.

B. To invest, reinvest and keep invested the proceeds of any or all property, real and personal, tangible and intangible, sold or otherwise disposed of, whether by way of exchange, liquidation or otherwise, by them in such bonds, stocks (including stocks of so-called "investment trusts"), securities, choses in action and/or other personal property, tangible and intangible, and/or in such real property as they in their sole and absolute discretion shall determine, whether or not the same shall be income yielding, and whether or not the same shall constitute investments then authorized for fiduciaries by the laws of the State of Missouri or any other State.

C. To hold and to continue to hold, so long as they in their sole and absolute discretion shall determine, and to invest and reinvest in, noninterest-bearing obligations issued at a discount and redeemable for fixed amounts increasing at stated intervals.

D. At any time and from time to time, to sell at public or private sale, and for such prices and upon such terms as they in their sole and absolute discretion shall determine, including on credit and, if on credit, for terms in excess of one year, any or all real property and/or any or all personal property, tangible and intangible, at any time held by them.

E. To permit any moneys at any time received or held by them to remain uninvested.

F. At any time and from time to time, to mortgage, exchange, partition and otherwise dispose of any or all property, real and personal, at any time held by them, and to lease the same for such term or terms as they in their sole and absolute discretion shall determine (including, without the permission of any Court of Judge, terms in excess of five years and terms extending beyond the duration of the trust hereby created).

G. To deposit, and to keep on deposit for such periods as they in their sole and absolute discretion shall determine, in savings and/or other bank accounts, any or all moneys at any time received or held by them.

H. To consent to and/or participate in and to dissent from and/or to oppose any agreement, merger, consolidation, reorganization or exchange affecting the whole or any part of my estate and/or of the principal of the trust hereby created, and to accept and hold any property which may be received as a result thereof.

I. To deposit any securities and/or other properties with any protective, reorganization or other committee, and to delegate discretionary power to any such committee, and to pay a share of the expenses and compensation of any such committee, and to pay any assessments levied with respect to any securities or other properties so deposited.

J. To exercise any conversion privileges and/or subscription rights available in connection with the whole or any part of my estate and/or of the principal of the trust hereby created.

K. To vote in person or by proxy on all stocks and other securities at any time held by them, and to delegate discretionary power to any proxies designated by them for such voting.

L. To compromise, settle and/or arbitrate any claim of mine or against me or of or against my estate or the trust hereby created, and to reduce the rate of interest on, to extend or otherwise modify and/or to foreclose upon default or otherwise enforce any obligation to me or my estate or the trust hereby created.

M. To abstain from enforcing any claim at any time held by them.

N. To borrow money for the purpose of paying taxes, making subscriptions, exercising options, paying assessments and for the accomplishment of any other purpose, and to pledge all or any portion of my estate and/or of the principal of the trust hereby created as security for such loans.

O. To enter into contracts in such form as they in their sole and absolute discretion shall determine with one or more individuals, firms, associations and/or corporations, providing for the rendering by such individuals, firms, associations and/or corporations of advice and counsel relating to and in connection with investments.

P. To employ and retain any individuals, firms, associations and/or corporations, on such terms as they in their sole and absolute discretion shall determine, to render clerical, bookkeeping, accounting, auditing and legal services.

Q. To register any securities and/or to deposit any moneys at any time constituting all or a part of my estate and/or of the principal of the trust hereby created, and/or to take and/or to hold title to any real property at any time constituting all or a part of my estate and/or of the principal of the trust hereby created, in the name or names of one or more of them, and/or in the name or names of one or more nominees, severally or jointly, without the addition of words indicating that such securities and/or moneys and/or real property are held or taken in a fiduciary capacity.

The foregoing powers shall be supplemental and not exclusive, it being my intention that my Executors and my Trustees shall have all of the general powers of fiduciaries, and, in addition, said special powers and all other powers reasonably to be implied therefrom or necessary for the proper exercise thereof. None of said powers shall be construed to limit in any manner any other thereof.

TWENTY-FIRST: I direct that, if and after the devise and the bequest provided for in Article TENTH hereof shall be set apart, then, in the administration of the balance of my estate then remaining, and in any event in the administration of the trust hereby created, to the extent permitted by law:

A. All dividends and other distributions in stock or other securities, whether of the corporation or association declaring or authorizing the same or otherwise, shall be deemed to be in whole principal, or in whole income, or in part principal and in part income, of said balance of my estate or of the trust hereby created as my Executors or my Trustees, as the case may be, other than my wife, shall in their sole and absolute discretion determine.

B. Any cumulative dividend accumulated prior to my death, or, if the stock with respect to which such dividend has accumulated shall have been acquired subsequent to my death, accumulated prior to the time of such acquisition, and any interest accrued prior to my death, or, if the obligation with respect to which such interest has accrued shall have been acquired subsequent to my death, accrued prior to the time of such acquisition, and the increase in the redemption price of any noninterest-bearing obligation issued at a discount and redeemable for fixed amounts increasing at stated intervals, shall respectively be deemed to be in whole principal, or in whole income, or in part principal and in part income, of said balance of my estate or of the trust hereby created as my Executors or my Trustees, as the case may be, other than my wife, shall in their sole and absolute discretion determine.

C. Only such part, if any, of the income from the securities at any time held in said balance of my estate or the trust hereby created as my Executors or my Trustees, as the case may be, other than my wife, shall in their sole and absolute discretion determine shall be applied as a sinking fund to offset the loss of the premium upon or market value of any such securities.

D. The costs incurred in connection with joining in or dissenting from and/or opposing any agreement, merger, consolidation, reorganization or exchange referred to in part H of Article TWENTIETH hereof, the expenses, compensation and assessments referred to in part I thereof, the costs incurred in connection with any compromise, settlement, arbitration, extension, modification, foreclosure or other enforcement referred to in part L thereof and the fees, compensation and expenses of the individuals, firms, associations and corporations referred to in parts O and P thereof shall respectively be charged in whole to principal, or in whole to income, or in part to principal and in part to income, of said balance of my estate or of the trust hereby created as my Executors or my Trustees, as the case may be, other than my wife, shall in their sole and absolute discretion determine.

E. Any receipt not hereinbefore in this Article TWENTY-FIRST referred to which could be deemed to be either principal or income shall be deemed to be in whole principal, or in whole income, or in part principal and in part income, of said balance of my estate or of the trust hereby created, and any cost not hereinbefore in this Article TWENTY-FIRST referred to which could be charged to either principal or income shall be charged in whole to principal, or in whole to income, or in part to principal and in part to income, of said balance of my estate or of the trust hereby created, as my Executors or my Trustees, as the case may be, other than my wife, shall in their sole and absolute discretion determine.

F. Upon the termination of the trust hereby created, any income which shall have accured, but which shall not have been collected, prior to the date of such termination shall not be apportioned and shall pass as income to the next succeeding interest or estate.

IN WITNESS WHEREOF, I have hereunto set my hand and seal this 14th day of January, 1959.

H S Truman (L.S.)

Harry Truman

The foregoing, consisting of twenty-two pages, including this page, each of the first twenty pages of which was initialed prior to the execution hereof by the above named Testator HARRY S. TRUMAN, was signed, sealed, published and declared by said Testator as and for his Last Will and Testament in our presence and hearing, and we thereupon, at his request, in his presence and in the presence of each other, subscribed our names as witnesses this 14th day of January 1959.

Arthur Mag   redising at Kansas City Mo
John W. Phellios residing at Kansas City, Mo
Ayrom K. Ellison residing at Kansas City, Mo.

CODICIL
TO
THE LAST WILL AND TESTAMENT
OF
HARRY S. TRUMAN

I, HARRY S. TRUMAN, being of sound mind and disposing memory, do hereby make, publish and declare this Codicil to my Last Will and Testament dated Jan. 14, 1959.

ITEM I

In addition to specific bequests made by me in my Last Will and Testament referred to, I hereby give to each of my nephews and niece and the nephew and nieces of ELIZABETH VIRGINIA, BESS WALLACE TRUMAN (Mrs. Harry S. Truman), who may survive me, the sum of One Thousand Dollars ($1000.00) each. In the event that any nephew or niece of either BESS WALLACE TRUMAN or myself, does not survive either of us, then such sum of One Thousand Dollars ($1000.00) shall be given to his or her child or children, in equal shares, and if he or she shall have no child or children surviving, such bequest shall lapse and return to my estate. The names of my nephews and nieces of myself and my wife to whom the sum of One Thousand Dollars ($1000.00) shall be given to each are as follows:

1. John Curtis Truman
2. Fred Truman
3. Martha Ann Truman Swoyer
4. Harry Arnold Truman
5. Gilbert Truman
6. David Bess's relation
7. Marion Brasher
8. Margo

In addition to the specific bequests made by me in my Will and as above made to the nephews and nieces of myself and Mrs. Bess Wallace Truman, I give and devise to the following greatnephews and greatnieces of myself and my wife the sum of Five Hundred Dollars ($500.00) to each, except to John Ross Truman, I give the sum of Five Dollars ($5.00). They are as follows:

Children of John Curtis Truman:

John Ross Truman	$ 5.00
Mary Martha Truman	500.00
Rita Marie Truman	500.00
Loretta Ann Truman	500.00
Gilbert Higbee Truman	500.00
Jean Ellen Truman	500.00

Children of Harry Arnold Truman:

Wenda Lee Truman	$500.00
Linda Kay Truman	500.00
Sue Ellen Truman	500.00

Child of Martha Ann Swoyer:

Karl Swoyer	$500.00

Child of Gilbert Truman:

Anita Luana Truman	$500.00

Children of Marian Wallace Brasher:

Cheryl Anne Brasher	$500.00
Elizabeth Marian Brasher	500.00
Richard Jay Wood Brasher	500.00
Lynne Frances Brasher	500.00
Pamela Sue Brasher	500.00

ITEM II

In addition to other specific bequests made by me in my Last Will and Testament and by this Codicil, I give to ROSE CONWAY, Secretary, the sum of One Thousand Dollars ($1000.00); to Mrs. Anne Smith the sum of Five Hundred Dollars ($500.00); to Frances Myers Williams the sum of Five Hundred Dollars ($500.00); to Mary Jo Nick the sum of Five Hundred Dollars ($500.00).

ITEM III

It is my will and desire, and I direct that my Executrix or Executor arrange and cause my remains to be laid to rest in the center of the plaza South of my office on the premises of THE HARRY S. TRUMAN LIBRARY, in Independence, Missouri. I further direct that a place be provided for the last resting place of Mrs. Truman. I direct that the slab covering the graves shall be level with the surrounding ground. If it is desired that an obelisk should be put at the head of the graves, and the Executrix or Executor shall so decide. It is my desire that a slab be placed over the graves, whether the obelisk is set up or not.

I would suggest that the slab over the graves, *which will lie flat*, have the following inscriptions:

HARRY S. TRUMAN
Born May 8, 1884
Lamar, Missouri

Married June 28, 1919
Daughter Born February 17, 1924
County Judge Eastern District
Jackson County
January 1, 1925
Presiding Judge, Jackson County
January 1, 1927-January 1, 1935
United States Senator, Missouri
January 3, 1935-January 12, 1945
Vice-President, United States
January 20, to April 12, 1945
President, United States
April 12, 1945-January 20, 1953

BESS WALLACE TRUMAN
Born February 13, 1885
Independence, Missouri
Married June 28, 1919
Daughter born February 17, 1924
Mary Margaret
First Lady, United States of America
April 12, 1945-January 20, 1953

ITEM IV

I hereby nominate and designate as attorneys for the Executrix or Executor, SAMUEL ROSENMAN, ARTHUR MAG, and RUFUS BURRUS, and direct that their compensation be fixed by the Judge of the Probate Court of Jackson County, Missouri.

IN WITNESS WHEREOF, I, HARRY S. TRUMAN, have to this the First Codicil to my Last Will and Testament, consisting of four (4) sheets of paper, subscribed my name this 23rd day of October, 1961.

Harry S. Truman
Harry S. Truman

The foregoing instrument, consisting of four (4) sheets of paper, was, at the date thereof, signed and declared by the said HARRY S. TRUMAN, to be the First Codicil to his Last Will and Testament, in the presence of us, who at his request and in his presence, and in the presence of each other have subscribed our names as witnesses thereto.

NAME: Arthur Mag
NAME: Ayram K. Ellison
John M. Phillips

ADDRESS: Kansas City Mo
ADDRESS: Kansas City Mo
Kansas City, Mo

SECOND CODICIL TO LAST WILL AND TESTAMENT
OF
HARRY S. TRUMAN

I, HARRY S. TRUMAN, being of sound mind and disposing memory, do hereby make, publish and declare this to be the second codicil to my Last Will and Testament dated January 14, 1959.

ITEM I
I hereby cancel any instruments under which I reserved title to the books located in my suite in the Harry S. Truman Library.

ITEM II
I hereby cancel Article FIFTH of my said Last Will and Testament, and I hereby amend Article THIRD and Article FOURTH of my said Last Will and Testament to cancel the words "the members of the committee created by the provisions of Article FIFTH hereof" and the words "the committee created pursuant to the provisions of Article FIFTH hereof", wherever said words are used and substitute in lieu thereof, in each case, the words "the Archivist of the United States".

ITEM III
I hereby cancel Article SEVENTEENTH of my said Last Will and Testament in in lieu thereof hereby substitute the following Article SEVENTEENTH:

SEVENTEENTH: The provisions herein made for my wife shall be in lieu of dower, homestead and all statutory marital rights she may have in my estate except such rights as she may have for maintenance at any time during the administration of my estate and except such rights as she may have to exempt property under the Missouri Statute.

ITEM IV
I hereby add the following Article TWENTY-FIRST to my said Last Will and Testament:

TWENTY-FIRST: I direct my Executors in making distributions from my Remaining Estate to allocate specific items of property to the various devises and bequests and fractions set forth from my Remaining Estate, as provided in my said will, and in so doing to determine the value of the property constituting my Remaining Estate, which property shall be valued at its fair market value as of the time of distribution.

ITEM V

I hereby republish, ratify and confirm all of the terms and provisions of my said Last Will and Testament as amended by the codicil thereto executed October 23, 1961, and as further amended by this second codicil thereto, consisting of two (2) sheets of paper.

IN WITNESS WHEREOF, I have hereunto set my hand and seal this 4th day of November, 1967.

Harry S. Truman (SEAL)

The foregoing instrument, consisting of two (2) sheets of paper, was, at the date thereof, signed and declared by the said HARRY S. TRUMAN, to be the second codicil to his Last Will and Testament, in the presence of us, who at his request and in his presence, and in the presence of each other have subscribed our names as witnesses thereto.

NAME: Arthur Mag   ADDRESS: Kansas City, Mo.
NAME: Donald H. Chisholm   ADDRESS: Kansas City, Mo.
NAME: Reese A. Gardiner   ADDRESS: Kansas City, Mo.

Facsimile of a section of the last page of the Will of Harry S. Truman.

SECOND CODICIL TO LAST WILL AND TESTAMENT OF HARRY S. TRUMAN-
Page Two

ITEM V

I hereby republish, ratify and confirm all of the terms and provisions of my said Last Will and Testament as amended by the codicil thereto executed October 23, 1961, and as further amended by this second codicil thereto, consisting of two (2) sheets of paper.

this _4th_ day of _November_, 1967. IN WITNESS WHEREOF, I have hereunto set my hand and seal

Harry Truman (SEAL)

Notes on the Will of Harry S. Truman

HARRY TRUMAN'S WILL, like those of Presidents Hoover, Eisenhower, and Lyndon Johnson, reflects the enactment by the Congress of a framework of legal authority, principally the 1955 Presidential Libraries Act, under which the Administrator of General Services may receive papers and other historical materials which a President or former President wishes to transfer to the Government, and also land, buildings, and equipment to house such collections. Though the theory has been challenged in recent litigation, this statute was clearly based on the traditional concept that such papers are the property of the President, who is free to give or to withhold them, who may transfer custody or possession of them to the Government without loss of his ownership, and who may attach conditions, acceptable to the Government, to his gifts.

During their lives Presidents Hoover, Truman, Eisenhower, and Lyndon Johnson all entered into written agreements with the Administrator looking to the establishment of such libraries. They transferred papers and other materials to the Government on the basis of those arrangements, and the Wills of each of them contain provisions designed to complete the transfer of additional items considered appropriate for these institutions.

Presidential papers are, of course, a unique subject matter affected by very special considerations. This is evident in paragraph 4th of President Truman's Will, which limits access to certain papers and explains the reasons for doing so. Presumably the letter agreements between the Presidents and the administrator also include various conditions which the former Presidents felt were desirable. Apparently both President Truman and President Eisenhower were pleased with their actual experience with the archivists working in their respective libraries. Provisions included in the Will of each for review of certain decisions by family members or trusted friends were eliminated in codicils which they later made.

President Truman's Will displays prominently the marks of modern tax planning. Tax considerations usually bulk large in the advice given to clients with an estate, for tax purposes, approaching $1,500,000, and the client, who ultimately makes the decisions, usually treats them as important too. On the basis of the evidence here, President Truman did.

The terms of the Will are designed to take full advantage of the marital deduction tax savings opportunity while avoiding any risk of unnecessary exposure to taxation at Mrs. Truman's death. Since the property which the President would own at the time of his death, and its precise value at that time (or six months later at the alternate valuation date), could not be known exactly at the time the Will was being prepared, the draftsmen could not rely simply upon some combination of gifts of specific amounts of money or particular property or even fractional shares of the residue, and still be sure of attaining the maximum tax advantage possible in the situation. To achieve precisely the right figure requires the use of a formula of some kind.

Formulas for this purpose are expressed in different ways. None of them make easy reading. The most common form is a gift in the will to the surviving spouse—widow or widower— which, with property passing to the spouse outside the will and qualifying for the marital deduction, will just equal the optimum gift for this purpose. The gift may be expressed as a dollar amount or as a fractional share of the property which comprises the residue of the estate. Either way the spouse is the recipient.

The draftsmen of President Truman's Will used a somewhat different approach, one which can be equally effective but which is probably less commonly seen in wills. This is a gift made in the will to a recipient, here a trust, which does *not* qualify for the marital deduction and which will not expose the property to potential taxation at the death of the surviving spouse. The gift is of an amount equal to the value of

A section of the front page of the Nov. 3, 1948 issue of the *Chicago Daily Tribune* **which erroneously announced the defeat of Truman.**

the property passing to the spouse outside the will and qualifying for the marital deduction. Since that amount can only be determined in the future, the gift must be expressed in a formula. Any remaining property passing under the will is then divided equally between the surviving spouse and a nonqualifying recipient. The latter need not be, but ordinarily would be, the same as the recipient of the formula gift.

The draftsmen of President Truman's Will were aware that he and Mrs. Truman held substantial amounts of property in their joint names. At the death of either, the survivor would become the sole owner automatically. The property would not be included in the probate estate of the other nor controlled by the terms of the other's will. To the extent that the value of such property must be included in the taxable estate of the first spouse to die, it would also qualify for the marital deduction. Article VIII creates an equalizing gift to a nonqualifying trust. Under Articles X through XIV the balance of the estate is divided equally between Mrs. Truman and nonqualifying recipients. According to one of Mr. Truman's attorneys, "In this manner President Truman's Will took the maximum advantage of the marital deduction without overqualifying."

Another interesting aspect of this Will are

the provisions of the first codicil with respect to the gravesite of President and Mrs. Truman. A number of Presidents, beginning with George Washington, have used their wills to express their wishes on this score. None have contained the detail of this one. The will may be an appropriate, though hardly necessary, place for instructions on the kind of marker to be used on the grave. It is not a good place for instructions on the kind of funeral or the desired place for burial, since it often will not be available when decisions on these subjects must be made.

Finally, a note of explanation about the legacies to the children of John Curtis Truman may be in order. Five of his six children were left $500 each; but one, John Ross Truman, was given only $5. On the surface, this suggests a difference in the President's feelings toward John Ross Truman, but there is a happier explanation. According to one of the attorneys for the estate, at the time the codicil was drawn John Ross Truman was attending a seminary with plans to become a Catholic priest in an order which required the vow of poverty. Knowing that President Truman decided that, since he would not be able to receive and enjoy the funds, the gift to him should be nominal.

DWIGHT D. EISENHOWER

D WIGHT DAVID EISENHOWER was born of Swiss-German stock on October 14, 1890, in a poor section of Denison, Texas. When Dwight was five months of age, his parents moved to Abilene, Kansas, where his father earned a small salary in a railroad machine shop and later as a mechanic in a creamery. The third of seven sons, Dwight acquired the nickname of Ike. Although christened David Dwight Eisenhower, his mother insisted on calling him Dwight since his father was David. To avoid the confusion, he later switched his name to Dwight David.

In Abilene the family first lived in a small house on South Second Street; in 1898 they purchased a house, three acres, and a barn on South Fourth Street. In high school, Ike was

an average student who took an active interest in sports. Graduating in 1909, he spent a year working at odd jobs around town before he took competitive exams for appointment to either West Point or Annapolis. He was admitted to West Point on June 14, 1911. Upon graduation in 1915, he ranked 61st scholastically and 95th in conduct among 164 cadets. Following his graduation he was stationed in Texas, where he met Mamie Geneva Doud, the daughter of a Denver meat packer. The two were married in the music room in her father's home in Denver on July 1, 1916, and on their honeymoon the bride met her husband's family for the first time.

Eisenhower served in World War I, attaining the rank of lieutenant colonel. He commanded Camp Colt at Gettysburg, Pennsylvania, a tank-training post. Although he received orders to go overseas, the war ended seven days before he was to embark. During the war their first child Doud Dwight, who died in infancy, was born. His surviving son, John, was born in 1922.

Eisenhower was transferred from Camp Colt to Fort Meade, Maryland, after the war, then to the Panama Canal Zone, and he was selected in 1925 for the General Staff School at Fort Leavenworth, Kansas, where he finished first among the 275 officers in the course. His next assignment took him to Washington, where he served from 1929 to 1935 in the office of the Secretary of War. While there he assisted Douglas MacArthur in dispersing the Bonus Marchers from the Anacostia Flats in Washington in 1932. In 1933 he became an aide to MacArthur in the Philippines. Shortly after Pearl Harbor he was brought back to Washington by General George Marshall, who assigned him to command the American forces in the European theater of operations. His diplomatic and military skills led to his appointment as Supreme Commander for the invasion of Europe.

Mamie Doud Eisenhower

Eisenhower advanced during the war from a one-star general in 1941 to a five-star general in 1944, a rank made permanent by Congress in 1946. May 8, 1945, ended the war in Europe with the German surrender, but Ike remained in Europe until November. Returning to Washington, he succeeded General Marshall as Chief of Staff.

In 1948 Eisenhower retired to become the president of Columbia University. In the fall he also wrote his story of the war, *Crusade in Europe*. His popularity was high, and he was mentioned as a possible candidate for President, but he was not interested at that time. He took leave from Columbia in 1951 to assume command over the newly created NATO forces in Europe. By 1952, his popularity had risen to a point where he was persuaded to run. In the Republican convention, Ike was chosen on the first ballot over Senator Robert A. Taft of Ohio. The Democrats nominated Governor Adlai Stevenson of Illinois. Eisenhower and his running mate, Richard M. Nixon won a sweeping victory.

Mamie Eisenhower was an accomplished hostess by the time she was in the White House. She avoided publicity and, being non-

Eisenhower political campaign button.

political herself, contributed little to the business of government aside from her role as First Lady. Having been transferred from Army post to Army post during Eisenhower's military career, the couple never owned a home until 1950, when they purchased a 189-acre farm three miles south of Gettysburg, Pennsylvania, near the General's early post at Camp Colt. It included a nine-room brick farmhouse on property which had been built a century before, and cost $24,000; another $16,000 was spent for machinery and pure-bred Black Angus cattle. Before Eisenhower retired, he spent another $100,000 on improving the property, including the addition of a 14-room house.

The Republican Party renominated Eisenhower in 1956; once again Ike trounced Adlai Stevenson. The first President to be limited by statute to two terms, he and Mamie retired to the Gettysburg farm. Eisenhower died on March 28, 1969. After lying in state at the Capitol Rotunda, his body was taken by train to Abilene, where it was buried in the chapel near the Museum and Library.

When in 1946 Congress voted to make Eisenhower General of the Army for life, provisions were included for an annual income of $19,000. His annual salary as president of Co-

Five-star pajamas worn by President Eisenhower during his illness in 1965.

lumbia University added $25,000. He cleared $476,250 for his book *Crusade in Europe*, thanks to favorable tax legislation. After eight years as President, with a salary of $100,000 per year, Eisenhower was able to spend a comfortable retirement, assured of income from his books, investments, and a $25,000 pension and up to $50,000 in office expenses, enacted by Congress in 1958, during his Administration. After his death his widow received a pension of $10,000 for his White House service.

The Eisenhower Museum, built at a cost of $500,000, contains a vast collection of mementoes, trophies, medals, and personal gifts valued in excess of $2,000,000. The museum was dedicated and opened by President Eisenhower on Veteran's Day, 1954. The Eisenhower Library, across from the Museum, was erected by contributions to preserve the documents, publications, and other historical material relating to the Eisenhower Administration. It was dedicated on May 1, 1962. The Eisenhower Home on Fourth Street in Abilene, which completes the complex, was donated by all the Eisenhower brothers to the Eisenhower Foundation in 1946. The chapel on the grounds that houses the remains of the President was built in later years.

Carved wooden elephant presented to President Eisenhower by the King of Thailand in 1960.

Text of the Will of Dwight D. Eisenhower

I, DWIGHT D. EISENHOWER of Gettysburg, Pennsylvania, do make, publish and declare this to be my Last Will and Testament, hereby revoking any and all Wills and Codicils thereto by me at any time heretofore made.

FIRST: I direct that all my just debts and funeral expenses be paid as soon as may be convenient after my death.

SECOND: I give and bequeath to:

(a) BRIGADIER GENERAL ROBERT LUDWIG SCHULZ, USA, 042115, c/o Adjutant General, United States Army, Washington, D. C., the sum of FIVE THOUSAND DOLLARS ($5,000), but if he predeceases me then I give and bequeath the sum of TWO THOUSAND FIVE HUNDRED DOLLARS ($2,500) to his descendants me surviving *per stirpes*;

(b) M/SGT. LEONARD D. DRY, USA, 36119802, c/o Adjutant General, United States Army, Washington, D. C., the sum of FIVE HUNDRED DOLLARS ($500), but if he predeceases me then I give and bequeath the sum of FIVE HUNDRED DOLLARS ($500) to his descendants me surviving *per stirpes*;

(c) MICHAEL J. McKEOGH, 3704 Sixty-fifth Street, Hyattsville, Maryland, the sum of ONE THOUSAND DOLLARS ($1,000) but if he predeceases me then I give and bequeath the sum of ONE THOUSAND DOLLARS ($1,000) to his descendants me surviving *per stirpes*; and

(d) M/SGT. JOHN MOANEY, JR., USA, 33068232, c/o Adjutant General, United States Army, Washington, D. C., the sum of FIVE THOUSAND DOLLARS ($5,000), but if he predeceases me then I give and bequeath the sum of ONE THOUSAND DOLLARS ($1,000) to his wife, DOLORES MOANEY, if she survives me.

THIRD: I give and bequeath all of my tangible personal property, except such "Writings" and "Uncompleted Writings" which are the subject of a certain License Agreement dated February 23, 1961, between Doubleday & Company, Inc., and myself, as follows:

(a) To the LOS ANGELES COUNTY MUSEUM OF ART (POLLY FIRESTONE WING), Exposition Park, Los Angeles, California, the portrait of me done by Andrew Wyeth in 1957.

(b) To my wife, MAMIE DOUD EISENHOWER, if she survives me, or if she does not survive me, then to my son, JOHN S. D. EISENHOWER, or if he does not survive me, then in equal shares to his children living on the date of my death:

1. All farm equipment, livestock and produce;

2. All furniture, furnishings and other articles of household use or ornament;

3. All automobiles and their accessories and equipment;

4. All clothing and other articles of personal use and adornment other than jewelry; and

5. All papers and other documentary materials which are excluded from the bequest hereinafter made to the United States of America.

(c) To the UNITED STATES OF AMERICA for deposit in the Eisenhower Presidential Library at Abilene, Kansas, all of my papers and other documentary materials, including books, still pictures, motion pictures and sound recordings, to be held by the UNITED STATES OF AMERICA for the same uses and upon the same terms and conditions as are set forth in my letter dated April 13, 1960, to the Honorable Franklin Floete, Administrator of General Services, Washington, D. C., excepting therefrom, however, those papers and other documentary materials which shall have been determined by me or shall be determined by my son, JOHN S. D. EISENHOWER, or in the event he predeceases me, by LIEUTENANT GENERAL A. J. GOODPASTER, to be of private or personal interest to me or to a member of my family.

(d) To the EISENHOWER FOUNDATION, Abilene, Kansas, all of the rest of my tangible personal property, including but not limited to my jewelry, sporting equipment, Steuben glass, office furniture, furnishings, pictures and other articles of office use or ornament, my souvenirs, medals, decorations, flags, swords, arms and equipment and other articles presented to me by any government or by any head or representative of a government or by any private, civic or public organization, and any bequests made under other provisions of this Article THIRD of my Last Will and Testament, which shall lapse or which the donee thereof shall disclaim, or which shall otherwise be an ineffective disposition thereunder.

(e) My Executors are hereby authorized and empowered in their absolute and sole discretion to determine the nature and allocation of my tangible personal property among the donees hereinabove named, and their decisions thereon shall be final and conclusive upon all persons and organizations interested in my Estate.

FOURTH: In the event my wife, MAMIE DOUD EISENHOWER, predeceases me, I give, devise and bequeath the real property owned by me and located in Gettysburg, Pennsylvania, together with all the buildings and improvements thereon and appurtenances thereto, to my son, JOHN S. D. EISENHOWER, if he survives me.

FIFTH: On February 25, 1961, I, as "the Author," entered into a License Agreement with Doubleday & Company, Inc., as "the Publisher," under which I granted and assigned to Doubleday & Company, Inc. certain rights to "Writings" and "Uncompleted Writings" of mine as therein defined. In the event that this License Agreement is in effect at the time of my death, I authorize my Executors, subject to the terms and conditions of said License Agreement, to transfer to Doubleday & Company, Inc., all such "Writings" of mine which are either uncompleted or, if completed, have not been delivered to Doubleday & Company, Inc.

SIXTH: I give and bequeath unto MERCANTILE-SAFE DEPOSIT AND TRUST COMPANY, of Baltimore, Maryland, and JOHN S. D. EISENHOWER, and their successors, as Trustees of the "Non-Marital Trust Share" of a certain Indenture of Trust created by me as Settlor on September 27, 1961, and as amended by me on May 5, 1965, all of my right, title and interest in that certain "License Agreement" dated February 25, 1961, between me as "the Author" and Doubleday & Company, Inc., of Garden City, New York, as "the Publisher," and I direct that all advances, royalties, earnings, recoveries and other payments made to my said Trustees pursuant to this Article of my Last Will and Testament and the aforementioned "License Agreement" shall constitute a full acquittance and discharge of Doubleday & Company, Inc.'s obligations with respect to such payments or the application thereof.

SEVENTH: All the rest, residue and remainder of the property, both real and personal and wheresoever situate, of which I may die seized or possessed and to which I may be entitled at the time of my death, and all property over which I have power of appointment and disposition, which powers I hereby exercise in favor of my general Estate, I give, devise and bequeath to the MERCANTILE-SAFE DEPOSIT AND TRUST COMPANY of Baltimore, Maryland, and JOHN S. D. EISENHOWER, and their successors, as Trustees, of a certain Indenture of Trust bearing date September 27, 1961, and as amended by Indenture dated May 5, 1965, between me, as Settlor, and said MERCANTILE-SAFE DEPOSIT AND TRUST COMPANY and JOHN S. D. EISENHOWER, as Trustees, as an addition to the principal of said Trust, to be held by said Trustees upon the trusts, terms and conditions set forth in said Indenture of Trust as amended.

EIGHTH: In addition to the powers vested by law in executors and trustees, I authorize my Executors and any fiduciary acting in my capacity hereunder to exercise the following powers in their absolute and sole discretion with respect to any income or principal received or held hereunder:

1. To determine what property is covered by general descriptions contained in this Will;

2. To retain, for such period of time as they wish, any property owned by me at the time of my death, without liability for any decrease in value;

3. To sell at public or private sale, upon such terms, giving credit, mortgaging it, pledging it or otherwise encumbering it, or to exchange any property, real or personal, and to invest and reinvest any funds in their hands in any kind of property whatsoever, real or personal, whether or not the same may be income-producing or be authorized by law for the investment of estate or trust funds, and without regard

to the proportion that such property, or other property of a similar character held, may bear to the entire Estate. Such power to sell and exchange shall include the sale of options, conversion privileges or subscription rights for additional securities;

4. To apportion between principal and income all stock and extraordinary cash dividends. In making such apportionment, I suggest that my Executors shall be guided by the following rules, but such suggestion is not binding and shall not control the absolute discretion accorded my Executors hereby:

(a) All dividends paid in cash, whether ordinary or extraordinary, and including dividends of wasting asset corporations and capital gains distributions of regulated investment companies, shall be income. Dividends which are receivable in cash or in stock of another corporation at the option of the stockholder shall be treated as cash dividends;

(b) Every dividend paid in stock of the declaring corporation, whether ordinary or extraordinary, shall be principal;

(c) All other dividends, payable in bonds or other property of the declaring corporation (or in stocks, bonds or other property of a non-declaring corporation) to the extent that they represent, or are charged against, earnings of the declaring corporation, regardless of when earned, shall be income;

(d) Notwithstanding the foregoing, any distributions made by a corporation, in complete or in partial liquidation or representing a substantial part of its total assets, shall be principal;

5. To vote, in person or by proxy, at corporate or other meetings, and to delegate their discretionary powers in connection therewith;

6. To sell, exchange, lease, mortgage, partition or improve any real estate owned by me alone, or jointly in common with others, or acquired by them, upon any terms, conditions and covenants, and to execute such deeds, leases, mortgages and other instruments relating to such property. Any mortgage or lease may be made for such period of time as they deem proper, without regard to the length of time of the administration of my Estate and without regard to any statutory restriction or requirement of approval of any court;

7. To borrow, in the name of my Executors, from themselves or from others, such sums of money, for such periods of time, at such rates of interest; and, if necessary, furnish any Estate property as security therefor;

8. To exercise options, conversion privileges or rights to subscribe for additional securities, and to make payments therefor;

9. To consent to, or participate in, dissolutions, reorganizations, consolidations, mergers, sales, leases, mortgages, transfers or other action or changes affecting securities held by them and, in connection therewith, to delegate their discretionary powers, including the right to deposit any securities with any protective committees, and to pay any necessary assessments, subscriptions or other expenses, and to charge the same against principal or income;

10. To extend or modify the terms of any bond and mortgage; to foreclose any mortgage or take title by deed in lieu of foreclosure or otherwise; to protect or redeem any property from forfeiture for non-payment of taxes or other liens; and, generally, to exercise as to such bond and mortgage or such property all powers that an absolute owner might exercise;

11. To make loans, secured or unsecured, in such amounts, upon such terms, at such rates of interest and to such persons, firms, corporations or other entities;

12. To register any property and hold the same in the name of their nominee, or to hold such property in unregistered form, and to keep such property anywhere that they shall select;

13. To compromise and adjust any claims or debts due to, or made against them, upon any terms and conditions, without prior authority from any court;

14. To amortize, or not to amortize, any investment which may be made or received by them at a premium, and to treat each such investment in a different manner so that they may amortize one such investment and need not amortize another such investment;

15. To do all such actions, take all such proceedings, and exercise all such rights and privileges with relation to a certain License Agreement referred to in Articles FIFTH and SIXTH of this my Last Will and Testament, and in connection therewith, to make, execute and deliver any instruments, to enter into any convenants or agreements, and to designate the "approved person" as provided in said License Agreement.

NINTH: I authorize and empower my Executors to claim administration expenses of my Estate as deductions for either income tax or estate tax purposes in such amount or amounts as my Executors, in my Executors' sole discretion, shall see fit, and to allocate the increased Federal estate tax payable by my Estate resulting from any election, entirely to principal, or entirely to income, or partly to each, as my Executors in their sole discretion shall determine.

TENTH: I authorize my Executors, in their sole discretion, to join with my spouse in filing any joint income, gift or other tax returns for any period prior to my death, and to pay out of the principal of my Estate all taxes, interest and penalties found to be due with respect to such returns.

ELEVENTH: On September 27, 1961, I, as Settlor, created an Indenture of Trust with the MERCANTILE-SAFE DEPOSIT AND TRUST COMPANY of Baltimore, Maryland, and my son, JOHN S. D. EISENHOWER, as Trustees, in which Indenture, which was amended on May 5, 1965, I directed said Trustees, and their successors, to pay over to the legal representative or representatives of my Estate such amount or amounts from the principal of the Trust Fund of the "Non-Marital Trust Share" of said Indenture if my wife, MAMIE DOUD EISENHOWER, survives me, or from the principal of the "Trust Estate" if my said wife, MAMIE DOUD EISENHOWER, predeceases me, as shall be stated by such legal representative or representatives, in a written instrument or instruments delivered to the Trustees, to be the amount needed to pay any and all legacies, debts, administration and funeral expenses and all estate, transfer, inheritance or other death taxes (including interest and penalties, if any) which shall have become payable to any taxing authority by reason of my death, upon or in relation to any property, whether such property passes under said Indenture of Trust or any amendment thereto, or under my Last Will and Testament or any Codicil thereto, and whether such property passes upon my death or at any time during my lifetime. I hereby authorize and empower my Executors to call upon said Trustees for such amount or amounts as may be required to pay any and all of the aforesaid items.

TWELFTH: I hereby nominate, constitute and appoint MERCANTILE-SAFE DEPOSIT AND TRUST COMPANY of Baltimore, Maryland; my son, JOHN S. D. EISENHOWER; and my friends, CLIFFORD R. ROBERTS and BARRY T. LEITHEAD, Executors of this my Will, and I direct that no bond or other security shall be required of them or any of them in such capacity or of any successor Executor appointed as hereinafter authorized in any court or place.

In the event one of more of my Executors (or their successors) named above shall die or refuse or for any reason be unable to serve or to continue serving as an Executor of this my Will, or having qualified shall resign for any reason whatsoever, which resignation is hereby authorized, the remaining Executors for the time being may and shall have the power to nominate and appoint a successor or successors, provided that no one objectionable either to my wife, MAMIE DOUD EISENHOWER, or to my son, JOHN S. D. EISENHOWER, shall be so appointed.

A majority of the acting Executors may from time to time exercise any of the powers, authorities and discretionary rights conferred upon my Executors by this my Will.

Any successor Executor at any time acting hereunder shall have the same powers, authorities and discretions as though named originally in this Will.

IN WITNESS WHEREOF, I have hereunto set my hand and seal this 25 day of May, in the year One Thousand Nine Hundred Sixty-five.

Dwight D. Eisenhower

SIGNED, SEALED, PUBLISHED AND DECLARED by the above-named Testator, DWIGHT D. EISENHOWER, as, for and to be his Last Will and Testament, in the presence of us and each of us, and we, at his request and in his presence and in the presence of each other, have hereunto subscribed our names as witnesses the day and year last above written.

Lillian H. Brown   residing at High Street
                          Cashtown Penn
Ethel M. Wetzel   residing at R. D. #3
                          Gettysburg, Pa.

Charles M. Mac
residing at 225 Lincolnway Ext
                          New Oxford, Pa.

CODICIL
to
Last Will and Testament
of
DWIGHT D. EISENHOWER

I, DWIGHT D. EISENHOWER, of Gettysburg, Pennsylvania, declare this to be a Codicil to my Last Will and Testament dated May 25, 1965.

FIRST: I revoke Sub-paragraph (c) of Paragraph THIRD of my said Will and in lieu thereof direct that the following Sub-paragraph be substituted:

" (c) To the UNITED STATES OF AMERICA for deposit in the Eisenhower Presidential Library at Abilene, Kansas, all of my papers and other documentary materials, including books, still pictures, motion pictures and sound recordings, to be held by the UNITED STATES OF AMERICA for the same uses and upon the same terms and conditions as are set forth in my letter dated April 13, 1960, to the Honorable Franklin Floete, Administrator of General Services, Washington, D. C., excepting therefrom, however, those papers and other documentary materials which shall have been determined by me to be of private or personal interest to me or to a member of my family."

SECOND: In all other respects I ratify and confirm my Will dated May 25, 1965.

IN WITNESS WHEREOF, I have hereunto set my hand and seal this 21 day of October, 1966.

Dwight D. Eisenhower
Dwight D. Eisenhower

SIGNED, SEALED, PUBLISHED AND
DECLARED by the above-named Testator,
DWIGHT D. EISENHOWER, as and for a
Codicil to his Last Will and Testament, in the
presence of us and each of us, and we, at his
request and in his presence and in the presence of each other, have hereunto subscribed our names as witnesses the day and
year last above written.

Ethel M. Wetzel   residing at R. D. #3
                                    Gettysburg, Pa.
Lillian H. Brown   residing at High Street
                                    Cashtown, Pa.
Charles W. May
residing at 225 Lincolnway East
                              New Oxford, Pa.

Eisenhower Home, Abilene, Kansas.

Notes on the Will of Dwight D. Eisenhower

AS ONE OF THE GROUP OF MODERN WILLS IN THIS SERIES, the Will of President Eisenhower shares the characteristics of others in that group. It contains a grant of broad powers to the Executors in their administration of the property. It makes a gift to the United States of America of papers and historical materials to be placed in a Presidential Library. It makes a gift of other mementoes to the Eisenhower Foundation formed to construct the museum which is adjacent to the Eisenhower Presidential Library in Abilene, Kansas. The Foundation has donated the museum structure and its contents to the United States, which received them under the procedure and authority discussed in the Notes to the Will of President Truman.

Like the Will of Herbert Hoover, this one employs a pourover provision to add assets to an existing *inter vivos* trust, the terms of which are not a matter of public record. These two wills illustrate the frequent use of this combination by persons active in public life. President Eisenhower's particular reasons for selecting this estate plan are not known.

The provisions of the Will suggest that tax considerations also affected the terms of the estate plan. Published accounts at the time of his death indicated a gross estate of approximately $2,870,000, and a net estate, after payment of outstanding obligations and costs of administration, of approximately $2,730,000. Estate and inheritance taxes would have further substantially reduced the amounts available for distribution.

The use of provisions qualifying for the marital deduction are a standard practice for married couples estates of this size. The references in the Will to a "Non-Marital Trust Share" of his *inter vivos* trust strongly imply

the existence of a Marital Share, that is, a gift that would qualify for the marital deduction. In fact, a marital deduction trust was established for Mrs. Eisenhower's benefit as part of the trust created in September 1961. The gift to a surviving spouse need not be in trust in order to qualify for the deduction. Use of the trust, however, assured sound investment and administrative management and relieved Mrs. Eisenhower of all such problems.

The Gettysburg Farm was owned jointly with Mrs. Eisenhower, and therefore she succeeded to it automatically at his death. She had made contributions to its purchase and renovation. The Farm's value at the time of his death would not have been subject to the federal estate tax in the proportion which her contributions bore to the total invested.

As did many of his predecessors, President Eisenhower remembered in his Will some of those who had provided close personal service to him during his life. Three of the individual legatees named in Article Second, Sgts. Dry, McKeogh, and Moaney, served with him during World War II and thereafter. The fourth individual legatee, Brig. Gen. Robert Schulz, was the President's military aide for many years after the war.

Sculptured head of President Eisenhower.

Article Eleventh is an interesting provision. It reflects the fact that Executors must pay legacies, debts, taxes, and the costs of administration in cash. If necessary, they may sell other assets to raise the funds required. Where both a will and an *inter vivos* trust are used to make property transfers, the necessary cash may be in the wrong place. It makes little sense to sell desirable assets which are part of the probate estate in order to obtain cash when the trust created by the testator has it in sufficient amounts.

All that is needed is a little coordination. One technique sometimes used is to authorize the trustee to buy assets from the Executor, thereby preserving assets desirable for the testator's purposes while shifting cash to the point needed. But there may be income tax disadvantages to casting these shifts in the form of a sale. The same purpose may be better achieved through Article Eleventh and its corollary in the trust instrument. As Article Eleventh re-

cites, the trust authorizes the trustees to pay over to the Executors amounts of cash needed for such purposes on the latters' request. The Will, in what may be an excess of caution, specifically authorizes the Executors to call upon the trustees for such amounts.

Article Eleventh also illustrates the pervasive effect of the marital deduction. To qualify for that tax benefit, property must "pass" to a surviving spouse. If it is used to pay taxes or other expenses, then it does not "pass" as required. Thus, a provision dealing with payment of debts, taxes, etc., and authorizing the fiduciaries to shift cash to meet these needs must specify that the cash be taken only from the "Non-Marital Trust Share." If that is not made explicit, then the trust provision might be interpreted as authorizing use of marital share funds in a way inconsistent with the requirements to qualify for the deduction. On such technical points, substantial differences in tax liability can turn.

President Eisenhower with a sugar-beet farmer.

JOHN F. KENNEDY

JOHN FITZGERALD KENNEDY was born the second of nine children in Brookline, Massachusetts, a suburb of Boston, on May 29, 1917. Of Irish ancestry, the family had risen to wealth and prominence, though at the time of his birth the family fortune was only modest. His maternal grandfather, from whom he received his middle name, had been mayor of Boston and his father, Joseph Kennedy, served as Ambassador to Great Britain. As the family fortune grew and the business centered more and more in New York, Joseph Kennedy moved his family to Bronxville, an affluent suburb of New York.

Kennedy's early education involved several schools, ending with his preparatory education at Choate. He entered Princeton University but was stricken with a case of jaundice in his freshman year and never returned; instead, he entered Harvard University. His senior year thesis at Harvard, concerning the conditions preceding World War II, became a popular book under the title *Why England Slept*. His *Profiles in Courage* was to win the Pulitzer Prize in biography in 1957.

After graduating from Harvard in 1940, Kennedy entered the Navy in World War II as a lieutenant. He was in command of a PT boat in the Solomon Islands when the vessel was cut in half by a Japanese destroyer. Two of the crew were killed, but the other 11 survived; Kennedy escaped with a back injury that was to plague him for the rest of his life.

At 28, Kennedy won a seat in the House

of Representatives for a poor district of Boston. He served three terms in Congress, then unseated Henry Cabot Lodge in the U.S. Senate in 1952. Early in the first of his two terms in the Senate he met Jacqueline Lee Bouvier at a dinner party in Washington, D.C.; they were married on September 12, 1953.

In 1956 he set his sights on the Vice Presidential nomination at the Democratic national convention. Kennedy jumped to a commanding lead over Kefauver on the second ballot, but before the results were announced the delegates were switching their votes and Kefauver beat Kennedy. The effort brought Kennedy into the national political limelight.

In 1957 the Kennedys purchased a house on N Street on Georgetown, D.C., for $78,000. Remodeling of the house cost an additional $20,000 and they sold the house in 1961 for $105,000. This was the only home they ever owned after their marriage. The 400-acre Virginia estate, Glen Ora, a mile and a half south of Middleburg, was rented as a resort after he was elected President.

At the Democratic national convention in 1960, Kennedy was nominated for President on the first ballot. Millions of viewers watched the TV debates between Vice President Nixon and Kennedy. Kennedy won the election, becoming the second Roman Catholic to become a Presidential candidate and the first to be elected to that office. He was also the youngest President and succeeded the oldest.

The Kennedys moved into the White House in 1961, but it was their home for only two years and 10 months. The family included the two children, Caroline and John Jr.; a third child born in the White House did not survive. During that time Mrs. Kennedy carried on an extensive program for refurbishing the White House. Patrons of the arts themselves, the Kennedys enriched the White House by persuading citizens to devote valuable pieces of art or items of fine furniture or to contribute funds for their acquisition with art treasures and conducted tours that were televised.

As a step in the reelection campaign in 1964 and to boost his popularity, Kennedy de-

Life preserver from the *Honey Fitz*, the Kennedy sailing yacht.

cided to make a short speaking trip to Texas. He arrived in Dallas on the morning of November 22, 1963, amid a warm welcoming crowd. As a motorcade containing President and Mrs. Kennedy, Vice President Johnson and Mrs. Johnson, and Texas Governor and Mrs. Connally headed for a luncheon meeting, an assassin fired three shots, two of which hit the President in the head. The President was rushed immediately to Parkland Hospital, where he was pronounced dead a half hour later.

A state funeral comparable to Lincoln's was held in Washington, D.C., as the caisson bore the remains to Arlington National Cemetery. An eternal flame marks his resting place. Shortly thereafter the National Cultural Center, started during the Eisenhower Administration, was renamed the John F. Kennedy Center for the Performing Arts. His papers and mementoes are deposited in the National Archives and Records Center and are to be housed in a proposed library and museum.

In addition to his $100,000 annual salary as President, which he was paid monthly, Kennedy also received a $50,000 expense allowance. (His widow receives a $10,000 pension.) His income from a trust fund was about $500,000 a year. This fund derived from the estate of Joseph P. Kennedy, which was estimated at between $200 and $400 million. Joseph Kennedy disposed of most of his fortune to his family before his death to avoid excessive inheritance taxes.

Text of the Will of John F. Kennedy

I, *JOHN F. KENNEDY*, married, and residing in the City of Boston, Commonwealth of Massachusetts, being of sound and disposing mind and memory, and mindful of the uncertainty of life, do hereby make, publish and declare this to be my Last Will and Testament.

FIRST

I hereby revoke any and all other Wills, Testaments, and Codicils heretofore made by me.

SECOND

I direct that all of my just debts and funeral expenses be paid as soon after my decease as may be convenient.

THIRD

I give and bequeath unto my wife, JACQUELINE B. KENNEDY, if she survives me, the sum of Twenty-Five Thousand ($25,000.00) Dollars, together with all of my personal effects, furniture, furnishings, silverware, dishes, china, glassware and linens, which I may own at the time of my death.

FOURTH

During my life, I have made substantial contributions to divers charities, causes and institutions of all faiths, both individually and through The Joseph P. Kennedy Jr. Foundation, which was established in honor of my late beloved brother. I am certain that the contributions which I and other members of my family have made to the Foundation will be applied after my death without bias or discrimination to the fulfillment of the Foundation's eleemosynary purposes.

FIFTH

I hereby direct my Executors to divide into two equal shares all of the rest, residue and remainder of my property, real, personal, and of any nature whatsoever and wheresoever situate, of which I shall die seized and possessed, and to which I shall be entitled at the time of my death, including without limitation any gifts and bequests heretofore made by me which may fail or lapse, and any property over which I may have the right of testamentary disposition, and I hereby give, devise, bequeath and dispose of the said two equal shares as follows:

[A] *As to One of Such Equal Shares - (Hereinafter Called "The First Equal Share")*

1. If my wife, JACQUELINE B. KENNEDY, survives me, then I give, devise and bequeath the First Equal Share unto my Executors and Trustees hereinafter named, In Trust, nevertheless, for the benefit of my said wife, to invest, reinvest and keep the same invested, and to collect and receive the rent, income and profits therefrom, and after deducting all proper reserves and expenses, to pay to my said

wife, in each calendar year, all of the net income thereof; such payments to be made in semi-annual or sooner installments, as my Trustees in their sole discretion may determine.

2. Upon the death of my said wife, the Trustees shall pay over the principal of the trust as it shall then exist, to such person or persons, including her own estate, and in such proportions as my said wife designates or appoints in and by her Last Will and Testament, under and by specific reference to this paragraph; and in default of such designation or appointment, the Trustees shall divide the same into as many equal parts as there shall be living at the death of my wife, children of mine and issue (taken collectively) of any predeceased child of mine, and shall pay one such equal part unto each such child, and one such equal part, in equal shares, per stirpes, unto such issue; and in default of all thereof, the same shall be paid to those persons to whom and in those proportions in which the same would have been distributed had I died immediately after the death of my wife, seized and possessed of said principal in my own right, intestate, domiciled in the Commonwealth of Massachusetts, and not survived by my father or mother.

3. Notwithstanding anything to the contrary in this Will contained, during the life of my said wife, the Trustees in their sole discretion may from time to time pay to my said wife out of the principal of the trust set up for her benefit, such sum or sums as the Trustees in their sole discretion may deem necessary to insure her health, welfare, or comfort, or to enable her to maintain the standard of living to which she is accustomed; provided, however, that such payments out of principal shall not aggregate in any one calendar year more than ten percent (10%) of the principal of the trust as it existed on the first day of said calendar year and computed at market or appraisal value as of the first day of said calendar year; and provided, further, that if said principal as so computed shall be less than One Thousand ($1,000.00) Dollars on the first day of said calendar year, the Trustees may in their sole discretion and without regard to said limitation of ten percent (10%), pay to my said wife all of said principal, even though such payment may terminate the trust.

The Trustees may exercise the discretion in this Paragraph "[A]-3" provided without regard to any other income or resources which my said wife may have from time to time, and without in anywise being accountable for the exercise of such discretion, but the Trustees may not be compelled to exercise such discretion.

4. In setting up the trust for the benefit of my said wife as in this Paragraph "[A]" provided, I direct that such First Equal Share shall be constituted of assets of my estate as are classified as "deductible" under the provisions of the United States Internal Revenue Code (Section 812(e), and the Regulations thereto (as the same or similar statutes and regulations may provide at the date of my death), before resort is had to "non-deductible" assets for such purpose.

5. If my said wife, JACQUELINE B. KENNEDY, does not survive me, then I direct that the First Equal Share shall be added to the Second Equal Share bequeathed and devised in Paragraph "[B]" of this Article "FIFTH", and shall be disposed of as part thereof.

[B] *As to the Remaining Equal Share - (Hereinafter Called "The Second Equal Share")*

I give, devise and bequeath the Second Equal Share, or if my said wife, JACQUELINE B. KENNEDY, shall not survive me, then also the First Equal Share, unto my Executors and Trustees hereinafter named, In Trust, nevertheless, to divide said Equal Share(s) into as many sub-shares as I shall leave me surviving children and issue (taken collectively) of any of my children who shall have predeceased me, and to hold and dispose of such equal sub-shares as follows:

1. To pay over one such equal sub-share, in equal parts, unto the issue living at the time of my death of any of my children who shall have predeceased me, such issue to take per stirpes and not per capita.

2(a). To set aside one such equal sub-share for the benefit of each of my children, and to invest, reinvest, and keep the same invested, and to collect and receive the rents, income and profits therefrom, and after deducting all proper reserves and expenses, to pay the net income thereof in each year to the child for whom such equal sub-share is so held in trust, in annual or sooner installments, as my Trustees in their sole discretion may determine, as long as such child shall live.

(b). Upon the death of such child, the trust for his or her benefit shall come to an end, and the principal of the trust as it shall then exist shall be paid unto the issue of such child living at his or her death, in equal shares, per stirpes and not per capita; and in default of such issue, the same shall be paid in equal shares unto my other children living at the termination of the trust and unto the issue then living of any of my children who shall have died prior to the termination of the trust, such issue to participate equally per capita in one equal share; and in default of all of the foregoing, such principal shall be paid unto those persons to whom and in those proportions in which the same would have been distributed had I died immediately upon the termination of the trust seized and possessed of said principal in my own right, intestate, domiciled in the Commonwealth of Massachusetts, and not survived by my father or mother.

(c). Notwithstanding anything to the contrary in this Will contained, and in addition to all other powers and authorities vested in the Trustees, I hereby empower the Trustees in their sole discretion, out of the principal of a trust set up herein for the benefit of a child of mine, to expend from time to time, for the benefit, health, welfare, or comfort of such child, or to enable him or her to maintain the standard of living to which such child may be accustomed, such sums as the Trustees in their sole discretion may determine; provided, however, that such expenditures out of principal shall not aggregate in any one calendar year more than twenty percent (20%) of the principal of said trust as it existed on the first day of said calendar year, and computed at market or appraisal value as of the first day of said calendar year; and provided, further, that if said principal as so computed shall be less than Five Hundred ($500.00) Dollars on the first day of said calendar year, the Trustees may in their sole discretion and without regard to said limitation of twenty percent (20%), expend all of said principal, even though such expenditure may terminate the trust.

The Trustees may exercise their discretion as in this Paragraph "[B]-2(c)" provided, without regard to any other income or resources which said child may have from time to time, and without in anywise being accountable for the exercise of such discretion, but the Trustees may not be compelled to exercise such discretion.

(d). In the event that a child of mine for whom a trust has been set up herein shall be a minor, then during the minority of such child, the Trustees shall from time to time apply so much of the net income of the trust as the Trustees in their sole discretion may determine, to the maintenance, support, education and welfare of such child, accumulating the balance of the net income until such child attains his or her majority, at which time all of the accumulated income shall be paid unto such child. Upon the death of such child before attaining his or her majority, the accumulated income shall be paid unto the persons and in the same proportions, manner and events provided in Paragraph "[B]-2(b)" of this Article "FIFTH" for the payment of principal upon the termination of the trust.

(e). In making any expenditure out of principal as provided in Paragraph "[B]-2(c) of this Article "FIFTH", and in applying the net income during the minority of a child, as provided in Paragraph "[B]-2(d)" of this Article "FIFTH", the Trustees may in their sole discretion make such expenditure or application direct or in the form of a payment to the parent, or to the guardian appointed under any jurisdiction either of the person or property of said child, or to an adult person with whom the child for whose benefit the trust is set up resides; or if such child is over the age of eighteen (18) years, then to such child; and the receipt of such parent, guardian, adult person, or child, as the case may be, shall discharge the Trustees and they shall not be responsible for the application of the principal or income by such parent, guardian, adult person, or child.

3. In the event that my wife, JACQUELINE B. KENNEDY, survives me, but I am not survived by any children or by any issue of a deceased child, then I give, devise and bequeath the Second Equal Share unto my said wife, to have and to hold unto herself absolutely and forever.

[C] In the event that neither my said wife, JACQUELINE B. KENNEDY, nor any of my children, nor any issue of my children survive me, then I give, devise and bequeath the First and Second Equal Shares to those persons to whom, and in those proportions in which the same would have been distributed had I died intestate, a widower, seized and possessed of such shares in my own right, domiciled in the Commonwealth of Massachusetts, and not survived by my father or mother.

[D] In the event that any part of my estate or of the principal of the trusts provided for in this Will shall become or be payable to a person under the age of twenty-one (21) years, said part shall vest absolutely in such person, notwithstanding minority.

During the minority of such person, and unless otherwise prevented by law, such part shall, in the sole discretion of the Executors or Trustees, remain in the custody of the Executors or Trustees, as Donees under a power of trust, until such minor attains the age of twenty-one (21) years. The Donees shall apply so much of the income or principal as the Donees, in their sole discretion, may deem necessary or advisable for the benefit of said minor, irrespective of any other source of support or maintenance or any other property which said minor has or may from time to time have.

The Donees are empowered to apply principal and income directly to the use of such minor, or to make any payment of principal or income to such minor, or to the parent, or to the guardian appointed under any jurisdiction of the person or property of such minor, or to an adult person with whom such minor resides. The receipt of such minor, parent, guardian, or person (as the case may be) shall discharge the Donees and they shall not be responsible for the application of the principal and income by such parent, guardian, person or beneficiary.

The Donees shall have all the investment and administrative powers conferred upon the Trustees hereunder. The Donees shall be entitled to receive as compensation the same commissions in respect of income and principal as are allowed to the Trustees, and they may deduct their commissions without judicial authorization.

SIXTH

I hereby authorize and empower my Executors and Trustees, as the case may be:

(a) In their sole discretion, to retain any and all property in the form they may receive it hereunder, although the same may not be of a character permitted for the investment of trust funds by the laws of any state.

(b) To invest, reinvest and keep invested all or any part of the principal of the trusts herein created in such property, real, personal and mixed, as in their sole discretion they may determine, although the same may not be of a character permitted for the investment of trust funds by the laws of any state, specifically including, but without limitation, the right to invest and reinvest in common and preferred stock, secured and unsecured debenture bonds or notes, mortgages, securities of every nature and description, oil, gas and mineral explorations and interests of all kinds and description, property of a speculative or wasting nature, and including further, but without limitation, the right in their sole discretion to invest, reinvest and keep invested such principal or any part thereof in the form of loans, secured or unsecured, to such persons, enterprises and entities and upon such terms and conditions as the Trustees or Executors may deem advisable.

(c) With reference to any real property which, or an interest in which, at any time constitutes part of my estate, or of the trusts herein created, to manage, control and protect the same; to dedicate streets, highways or alleys and to vacate any subdivision or part thereof; to subdivide and resubdivide such property as often as desired, to construct buildings or other improvements on such property, to repair, remodel, tear down and rebuild or enlarge any building at any time thereon, to contract to sell, or grant options to purchase, to sell on any terms and to convey the same or any part thereof to a successor or successors in trust, and to grant to such successor or successors in trust all the title, estate, powers and authorities vested in the Trustees, to lease said property or any part thereof from time to time, to commence *in praesenti* or *in futuro* and upon any terms and for any period or periods of time, even for periods extending beyond the duration of the trusts, and to renew or extend the leases upon any terms and for any period or periods of time, and to amend, change or modify leases and the terms and provisions thereof at any time or times hereafter.

(d) To retain any property at any time held by them without regard to the proportion such property or property of a similar character so held may bear to the entire amount of the trust estates.

(e) To invest the principal of each trust hereby created separately, or to invest the principal of two or more such trusts together.

(f) To hold uninvested any moneys constituting part of my estate or the trust funds for such time as in their discretion they may deem advisable, without any liability to pay interest thereon and without any liability for not investing such moneys.

(g) To create such reserves out of income, as in their sole discretion they may deem advisable, for depreciation, obsolescence, amortization, or to insure the prompt payment of taxes and other obligations, and to restore to income such reserves as may be unused.

(h) To charge losses, deductions and expenses or any part therof to principal or to income, as in their sole discretion they may determine to be advisable or proper.

(i) In their sole discretion, to distribute income at any time during the administration of my estate, and to pay interest on any bequest or devise made herein, at such rate as in their sole discretion they may determine.

(j) To associate themselves and to become and act as copartners, general or limited, or as joint adventurers, in any copartnership, venture or enterprise, with and at the risk of the assets of my general estate or the trusts, or any thereof, herein created; to incorporate under any jurisdiction any business or enterprise which I may own or in which I may be engaged at the time of my death, or to join with others in the incorporation in any jurisdiction of any business or enterprise in which I may have an interest at the time of my death, or in which my estate or the trusts or any thereof may from time to time have an interest, and to hold and treat the shares of any such corporation as an asset of my estate or as part of the principal of any trust herein created; to continue and to participate in, manage, operate and engage in any business, venture or enterprise which I may own or in which I may have an interest at the time of my death, or in which I may be associated with others, even though to do so, the Executors or Trustees may be, become and act as copartners, general or limited, or as co-adventurers or otherwise; and in connection with any and all of the foregoing, to borrow funds from time to time for the use and benefit of such business, and to pledge, mortgage, hypothecate and encumber any and all assets of said business, my estate, and the principal of the trusts herein created, as security for such loan or loans, this power to borrow money being in addition to and not in limitation of the power and authority to borrow which the Executors or Trustees may otherwise have under this Article "SIXTH".

(k) In their sole discretion, to retain as principal or to credit to and pay out as net income hereunder all or any part of the net gains and profits derived from the sale, exchange, or other disposition of any property belonging to said trusts, as the Trustees in their sole discretion may from time to time determine. Any part of such net gains and profits not credited or paid out as net income hereunder pursuant to such discretion shall be and remain principal hereunder.

The discretions and directions herein given to the Trustees shall be in addition to and not in limitation of the discretions given in Paragraphs "[A]-3" and "[B]-2(c)" of Article "FIFTH" hereof.

(1) From time to time, to borrow such sum or sums of money as they may deem necessary or proper (i) to provide moneys with which to pay any transfer, legacy, succession or inheritance taxes or death duties to whomsoever payable; (ii) in connection with the administration of my estate; (iii) for the maintenance, protection, or advancement of any property which may form part of my estate or the principal of the trusts herein created, including any shares of stock of any corporation or any interest of any nature or description whatsoever in any enterprise; or (iv) for the use or benefit of any business operated by the Trustees—all upon such terms and conditions as in their discretion the Executors and Trustees may determine; and for the sum or sums so borrowed, to execute and deliver promissory notes or other obligations in such form as they may determine, and to secure the payment of any amounts so borrowed by mortgage, pledge, hypothecation, or encumbrance of any real or personal property of which I may die seized or possessed, or which at any time may form part of my estate or the trusts herein created.

(m) From time to time to sell, lease, exchange, or otherwise dispose of, at public or private sale, any real or personal property, or any interest therein, which may at any time belong to my estate or to the trusts herein created, upon such term or terms, including credit, secured or unsecured, as they may determine in their sole discretion to be for the best interests of my estate or of such trusts, and to accept in payment or exchange, property, cash, securities, bonds, notes, or mortgages— although the same may not be of a character permitted for the investment of trust funds by the laws of any state; and to execute, acknowledge, and deliver any good or sufficient deeds, conveyances, leases, assignments and other instruments that may be necessary with respect to the sale, lease, exchange or disposition of property.

(n) To renew or extend the time of payment of any obligation, secured or unsecured, payable to or.by my estate, for as long a period or periods and on such terms as they may determine, and to settle, adjust, compromise and arbitrate claims or demands in favor of, or against, my estate or the trusts herein created—all upon such terms as they may deem advisable.

(o) With respect to any securities forming part of my estate or the trusts herein created, to vote upon any proposition or election at any meeting, and to grant proxies, discretionary or otherwise to vote at any meeting; to join in or become parties to any reorganization, readjustment, merger, voting trust, consolidation or exchange, to deposit any such securities with any committee, depository, trustee or otherwise; and to pay out such fees, expenses or assessments incurred in connection therewith, and to charge the same to principal or income of my estate or the trusts to which such securities may belong, as the Executors or Trustees may determine; to exercise conversion, subscription or other rights, or to sell or abandon such rights; and to receive and hold any new securities or other property issued or delivered as a result of any such reorganization, readjustment, merger, voting trust, consolidation, exchange or exercise of conversion, subscription, or other rights, although the same may not be of a character permitted for the investment of trust funds by the laws of any state; and generally, to take all action in respect of any securities belonging to my estate or the trusts hereunder, as the Executors or Trustees might or could do as absolute owners thereof.

(p) Unless otherwise prevented by law, to cause any securities or other property to be held in bearer form, or to be registered and held in the name of a nominee.

(q) To advise with counsel, who may be counsel for any person interested in the estate or in the trusts herein created, and the Executors or Trustees shall not be liable for any action taken or omitted to be taken upon the advice of counsel.

(r) If they so deem it advisable, to assign, transfer and convey all or any part of the property belonging to my estate or to the trusts herein created, to a corporation organized by them in any jurisdiction, in exchange for the stock, bonds, debentures, notes or securities of such corporation, and to distribute, hold or retain the same in accordance with the provisions made by me herein for the disposition of the property so assigned, transferred or conveyed to said corporation.

(s) To make any division or distribution of my estate, or the principal of the trusts herein created, in kind at the then market value of the property, or partly in kind and partly in money, and to cause the respective shares to be composed of property similar to or different from other shares.

(t) In their sole discretion, and insofar as permitted by law, to file Federal or State Income Tax Returns jointly with my wife, JACQUELINE B. KENNEDY.

(u) Notwithstanding anything to the contrary in this Will contained, with respect to the trust set up for the benefit of my wife, JACQUELINE B. KENNEDY, in Paragraph "[A]" of Article "FIFTH" hereof (a) the Trustees shall and are hereby directed to convert into income-producing property any unproductive property forming part of the principal of said trust within a reasonable time after the same becomes unproductive, or if unproductive at the time of the receipt thereof by the Trustees, then within a reasonable time after such receipt; and (b) the Trustees shall not hold uninvested beyond a reasonable time, moneys belonging to the principal of said trust.

SEVENTH

(a) The Executors or Trustees shall make no deduction from, nor addition to, income by reason of the purchase or sale of securities at a premium or discount.

(b) All dividends received by the Executors or Trustees in stock of a corporation or association declaring the same and declared in respect of any stock constituting any part of my estate or the principal of the trusts hereunder, all liquidating dividends, and all rights to subscribe to new or additional stock or other securities, and the securities or other property received upon the exercise of any such rights, and the proceeds of the sale of any such rights, shall be deemed principal. All other dividends received by the Executors or Trustees shall be treated as income and distributed accordingly. The Executors or Trustees shall have power to determine whether, and if at all, to what extent, any dividend received by them is a liquidating dividend.

(c) Persons dealing with my estate or the trusts herein created shall be under no obligation to see to the proper application of money paid or property delivered to the Executors or Trustees, or to inquire into the authority of the Executors or Trustees as to any transaction, and the receipt of the Executors or Trustees for any money or thing paid or transferred or delivered to them shall be a sufficient discharge to the person or persons paying, transferring or delivering the same, or from all liability to see to the application thereof.

(d) Every deed, trust deed, mortgage, lease, contract or other instrument executed by the Trustees in relation to any property belonging to the trusts herein shall be conclusive evidence in favor of every person relying upon or claiming under any such conveyance, lease or other instrument (i) that at the time of the delivery thereof the trusts created in this Last Will and Testament were in full force and effect; (ii) that such conveyance or other instrument was executed by the Trustees in accordance with the terms, conditions and limitations contained in this Last Will and Testament, and is binding upon all beneficiaries thereunder; (iii) that the Trustees were duly authorized and empowered to execute and deliver such deed, trust deed, mortgage, lease, contract or other instrument; and (iv) if the conveyance is one made by or to a successor or successors in trust hereunder, that such successor or successors in trust have been properly appointed and is or are fully vested with all the title, estate, rights, powers, authorities, duties and obligations of its, his or their predecessors in trust.

EIGHTH

I direct that all estate, inheritance, succession, legacy, transfer taxes or other taxes of the same nature, which may be payable by reason of my death, including interest and penalties thereon, with respect to property or assets comprising my estate for such tax purposes, whether or not such taxes are payable by my estate or by any devisee, legatee, recipient or beneficiary of any such property or assets, shall be paid entirely as an administration expense out of such part of my residuary estate as passes to my Trustees in Paragraph "[B]" of Article "FIFTH" of this Last Will and Testament, without any right of reimbursement from any devisee, legatee, recipient or beneficiary of such property or assets.

NINTH

I hereby nominate, constitute and appoint my wife, JACQUELINE B. KENNEDY, and my brothers, ROBERT F. KENNEDY and EDWARD M. KENNEDY, as Executors of, and Trustees under, this my Last Will and Testament; and if for any reason at any time any one of them does not qualify or is unable or unwilling to serve as such Executor or as such Trustee, I hereby nominate, constitute and appoint the following, in the order named, as Executrix or Trustee of this my Last Will and Testament (as the case may be) to fill any such vacancy: my sisters, EUNICE K. SHRIVER, PATRICIA LAWFORD and JEAN KENNEDY.

I direct that no bond be required of the Executors or Trustees in this or any other jurisdiction, and that no inventory of my estate need be filed.

Insofar as may be permitted by law, no Executor or Trustee shall be liable for any act or omission in connection with the administration of my estate or of the trusts herein created, or the exercise of any of the powers and discretions hereinbefore provided for, nor for any loss or injury to any property held in or under my estate or said trusts, except for his or her actual fraud, and no Executor or Trustee shall be responsible for any act or omission of any other Executor or Trustee.

Any Executor or Trustee acting under this Will may at any time and from time to time, be revocable power of attorney executed under seal, delegate to the other Executors or Trustees (as the case may be) full exercise of all or any of the powers vested in such delegating Executor or Trustee.

I hereby direct that the Executors and/or Trustees, unless otherwise prevented by law, shall act by a majority vote.

IN WITNESS WHEREOF, I have hereunto subscribed my name and affixed my seal to this, my Last Will and Testament, this 18th day of June, in the year one thousand nine hundred fifty-four.

John F. Kennedy

The foregoing instrument, consisting of this and sixteen (16) preceding pages, was subscribed by JOHN F. KENNEDY, the Testator, in the City of Washington, D. C., on the 18th day of June, in the year one thousand nine hundred and fifty-four, in the presence of us and each of us, and at the same time and place was subscribed, published and declared by him to be his Last Will and Testament, and we, at his request, and in his presence, and in the presence of each other, signed our names hereto as subscribing witnesses hereof.

T. J. Reardon Jr.   Residing at 3134 Dumbarton Ave N.W.
                                                          Washington, D. C.
Theodore C. Sorensen   Residing at 1105 57th Ave. S.E.
                                                          Washington, D. C.
Evelyn Lincoln   Residing at 3132-16th St. N.W.
                                                          Washington 10, D. C.

Notes on the Will of John F. Kennedy

THE WILL OF PRESIDENT KENNEDY WAS EXECUTED IN 1954, when he was still in his first term in the United States Senate and when he had been married for less than a year. Since his Presidency was still in the future, this Will, unlike those of other recent Presidents, says nothing on the subject of Presidential papers and other materials. After President Kennedy's death, members of his family entered into an agreement with the Administrator of General Services for the transfer of these materials to the Government. However, as of this writing, a site for a Kennedy Library and Museum has not been finally determined.

Tax considerations are evident in the terms of this Will, though apparently neither the draftsman nor the client was concerned about achieving the last possible dollar of tax saving. Both the gifts outright under Article Third and in trust under Article Fifth [A] qualify for the marital deduction. However, concern for

Drum used to muffle the cadence for the funeral of John F. Kennedy.

minimizing taxes at Mrs. Kennedy's death was shown only if both she and a child or children survived the testator—as, of course, they did. In that situation, the terms of the trust of "The Second Equal Share" (Article Fifth [B]) avoid a tax on that property at the time of her death.

There are a variety of ways of making a gift to a surviving spouse that will qualify for the marital deduction. The provisions of Article Fifth [A] creating the trust of "The First Equal Share" is an example of one method frequently used. Though the property is held by a trustee rather than the spouse, the transfer will qualify if the surviving spouse is given a right to all of the income for life and a general power of appointment over the trust principal. Building upon the language of the statute, the Regulations issued by the Treasury Department impose a number of subsidiary requirements designed to assure that the income to be received will be real as well as theoretical. Some of these conflict at points with the sweeping discretion that is now frequently given to trustees by the instruments appointing them. Thus, to preserve the desired tax advantage, it becomes necessary to insert provisions such as paragraph (u) of Article Sixth to qualify or contradict some of the prior paragraphs in the same Article.

Though not required for tax purposes, another provision of this trust illustrates a highly desirable technique to build flexibility into a property arrangement that could last for many years. Paragraph 3 of Article Fifth [A] confers discretion on the trustees to pay principal, as well as income, to President Kennedy's widow for the purposes specified. Too many trusts have been created without sufficient regard for the uncertainties of the future. Changes in the needs of the beneficiary, or in the purchasing power of the dollar, or in the return realized from trust investments, can convert what was thought at the time of writing the instrument to be a generous provision for a beneficiary into one which is grossly inadequate. Unless the trustees are given explicit authority to enlarge the amounts payable, they are powerless to remedy a bad situation even though they believe the creator of the trust would have authorized the adjustment had he foreseen the problem. Here such discretion has been given, though it is unlikely that it has had to be used much.

The Notes to the Will of President Buchanan discussed some of the problems created by ownership of property by minors and the use of the trust device to simplify or avoid them. The trust handles nicely the investment and management of property while avoiding the legal restrictions of a guardianship. However, when it comes to use of the funds for the minor the difficulties are revived. Trustees typically make distributions to adults and are protected by the receipts which they give. Can the trustee rely on the receipt of a minor? If not, must he retain the funds until majority, spend them himself for the minor's benefit, or have a guardian appointed for the minor after all? If so, the value of the trust solution is seriously impaired.

Trustees tend to feel more comfortable with distributions during minority if the instrument includes a provision of the type illustrated by subparagraph (e) of paragraph 2 of Article Fifth [B]. Known as a "facility of payment clause" this provision clearly authorizes a choice of method of making payment and possible recipients for it that ought to meet smoothly any possible future needs or circumstances.

Article Fourth of President Kennedy's Will is unusual. It makes no gift, but refers to gifts made in the past to a family foundation. It expresses confidence with respect to the way in which these past gifts will be used or distributed in the future, but as to a gift already

complete a testator can only express a hope rather than impose a legally binding obligation on the Foundation to follow his wishes. Perhaps the provision was included here as an indirect explanation of the failure to make charitable gifts in this Will. In the latter respect, President Kennedy's action was consistent with that of most of his predecessors. Though many of them were wealthy men, only a few made gifts to charitable or public purposes in their wills. Presumably, many of them made substantial contributions during their lives.

The reference to the Joseph P. Kennedy Jr. Foundation illustrates another modern phenomenon, the private charitable foundation. The creation of a family-controlled foundation permits a transfer of fund earmarked ultimately for charitable purposes without loss of control of the assets themselves. Most such foundations conduct no programs of public benefit themselves but perform their function in dispersing funds to organizations which do so, or to individuals in need of help. Since 1969 these foundations have been subject to a series of new requirements imposed by the Congress to assure that the potential benefit of funds held by such foundations will be made promptly available for public purposes.

The Will of President Kennedy deserves high marks in many respects. One of these is readability. Its organization of a complicated set of ideas, expressed in language which is precise yet simple, make it one of the better samples of will drafting in this book.

Facsimilie of a section of the last page of the Will.

IN WITNESS WHEREOF, I have hereunto subscribed my name and affixed my seal to this, my Last Will and Testament, this 18th day of June, in the year one thousand nine hundred fifty-four.

LYNDON B. JOHNSON

O F BRITISH ANCESTRY, LYNDON BAINES JOHNSON WAS BORN AUGUST 27, 1908, in the hill country of southwest Texas near Stonewall, the oldest of the five children of Samuel Ealy and Rebekah Baines Johnson. His father had been a state legislator, school teacher, and rancher. His mother was a reporter for her father's newspaper and had met Samuel E. Johnson, Jr., while conducting an interview.

Lyndon's family had lived in Texas since 1846, when his grandfather, Sam Ealy Johnson, Sr., moved from Alabama to Texas with his parents at the age of eight. The grandfather had been a cattle driver, an Indian fighter, and a Confederate soldier, and became a member of the Texas legislature. He and his brothers built the fort that grew into the community known later as Johnson City.

When Lyndon was five, his family moved to a house near Johnson City, where he grew up and attended a local school. He was not born to wealth and as a boy worked as a shoeshine boy, on a highway construction gang, as a helper in the newspaper printer's office, and at various other jobs. After graduating from Johnson City High School at 15, he worked in California for two years. Returning home, Lyndon was persuaded by his mother, herself college-educated, to attend college. He entered Southwest Texas State Teachers College in San Marcos. He took off one year and taught Mexican-American children at Cotulla, Texas. Graduating from college in 1930, he taught debating and public speaking at a Houston high school for two years.

His political career started in 1932, when he became secretary to Richard M. Kleberg, a Congressman, lawyer, banker, and cattleman. The job brought Johnson to Washington, where he worked in the House of Representatives and came in contact with Franklin D. Roosevelt. In 1935 the President appointed him Texas State Director of the National Youth Administration.

On a visit to Austin, Texas, in 1934, he had met Claudia Alta Taylor, a graduate in journalism from the University of Texas and the daughter of a rich East Texan. The two were married following a two-month courtship.

In 1937, at the age of 29, Johnson gathered his savings, borrowed more from his father-in-law, and won the seat in the House of Representatives vacated by the death of Congressman James P. Buchanan of the Austin district. Following Pearl Harbor, Johnson joined the Navy as a reserve officer with the rank of lieutenant commander. He was sent on a hazardous air mission over New Guinea for

which he was awarded a Silver Star. After seven months he returned with other Congressmen whom Roosevelt had recalled from military service. He remained in the House of Representatives until 1949, serving almost six terms.

In 1948 Johnson ran for the U.S. Senate and beat ex-Governor Coke Stevenson in the Democratic primary runoff by a mere 87 votes. In November he beat his Republican opponent and Johnson took his seat in the Senate in 1949, where he served continuously until 1961. After three years' service he was elected Democratic minority whip. At the age of 44, he became the youngest minority leader in the history of the Senate in 1953 and majority leader in 1955.

When the Democratic national convention met in 1960, Johnson lost the nomination to John F. Kennedy. Johnson then readily accepted the Vice Presidential nomination to the surprise of his friends. With Johnson's Southern support and Kennedy's appeal in the North, the ticket won a narrow victory.

With the assassination of John F. Kennedy

Birthplace of President Lyndon Baines Johnson.

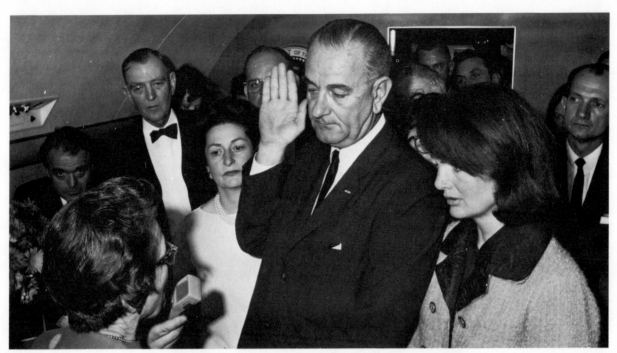

Lyndon Baines Johnson taking the oath of office on board
the Presidental plane at Dallas airport, November 22, 1963.

on November 22, 1963, Johnson became President. Mrs. Johnson, known to most Americans as "Lady Bird," a nickname given her in childhood, assumed her own identity in the White House. Two teen-age daughters, Lynda Bird and Luci Baines, completed the family household.

When the Republicans met in 1964, they chose Barry Goldwater as their candidate. Against him stood Lyndon Johnson, a seasoned and professional politician. The campaign was intense, but Johnson, won the election by the largest popular margin in American history— more than 15,000,000 votes. However, the Vietnam War divided the American people more bitterly than perhaps any conflict since the Civil War. Johnson's failure to resolve the war by the time of the 1968 campaign caused him to announce that he would not run for reelection.

On January 20, 1969, Johnson and his family returned to the L.B.J. Ranch at Stonewall, Texas, where he devoted his full time and energy to the planning and building of the Lyndon Baines Johnson Library and Museum, which houses the Presidential papers and memorabilia he donated to the National Ar-

chives and Records Center in 1965.

Johnson died January 22, 1973. His body was flown to Washington, D.C., and passed in a motorcade procession to the Capitol, where he lay in state. The funeral was held the following day in the National City Christian Church and he was flown back to the L.B.J. Ranch. There he lies buried beside his relatives in the family cemetery on the Pedernales River. The Johnson home and the 200 adjoining acres of the L.B.J. Ranch were donated to the National Park Service with the stipulation that Mrs. Johnson could continue to live at the ranch.

Johnson built up a multimillion-dollar fortune in real estate and television stations. His wife had inherited 3,800 acres of land in Alabama, and during his Vice Presidency Johnson added more than 12,000 acres of Texas land. In one transaction alone, he and a partner paid Texas Christian University $500,000 for a large ranch which it owned. His salary as Vice President was $35,000 and as President, $100,000. His Presidential pension was $25,000 a year plus an office and $50,000 a year for office help. He also had unlimited free mailing privileges. His widow's Presidential pension is $10,000 per annum.

Text of the Will of Lyndon B. Johnson

THE STATE OF TEXAS

                                    KNOW ALL MEN BY THESE PRESENTS:

COUNTY OF BLANCO

That I, LYNDON B. JOHNSON, of Blanco County, Texas, being of sound and disposing mind and memory, do make, publish and declare this to be my Last Will and Testament, hereby revoking all other wills and codicils by me heretofore made.

SECTION I.

In this will I am disposing of my interest in the community estate of my wife, CLAUDIA T. JOHNSON, and me. I am not endeavoring to dispose of the interest of my wife in our community estate except such interest, if any, as she might have in my papers in case I have not disposed of all of my interest therein during my lifetime. Unless such papers are my separate property, I own no separate property.

SECTION II.

In the administration of my estate and of each trust established hereunder and in connection with the construction of this will, the following shall obtain:

(a) The word "executor" shall embrace both the singular and the plural.

(b) The word "trustee" shall embrace both the singular and the plural.

(c) The word "child" and the word "children" shall embrace both the singular and the plural and shall also include an adopted child or adopted children.

(d) The word "descendant" and the word "descendants" shall embrace both the singular and the plural and shall include anyone adopted into the line of descent as well as lineal descendants by blood.

(e) The masculine gender whenever used shall also embrace the feminine and neuter genders as the context of this will permits.

(f) A person shall be deemed to have survived or be living at the time of the death of another person or at the time of the occurrence of a specified event if at that time such person was en ventre sa mere and survives birth.

(g) The word "corpus" as used herein shall include not only principal and accumulations to principal but also shall include any undistributed or accrued income.

(h) The word "property" and the word "assets" as used herein shall be construed to include money.

(i) The independent trustee shall be my wife, CLAUDIA T. JOHNSON, while she is acting as a trustee and thereafter shall be the trustee or trustees acting hereunder who is not or who are not related by blood or marriage to any beneficiary of the trusts created in this will.

SECTION III.

I direct that all of my just debts and costs of administering my estate and all expenses of my last illness, funeral and burial be paid in full as soon as convenient out of property owned by me at the time of my death, except that any debt which does not mature during the administration of my estate and which is secured by a mortgage, pledge or similar encumbrance on property owned by me at the time of my death shall not be paid but such property shall pass under this will subject to such mortgage, pledge or similar encumbrance.

SECTION IV.

All federal and state estate, inheritance or succession taxes imposed upon my taxable estate, whether passing under this will or not, or on beneficiaries of my estate, including the portion of any such tax as is attributable to the proceeds of life insurance on my life receivable by a beneficiary other than my executor, shall be paid in full as soon as convenient out of property owned by me at the time of my death. In discharging the foregoing direction, my executor may arrange for payment of all such taxes and duties imposed upon my taxable estate, or any beneficiary thereof, upon such terms and conditions as he may determine for the best interest of my estate. My estate shall be entitled to no reimbursement for any such taxes paid by my executor on behalf of any beneficiary of my estate.

SECTION V.

I give and bequeath unto my wife, CLAUDIA T. JOHNSON, if she survives me, all of my interest in our household and kitchen furniture, furnishings and fixtures, personal automobiles, musical instruments, books, pictures, jewelry, silverware, china, crystal, wearing apparel, family stores and all other similar articles of tangible personal property of which I may die seized and possessed.

If my wife should not survive me, I direct that my executor in his absolute and sole discretion may divide and partition the property mentioned in this Section V, or any part thereof, between my children, LYNDA BIRD JOHNSON ROBB and LUCI BAINES JOHNSON NUGENT, share and share alike, or sell and distribute the proceeds of sale or distribute in kind the property mentioned in this Section V, or any part thereof, as a part of the residue of my estate.

If my wife and a daughter of mine should not survive me, I direct that my executor in his absolute and sole discretion may divide any partition the property mentioned in this Section V, or any part thereof, between my surviving daughter and the children, if any, of my deceased daughter, in such manner as he may in his absolute and sole discretion determine, or sell and distribute the proceeds of sale or distribute in kind the property mentioned in this Section V, or any part thereof, as a part of the residue of my estate.

If my wife and both of my daughters should not survive me, I direct that my executor in his absolute and sole discretion may divide and partition the property mentioned in this Section V, or any part thereof, among the children, if any, of my daughters in such manner as he may in his absolute and sole discretion determine, or sell and distribute the proceeds of sale or distribute in kind the property mentioned in this Section V. or any part thereof, as a part of the residue of my estate.

The decision of my executor as to what property is included within the provisions of this Section V, or as to the disposition to be made of same within the provisions of this Section V shall be binding and conclusive on all interested parties.

SECTION VI.

I give and bequeath the following specified sums to the individuals named below who survive me:

(a) To my sister, LUCIA ALEXANDER, the sum of Ten Thousand Dollars ($10,000);

(b) To my sister, REBEKAH BOBBITT, the sum of Five Thousand Dollars ($5,000);

(c) To my brother, SAM HOUSTON JOHNSON, the sum of Five Thousand Dollars ($5,000);

(d) To YOLANDA BOOZER, the sum of Three Thousand Dollars ($3,000);

(d) To JAMES DAVIS, the sum of Three Thousand Dollars ($3,000);

(f) To MARY DAVIS, the sum of Three Thousand Dollars ($3,000);

(g) To MARIE FEHMER, the sum of Three Thousand Dollars ($3,000);

(h) To ASHTON GONELLA, the sum of Three Thousand Dollars ($3,000);

(i) To DOROTHY NICHOLS, the sum of Three Thousand Dollars ($3,000);

(j) To MARY RATHER, the sum of Three Thousand Dollars ($3,000);

(k) To JUANITA ROBERTS, the sum of Three Thousand Dollars ($3,000);

(l) To MILDREN STEGALL, the sum of Three Thousand Dollars ($3,000);

(m) To MARY MARGARET WILEY VALENTI, the sum of Three Thousand Dollars ($3,000);

(n) To KOO VOO WONG the sum of Three Thousand Dollars ($3,000);

(o) To ZEPHYR WRIGHT, the sum of Three Thousand Dollars ($3,000);

SECTION VII

I give and bequeath to my friends, DALE MALACHEK and JEWEL MALACHEK or the survivor of them the sum of Twenty-five Thousand Dollars ($25,000).

SECTION VIII

My executor in his absolute and sole discretion may satisfy the gifts made in Sections VI and VII in cash or in property of an equivalent value or in a combination of cash and property of an equivalent value.

SECTION IX.

I give and bequeath, including *any community interest* that my wife, CLAUDIA T. JOHNSON, may have therein, to the United States of America for inclusion in the Presidential Archival Depository known or to be known as the LYNDON BAINES JOHNSON LIBRARY for administration therein by its authorities, all of my Presidential and other papers, documents, historical materials, mementos, objects of art and other memorabilia, including but not limited to books, motion pictures, still pictures, and sound records (all of which are hereinafter called "materials") of which I die seized or possessed and which relate to my life and work, *subject to the conditions* set forth in the letter dated August 13, 1965, signed by me and addressed to Lawson B. Knott, Jr., Administrator of General Services Administration of the United States of America, concerning the establishment of said *Presidential Archival Depository*; provided, however, the gift hereby made is without any reservation of any intervening interest or right to the actual possession or enjoyment of said materials in my estate or my family. I hereby complete the gift of such materials not otherwise previously transferred during my lifetime as proposed in my said letter of August 13, 1965, and I hereby incorporate by reference said letter in this my last will and testament. The gift of such materials of which I may die seized or possessed is made by this provision of this my last will and testament in lieu of a Deed of Gift with respect to such property executed during my lifetime.

SECTION X.

All of the **rest and residue of my estate of every kind** and character, real, personal and mixed of which I may die seized and possessed or to which I may be entitled at the time of my death, I give, devise and bequeath unto my wife, **CLAUDIA T. JOHNSON**, and her substitute or successor trustees or trustee, IN TRUST, for the following uses and purposes and subject to the following provisions:

(a) **Upon my** death, the trustee shall divide and partition the trust property into *two parts* of equal value. One of said parts shall be designated as *THE LYNDA BIRD JOHNSON ROBB TRUST* and shall represent and be held and administered for the benefit of my daughter, LYNDA BIRD JOHNSON ROBB, born 1944 and the descendants of my said daughter all as hereinafter more particularized. The other of said parts shall be designated *THE LUCI BAINES JOHNSON NUGENT TRUST* and shall represent and be held and administered for the benefit of my daughter, LUCI BAINES JOHNSON NUGENT, born 1947 and the descendants of my said daughter, all as hereinafter more particularized. Each of said trusts shall be held and administered as a separate and distinct trust, subject to and governed by the provisions hereinafter set forth. If, however, at the time of my death, either child of mine above named should be dead without descendants her surviving, then the trust which would otherwise be created hereunder and designated by the name of the particular deceased child of mine shall not be created and the assets and property which would otherwise be allocated and partitioned to the trust not so created shall become and be a part of the other trust authorized to be created hereunder.

(b) The trustee, if and while the particular child of mine whose name designates the particular trust is living and during the continuance of that trust, shall pay at such intervals as the independent trustee may determine unto the particular child of mine whose name designates the particular trust so much of the net income of the particular trust as the independent trustee may in his absolute and sole discretion deem appropriate and determine to distribute unto the particular child of mind whose name designates the particular trust.

(c) Subject to the provisions of subdivision (b) of this Section X, the trustee, during the life of the particular child of mine whose name designates the particular trust and during the continuance of that particular trust, shall distribute at such intervals as the independent trustee may determine to the descendants of the particular child of mind whose name designates the particular trust in such proportions as the independent trustee may determine, which need not be equal as between or among beneficiaries, so much of the net income of the particular trust as the independent trustee in his absolute and sole discretion may deem appropriate and determine to distribute to the descendants of the particular child of mine whose name designates the particular trust.

(d) Any income not distributed as hereinabove provided shall be accumulated and added to the corpus of the particular trust.

(e) Upon the attainment of the age of thirty (30) years by the particular child of mine whose name designates the particular trust, that particular trust shall terminate and all of the assets and property comprising the corpus of the same shall be delivered and distributed in fee simple and free of trust unto the particular child of mind whose name designates that particular trust.

(f) If the particular child of mind whose name designates the particular trust should predecease me leaving descendants surviving at the time of my death, or if she should survive me but die prior to attaining the age necessary under the terms hereof to become entitled to distribution and delivery in fee simple and free of trust of the assets and property comprising the corpus of that particular trust leaving descendants her surviving, the assets and property comprising the corpus of the trust designated by the name of that particular deceased child of mine shall be retained in trust until the youngest of the children of the particular deceased child of mine whose name designates the particular trust attains the age of twenty-five (25) years, and during that period the net income of that particular trust or so much thereof as the independent trustee may deem appropriate shall be distributed in such proportions as the independent trustee may determine, which need not be equal as between or among beneficiaries, unto the descendants of the particular deceased child of mine whose name designates the particular trust. Any income not distributed as hereinabove provided shall be accumulated and added to the corpus of the particular trust. Upon the attainment of the age of twenty-five (25) years by the youngest of the children then living of the particular deceased child of mine whose name designates the particular trust, the trustee shall deliver and distribute in fee simple and free of trust all of the assets and property then comprising the corpus of that particular trust unto the children and the descendants of any deceased children of the particular deceased child of mine whose name designates that particular trust, per stirpes and not per capita.

(g) If any child of mine should die after I die leaving no descendants surviving, or if any child of mine should die before my death, leaving descendants surviving me, or after my death leaving descendants surviving, and all of the descendants of that particular child of mine should die before becoming entitled hereunder to actual distribution and delivery in fee simple of all of the assets and property comprising the corpus of the trust bearing the name of that particular child of mine, said trust shall terminate and the assets and property comprising the corpus of the same shall be incorporated and merged into the other trust created hereunder; but if the other trust created hereunder has been theretofore finally terminated hereunder, the assets and property which said trust theretofore finally terminated would otherwise have been entitled to receive hereunder if it had not been theretofore finally terminated shall vest in and be delivered in fee simple and free of trust unto those persons who, and in such proportions as said persons were entitled under this will to distribution and delivery in fee simple of the assets and property comprising the corpus of the trust theretofore finally terminated at the time of its final termination and the heirs, executors and administrators of said respective persons.

(h) If at any time during the life of any trust created hereunder all of my children and descendants should be dead, any trust existing hereunder shall terminate and all of the assets and property comprising the corpus of the same shall be delivered and distributed in fee simple and free of trust unto THE JOHNSON CITY FOUNDATION, to be held and administered and/or distributed in furtherance in the State of Texas of the general purposes of said Foundation.

(i) Anything in this will to the contrary notwithstanding, I direct that all trusts herein created shall in all events terminate not later than twenty (20) years from and after the death of the survivor of the following parties, to wit: my wife, CLAUDIA T. JOHNSON, and all of my children and descendants living at the time of my death, and upon such termination of any such trust the assets and property comprising the corpus of same shall be delivered and distributed in fee simple and free of trust unto those persons who at the time of such termination constitute the beneficiaries of the particular trust estate, in the respective proportions of the presumptive interest of said respective beneficiaries in the particular trust estate at the time of such termination.

(j) If at any time during the life of any trust herein created the net income which may be distributed under the terms hereof, together with income from other sources which may be available for such pruposes, shall not be adequate in the opinion of the independent trustee for the proper and appropriate education, maintenance and support of any beneficiary of the particular trust to whom income may be distributed at the time of the particular supplemental distribution, the independent trustee in his absolute and sole discretion may supplement the same out of the corpus of the particular trust to such extent and in such manner as he may deem necessary and appropriate for such purposes, and the amount of such supplemental distribution shall be charged against the presumptive share, if any, of the particular beneficiary of the particular trust.

SECTION XI.

The trustee of the trusts created herein, his substitute or successor trustees or trustee, all for the purpose of conserving, managing, disposing of and investing the assets and properties from time to time comprising the corpus of any trust created herein (hereinafter sometimes referred to as "properties"), shall have and exercise the following rights, powers and privileges, and shall be subject to the following conditions, duties, provisions and limitations:

(a) *Partitions and Distributions.* The trustee shall have full power and authority to make all partitions, divisions and distributions contemplated by any of the provisions of this will. He may make such partitions, divisions and distributions by allocating properties proportionately in kind or by allocating undivided interests therein or by making distributions partly in cash and partly in kind, at valuations to be fairly and reasonably determined by him. The trustee is also empowered to sell such properties as he may deem necessary or appropriate for the purpose of making such partitions, divisions or distributions. The actual partitions, divisions and distributions made by the trustee shall be binding and conclusive on all interested parties.

(b) *Conservation of Trust Properties*. The trustee shall have full power and authority to hold, manage and conserve for any period of time the properties owned by me at the time of my death which become a part of any trust created herein and any and all properties coming into his hands as trustee through the liquidation of any corporation, partnership or joint venture in which any trust has an interest, or otherwise. In connection with the management and conservation of such properties the trustee shall have the same powers in that respect as are accorded him in this will with respect to properties acquired as an investment. At all times the trustee shall have full power and authority to hold, manage and conserve any and all properties owned by any trust, and to that end he may take all action deemed necessary or appropriate for said purposes and may exercise all of the rights and powers that a prudent owner of any such property would have and exercise in managing and conserving property of a like kind.

(c) *Investment in Securities*. The trustee may purchase or otherwise acquire, upon such terms and conditions as he may deem appropriate stocks, stock rights, warrants, bonds, debentures, convertible debentures, notes, certificates of interest, certificates of indebtedness, or any other thing of value issued by any person, firm, association, trust, corporation or body politic whatsoever, except that the trustee shall not acquire by purchase any securities issued by the corporate trustee or any affiliate of the corporate trustee.

(d) *Investment and Investment Powers*. The trustee may acquire, upon such terms and conditions as he may deem appropriate, real and tangible personal property of any kind or character; he may purchase or otherwise acquire oil, gas and other mineral properties, whether similar or dissimilar, of any kind or character, may make and release oil, gas and other mineral leases, whether similar or dissimilar, and subleases and farmouts, may enter into development and drilling contracts, may explore, develop, operate and produce oil, gas and other mineral properties, whether similar or dissimilar, and may enter into unitization agreements, operating contracts and agreements for the present or future pooling of any interest in oil, gas or other mineral properties, whether similar or dissimilar; he may carry on and conduct a ranching business and in connection therewith shall have and exercise all of the powers and privileges that a prudent individual would have in carrying on and conducting his own ranching business including but not limited to the purchase and sale of all kinds of livestock, the hiring and discharging of employees, the growing or purchase of feeds, the leasing of ranch lands, the improvement of breeding herds and the conservation of soil and water; he may sell for cash or credit or for part cash and part credit, exchange, hold, dispose of, lease for any period of time, improve, repair, maintain, work, develop, operate, use, mortgage or pledge all or any part of the funds, assets and property constituting from time to time any part of any trust; engage in and carry on any business or undertaking and enter into any. partnership with any person, firm or corporation and any trustee under any other trust; borrow money; enter into contracts; execute obligations, negotiable and nonnegotiable; vote shares of stock in person or by proxy, with or without power of substitution; alone or with others to form, reorganize or extend the life of any corporation and exercise and perform any and all rights, privileges and powers inuring to the holder of any stock or securities comprising at any time a part of any trust estate; sue and be sued; settle, compromise or adjust by arbitration or otherwise any dispute or controversy in favor of or against any trust estate; waive or release rights of any kind; appoint, remove and act through agents, managers and employees and confer upon them such power and authority as he may deem necessary or desirable; pay all reasonable expenses; execute and deliver any deeds, conveyances, leases, contracts or written instruments of any character appropriate to any of his powers or privileges.

(e) *Selection and Retention of Investments*. Any property constituting a part of my estate at the time of my death and which becomes a part of the properties of any trust created herein and any property acquired by the trustee as herein provided and from time to time constituting any part of the particular trust shall be deemed a proper investment, and the trustee shall be under no obligation to dispose of or convert any such property. Investments need not be diversified, may be of a wasting nature, and may be made or retained with a view to possible increase in value. The trustee may invest and reinvest all funds available for investment or reinvestment from time to time or at such times as he may deem advisable in such investments as he is permitted to make pursuant to the terms of this will. He is expressly authorized to invest in unproductive property if in his judgment the best interest of the beneficiaries of the particular trust will be served thereby. The trustee, except as herein otherwise specifically provided, shall have as wide latitude in the selection, retention and making of investments as an individual would have in retaining or investing his own funds, and shall not be limited to nor be bound or governed by the laws or regulations of the State of Texas or any other state or country in respect of investments by trustees except to the extent that the application of such laws may not be waived.

(f) *Duration and Extent of Powers*. The trustee with respect to any and all power and authority conferred upon him by this will shall have the right and power to exercise any such power or authority in a manner so as to bind any trust created herein, even though any agreement, contract, lease, note or other evidence of indebtedness, or any other written instrument executed by him pursuant to the power and authority conferred upon him is not performable until after the expiration of the particular trust or may extend beyond the duration of such trust or may not become due and payable during the duration of the particular trust, it being the intent hereof that the trustee in binding and committing any trust pursuant to the power and authority herein conferred upon him shall have and possess with respect to such power and authority the same rights as if he were the individual owner of the property affected by the exercise of such power and authority.

(g) *Power to Determine Income and Principal*. Stock dividends and capital gains shall be treated as corpus. Except as herein otherwise specifically provided, the trustee shall have full power and authority to determine the manner in which expenses are to be borne and in which receipts are to be credited as between principal and income and to determine what shall constitute income or net income and what shall constitute corpus or principal and to withhold from income such reserves for depreciation or depletion as he may deem fair and equitable. In determining such matters, the trustee may give consideration to the provisions of Articles 26 to 36, inclusive, of the Texas Trust Act, but shall not be bound by such provisions.

(h) *Payments and Distributions*. All payments of income and distributions of principal to the beneficiary or beneficiaries of the particular trust as and when such payments or distributions are made, shall be made to such beneficiary or beneficiaries in person or upon their personal receipts, except that in the case of beneficiaries who shall not have attained their majority or who shall be under other disability, payments of income may be made to the parent, custodian, natural guardian or legal guardian of such beneficiaries, or may be made directly to or expended and used for the education, maintenance or support of such beneficiaries without the intervention of any legal guardian or other legal representative, and distributions of principal shall be made to the legal guardian of such beneficiaries.

(i) *Decisions of Trustee*. In each case in which discretionary power is vested in the trustee his express or implied decision or action in the exercise thereof shall be final and conclusive and be binding upon all beneficiaries hereunder and upon all persons whomsoever. In like manner, the express or implied decision or action of the independent trustee in the exercise of the discretion herein conferred upon him shall be binding and conclusive upon all beneficiaries hereunder and upon all persons whomsoever.

(j) *Accounting Reports and Responsibilities*. The trustee shall annually, or more frequently if he should so elect, render an accounting and report on the affairs of each trust then existing hereunder to each then income beneficiary. If any beneficiary has not reached his majority or is under other disability, the report or accounting which would otherwise be made to such beneficiary shall be made to his parent, natural guardian or legal guardian. Any trustee succeeding to the trusteeship shall be under no duty whatsoever to have an audit made of the books, records and affairs of the trusts then existing hereunder and upon his succession to the trusteeship may rely upon and accept as conclusive such audit or audits as may have been made by the prior trustees, and any and all trusts created herein shall exonerate and hold any trustee harmless from not having, upon his succession to the trusteeship, an audit made of the books, records and affairs of the trusts existing hereunder at the time of his succession to a trusteeship.

(k) *Governing Law - Cumulative and General Powers.* This trust shall be governed by the laws of the State of Texas, except to the extent that the same are inconsistent with the provisions of this will, in which event the provisions of this will shall govern. Except as herein otherwise provided, the powers conferred upon the trustee herein shall not be construed as in limitation of any authority conferred by law but shall be construed as in addition thereto. In general, the trustee shall have and exercise all such rights, powers and authority as persons owning similar property in their own right may lawfully have and exercise and shall have full power and authority to execute and deliver any and all instruments requisite to the exercise of such rights and powers.

SECTION XII.

Upon the death, resignation, failure, refusal or inability of my wife, CLAUDIA T. JOHNSON, to act as trustee, I direct that DONALD S. THOMAS, Austin, Texas, and J. W. BULLION, Dallas, Texas, shall become and be the trustees hereunder. Thereafter, in case of the death, resignation, failure, refusal or inability to act of any trustee acting hereunder, the remaining trustee shall appoint another trustee to serve with him, all to the end that there shall always be two trustees acting hereunder, subject to the condition, however, that at all times when two trustees are acting hereunder one of them must be a person who is not related by either blood or marriage to any beneficiary of the trusts created in this will.

If, however, all trusteeships should become vacant, I direct that CAPITAL NATIONAL BANK, Austin, Texas, and its successors shall become and be the trustee hereunder. Should CAPITAL NATIONAL BANK or any successor to that bank or any substitute or successor corporate trustee resign, fail, refuse or become unable to act hereunder, I direct that any court of competent jurisdiction, upon proper application made therefor and upon such service of process as the court may direct, may be decree appoint as sole trustee hereunder any trust corporation or national bank in the State of Texas possessing trust powers and having not less than Ten Million Dollars ($10,000,000) unimpaired capital and surplus.

No trustee named in this will nor any substitute or successor corporate trustee possessing the qualifications hereinabove designated shall be required to furnish bond or other security. Any successor trustee appointed by the remaining trustee as herein provided shall be required to furnish bond or other security only if, as and to the extent specified in the instrument of appointment.

Any trustee acting hereunder other than my wife, CLAUDIA T. JOHNSON, shall be entitled to reasonable compensation for services as such. No trustee shall be liable hereunder except for willful misconduct or personal dishonesty.

SECTION XIII.

Each trust created by this will is a spendthrift trust and no beneficiary of any trust created herein shall have the right or power to anticipate, by assignment or otherwise, any income or corpus given to such beneficiary by this will or any portion thereof, nor in advance of actually receiving the same shall have the right or power to sell, transfer, encumber, or in anywise charge same; nor shall such income or corpus or any portion of same be subject to any execution, garnishment, attachment, insolvency, bankruptcy or other legal proceedings of any character, or legal sequestration, levy or sale, or in any event or manner be applicable or subject, voluntarily or involuntarily, to the payment of such beneficiary's debts.

SECTION XIV.

If at the time of my death all of my children and descendants should be dead, I give, devise and bequeath all of said rest and residue of my estate to THE JOHNSON CITY FOUNDATION to be held and administered and/or distributed in furtherance in the State of Texas of the general purposes of said Foundation.

SECTION XV.

I constitute and appoint my wife, CLAUDIA T. JOHNSON, independent executor without bond of this my last will and testament. In case of the death, resignation, failure or inability of my wife to act as executor, I constitute and appoint DONALD S. THOMAS and J. W. BULLION, or such one of them as shall qualify, independent executors or independent executor, as the case may be, of this my last will and testament. Should DONALD S. THOMAS and J. W. BULLION die, resign, fail or become unable to act as executor hereunder, I constitute and appoint CAPITAL NATIONAL BANK and its successors independent executor without bond of this my last will and testament.

I direct that no action be had in the probate court respecting my estate other than to probate this will and return and record an inventory and appraisement of my estate and list of claims.

SECTION XVI.

During the administration of my estate my executor from time to time shall have and exercise the following rights, powers and privileges and shall be subject to the following duties, responsibilities, conditions and limitations:

(a) My executor may in his absolute and sole discretion join with my wife, CLAUDIA T. JOHNSON, or with her legal representative in executing any federal or state joint income tax returns to the fullest extent permitted by any of the applicable tax statutes. My executor may further pay out of property owned by me at the time of my death such part or all of any tax, interest or penalty due or shown to be due upon or by reason of any or all of such joint returns without any duty whatsoever to allocate to or to recover from my wife or her estate any such tax, interest or penalty so paid by her.

(b) My executor is authorized to claim expenses which may be deductible either from my gross estate in computing the estate tax or from gross income in computing income taxes as either estate or income tax deductions and make such adjustment of tax between principal and income as he may think equitable. Any determination so made by my executor shall be binding and conclusive upon all interested parties.

(c) My executor shall have full power and authority to pay all costs, taxes, expenses and charges in connection with his administration of my estate and to reimburse himself for any and all actual expenses which he may reasonably incur in the administration of my estate.

(d) No executor shall be liable for any action taken or not taken or for any loss or depreciation in value of any property in my estate whether due to an error in judgment or otherwise where such executor has exercised good faith and ordinary diligence in the exercise of his duties, and no executor shall be liable for any mistake of law or fact.

(e) Except to the extent that the same are not consistent with the provisions of this Section XVI, in which event the provisions of this section shall control, my executor shall have and exercise all of the rights, powers and privileges and be subject to all of the duties, responsibilities, conditions and limitations conferred and imposed upon the trustee in Section XI.

This I make and publish as my Last Will and Testament, hereunto subscribing my name in the presence of Robert North and Mike Howard, who have, at my request and in my presence and in the presence of each other, also subscribed their names as attesting witnesses, all on this 25th day of July 1972.

Lyndon B. Johnson
Lyndon B. Johnson

We, the undersigned persons of lawful age, have on this day, at the request of LYNDON B. JOHNSON, witnessed his signature to the foregoing Last Will and Testament in the presence of each of us, and we have, at the same time and in his presence and in the presence of each other, subscribed our names hereto as attesting witnesses.

549 Graham Rd
San Antonio Tex
Address
P. O. Box 226
Stonewall, Texas
Address
Robert North
Witness
Mike Howard
Witness

THE STATE OF TEXAS
COUNTY OF BEXAR

BEFORE ME, the undersigned authority, on this day personally appeared LYNDON B. JOHNSON, Mike Howard and Robert North, known to me to be the testator and witnesses, respectively, whose names are subscribed to the annexed and foregoing instrument in their respective capacities, and all of said persons being by me duly sworn the said LYNDON B. JOHNSON, Testator, declared to me and to the said witnesses in my presence that said instrument is his Last Will and Testament and that he had willingly made and executed it as his free act and deed and for the purposes therein expressed; and the said witnesses, each on his oath, stated to me in the presence and hearing of the said Testator that the said Testator had declared to them that the said instrument is his Last Will and Testament and that he executed the same as such and wanted each of them to sign it as a witness; and upon their oaths each witness stated further that they did sign the same as witnesses in the presence of the said Testator and at his request; and that he was at that time over eighteen years of age and was of sound mind; and that each of said witnesses was then at least fourteen years of age.

Lyndon B. Johnson
Lyndon B. Johnson

Mike Howard
Witness

Robert North
Witness

SUBSCRIBED AND ACKNOWLEDGED BEFORE ME by the said LYNDON B. JOHNSON, Testator, and subscribed and sworn to before me by the said Mike Howard and Robert North witnesses, this 25th day of July, 1972.

Elizabeth P. Hall
Notary Public, Bexar County, Texas

My commission expires
June 1, 1973.

(seal)

Notes on the Will of Lyndon B. Johnson

TEXAS IS ONE OF EIGHT STATES WHICH HAVE A SPECIAL SYSTEM OF LAW with respect to property acquired by a married couple through the efforts of either during the period of marriage. Such property is called community property, and is treated as belonging to both husband and wife in equal shares at all times. This differs radically from the system in the other 42 states, which recognizes separate ownership by either spouse without regard to when or how property is acquired. (The widespread practice of many married couples in those states who routinely put assets into joint ownership is inspired by sentiments similar to those on which the community property system is based. The results, however, are not the same, and the practice can develop serious disadvantages as the value of assets held jointly mounts.)

Lyndon Johnson was the first President whose permanent home was located in a community-property state. As a result, his Will is distinctly different from that of any other President. Under the community-property system, Mrs. Johnson owned 50 percent of their community property from the time it was acquired. Section I of President Johnson's Will makes clear that it purports to deal only with his share of that property. It is possible for the will of a husband or wife to attempt to dispose of the other's share of community property, but those provisions will be effective only if the other assents. President Johnson's Will does so only with respect to any share which Mrs. Johnson might have in his papers. It is also possible for either a husband or wife or both to own property which is not community property (usually described as separate property), either because it was acquired before marriage, or by gift or inheritance after marriage. The will of the owner of separate property controls all of it. However, this Will explicitly disclaims ownership of any separate property with the possible exception of President Johnson's papers.

The community-property system affects the preparation of the will in several important ways. Since a surviving spouse is protected through his or her share in the community property, the law does not require that anything more be added to it from the other's property. Of course, it does not foreclose such addition either; but as a practical matter estate planning for wealthy couples with substantial amounts of community property begins from the premise that each already owns substantial wealth to which it may or may not be desirable to add. Here the only gift made to Mrs. Johnson for her own benefit was that made to her in Section V of the furnishings and equipment of their home.

Community property also has a different, though ultimately similar, status in the federal tax system. The marital deduction is not available for gifts of community property to a surviving spouse. The effect on federal estate tax liabilities is, however, equivalent to a gift to a spouse in a non-community-property state of the amount qualifying for the maximum marital deduction. The mechanics of arriving at the tax liabilities are different, but the results are comparable. In fact, the legislation creating the marital deduction, and related tax provisions for husband and wife, arose out of a desire to equalize tax treatment of those who do not live in community-property states with that of those who do.

On its face, President Johnson's Will, making comparatively insignificant provisions for his wife, appears quite different from those of Presidents Roosevelt, Truman, Kennedy, and, probably Eisenhower, all of whom were also survived by their wives and one or more children. Set in the community-property context, however, it can be seen to produce a pattern of distribution very similar to that of those men. Presidential papers and modest legacies to non-family members aside, the widow takes approximately half the property, and the other half (less taxes, debts, costs of administration) is given to or held in trust for the President's descendants. In this respect, estate planning for Presidents is like estate planning for any other client with substantial wealth and similar family. President Johnson's Will does not employ the trust device to save potential taxes at the death of either of his children, as does that of President Franklin Roosevelt. Apparently, the trusts for his daughters were conceived as primarily protective arrangements for them while they were still comparatively young, for the trusts terminate as each reaches the age of 30—reached by his daughter Lynda Robb in 1974, and to be reached by his daughter Luci Nugent in 1977.

Another respect in which President Johnson's Will differs from those of all his predecessors is in his appointment of Mrs. Johnson as *independent* Executor. The adjective has a special significance representing an alternative method of estate administration available historically only in Texas, two or three other states, and the District of Columbia, though not necessarily under precisely that name. The effect is to relieve an Executor from continuing supervision by the court which appoints him. The value of court supervision as a form of protection for the interests of those with rights in an estate ranges from absolutely essential to zero. An efficient legal system should offer a choice of methods of estate administration, and that is one of the purposes of the Uniform Probate Code which has been enacted in substantial measure in 10 states and is currently under consideration in many more. Unfortunately, the legal machinery in many states is not as flexible as it could and should be. Through his designation of her as independent Executor, President Johnson demonstrated confidence in Mrs. Johnson's judgment, diligence, and honesty. He also chose a system of administration which he thought would be simpler, less expensive, and more private.

President Johnson's Will, like those of his contemporary Presidents, is the handiwork of an experienced professional draftsman of such instruments. It reveals its source in many ways. One of these is systematic coverage of most, if not all, sequences of events that could occur, however improbable such events may be. Another is the comprehensive grant of powers to the trustee and Executor. Added up, these authorize the trustee or Executor to take any action thought desirable in the management of the estate or trust property. The specific reference to investment in development of mineral interests and in ranching is probably more common in wills drawn in the Southwestern United States.

Section II, which sets out nine paragraphs of definitions and usage applicable to this document, is characteristic of a professionally drawn instrument. Sections XII and XV make provision for filling vacancies in the offices of Executor or trustee so that it should never be necessary to resort to a court appointment.

Paragraph (i) of Section X is a savings clause included to forestall a challenge to provisions of the Will as being in violation of the Rule Against Perpetuities. The Rule has been evolving over three centuries. Its purpose may be easily stated in general terms: to limit to a decent period the time during which the wishes of a dead testator will control property which he formerly owned. However the details of its application to particular situations have proved so difficult and eccentric that law students and lawyers alike regard it with trepidation.

A savings clause protects the client's instrument against any unpleasant surprise from this quarter. It also permits deliberate use of provisions which would otherwise be defective under the Rule. Thus here, the provisions of paragraph (f) of Section X, postponing distribution until the youngest descendant of a daughter reached age 25, could be vulnerable, were it not for the savings clause.

Section XIII is a spendthrift clause. It prevents beneficiaries from selling or giving away their interests before they have actually received them from the trustee. It also shelters those interests from the remedies which unpaid creditors generally may employ against assets of their debtors. The effect is to create a privileged class, beneficiaries of spendthrift trusts, who are able to enjoy the benefits of wealth without all of the responsibilities that usually accompany it. Perhaps some beneficiaries, known to be unable to resist running up bills far beyond their current means, should be protected in this way. However, automatic inclusion of such a provision, without discussion of the question with the client, and without specific instructions to do so to create protection thought to be needed, is an undesirable, though unfortunately common, drafting practice. The odds are large that that is what happened here.

Examination of the end of the Will discloses that President Johnson and the witnesses all signed twice, the second time before a notary public who also signed and affixed his seal. Though not necessary to make a valid will, the second signing before a notary simplifies the filing of the Will for probate after the testator's death. In one form or another the witnesses must give their testimony about the ceremony of signing. Through the procedure used here, they (and the testator) do so under oath before a notary who makes this record. All that is necessary then, after the testator's death, is to file the will in the appropriate court with the notary's certificate attached. At that point there is no need to take the witnesses' testimony again.

This device, called a self-proved will, is authorized in some states, though probably not a majority. Wherever that authority exists, the device does simplify the offer of a will for probate at some undetermined future time when the witnesses may be difficult to find or to account for.

Facsimile of a section of the Will of Lyndon B. Johnson.

THE STATE OF TEXAS

COUNTY OF BEXAR

BEFORE ME, the undersigned authority, on this day personally appeared LYNDON B. JOHNSON, _Mike Howard_ and _Robert North_, known to me to be the testator and witnesses, respectively, whose names are subscribed to the annexed and foregoing instrument in their respective capacities, and all of said persons being by me duly sworn the said LYNDON B. JOHNSON, Testator, declared to me and to the said witnesses in my presence that said instrument is his Last Will and Testament and that he had willingly made and executed it as his free act and deed and for the purposes therein expressed; and the said witnesses, each on his oath, stated to me in the presence and hearing of the said Testator that the said Testator had declared to them that the said instrument is his Last Will and Testament and that he executed the same as such and wanted each of them to sign it as a witness; and upon their oaths each witness stated further that they did sign the same as witnesses in the presence of the said Testator and at his request; and that he was at that time over eighteen years of age and was of sound mind; and that each of said witnesses was then at least fourteen years of age.

Lyndon B. Johnson

Notes on Dying Without a Will

FOUR PRESIDENTS, LINCOLN, ANDREW JOHNSON, GRANT, AND GARFIELD, died intestate——that is, without leaving a valid will. Their property which could have been distributed under a will passed instead to the surviving members of their families under the intestate laws of the states in which they were domiciled. These laws provide a set of rules to govern succession to property whose former owners have died without creating any scheme of disposition of their own; also serve to fill gaps in schemes which have been provided but which have proved to be incomplete.

Necessarily, such a set of rules must be comparatively simple and rigid. It cannot take into account the variety of factors which individuals can, and often do, consider in devising an estate plan for their particular property and family. In fact, the intestate laws rest almost entirely on the single factor of closeness of family relation to the deceased. Thus, a surviving spouse and children are preferred to parents and brothers and sisters; the latter are preferred to more remote relativeness, etc. Undoubtedly, this pattern coincides with the preferences of most people, but the intestate rules apply in the same way to estates of all sizes and create shares payable outright to the recipients without regard to their ages, financial needs or resources, physical condition, mental capacity, or experience in money management. These statutes perform an important function in assuring an orderly disposition of all estates, but, except in rare instances, they are a poor substitute for an individually designed estate plan. They serve the needs and wishes of individual property owners and their families about as well as a single size of clothing would fit all adult members of the population.

All four of these Presidents were survived by a widow and one or more children. The intestate rules are perhaps most open to criticism in this situation for, then and now, they typically produce a division of the property between the widow and the children. More often than not though such a division makes poor sense. If the children are adult and self-supporting, the needs of the widow should usually be treated as preeminent. Husbands making wills typically do this, as do the numerous adult children who voluntarily sign over to a surviving parent their intestate share of an estate of modest size. When the children are minors the disadvantages of intestacy become even more evident. Minors' interests are usually best served by a surviving parent able to use all available assets for the benefit of the whole family, but a minor's intestate share cannot be so treated. It belongs to the minor alone whose very status as a minor prevents the voluntary sharing possible for an adult child. Instead, appointment of a guardian of the estate of the minor will usually be required. Then the guardian, who may be the surviving parent, must observe court-directed procedures and be subject to restrictions on the way the funds may be invested and the uses to which they may be put.

Admittedly, there are circumstances in which the children and a surviving spouse should share the property. Where the estate is large, tax considerations and the existence of an excess over the widow's forseeable needs may both suggest a division——though not necessarily in the form prescribed by the statute. In the case of a second marriage, where the present husband or wife is not the parent of one or more of the children, there is substantially less assurance that property left to the spouse will pass ultimately to the children. These two situations aside (and absent some other special factor influencing the particular husband and father), the family, now reduced to a widowed mother and her children, is ordinarily best served by a disposition which makes her the sole or principal recipient of the property. Intestate statutes recently enacted in a few states are moving in that direction.

Under Illinois law, Lincoln's estate——to take one Presidential example——was divided into equal thirds, for his middle-aged widow, his son, Robert, who had just graduated from college, and his son, Tad, a 12-year old boy. A modern estate planner would be chagrinned if he could not suggest a plan more likely to care for each family member fairly and also to achieve the goals which a husband and father typically has for his family. Lincoln was free, of course, to divide his estate into equal thirds for his widow and two children, precisely as the statute did, but there is no evidence that such a division was his conscious choice. Rather, that result was produced by his inaction which had the effect of allowing the Illinois legislature to plan his estate by default.

Death without a will may also create unnecessary problems or costs in settling an estate or managing its assets. The court must appoint an administrator who may or may not be someone the intestate would have chosen. Bond, which might have been waived, will probably be required. Lacking a grant of specific powers in the will, the administrator may be inhibited in applying his best judgment to the management of the property or may be put to the expense and delay of obtaining court approval for quite ordinary transactions. Here too, enactment of modern statutes, such as the Uniform Probate Code, is serving in a few states to minimize these difficulties. Perhaps most important, death intestate precludes any opportunity to use the trust device with its potential for family protection, adaptability to changing circumstances, and the use of complex patterns of distribution effected over many years.

Given their property and family situations, the failure of these four Presidents to make a will seems thoughtless at best, perhaps even irresponsible. One may wonder that these chief executives of the nation, so respected and effective in other ways, could have failed to perform this simple obligation owed to their immediate families. Yet, like the Presidential testators whose wills are reproduced in this book, these Presidents too are typical. A significant fraction of our population dies intestate. People of all ages, means, educational backgrounds, and family circumstances are represented. Making a will is an opportunity to provide a final, thoughtful expression of love and of one's personality, but, for a variety of reasons, many fail to take advantage of it. It should not be too surprising then that a small proportion, 4 of 35, of our Presidents should have neglected it too.

Index

Abilene, Kansas, 234, 236
Adams, Abigail, 32, 33, 36, 54; Abigail, grand-daughter, 34; Abigail Brown, 61; Charles, 34; Charles Francis, 55, 58, 59, 60, 61, 62, 64; Charles Francis, son, 60, 142; Elizabeth Coombs, 34, 59; Henry, 32; Henry Brooks, 61; Isaac Hull, 34, 59
Adams, John, 38, 41, 54, 62, 79, 195, 212; colonial legislature of Massachusetts, 33; Commissioner to France, 33; estate, 33, 36; executors, 35, 36; land holdings, 34; library, 34, 35; law practice, 33; family fortune, 32, 33; Minister to Great Britain, 33; Presidency, 33; private papers, 35; salary, 33; Stuart portrait, 55, 60; Vice President, 33;
Adams, John, father of President John, 32, 61
Adams, John Quincy, 33, 34, 35, 36; bequests, 60-62, 64; burial, 55; in Congress, 54, 55; diaries, 55, 65; estate, 55; executors, 56, 59, 62; financial problems, 55; fortune, 55; land holdings, 55, 56, 58, 64; library, 60, 65; Massachusetts Senate, 54; Minister to Netherlands, Russia, Great Britain, 54, 55; papers, 55, 60, 65; Presidency, 36, 54, 55; real estate, 55-59; salary, 55; Secretary of State, 36, 55; trusts & trustees, 59
Adams, John Quincy, son of Charles Francis, 60, 61, 62; John Quincy, son of Thomas B., 59; Joseph, 32; Joseph Harrod, 34, 59, 61; Louisa Catherine, granddaughter of John Quincy, 55; Louisa Catherine, wife of John Quincy, 54, 56, 57, 59, 62; Mary Catherine, 61; Mary Louisa, 55, 57-62; Susanna Boylston, 32; Thomas Boylston, 34, 35, 36, 55, 59
Adams family interests, 64, 65
Aiken, Charles A., 110; Mary M., 110
Alaska, 179
Albemarle County, Va., 37, 39, 40
Alexander, Lucia, 266
Alexandria, Va., 19, 26, 29; Academy, 20
All Souls Unitarian Church, Washington, D.C., 172
Allegheny College, Pa., 158
Allen, Lewis W., 141
Ambrose, John, 94
American Bar Association, 169
American Colonization Society, 45, 46, 47
American Horticultural Society, 30
American Relief Committee, 188
Amherst College, 184
Appleton, Jane Means see Pierce, Jane
Archivist of the U.S., 215, 216, 217, 230
Arlington National Cemetary, 169, 248
Armstrong, Robert, 67, 70
Arthur, Chester Alan, 129, 135, 168; Collector of customs, 137; education, 136; executors, 138, 140; fortune, 137; income, 137; investments, 138, 140; lawyer, 136, 137; New York militia, 137; Presidency, 137; Quartermaster General, 137; real estate, 137-139; salary, 137; servants, 137, 138; trusts & trustees, 138, 140; Vice President, 137, 140
Arthur, Chester Alan, son, 137, 138, 140; Ellen Herndon, daughter, 137, 138, 140; Ellen Herndon, wife, 136, 137; Malvina, 136; William, 136
Ash Lawn, Va., 50
Ashfield, Va., 51
Ashton, Ann, 26
Assassinations, 124, 135, 159, 248
Atlanta, march on, 147
Australia, 188
Axson, Ellen see Wilson, Ellen
Baldwin, Nelly, 45
Ball, Francis, 26; Mary, 15
Bank failure, 129
Baruch, Bernard, 175
Baton Rouge, La., 98
Belmont College, 146
Beneficiaries, 36
Berkeley, Va. plantation, 78, 79
Bibby, Gouverneur S., 52
Birchard, Sardis, 130
Bishop, Thomas, 24

Black Hawk War, 97, 122
Blaine, James G., 131, 135, 137
Blair, Frank, 67, 68
Blair House, 214
Blanchin, General J. B. & Co., 67, 68
Blooming Grove, Ohio, 178
Bobbitt, Rebekah, 266
Bolling, William H., 175
Bonus marchers, 235
Booth, John Wilkes, 124
Boston, 58, 59, 62
Boston massacre, 33
Boston police strike, 184
Bouvier, Jacqueline Lee see Kennedy, Jacqueline B.
Bowdoin College, 108
Boys Clubs of America, 189
Braintree, Mass. see Quincy, Mass.
Brasher, Marian Wallace, 228
Breckinridge, John C., 128
British & Indian War, 67, 69
Brookline, Mass., 247
Brush, Louis H., 179
Bryan, William Jennings, 169
Bryn Mawr College, 174, 175
Buchan, Earl of, 23
Buchanan, Edward Y., 116, 117, 118; James, father, 114
Buchanan, James, 128, 260; bequests, 116; candidacies, 115, 120; codicils, 118-119; in Congress, 115; education, 114; executors, 116-118, 120; fortune, 115; funeral, 116; income, 114; lawyer, 115; Minister to Russia, England, 115; nephews & nieces, 117, 120; papers, 118, 120; Presidency, 115; real estate, 117, 121; salary, 115; servants, 115, 116, 119; Secretary of State, 115; trust, 120
Buchanan, James P., 262
Buffalo, N.Y., 102, 103, 104, 141
Buffalo Historical Society, 103
Buffalo Orphans Asylum, 104, 106
"Bull Moose", 163
Bullion, J.W., 274, 275
Bureau of the Census, 11
Burnet, Findlay & Harrison, 82
Burnet, Jacob, 80
Butler, Benjamin F., 73, 74, 75
Byrd, William, 23
Caldwell, N.J., 141
California, 188
Campbell, Parson, 49
Campobello, N.B., 189, 205
Canada, 136, 169, 170
Cantine, Christina, 75
Canton, Ohio, 158, 159
Cape Cod, 142
Carow, Edith Kermit see Roosevelt, Edith Kermit
Carter, Betty, 26; Charles, 23; Robert "King", 78
Cass, Lewis, 115
Chesapeake Bay, 42
Childress, Sarah see Polk, Sarah
Childs, George, 128
Chinese Imperial Bureau of Mines, 188
Christian, Letitia see Tyler, Letitia
Cincinnati, Ohio, 78, 81, 84, 130, 133, 146, 168, 169; University of, 168
Civil War, 86, 90, 123, 128, 130, 135, 137, 141, 147, 158, 263
Clark, Susanna Boylston, 34
Clary, Joseph, 102
Clay, Henry, 55, 92
Cleveland, Esther, 142, 143; Frances F., 142-145; Francis G., 143
Cleveland, Grover, 147; Assistant District Attorney, 141; bequests, 143, 145; burial, 142, 143; education, 141; estate, 142; executor, 143; Governor of New York, 142; homes, 142; lawyer, 141, 142; legacies, 143; Mayor of Buffalo, 142; name, 141; New York Institute for the Blind, 141; nominations, 142; Presidency, 142; salary, 142; Sheriff, 141
Cleveland, Marion, 143; Richard F., father, 141; son, 143; Rose, 142; Ruth, 142
Cleveland Memorial Tower, 142
Cleves, Ohio, 81, 82, 83
Clinton, George, 23
Codicils, 1, 48

Coffee, Andrew Jackson, 69; John, 69
Coleman, Ann, 114
Colombia, 79
Columbia, Tenn., 92, 93
Columbia Law School, 162, 197
Columbia University, 235
Columbian Exposition, 92
Community property, 278
Concord, N. H., 109, 111
Concord Public Library, 111
Confederate Congress, 86
Confederate States, 86
Congress, U.S., 38, 43, 55, 67, 70, 85, 91, 175; appropriations, 50, 73, 169; grant, 51. See also Library of Congress
Conkling, Roscoe, 137
Connally, John B., 248
Connelly, Matthew, 217
Constitution, frigate, 43, 46, 60
Constitutional Convention, 42; proceedings 45, 47
Continental Congress, 42, 45, 49
Coolidge, Calvin, 11, 189; estate, 185; Governor of Massachusetts, 184; homes, 185; investments, 185; land holdings, 185; lawyer, 184; local & state politics, 184; name, 184; newspaper column, 185; oath of office, 185; Presidency, 185; salary, 185; Vice President, 185
Coolidge, Grace, 184, 186, 187; John, ancestor, 184, son, 186, 187; Joseph, 40
Cooper, Thomas, 61
Court of St. James, 115
Craik, Dr. James, 17, 24
Culpeper, Lord, 15
Custis, Daniel Parke, 16, 29; Eleanor Parke see Lewis, Eleanor Parke; George Washington Parke, 25, 26, 27; Martha Dandridge, see Washington, Martha
Cypress Grove Plantation, 98
Dallas, Tex., 248
Dana, Francis, 54
Dandridge, Bartholomew, estate, 22, 23; Frances, Jones, 16; John, father of Martha Washington, 16; John, son of Bartholomew, 22; Mary, 22
Daniel, Margaret Truman, 214, 216, 217, 218, 219
Dark Horse candidates, 92
Daughters of the American Revolution, 147
Daugherty, Harry M., 179
Davidson College, N.C., 174
Davis, David, 124; Jackson, 128
De Wolfe, Florence Kling see Harding, Florence Kling; Marshall Eugene, 178
Declaration of Independence, 33, 37, 78
Delano, Sarah see Roosevelt, Sarah Delano
Delaware, Ohio, 130
Democratic Convention 1852, 109; 1856, 115; 1912, 175; 1936, 198; 1956, 248; 1960, 248, 262
Democratic party, 91, 115, 126, 142, 175
Dennison, Robert, 217
Dent, Frederick, 127; Julia see Grant, Julia
Depression, 73, 79, 189, 198
Descendants, 140
Devin, Sarah H., 149
Dewey, Thomas E., 198, 214
Dickinson College, 114
Dimmick, Mary Scott Lord see Harrison, Mary Lord
Dinwiddie, Robert, 16
Disciples of Christ, 134
District of Columbia, university in, 21, 30; establishment & financing, 21-22, 30. See also Washington, D.C.
Donelson, Andrew Jackson, 69, 70, 71; Rachel see Jackson, Rachel
Donelson family, 71
Doubleday & Co., 237, 238
Doud, Mamie Geneva see Eisenhower, Mamie
Douglas, Stephen A., 123
Dower Negroes, 19
Drew, Steven & William, 81
Drexel, Joseph, 128
Dry, Leonard D., 237, 245
East Aurora, N.Y., 102
Eaton, Bettie H., 149
Edison, Thomas, 179

Education of orphans, 20
Eisenhower, David, 234
Eisenhower, Dwight D., 12, 187, 189, 195, 212
    232, 278; bequests, 237; burial, 236;
    Chief of Staff, 235; codicil, 243; education,
    234; estate, 240, 245; executors, 238-242,
    245, 246; homes, 236, 245; income, 236;
    investments, 239-241; military career,
    235, 236; name, 234; NATO forces, 235;
    papers, 236, 238, 243, 245; pension, 236;
    Presidency, 235; President Columbia Uni-
    versity, 235; property, disposition & trans-
    fer, 239, 240, 246; salary, 236; stocks,
    bonds & securities, 240, 241; Supreme
    Commander, 235; taxes, 241, 242, 245,
    246; trusts & trustees, 239, 242, 245, 246;
    World War I, 234; World War II, 235, 245;
    writings, 235-239
Eisenhower, John S. D., 235, 237, 238, 239,
    242; Mamie Doud, 234-238, 241, 242,
    245
Eisenhower Foundation, 236, 238, 245
Eisenhower Museum, 236, 245
Eisenhower Presidential Library, 236, 238, 243
Elliot, Jesse D., Commodore, 46, 61
Ely, Northcut, 190, 191, 192
Equal portions, 36
Eppes, Francis, 39; Francis, John W., 39; Mary,
    39
"Era of Good Feelings", 50
Erie County, N.Y., 141
Estate administration, 13, 173
Ewing, George W., 46
Executive Branch, reorganization, 189
Executive mansion, 43
Executors, 13, 90, 120, 140, 168, 196, 242, 246,
    279
Fairfax, Bryan, 17, 24
Fairfax County Courthouse, Va., 31
Fairfield, Vt., 36
Fayetteville, N.Y., 141
Federalists, 114
Fee tail interest, 64
Fiduciaries, 195, 196
Fillmore, Abigail, 102, 107; Calvin T., 104, 106;
    Caroline C., 103-107; Cyrus, 104; Mary
    Abigail, 103
Fillmore, Millard, 140; apprenticeship, 102;
    bonds, 106; codicils, 105-107; Comptroller
    of N.Y., 103; in Congress, 103; education,
    102; estate, 103-105; executors, 104, 105;
    homes, 103; land holdings, 104, 106;
    lawyer, 102; N.Y. State Legislature, 102;
    papers, 103; philanthropist, 103; Presi-
    dency, 103; salary, 103; Vice President,
    103
Fillmore, Millard Powers, 103, 104, 105, 106;
    Miranda, 104; Nathaniel, 102; Phoebe Mil-
    lard, 102
Findlay, James, 80
Firestone, Harvey, 179
First Presbyterian Church, Indianapolis, 155
Fish, Hamilton, 128
Folsom, Mary Frances see Cleveland, Frances
    F.
Food Administration, U.S., 189
Foraker, Joseph, 179
Ford, Henry, 179
Ford's Theatre, 124
Fort Harrison, 97
Foundations, 260
Franklin, Benjamin, 17, 24, 38
Franklin D. Roosevelt Library, 198, 203
Free Soil party, 73
Fremont, John C., 115, 123, 134
Fremont, Ohio, 130, 131
French, Seth B., 139
French & Indian Wars, 16
Frothingham, Nathaniel L., 61
Galena, Ill., 128
Galt, Edith Bolling see Wilson, Edith; William C.,
    99
Gardiner, Alexander, 87; David L., 89; Julia see
    Tyler, Julia Gardiner
Garfield, Abram, 134; Eliza, Ballou, 134, 135
Garfield, James Abram, 11, 128, 137; assassina-
    tion, 135; in Congress, 135; education,
    134; estate, 135; farm in Mentor, Ohio,
    135; insurance policy, 135; lawyer, 134;

memorials, 135; military career, 135; Ohio
    State Senate, 135; Presidency, 135; Pres-
    ident of Hiram College, 134; salary, 135
Garfield, Lucretia, 134, 135; pension, 135
Garrett, Alexander, 39, 40
General Services of the U.S., Administrator, 14,
    215, 232, 238, 243, 259, 267
Gettysburg, Pa., 235, 236, 245
George, Benjamin Pierce, 111
Georgetown, Ohio, 127
Georgia Warm Springs Foundation, 199, 200,
    201
Germany, food supply, 189
Gifts, 12, 13, 232, 245
Gilder, Richard Watson, 143
Goldsmiths Company, Edinburgh, 24
Goldwater, Barry, 263
Goodhue, Grace see Coolidge, Grace
Goodpaster, A. J., 238
Gouverneur, Maria, 50, 51, 53; Samuel, L., 51-
    53
Graham, Daniel, 95
Grant, Jesse, 127; Julia, 127, 128; Nellie, 128
Grant, Ulysses S., 11, 135, 137, 168, 169; be-
    quests to the government, 129; consi-
    dered a failure, 128; education, 127; fi-
    nancial problems, 128, 129; houses, 128;
    income, 128; library, 128; Memoirs, 129;
    military career, 127, 128; name, 127; na-
    tional recognition, 129; pension, 129;
    Presidency, 128; real estate, 129; salary,
    128; State funeral, 129
Grant's tomb, 129
Green, Sarah, 24
Greeneville, Tenn., 125, 126
Greenway, Va., 85, 87
Groton, 197
Grover, Stephen, 141
Grundy, Felix, 91, 93
Guardians & guardianship, 120, 139, 150, 153,
    157
Guiteau, Charles J., 135
Gurley, Ralph Randolph, 45, 46
Hackett, Henry T., 204, 209
Hall, Nathan K., 105
Hamilton, Alexander, 38
Hammond, Mildred, 26
Hampden-Sydney College, 78
Hampton, Va., 87, 88, 90
Hancock, Winfield, 135
Hanna, Mark, 159
Hardin County, Ky., 122
Harding, Abigail V., 180; Florence Kling, 178-
    181, 183, grandchildren, 181; George
    Tryon, 180, 181; George Tryon Jr., 180,
    181
Harding, Warren Gamaliel, 169, 184, 185, 189;
    bequests, 180, 181; brother & sisters,
    181; education, 178; estate, 179, 183;
    executor, 180, 182; funeral, 179; govern-
    ment bonds & securities, 180; invest-
    ments, 183; journalist, 178; Lieutenant
    Governor, 178; local politics, 178;
    memorabilia, 179, 181; nephews &
    nieces, 181; nomination Governor of Ohio,
    175, 176; papers, 179; pastimes, 179;
    Presidency, 179; real estate, 180; speak-
    ing tour 1923, 179; stocks, 179, 180, 181;
    trusts & trustees, 180, 183
Harding Memorial Association, 179
Harding Publishing Company, 179, 180, 183
Harris, Julia, 104, 105; M. L., 152
Harrison, Anna, 78, 79, 81
Harrison, Benjamin, 13; bequests, 148-152,
    154-155; codicil, 147; Court crier, 146;
    education, 146; estate 147; executor, 154,
    157; family discord, 147, 156, 157; family
    portraits, 152; homes, 146, 147, 150, 153,
    156; Indiana volunteer infantry, 147; in-
    vestments, 154; land holdings, 150;
    lawyer, 146, 147; papers, 151, 152; Pres-
    idency, 147; residuary estate, 148, 154,
    156, 157; salary, 146; Supreme Court,
    147; trusts & trustees, 148, 153; Ven-
    ezuela border dispute, 147
Harrison, Benjamin, father, 78, 81; brother, 81;
    son, 82, 83; Benjamin Jr., 149; Betsey
    see Short, Betsey; Caroline Scott, 146,
    147; Elizabeth, 148, 150-154, 156; John

Cleves, 82; John Scott, 81, 82, 146;
    Marthena, 149, 153; Mary Lord, 147-157;
    Mary Saunders, 153; Mary Scott, 147,
    149, see also McKee, Mary Harrison;
    Russell B., 147, 149, 150-152, 156, 157;
    Symmes, 81
Harrison, William Henry, 85, 120, 142, 146, 151,
    163; campaign of 1840, 79; debts, 79;
    education, 78; estate, 84; executors, 80;
    Governor of Indiana Territory, 79; grand-
    son Benjamin, 146; imperfection of will,
    84; land holdings & real estate, 78, 80-84;
    medical studies, 78; military service, 78,
    79; Minister to Colombia, 79; papers, 79, 83;
    Presidency, 79; salary, 79; Secretary & del-
    egate of Northwest Territory, 79; U.S.
    Senator, 79; Will, fragment of, 83
Harrison, William Henry, son, 81; William Henry,
    grandson, 149, 153
Harry S. Truman Library, Independence, Mo.,
    214, 215, 216, 228, 230
Harvard University, 32, 33, 54, 162, 197, 248
Hastings, Anna, 143; Frank S., 143, 144; Mary,
    143; Richard, 143
Hawthorne, Nathaniel, 108; children, 110
Hay, Elizabeth K., 51
Hayes, Birchard A., 131, 132; Fanny, 131, 132;
    Lucy (Lemonade Lucy), 130, 131, 133;
    Rutherford, 130
Hayes, Rutherford B., 137, 169; in Congress,
    130, 131; education, 130; executors, 132,
    133; Governor of Ohio, 131; hard-money
    position, 131; lawyer, 130, 133; military
    career, 130; philanthropic works, 131;
    Presidency, 131, 133; salary, 131; trusts
    & trustees, 132, 133
Hayes, Rutherford P., 131, 132; Scott Russell,
    131-133; Sophia Birchard, 130; Webb C.,
    131, 132
Haynie, Sally B., 24
Henry, Harriet B., 117; J. Buchanan, 116-118;
    Lou see Hoover, Lou
Herbert Hoover Memorial Park, Library & Birth-
    place Foundation, 189, 191, 192
The Hermitage, 67, 68; as museum, 71
Herndon, Ellen Lewis see Arthur, Ellen Herndon
Herron, Helen see Taft, Helen H.; John V., 169
Hillsborough, N.H., 108
Hiram College, 134
Hobart, Garret A., 159
Hoes, Hannah see Van Buren, Hannah
Holliday, John H., 152
Hood, John, 23
Hoover, Allan, 189, 190, 191, 192
Hoover, Herbert, 12, 187, 212, 232, 245; Ameri-
    can Relief Committee, 188; Australia, 188;
    bequests, 191; burial, 189, 193; charities,
    189; China, 188; executors, 191, 196;
    Food Administration, 189; food sup-
    ply of Germany, 189; homes, 189; in-
    vestments, 193, 196; memorials, 189; min-
    ing engineer, 188; multi-millionaire, 189;
    papers, 189; pension, 189; Presidency, 189;
    property, transfer of, 193, 194; public ser-
    vice, 189; residuary estate, 192; salary, 188,
    189; secretarial staff, 189, 190; Secretary of
    Commerce, 189; taxes, 194; travels, 188;
    trusts & trustees, 190, 192, 193, 195, 196;
    writings, 188, 189
Hoover, Herbert Jr., 190, 191, 192; Huldah Min-
    ton, 188; Jesse Clark, 188; Lou, 188, 189;
    Margaret C., 191; Margaret W., 191
Hoover Foundation, Inc., 191, 192
Hoover Institute & Library on War, Revolution &
    Peace, 189, 191, 192
Hopkins, James, 114
House, James, 81
House of Representatives, U.S. see Congress,
    U.S.
Hull, Isaac, 60
Hunter's Hill, Tenn., 67
Hyde Park, N.Y., 197, 198, 203
Illinois Legislature, 123
Independence, Mo., 213, 214
Indiana, 80, 122, 147
Indiana Territory, 79
Indianapolis, 146, 147
Indianapolis Orphan Asylum, 149
Indians, 66, 78, 79, 98

Inman, Henry, 73
Intestate statutes, 11
Jackson, Andrew, father, 66
Jackson, Andrew, 55, 72, 91, 115; bequests, 69, 70; in Congress, 67; on Constitution, 69; debts, 67, 68, 71; education, 66; estate, 67; executor, 70; financial problems, 67; land holdings, 67; lawyer, 66, 67; personal characteristics, 71; Presidency, 67, 71; salary, 67
Jackson, Andrew, Jr., 67, 68, 69, 70, 71; Rachel, granddaughter, 69, wife, 66, 67; Samuel, 69; Sarah, 69
Jackson County, Mo., 214
Jay Treaty, 54
Jefferson, Lucy, 38; Peter, 37
Jefferson, Thomas, 46, 47, 48, 49, 50, 53; architect & draftsman, 37, 41; business papers, 40; codicil, 40; creditors, 41; education, 37; estate, 38, 41; executors, 40, 41; financial problems, 37, 38; Governor of Virginia, 37, 49; Justice of the Peace & Vestryman, 37; land holdings, 37, 39; lawyer, 41; library, 38, 40, 48; Minister to France, 38; salary, 38; Secretary of State, 38; Presidency, 38; slaves, 37, 38; trusts & trustees, 41; Vice President, 38
John F. Kennedy Center for the Performing Arts, 248
Johns Hopkins University, 174, 175
Johnson, Abigail Louisa Smith, 34
Johnson, Andrew, 11, 103, 128; in Congress, 125, 126; estate, 126; fortune, 126; gift of new carriage, 126; Governor of Tennessee, 125; impeached, 126; library, 126; in local politics, 125; papers, 126; Presidency, 126; real estate, 126; salary, 126; tailor, 125
Johnson, Andrew, family: Andrew Jr., 126; Eliza McCardle, 125, 126; Jacob, 125; Mary McDonough, 125; William, 125
Johnson, Louisa Catherine see Adams, Louisa Catherine; Mary McDonough, 125; Olive A., 104, 105
Johnson, Lyndon Baines, 12, 187, 212, 232, 248; bequests, 265-267; burial, 263; in Congress, 262; education, 261; estate, 264, 265; executors, 275, 279; fortune, 263; funeral, 263; grandchildren, 266, 268, 269; income from estate, 270, 273, 275; investments, 271, 272; land holdings, 263; Lieutenant-Commander, Navy, 262; mineral properties, 271; papers, 263, 264, 278; pension, 263; Presidency, 263; property, disposition & distribution, 270-273; real estate, 263; salary, 263; stocks, bonds & securities, 271, 272; taxes, 265, 275, 276, 278, 279; teacher, 261, 262; trusts & trustees, 268-275, 279; Vice President, 262; Vietnam War, 263; World War II, 262
Johnson, Lyndon, family: Claudia T. (Lady Bird), 262-267, 270, 274, 275, 278; Luci Baines see Nugent, Luci Baines; Lynda Bird see Robb, Lynda Bird Johnson; Rebekah Baines, 261; Sam Ealy Sr., 261; Sam Houston, 266; Samuel Ealy, 261
Johnson City, 261
Johnson City Foundation, 270, 275
Johnston, Harriet Lane, 115, 116, 117, 119, 120. See also Lane, Harriet
Johnston, Henry E., 115, 117, 119
Jones, Joseph, 50
Joseph P. Kennedy Jr. Foundation, 249, 260
Kansas City School of Law, 214
Kefauver, Estes, 248
Kelberg, Richard M., 262
Kennedy, Caroline, 248; Edward M., 258; Jacqueline B., 248-252, 256, 258; Jean, 258
Kennedy, John F., 12, 107, 187, 262, 278; assassination, 248, 262; back injury, 247; charities, 249, 260; children, trust for, 251, 252; Choate, 247; in Congress, 247, 248, 259; education, 247; executors, 249; family fortune, 247; funeral, 248; gifts, 250, 259, 260; homes, 248; income from estate, 254, 256, 259; investments, 253, 256; papers, 248; pension, 248; Presidency, 248, 259; papers, 259; property, disposition of, 255, 256; PT boat commander, 247; real estate, 253, 254; reelection campaign, 248; residuary estate, 257; salary, 248; stocks, bonds & securities, 256, 257; taxes, 257, 259; trust funds, 248, 253; trusts & trustees, 249-251, 253, 254, 256, 257, 259, 260; World War II, 247; writings, 247
Kennedy, John Jr., 248; Joseph P., 247, 248; Robert F., 258
Kennedy Library, 248, 259
Kentucky, 81
Kenyon College, 130
Kinderhook, N.Y., 72
Know-Nothing party, 103
Knox, Jane see Polk, Jane Knox
Kortright, Elizabeth see Monroe, Elizabeth K.
L.B.J. Ranch, 263
Ladies Hermitage Association, 71
Lafayette, Marquis de, 24, 50, 69, 110, 111
Lafayette, George Washington, 70
Lake County Historical Society, 135
Lamar, Mo., 213
Lancaster, Pa., 114, 115, 116
Land holdings 12; early descriptions, 84
Landon, Alfred M., 198
Lane, Harriet, 114, 115. See also Johnston, Harriet Lane; James B., 117, 118; Jane B., 117; Martha J., 118
Latrobe, Benjamin, 16
Law, Elizabeth Parke, 27
Lawford, Patricia, 258
Lawnfield, Mentor, Ohio, 135
Le Hand, Marguerite A., 205, 211
League of Nations, 175
Lear, Tobias, 16, 24, 25, 29
Lee, Alice Hathaway see Roosevelt, Alice Hathaway
Leithead, Barry T., 242
Lewis, Betty, 23, 25, 26; Eleanor Parke, 26, 27, 29; Fielding, 26; George, 17, 24, 26; Howell, 26; Lawrence, 25-27, 29; Robert, 26
Liberia, 48
Liberty-Hall Academy, 22
Library of Congress, 17, 31, 83, 86, 109, 124, 126, 163, 170, 175
Lincoln, Abraham, 11, 103, 115, 126, 135; assassination, 124; campaigns, 123; Captain of volunteers, 122; in Congress, 123; education, 122; estate, 124; fortune, 124; Illinois Legislature, 123; lawyer, 123; papers, 124; parents, 122; personal description, 123; Presidency, 123; salary, 124; speeches, 123
Lincoln, Mary Todd, 123, 124; Robert Todd, 124; Thomas "Tad", 123, 124; William Wallace, 123
Lincoln Memorial, 124
Lindenwald, N.Y., 73, 75, 77
Livingston, Robert R., 50
Lloyd, David D., 217
Lodge, Henry Cabot, 248
Longfellow, Henry Wadsworth, 108
Longworth, Alice Roosevelt, 163, 164
Longworth, Nicholas, 163
Los Angeles County Museum of Art, 237
Louisa County, Va., 44
Louisiana Purchase, 38, 50
Lourie, James I., 136
Louisville, Ky., 97, 99
Lyndon Baines Johnson Library & Museum, 263, 267
MacArthur, Douglas, 235
MacCracken, Henry Noble, 185
Madison, Ambrose, 45
Madison, Dolley, 42, 44, 45, 46, 47, 48, 72, 115; fortune, 43
Madison, James, 40, 54, 79; codicil, 46, 48; on Constitutional Convention: proceedings & their publication, 45, 47; records of debates, 47, 48; in Continental Congress, 42; debts, 43; education, 42; estate, 43; executor, 46; land holdings, 44, 46; library, 45, 48; nephews & nieces, 44, 47; papers, 43, 45, 48; Presidency, 43; public life, 42; salary, 43; Secretary of State, 43; trusts & trustees 46, 48; writings, 47
Madison, John, 42; Nelly Conway, 42; Robert S., 45

Mahoning County, Ohio, 158
Malachek, Dale & Jewel, 267
Maloney, Thomas, 126
Manning, Helen Taft, 170
Marion, Ohio, 178, 179
Marion Park Commission, 181
Marion Star, 178, 179, 180, 181
Marital deductions, 12, 133, 245, 246, 259, 278
Marks, Anne Scott, 40
Married Women's Property Acts, 41, 145
Marshall, George, 235; John, 29
Martin, Thomas, 42
Massachusetts, inheritance laws, 64
Massachusetts Federalists, 54
Massachusetts Historical Society, 65
Massachusetts House of Representatives, 60
Massachusetts Senate, 54
Matson, John, 81
McCardle, Eliza see Johnson, Eliza McCardle
McClellan, George B., 123
McElroy, Mary E., 137, 139
McGehee, Edward, 100
McIntosh, Caroline Carmichael see Fillmore, Caroline C.
McKee, Benjamin Harrison, 148, 152; James R., 147; Mary, Harrison, 151, 157, see also Harrison, Mary Scott; Mary Lodge, 149
McKeogh, Michael J., 237, 245
McKinley, Helen, 160
McKinley, Ida S., 158, 159, 160, 161
McKinley, William, 163, 168; assassination, 159; campaigns, 159; in Congress, 158; education, 158; estate, 159; financial problems, 159; Governor of Ohio, 158; homes, 159; imperfection of will, 161; lawyer, 158; mementos, 159; mother, 160, 161; nomination, 159; Presidency, 159; salary, 159; savings, 159; Union Army, 158
McKinley, William Sr., 158
McMurdo, John, 85
Mecklenburg County, N.C., 91
Mexican War, 98, 101, 109, 111, 127
Miami University, Oxford, Ohio, 146
Mickle, Andrew H., 51, 52
Millard, Phoebe see Fillmore, Phoebe Millard
Miller, Charles E., 139; W. H. H., 152
Minors in wills, 14, 36, 90, 120-21, 139, 140, 143, 145, 148, 150, 153, 157, 164, 252, 253
Minot, Josiah, 110, 112
Mississippi plantation, 67, 68
Mississippi River, 98
Missouri Compromise, 123
Moaney, John Jr., 237, 245
Monticello, Va., 37, 38, 40, 41
Montpellier, Va., 42, 43, 47, 48
Monroe, Elizabeth see Hay, Elizabeth K.; Elizabeth Jones, 49; Elizabeth Kortright, 49
Monroe, James, 36; burial, 50; codicil, 51, 53; creditors, 53; debts, 51, 53; education, 49; estate, 53; executor, 51; financial problems, 50; homes, 50; House of Delegates, Virginia, 48; land holdings, 50, 53; lawyer, 49; Minister to France, 50; Presidency, 50; public service, 50; in Revolutionary War, 49; salary, 50; Secretary of State, 50; U.S. Senator, 50; validity of will, 53; writings, 51
Monroe, James, Captain, 51; Maria, see Gouverneur, Maria; Spence, 49
Moore, Benjamin Pierce, 111; Roy D., 179
Morgan, J. P., 128
Morris, Anna H., 149
Mount Vernon, Va., 15, 16, 25, 26, 27, 29
Mount Vernon Ladies Association, 30
Murphy, Charles S., 217
Nashville, 66, 71, 91, 92, 93, 96
National Archives & Records Service, 216, 217, 248, 263
National Cathedral, Washington, D.C., 175
National Cultural Center, 248
National Park Service, 126, 263
National Trust for Historic Preservation, 29, 175
National War Labor Board, 169
National Youth Administration, 262
NATO forces, 235
Navigation of James & Potomac rivers, 20
Negroes see Slaves
Negroes rights, 136

New Hampshire, 108, 111
New Jersey, College of, 42
New Orleans, 69
New Salem, Ill., 122
New York Assembly, 162
New York City, 50, 53, 61, 70, 72, 74, 128, 142, 162, 163; customs house, 137
New York Institute for the Blind, 141
New York State laws, 104, 105, 107; Library, 17; politics, 137; Senate, 73
Newman, Reuben & James, 46
Niles, Ohio, 158
Nixon, Richard M., 248
Nobel Peace Prize, 163
Norfolk County, Mass., 57, 58, 63
North Bend, Ohio, 78, 79, 81, 82, 83, 84, 146
North Carolina, 66, 91; University of, 91
Northampton, Mass., 184, 185
Northwest Territory, 78, 79
Nugent, Luci Baines Johnson, 263, 265, 266, 268, 279
Oak Hill, Va., 50, 53
O'Connor, Basil, 204, 209
Octagon House, 43
Ohio, 79
Ohio Central College, 178
Ohio General Assembly, 84
Ohio Historical Society, 179
Ohio State Senate, 135
Ohio Superior Court, 168
Orange, Ohio, 134
Orange County, Va., 42, 44, 97
Oregon, 92
Overton, John, 66
Oxford Female Institute, 146
Oyster Bay, N.Y., 162, 163
Panama Canal Zone, 235
Pan-American exposition, 159
Panic of 1819, 50
Panic of 1873, 126
Paris Peace Conference, 175
Parker, Elizabeth Scott, 149, 150
Parkman, Dr. George, 61
Parks, Harriot, 26
Patent Office, U.S., 60
Patterson, Andrew Johnson, 126; Martha Johnson, 126
Payne, John C., 45
Peace Conference, second international, 163
Peake, Humphrey, 25
Pearl Harbor, 235, 262
Pendergast, Tom, 214
Pendleton, Philip, 16, 22
Pennsylvania Legislature, 114
Peter, Martha Parke, 27
Philadelphia College of Physicians & Surgeons, 78
Philippine Commission, 168
Philippines, 235
Pierce, Anna Kendrick, 108; Benjamin, father, 108, son, 109; Frank Hawthorne, 111, 112
Pierce, Franklin, 103, 107, 115, 120; & alcohol, 113; bequests, 110-112; children, 108, 109, 113; in Congress, 108, 109; education, 108; estate, 109; executor, 110, 112; inauguration, 109, 113; lawyer, 108, 109; military service, 109; nephews & nieces, 110; in N.H. Legislature, 108; papers, 109; Presidency, 109
Pierce, Henry D., 110, 111; Jane, 108, 109, 113; Kirk Dearborn, 110, 111; Susan T., 110; Thomas B., 111
Plymouth, Vt., 184, 185
Point Pleasant, Ohio, 127
Political patronage, 137
Polk, James Knox, 109, 115; burial, 92, 93, 94; campaign, 92; in Congress, 91; education, 91; estate, 92, 94; Governor of Tennessee, 91; land holdings, 93, 94; lawyer, 91; nomination, 91, 92; praising his wife, 94; Presidency, 92, 96; real estate, 94; salary, 92; State legislator, 91; trust 94, 96; will not honored, 92
Polk, Jane Knox, 91, 92, 93; Marshall T., 93; Samuel, 91; Sarah, 91-94, 96; William H., 93
Polk Place, 91, 92, 93, 96
Poplar Grove, Tenn., 67
Potomac Company, 20, 27

Power of appointment, 167
Powers, Abigail see Fillmore, Abigail; Hiram, 73, 74
Pratt, Julius, 60
Presbyterian Church, Lancaster, Pa., 115, 116
Presidential families, 11, 12; financial situations, 11, 13; homes, 96, 103, 109 see also under individual presidents; Libraries Act, 212, 232; papers, 14, 173, 212, 232 see also under individual presidents; pension, 175; salary increase, 128
Presidents' deaths in office, 79, 98, 124, 135, 159, 199, 214, 248
Preston, Captain, 33
Price, William M., 50, 51, 52
Princeton, N.J., 142
Princeton University, 42, 142. 174. 175, 247; library, 45
Probate Court, 183
Progressive party, 163, 175
Prohibition, 179
Property, disposition & transfer of, 12, 13, see also under individual presidents
Pulitzer Prize, 247
Queen's College, Belfast, 136
Quincy, John, 33, 61; Jonah, 35; Norton, 34, 61
Quincy, Mass., 32, 33, 36, 54, 55, 56, 59, 61; Adams family tomb, 62; bequests to, 62
Raleigh, N.C., 125
Randolph, Jane, 37; Martha Jefferson, 38-40; Thomas Jefferson, 39, 40, 46; Thomas Mann, 38-40, debts & creditors, 39, 41
Real estate, co-ownership, 127
Reed, Mary L., 119; William B., 118, 119
Remsberg, Charity M., 180
Republican Convention 1860, 123; 1868, 128; 1876, 131; 1880, 135, 137; 1884, 137, 158; 1896, 159; 1900, 159; 1908, 169; 1912, 175, 179; 1916, 179; 1920, 179, 184; 1928, 189; 1952, 235; 1956, 236
Republican party, 115, 126, 128, 131, 136, 147, 158, 159, 163, 175
Residuary clause, 84
Revolutionary War, 16, 20, 21, 25, 49, 66, 91, 97, 108
Richmond, Va., 85, 86, 90
Rifle Company of New Orleans, 67, 69
Ringgold, Tench, 51, 52
Robb, Lynda Bird Johnson, 263, 265, 266, 268, 279
Roberts, Clifford R., 242
Roberts, Lewis, 66
Robertson, Donald, 42
Robinson, Joseph, 111
Rogers, Bowen & Rogers, 141
Rollins, Daniel G., 139
Roosevelt, Alice see Longworth, Alice Roosevelt; Alice Hathaway, 162; Anna Eleanor, 197-201, 203-207, 211, 212; Edith Kermit, 163-165, 167
Roosevelt, Franklin Delano, 12, 14, 65, 107, 189, 214, 235, 267, 278, 279; Assistant Secretary of the Navy, 197; bequests, 200, 201, 205; burial, 198, 200; campaigns, 198; children & grandchildren, 198, 201-203, 205-207, 211, 212; education, 197; estate, 199; executors, 200, 201, 208-210; fortune, 199; Governor of New York, 198; homes, 198, 199; investments, 199; library, 198, 203; papers, 212; polio, 198; Presidency, 198; property, transfer & distribution, 204-206, 207, 208, 210, 211; residuary estate, 199, 204, 211; servants, 200· stamp collection, 199; State Senator, 197; stocks, bonds & securities, 208; taxes, 200, 201, 212; trust funds, 205-209, 211, 212; trusts & trustees, 201, 204, 206, 208-210
Roosevelt, George Emlen, 165; James, father, 197; James, son, 204, 209; Martha Bulloch, 162
Roosevelt, Theodore, 13, 159, 168, 169, 175, 183, 195, 197; Assistant Secretary of the Navy, 163; burial, 163; cattle venture, 163; diaries, 163; education, 162; estate, 163, 165; executors, 164, 165, 167; Governor of New York, 163; inheritance, 162; investments, 165, 168; New York Assembly, 162; Nobel Peace Prize, 163; Police Commissioner,

N.Y. City, 163; Presidency, 163; property, administration of, 167; real estate, 165; Spanish-American War, 163; trusts & trustees, 164-167; U.S. Civil Service Commission, 163; Vice President, 163; writings, 162, 163
Roosevelt, Theodore, father, 162; Jr., 165
Rosenman, Samuel I., 217, 229
Rough Riders, 163
Rudolph, Joseph, 135; Lucretia see Garfield, Lucretia
Sagamore Hill, 162, 163
St. James Church, Hyde Park, N.Y., 200
St. Louis, Mo., 127, 128
St. Paul's Episcopal Church, Marion, Ohio, 181
Sample, James, 88
Sartoris, Algernon Frederick, 128
Saxton, Ida see McKinley, Ida S.
Schaffner, Charles D., 182
Schenectady, N.Y., 136
Schulz, Robert Ludwig, 237, 245
Scott, Caroline Lavinia see Harrison, Caroline Scott; Winfield, 103, 109, 136
Seminole Indians, 98
Senate, U.S. see Congress, U.S.
Shenandoah National Park, 189
Shepard, Anna, 61; Thomas, 61
Sherman, John, 135; William T., 147
Sherwood Forest, Va., 86, 87
Short, Betsey, 81; John C., 81
Shriver, Eunice K., 258
Silvester, Francis, 72
Singleton, Angelica see Van Buren, Angelica
Skelton, Martha Wayles, 37
Slavery, 60
Slaves, 16, 19, 20, 22, 23, 30, 37, 44, 50, 67, 68, 69, 86, 88, 98, 99; emigration to Africa, 47-48; freeing of, 94
Smith, Abigail, 33, 34; Al, 189, 198; John Adams, 34; Katharine Louisa, 34; Louisa Catherine, 62; Margaret see Taylor, Margaret; Walter, 97; William, 34; William Sr., 33
Smithsonian Institution, 17, 43, 55, 115, 128, 129, 175, 179
Souers, Sidney, 217
South Carolina, 66, 70
Southwest Texas State Teachers College, 261
Spanish-American War, 163
The Spanish Cottage, 98
Spiegel Grove, Fremont, Ohio, 131, 132; as museum 133
Spotswood, Elizabeth, 26
Springfield, Ill., 123
Springfield, Ky., 98
Stanford University, 188, 189
Stanton, Edwin M., 126, 128
Stark County Historical Society, 159
Staunton, Va., 174, 175
Stevenson, Adlai, 235, 236; Coke, 262
Stock market crash, 189
Stockton, Philip, 82, 83; Robert F., 142
Stone, Malvina see Arthur, Malvina
Stonewall, Tex., 261, 263
Stuart, Dr. David, 17, 24; Eleanor, 24
Summerhill, N.Y., 102
Supreme Court, U.S., 28, 29, 126, 147, 168, 170
Swarr, Hiram B., 117, 118
Swoyer, Martha Ann, 228
Symmes, Anna Tuthill see Harrison, Anna
Taft, Alphonso, 168; Charles Phelps, 170; Helen H., 169, 170; Horace D., 171, 172; Robert Alphonse, 170
Taft, William Howard, 163, 175, 179, 235; bequests, 170; burial, 169; Chief Justice, 169; codicils, 171, 172; education, 168; estate, 169, 170; executor, 170; Federal circuit judge, 168; homes, 169; Internal revenue collector, 168; lawyer, 168; mementos, 169; papers, 170, 173; Philippine Commission, 168; Presidency, 168, 169; real estate, 170; residuary estate, 173; salary, 168, 169; Secretary of War, 168; Solicitor General, 168
Taft School Foundation, Watertown, Conn., 171, 172
Taxable estates, 12
Taxes, 12-14, 167. See also under individual presidents
Taylor, Ann M. see Wood, Ann M.; Claudia Alta,

see Johnson, Claudia T.; Margaret, 97-99; Mary Elizabeth, 99, 100; Richard, father, 97, son, 98-100

Taylor, Zachary, 103, 115; burial, 98; career in U.S. Army, 97, 98; estate, 98, 101; executor, 100; family plot, 98; "Old Rough & Ready", 98; plantation owner, 99, 100; Presidency, 98; real estate, 99; servants, 99, 100; stocks, 99

Teapot Dome scandal, 179

Tecumseh, 79

Tennessee, 66, 67, 69, 71, 91, 92, 94; House of Representatives, 125; state of, as trustee, 94, 96; Superior Court, 67

Tenure of Office Act, 126

Texas, 92

Texas Christian University, 263

Texas Trust Act, 273

Thames, battle of, 79

Thomas, Donald S., 274, 275

Thornton, Boswell, 44; Jane, 26; Mary S., 82

Tibbott, E. Frank, 149

Tiffany, Louis Comfort, 137

Tilden, Samuel J., 131

Todd, Dolley Payne see Madison, Dolley; John Payne, 46, 48; Mary see Lincoln, Mary Todd

Torrence, George P., 81

Treaty of Paris, 33

Trinity Baptist Church, Marion, Ohio, 181

Trist, Nicholas P., 39, 40

Truman, Bess Wallace, 213, 214, 216-218, 220, 222, 226-228; Gilbert, 228; Harry Arnold, 228

Truman, Harry S., 12, 187, 189, 196, 198, 212, 245, 278; burial, 214, 228; in Congress, 214; campaign, 214; codicils, 227-231, 233; executors, 215, 221-223, 225, 228; farmer, 213; financial problems, 214; grandchildren, 220, 221; haberdashery, 214; homes, 213, 214; investments, 223, 224; Jackson County, Mo., elective offices, 214; library, 214; Memoirs, 214; Missouri artillery, 213; name, 213; nephews & nieces, 227, 228; papers, 215-217; pension, 214; Presidency, 214; property, disposition of, 224; residuary estate, 218; salary, 214; secretaries & servants, 228; stocks & securities, 224, 225; taxes, 218, 219, 224, 232; trusts & trustees, 218-226; Vice President, 214; World War I, 213; World War II, 214

Truman, John Anderson, 213; John Curtis, 228, 233; John Ross, 228, 233; Margaret see Daniel, Margaret Truman; Martha Ellen, 213

Trumbull, John, 61

Trust administration, 168, 183, 195, 196, 204

Trusts & trustees, 13, 36, 39, 94, 96, 140, 192, 195, 196, 204, 209, 210, 239, 246, 259, 260, 273, 275

Tuttle, Anna, 82, 83

Twain, Mark, 129

Tyler, David G., 88

Tyler, John, 145; burial, 86, 87, 90; children, 87, 90; and Civil War, 86; codicil, 88; debts, 86, 88; education, 85; estate, 87; executors, 88, 90; Governor of Virginia, 85; in gunship explosion, 86; land holdings, 86-89; lawyer, 85; papers, 86, 88; Presidency, 85; real estate, 90; relations with Congress, 86; on remarriage of widow, 87, 88, 90; salary, 86; servants, 88; Vice President, 85, 86; Virginia Legislature, 85

Tyler, John, father, 85, son, 88; Julia, daughter, 88; Julia Gardiner, 86-90, 145; Letitia, 85, 86, 90; Lyon G., 86; Mary Armstead, 85; Robert, 88, 89; Tazewell, 88, 89

Unemployment, 73

Uniform Probate Code, 196, 279

Uniform Simultaneous Death Act, 173

Uniform Testamentary Additions to Trust Act, 195

Uniform Trustee's Powers Act, 196

Union College, Schenectady, N.Y., 136

Union Seminary, Ohio, 158

Uniontown, Pa., College, 45

United Nations International Children's Emergency Fund, 189

U.S. Army, 97

U.S. Bank, 72

U.S. Congress see Congress, U.S.

U.S. Food Administration see Food Administration, U.S.

U.S. Supreme Court see Supreme Court, U.S.

Valley Forge, 49

Van Buren, Abraham, father of Martin Van Buren, 72, son of Martin Van Buren, 72, 74, 75; Angelica Singleton, 72, 73; Dirike, 75; Edward Livingston, 74; Hannah, 72; Jane Ann, 75; John, 74, 75; Lawrence, 75, Lucretia, 75

Van Buren, Martin, 79; advances to his sons, 74, 77; ancestors, 73; education, 72; estate, 73, 77; executors, 74-76; grandchildren, 74; imbalance in will, 77; lawyer, 72; library, 74; N.Y. State Governor & Senator, 72; Presidency, 72, 73; real estate, 75; salary, 72, 73; Secretary of State, 72; U.S. Bank, 72; U.S. Senator, 72; Vice President, 72

Van Buren, Martin, grandson, 74; Martin, nephew, 75; Singleton, 74; Smith Thompson, 74, 75, 77

Vanderbilt, William H., 128, 129

Venezuela, 147

Vermont, 136

Versailles Treaty, 175

Vice President, succession to presidency, 85-86, 90, 137, 214, 262-3

Vietnam War, 263

Vincennes, Ind., 79, 80

Virginia, University of, 38, 40, 45, 48, 174; library, 41, 45

Virginia Council, 78

Virginia laws, 19, 20

Virginia Legislature, 38, 49, 85

Virginia militia, 16

Virginia State Constitutional Convention, 42, 49

Votaw, Carolyn, 180

Walker, Ann, 24; Robert L., 159

Wallace, Elizabeth (Bess) see Truman, Bess Wallace

Waller, William, 88

War of 1812, 50, 97

Ward, Ferdinand, 128

Washington, Augustine, 15, 26; Bushrod, 16, 23-27, 29, 47, at Supreme Court, 29; Charles, 17, 24, 27; Charles Augustine, 27; Corbin, 26; Elizabeth, 24

Washington, George, 12, 13, 14, 32, 41, 47, 49, 61, 64, 70, 212, 233; bequests, 20-22, 30; bequests for public uses, 21; as businessman, 16-17; compensation for services, 21; education, 15; estate, 16, 25, 26, 30; executors, 27, 30; family vault, 27, 90; funeral, 27; income, 16; land holdings, 16-17, 23, 27, 29, 30; military service, 16, 20, 21, 25; private papers & library, 23; Presidency, 16, 19, 20, 30; record-keeping, 16; slaves, 16, 19, 20, 22, 23, 30; swords, 17, 24; will, physical characteristics & history, 29-31; will, printing, 30

Washington, George Augustine, 27; George Fayette, 25, 27; George Steptoe, 16, 24, 26, 27; Hannah, 24; Jane, 26; John Augustine, 26; Lawrence, 15, 24; Lawrence Augustine, 22, 25, 26; Maria, 27; Martha,

16, 19, 23, 25, 27, 29, 30, grandchildren, 16, 25, 26, will, 30, 31; Robert, 17, 24; Samuel, 17, 26, estate of, 22; Samuel, son of Charles, 26, 27; Thornton, 26, estate, 22; William Augustine, 17, 23, 24, 26, 27 26, 27

Washington, D.C., 26, 43, 44, 48, 50, 56, 57, 59, 128; Blair House, 214; Ebbett House, 159; See also District of Columbia

Washington-Spencer grant, 15

Wayles, John, 37

Wealth, forms of, 12

Weaver, Jessie Magaw, 117

Webb, Isaac, 130; Lucy see Hayes, Lucy

Wellington, Va., 29

Wesleyan Female College, 130

Wesleyan University, 174

West Branch, Iowa, 188, 189, 193

West Point, Military Academy, 93, 127, 213, 234

Western frontier, 127

Western Reserve Historical Society, 135

Westmoreland County, Va., 49

Weymouth, Mass., 33

Wheatland, Pa., 115, 116, 119

Whig party, 79, 85, 91, 98, 103, 115, 123

Whipple, Thomas J., 111

White, Chief Justice, 169

White House, 33, 50, 72, 86, 114, 115, 120, 123, 124; birth in, 142; collections, 73, 147; liquor, 131; redecoration & renovation, 126, 137, 189, 214, 248; upkeep, 86; weddings in, 50, 90, 128, 142, 145, 163

Whiteman, Lewis, 81

William & Mary College, 37, 49, 85

Williams, Willard, 111

Williams College, 134, 135

Williamsburg, raid on Governor's palace, 49

Willis, Nelly C., 44

Willkie, Wendell, 198

Wills, anti-lapse statute, 113; characteristics, 11; drafting & draftsmen, 12, 13, 140, 157, 167, 183, 195, 211, 212, 232, 260, 279; imperfections, 77, 84, 92, 161; instructions for funerals, 233; interpretation, 101, 195; language & terms, 13, 212, 264; lawyers and, 13; legal effects, 96, 101; restrictions on duration, 94; rule against perpetuities, 279; savings clause, 269, 279; second marriages, 107; self-proved, 277, 280; spendthrift clause, 275, 279, 280; standardized form, 13; survival of legatees, 172; tax, 12, 13, see also under individual Presidents

Wilson, Edith, 175, 176, 177; Eleanor, 174; Ellen, 174; James, 174; Jessie, 174; Margaret, 174, 176; Thomas, 24

Wilson, Woodrow, 163, 169, 188, 197; daughters, 174, 176, 177; death, 175; education, 174; estate, 175; executor, 176; Fourteen Points, 175; Governor of New Jersey, 175; homes, 174, 175; income, 174; lawyer, 174; library, 175; mementos, 175; name, 174, 177; papers, 175; Presidency, 175; President of Princeton University, 174; salary, 175; speeches, 175; thesis, 174; writings, 175, 177

Windt, Caroline Amelia de, 34

Witnesses, 84

Women, legal status, 41

Women's Christian Temperance Union, 131

Wood, Ann M., 99, 100

Woodbury, Levi, 109

Woodlawn, Va., 29

World War I, 175, 188, 189, 213, 234, 235

World War II, 214, 235

Wythe, George, 37

Yale University, 168, 169, 170, 171, 172

Yates, Maria T., 117

Young, Martha Ellen see Truman, Martha Ellen